Planter Raj to Swaraj

Freedom Struggle and Electoral Politics in Assam, 1826–1947

Planter Raj to Swaraj

Freedom Struggle and Electoral Politics

in Assam, 1826–1947

AMALENDU GUHA

Tulika Books

First published by ICHR in January 1977
Reprinted by People's Publishing House in August 1988

This revised edition published in 2006 by
Tulika Books
44 (first floor), Shahpur Jat, New Delhi 110 049, India

First edition (hardback), 2006
Second edition (paperback), 2012
Third edition (paperback), 2014

Fourth edition (paperback), 2019

ISBN: 978-93-82381-34-1

Printed at Chaman Offset, Delhi 110 002.

In memory of my father

JAMINISUNDAR GUHA (1873–1950)

of Manipur

Foreword, First Edition

The Indian Council of Historical Research was presented with a request from the Minister for Education and Social Welfare, which he had received in 1972 from Shri Raj Bahadur, then Union Minister for Parliamentary Affairs, and Shri K.C. Pant, then Union Minister for Home Affairs, for bringing out a series of books on the role of the central and state legislatures during our freedom struggle, to mark the Twenty-fifth Anniversary of India's attainment of independence.

The Council gladly accepted this assignment, and Professor Manoranjan Jha's *Role of the Central Legislatures in the Freedom Struggle* and Dr Amit Kumar Gupta's *North West Frontier Province Legislature and Freedom Struggle 1932-47* have already been published as a result of its efforts. The third book to come out in this series is the present work on the Assam legislature by Amalendu Guha, Professor of Economic History at the Centre for Studies in Social Sciences, Calcutta. The book has been written in consultation with an Editorial Board for the entire project, under the chairmanship of Professor S. Gopal, but, like all the other authors in this project, Dr Guha has been given complete academic freedom to express views based on his research.

Professor Guha has not only presented a detailed account of the evolution of the provincial legislature of Assam in the context of general political developments in the province, but has also provided valuable background for an understanding of the colonial socio-economic structure. He has discussed the politics of anti-imperialism both in the legislature and outside it, and marked shifts within the national movement in economic objectives and political ideas, particularly in the context of peasant and labour problems. Thus, the book, which is based on massive research, may be read as an authentic record of the role of Assam in the development of the Indian national movement, with a focus not restricted to only the leading party in the national movement, but also embracing other trends and elements, all of which together struggled in their own ways for liberation from colonialism.

The author has utilized the broadest possible range of sources in the relevant regional languages in local archives and private collections, and given a very full bibliography of published literature. Also of note is the use of quantitative data and statistics in elucidating the role of colonialism in stultifying the development of society and economy in northeast India, as well as the role of anti-colonial elements in endeavouring to break the colonial stranglehold.

1977 is the centenary year of the birth of Tarunram Phookan, a leading nationalist of old Assam. Like Chittaranjan Das in Bengal, he mobilized the middle class of Assam to combat imperial authority both within the legislature and outside it. It is fitting that this volume, which recounts the nature of the broader mobilization that followed, should be published in this year.

I thank the author and all those who assisted him in completing the work, as well as the members of the Editorial Board for scrutinizing the manuscript of this book in detail, and Professor Syed Nurul Hasan, Education Minister, for sponsoring this project.

New Delhi   R.S. SHARMA
1 January 1977   Chairman, Indian Council of Historical Research

Prologue, First Edition

This book on Assam – that is, present Assam, Nagaland, Meghalaya and Mizoram – comes alphabetically first in a series in which the role of legislatures in the history of the freedom struggle and political change in the eleven provinces of British India will be examined. I have stretched the period a little backward to begin from 1926, the year of the British annexation of Assam, and have carried the analysis to 1950. The Frontier Tracts (present Arunachal Pradesh) and the state of Manipur, which had some links with Assam, are however outside the scope of this study.

The historiography of modern Assam, as it stands today, practically stops at 1858. E.A. Gait, for example, devotes less than forty of the 400 and odd pages of his book – a lucid work in the tradition of imperialist historiography – to the post -1858 period. He stops short of the Non-Cooperation era even in the second edition that was brought out in 1926. K.N. Dutt's *Landmarks of the Freedom Movement in Assam* is but a bare 136-page outline, useful but inadequately documented. No other publication on the subject deserves mention here. Assam is one of those provinces where even an officially sponsored history of the local freedom movement has yet to come out. This lag, therefore, has forced me to look also for the wood so that I may not miss the trees. Chronicling has received no less importance in this study than analysis, particularly while dealing with the last phase of the freedom struggle.

My chief task has been to build the narrative chronologically for the century-and-a-quarter under review and, at the same time, to treat it thematically as well. In the resultant periodization, four distinct periods have emerged. Three chapters, one each, cover the first three periods – the years 1826–73, 1874-1905 and 1906–20. The major task in these chapters has been to provide the background for an understanding of the colonial socio-economic structure that was shaken in the political turmoil of the Gandhi epoch to follow. In the remaining five chapters, covering this last period of about three decades, the emphasis shifts somewhat from society and the economy to the politics of anti-imperialism both in the legislature and outside it. The shifts within the national movement in political ideals and economic objectives, particularly in the context of the peasant and labour problems, have not been lost sight of.

The main focus after 1905 is on all political activities centering round or opposed to the legislature that existed for the province. Hence, in my choice of source materials, over 50,000 printed pages of relevant legislative debates and interpellations have been more important than unpublished government records for the same period. These have, of course, been supplemented by other usual primary and secondary sources. Proceedings of legislatures have one advantage – that they carry not only the official but also other versions of events on record. Though not fortunate enough in my search for local private papers, I was nevertheless able to unearth a bundle of such papers labelled 'leaders' correspondence' in the APCC archives of Congress Bhavan, Gauhati. I have amply used this material to make up for the dearth of official records for the decade 1937–47, to which it relates.

Individual freedom-fighters or legislators not receiving adequate coverage in this book were not necessarily persons with a marginal role in the history of the period under review. This only means that either the necessary information was not available or the relevant micro-details were not found necessary for answering the questions raised.

Writing about the pre-independence decade has been the most difficult, yet exciting part of my task. Many of the actors and witnesses of this stormy phase of our history are still present amidst us, with all their sensitivities to what concerns them. This makes the use of a range of relevant materials for this study all the more difficult. Despite this limitation, I have not fought shy of devoting as much as one-third of the space of this book in this decade. I am nevertheless aware that, for a proper assessment of the events of this decade, more research will have to be conducted at the grass-roots level. Mine is spade work in anticipation of future research.

Errors of fact or interpretation, if any, remain mine alone.

Calcutta   AMALENDU GUHA
1 January 1977

Acknowledgements, First Edition

I am honoured that the Indian Council of Historical Research, New Delhi, which commissioned me for this study has accepted it for publication. For financial support during the three-and-a-half years I worked on the book, I have a debt of gratitude both to the Indian Council of Historical Research as well as to the Centre for studies in Social Sciences, Calcutta, I joined in November 1973. For promoting my release and for facilitating my taking up of the new assignment, my thanks are due to the Gokhale Institute of Politics and Economics, Poona.

I am grateful to Arvind N. Das, currently of the National Labour Institute, New Delhi and Manorama Sharma, of the Department of History, Dibrugarh University, Assam, for the research assistance they provided, each for six months, for collecting, arranging and even assimilating the materials. Thanks are due for their ungrudging help in the matter of access to some materials to Pabitrakumar Deka, A.C. Bhuyan and Homen Bargohain of Gauhati; and to Arun Ghosh, Kulanath Gogoi, Govindalal Ray and Anuradha Chanda of Calcutta. I take this opportunity also to thank my wife, Anima Guha, for sharing with me some of the stresses and strains that the writing of this book involved. The Cartography Section of my Centre is to be collectively thanked for preparing the map accompanying this book.

My friends and colleagues, S.K. Chaube, Amales Tripathi, Safiq Naqvi, M.S. Prabhakar, Sabyasachi Bhattacharya, Bipan Chandra and Barun De read and commented on portions of the manuscript. Their is scrutiny helped me avoid certain errors of judgement and style at the stage of revision. Barun and Bipan influenced considerably the rewriting of my final chapters, through their seminal ideas on some important aspects of Indian nationalism. For editorial help at the final stage, I am indebted to A.K. Gupta and N.C. Chatterjee of the Indian Council of Historical Research. My thanks go to my countless friends on the staff of various libraries at Poona, Bombay, Delhi, Calcutta, Shillong, Gauhati and Tezpur I visited in course of my work. My thanks also go to Sudhamay Sengupta, R. Girija and Gouri Banerjee who typed the manuscript.

Contents

List of Tables

List of Abbreviations

ACOER	*Assam Congress Opium Enquiry Report* (1925)
Ad. Rep.	*Administration Report* (Annual)
AICC	All India Congress Committee
AISF	All India Students Federation
AITUC	All India Trade Union Congress
ALAP	*Assam Legislative Assembly Proceedings*
ALCP	*Assam Legislative Council Proceedings*
ALECR	*Assam Labour Enquiry Committee Report*, 1921–22
AOC	Assam Oil Company Limited
APCC	Assam Pradesh (Provincial) Congress Committee
APTUC	Assam Provincial Trade Union Congress
AS	*Assam Secretariat Files* (at Assam State Archives, Shillong; now shifted to Gauhati)
BPCC	Bengal Provincial Congress Committee
CID	Criminal Investigation Department
CP	Central Provinces
CPI	Communist Party of India
CrPC	Criminal Penal Code
DCC	District Congress Committee
DIR	Defence of India Rules
DPI	Director of Public Instruction
DHAS	Department of Historical and Antiquarian Studies (Government of Assam, Gauhati)
EBALCP	*Eastern Bengal and Assam Legislative Council Proceedings*
GI	Government of India
IAR	*Indian Annual Register*

ICS	Indian Civil Service
IESHR	*Indian Economic and Social History Review*
ILCP	*Imperial (Indian) Legislative Council Proceedings*
Imp. Gaz.	*Imperial Gazetteer of India*
INA	Indian National Army
INTUC	Indian National Trade Union Congress
IPC	Indian Penal Code
ITA	Indian Tea Association
K.W.	keep with (certain confidential Home Department files were so marked)
LSG	Local Self Government
MLA	Member, Legislative Assembly
MLC	Member, Legislative Council
NAI	National Archives of India
n.d.	no date
NMML	Nehru Memorial Museum and Library
NNC	Naga National Council
OEHFM	Office of the Editor of the History of Freedom Movement, Government of Assam
Pol. Proc.	*Political Proceedings*
RCPI	Revolutionary Communist Party of India
RIAF	Royal Indian Air Force
RIN	Royal Indian Navy
RPC	*Rajendra Prasad Collection*
RTC	Round Table Conference
TE	Tea Estate

Note on Spelling

In matters of transliteration and the spelling of proper names, absolute consistency has not been aimed at. Anglicized spellings of several surnames (e.g., Barua, Borooah, Baruah, Barooah; Bardaloi, Bardoloi; Phookan, Phukan, etc.) are varied in usage; such spellings in a person's name often underwent changes even within his or her own lifetime. Hence, what has been attempted in this book is only to maintain the same spelling of a proper name all through, except in quotes.

In the matter of transliteration from Indian languages, all borrowed English words (e.g., 'Congress') have been retained in their original form, and a simplified system of transliteration has been improvized to avoid diacritical marks.

Introduction, Revised Edition

A work like this, for better or worse, acquires over the years a certain position and occupies a recognized space in the intellectual history of a people. Eschewing false vanity, I may even mention that some view this book as somewhat of a 'classic'. In the nearly three decades since its publication, the work has been used by scholars and others as a source book, a reference point, a point of departure and debate. It has also generated very strong disagreement for other explorations of corresponding themes. Indeed, it has even been the subject of a book-length polemic, published in the Assamese language.

The book having been out of print for quite some time, I was under pressure from young scholars to take a personal initiative to get it republished. I had the necessary permission from its original publishers, the Indian Council of Historical Research, to do so. But then I was caught in a dilemma. Should I go in for a thorough revision with the advantages of hindsight gained over the last thirty years or so, or for a mere reprint? I rejected both ideas, and for good reasons. Any attempt to thoroughly revise the work would have merely increased its bulk through padding, since my old perception still holds the ground in the absence of fresh empirical data warranting a new interpretation.

However, apart from taking care of printing mistakes and slips, further minor emendments of a few sentences of the original text have been necessary, for the sake of clarity and to avoid ambiguities. Besides, some matters have been shifted from the footnotes and incorporated into the main text, where they should have belonged. A few new footnotes have also been added. In short, my perception as of 1977 is preserved as a document, the emendments in this second edition being only marginal. Incidentally, it may be noted that the three-volume *Political History of Assam* (1,200 pages) corroborates, for the same colonial period, my major findings. History-writing by others from their respective points of view will continue; and, in due course, I believe, a consensus will emerge that is established as the core of historical truth, my own findings inclusive. This, at the least, is my belief.

What follows is a retrospect, a look back as an author re-reading his book and explaining how it came to be written, the doors it opens to avenues that could have been further explored and could still be explored by other scholars. I have only one regret, that I could not give more space to the movements of the plains tribes, hill tribes and other backward communities. However, it is gratifying to note that several of our younger scholars, having taken cue from my work, are now exploring these avenues.

I was invited by the Indian Council of Historical Research (ICHR) to write a book on an allotted theme – the role of Assam's legislature in the Indian freedom struggle – as a part of a national project encompassing the legislatures of all the British-Indian Provinces and the Central legislature. At first I hesitated to accept the invitation. By training an economist, I was then researching such topics as the growth of raw cotton output in western India during the nineteenth century, and its processing and marketing. Besides, the legislature as a focal point – I was afraid – would force me to tell too dull a story of the freedom movement, if not extended to its several other dimensions. However, given the assurance that I could digress to discuss other related socio-economic issues as well, and that my academic freedom to do so would not be interfered with, I seized the opportunity to make my home province better understood outside.

For fact-finding, I had to consult varied sources, some of which were not so easily available, as mentioned in my appended bibliography. Beyond the recorded facts, there were also my own historical and political perspectives. The facts themselves, as gleaned from selected sources, could be questionable. These, having their own inbuilt biases and contradicting each other, needed to be scrutinized and carefully divested of such anomalies for acceptance as truth. In doing so, the historian applies his mind, his own standards of judgement. He also takes the help of reasonable imagination to fill up gaps in the gleaned information, if any. This is the historical craft I followed. Interviews were used only to have a 'feel' of the period or for reinforcing certain recorded information. Thus my own values also influenced my narrative of what happened in Assam during its colonial past. Incidentally, I was myself a participant-observer during the last decade of the freedom struggle, and that experience too underlay my work.

I believe that history is made by the people, not by individuals glorified as heroes or demonized, although, at crucial junctures, they too play important roles. However, in the absence of adequate material for a people's history, I had to tread the elitist path. I made an attempt, nevertheless, to keep the interests of the toiling masses uppermost in my perspective. Unlike traditional historians, I also made use of the available quantitative data alongside the qualitative. This was done so that I could steer clear of the hyperboles and rhetoric resorted to by some of my peers (Saikia 2000; Barooah 1997). My terse comments on the leaders were discontinuous and not consolidated at one place. This resulted in a misunderstanding that an overall critical evaluation was neglected. In fact, I allowed my chronologically presented data to talk more than myself.

The way we did our job in the early 1970s, searching for 'facts' in archival records and sitting for hours in libraries making notes – indeed, the very act of writing a book and getting it typed – is probably now considered quite archaic. Sweeping changes have now taken place in the infrastructure for research and writing. Someone who is computer-illiterate like myself, cannot but wonder about the consequences, were these conveniences available in our days. Facilities like photocopying of archival documents and rare books were not easily available and, when available, were expensive. Articles were hand-written, followed by meticulous typing in triplicate. Editorial emendments were laborious, involving correction fluid. This involved a significant cost in terms of the time spent on editorial actions that are trivially achieved today with a personal computer.

The other major change that has altered the mechanics of doing research is the internet, the access to information that it provides and the speed with which it may be disseminated. Without these tools our progress was slower and we did not have the breadth of access that today's academics possess. Did all this affect the quality of our work? Probably not. Did it slow down our progress considerably? Most definitely so. That is why, while dealing with my topic, I had to limit its parameters so that I could finish the job on time, yet expecting that further research would follow to explore the area beyond them.

Despite near-unanimity about the importance *and* quality of my research, there were reservations, too, among reviewers of my book. Much of the polemics related to a perception that I had not been sufficiently appreciative of Gopinath Bardoloi's heroic role in saving Assam from inclusion in Pakistan. Perhaps I was expected to be more eloquent in this respect, as a biographer would have been.

Should credit go to Bardoloi alone for saving Assam? Surely not. His peers in the APCC also were equally seized with the issue, and played their respective roles individually and collectively. There was an immediate and spontaneous outburst of protests against the British Cabinet Mission's Grouping Plan. A popular upsurge in Assam led by Congressmen, socialists, communists and others took place at the grassroots, even as the Congress leaders were seriously considering it.

It provided for a three-tier confederation of all the provinces of India, grouped into three sections, and the princely states. It also provided for a province's right to quit its allotted section after the first elections under the new constitution were over. Though the national leaders found the offer worth considering, the people did not. They saw in it the danger of irrevocable inclusion into Pakistan. Under popular pressure, the AICC's resolution accepting the plan had to be drastically modified more than once at its drafting stage, to make it acceptable to the people. Finally, it was passed, by 99 to 52 votes, on 5 January 1947, with a *proviso*. In that *proviso* the AICC reserved the right to direct its Working Committee to advise a province to take appropriate action whenever circumstances so required, keeping in view the basic principle of provincial autonomy and the wishes of the people concerned. M. Tayyebulla, APCC president, was personally satisfied that this was enough guarantee against Assam's inclusion into Pakistan or a greater Bengal. He voted for the resolution. But of the other AICC members from Assam, one abstained and six voted against.

In fact, following the advice of Jawaharlal Nehru and Sardar Vallabhbhai Patel, the Assam Legislative Assembly, led by Bardoloi, had already passed a resolution in July 1946, expressing the will of the people in advance. It directed its members in the Constituent Assembly to shun the allotted section for framing, independently of it, Assam's provincial constitution. It was under such circumstances that the Muslim League's reiteration of its Pakistan demand and rejection of the plan led to its burial. India was vivisected. So was Punjab, Bengal and Assam. While narrating the facts of the episode, Bardoloi's role was certainly not understated.

It was on other issues like his rightist Gandhian labour policy, his handling of strikes in Digboi and Arunabund Tea Estate, and his withdrawal of the 'Assam Tea Garden Labourers' Freedom of Movement Bill' at the European party's request that I expressed my disapproval, and rightly. The facts talked more than I myself did. His hesitation to resign despite his party's anti-war stand – I argued – was not because of his 'lust for power', but to buy time to spell out and notify the newly adopted rigid policy on the Line system to protect tribal lands. Some of his contributions had to be unfortunately left out, simply because 'loading a whole elephant into a casket' was not possible. All said, while assessing Bardoloi's leadership in different contexts, I was not miserly.

About his first ministry I wrote: 'Bardoloi knew his game of politics too well . . . his personal qualities and the abilities of his colleague, Fakhruddin Ali Ahmed, made up for his team's shortcomings, . . . he had enough gifts of leadership to have his way at every critical stage and with popular support . . . he could always strike a balance between national and narrow Assamese interests' (Guha 1977, p. 232).

A British historian suggested that the Act of 1935 had 'granted almost full self-government in the Provinces' and that 'Indian politicians had prizes worth fighting for'. My retort was 'Bardoloi, the Congress politician and statesman, would not have chosen to give a walkover to Saadulla to form five of the six ministries during the period from 1937 to 1946 had the prize been worth fighting for, or if the nationalist struggle had only been a fight for prizes' (ibid., p. 336).

A more serious allegation was that my account of Assamese–Bengali relations was not impartial. Admittedly, my focus was not on Bengal but on Assam, particularly its Brahmaputra Valley. I did indicate that the imposition of Bengali as the only recognized language during 1836–73, an incessant influx of Bengali migrants, mutual territory claims of the two neighbouring provinces, competition for jobs, and, above all, lack of empathy of the Bengali middle-class leaders towards their neighbour's legitimate demands – all these factors were responsible for the genesis of Assamese chauvinism from the 1920s. For, Assamese sons of the soil were at the receiving end in their own homeland.

The situation of the Bengalis was quite different. They formed the major linguistic group in the province and a viable minority in the Brahmaputra Valley, yet outnumbering the Assamese in its urban sector. Besides, the Surma Valley

Bengalis were sons of the soil in their own right. They were not an endangered species. Under such circumstances, their Hindu–Bengali chauvinism does not appear to have taken the form of frenzied and visceral mobilizations. It found expression in domineering and contemptuous attitudes to the people of the other valley (ibid., p. 76 and 79).

As to the influx of migrants from Bengal into colonial Assam and the Sylhet question, my 1977 perception still holds good. By now they have already been assimilated to the mainstream Assamese society, mostly through linguistic conversion, despite past conflicts.

The British 'divide and rule' policy was revealed in Sir A. Frazer's secret note of 7 February 1904, quoted in my book as a footnote. He wrote that since overpopulated Eastern Bengal needed room for expansion, it could expand only towards the east. 'So far from hindering the national development,' he continued, 'we are really giving it greater scope and *enabling Bengal to absorb Assam*' (ibid., p. 71).

A section of middle-class Hindu–Bengali leaders, however, did not take up the bait. They reacted otherwise. They vehemently opposed the merger of Assam proper with Bengal or any part thereof. For, in their perception, it was a 'savage', wild territory. This attitude was a spoke in the wheel of the concept of 'greater Bengal', which was welcome to their Muslim counterparts and Frazer.

Perhaps it was the aforesaid anti-Assamese feelings and domineering attitude of Bengali leaders that influenced the Assamese leaders' decision to keep aloof from the former's anti-Partition movement. This theme remains unresearched by historians of Assam, myself included. It needs to be researched, and dispassionately.

Did my Bengali roots influence my perspective and interpretation? Opinions differ. While my book was well-received in general, a couple of historians found it to be subtly pro-Bengali and anti-Assamese in spirit and tone (Barooah 1997; Saikia, *Gariiyasii*, VI, May and September 1999), while still others complained that I was reticent in discussing the problems of the Bengalis of the Brahmaputra Valley. One reviewer blamed me for not throwing enough light on 'the connivance of certain influential politicians' to hand over Sylhet to Pakistan 'on a platter as it were' (*The Hindu*, international edition, 23 September 1989). Yet another scholar, without prejudice, commented: 'He de-Bengalized himself and wrote the chronicle of the exploitation of subaltern classes in Assam as an insider, as an Assamese' (Mitra 2005, p. 245). It is for the readers to judge the validity of such statements. However, it is possible that even an honest, dispassionate historian's perception might get unconsciously derailed because of his ethnic or class identity.

A pertinent point was raised by another reviewer (*The Economic and Political Weekly*, 1 April 1978). He rightly observed my reticence to analyse the 'exact relationship between the "regional" and the "national" big bourgeoisie', and also the 'class character of the Congress leadership on the national scale', which failed 'to solve the national question with wisdom'. Yes, it was my informed and wise decision not to theorize on this problematic issue. Instead, I illustrated, with select data, how the national leaders handled the aspirations of small national groups, hoping that readers would draw the right conclusions from them.

Within the colonial superstructure based on a feudal socio-economic society, capitalist growth was fragmented, weak and uneven. The pan-Indian big bourgeoisie – big corporate houses – were inclusivist and integrative in outlook, whereas the regional bourgeoisie were exclusivist and inward-looking, tied down as they were to their small interests. The former stood for a national free market and single nationhood; the latter, for a protected segment in that market and coordinated, autonomized plural nationalism. The one-nation ideology of the Congress in our multi-nationality country could not reconcile these diverse interests. Besides, the big bourgeoisie's hegemonization process was also weakened by feudal and semi-feudal interests, Hindu–Muslim disunity, casteism and tribalism. As a result, the national question remained – and still remains – unresolved.

Yet, what the Congress achieved was not small. The bourgeois Congress Party formally emerged as the leader of a multi-class national front against imperialism and fascism. Until 1946, there was no major lack of trust between its high command and the APCC. The latter, in that election year, pledged to halt the influx of migrants from Bengal, the separation of Sylhet and Cachar plains from Assam, and to reorganize the province's territorial boundary on the basis of Assamese language and culture. It won the poll (Guha 1977, p. 302). Its election manifesto had the high command's blessings.

Given the weak big bourgeois hegemony over the civil society, a *section* of the national leadership did tend to domineer or ridiculously misinterpret the aspirations of small national groups, as Rajendra Prasad did (ibid., pp. 258–59), but not always. In 1938, against Abul Kalam Azad's stiff opposition, it was Subhas Chandra Bose, Patel and Gandhiji who helped Bardoloi form Assam's first Congress coalition ministry. Nehru had no doubt about the legitimacy of Assamese aspirations to preserve their own culture and language in their own homeland. He also agreed on the desirability of separating Sylhet. It was Nehru and Patel who did effectively suggest the escape route for Assam to get out of the Cabinet Mission's road map. Above all, Gandhiji advised Bardoloi to revolt against the Congress high command if it meddled with Assam's autonomy on the eve of independence (ibid., pp. 258–59, 311 and 313).

The tendency to dominate and browbeat was a post-independence phenomenon, after the leadership's concern visibly shifted from decentralization of power and regional autonomy, to over-centralization for India's quick development as a planned, integrated economy.

To conclude, the history of the freedom struggle in India revolved around the Congress Party, and allies and rivals. Because of its big bourgeois class character, of its leadership the Congress Party had its limitations. That is why it could not be expected to fulfil its democratic tasks. Neither the national question nor the mass illiteracy problem has been solved during the half-century since we became a republic. Rather than the Congress, it is the socialists and communists who are to blame for their inability, so far, to head a coalition of the toiling classes to usher in a people's democracy in India, with the maximum possible autonomy for its regional national groups and without endangering our unity in diversity.

I am much indebted to the Omeo Kumar Das Institute of Social Change and Development of Guwahati, and its Director, Abu Nasar Saied Ahmed, for the encouragement and material support I received, without which this revised text of my book could not have been readied for publication. My thanks to all the members of the OKD family for their ungrudging and varied help, and for making me feel like I had been adopted into the Institute when I was working on my manuscript. For the excellent secretarial assistance and desktop printing, I owe a special word of appreciation to Ratna Bhuyan, Pranita Kalita and to Bornali Kalita.

My thanks to Indira Chandrasekhar of Tulika Books for bringing out this new edition of my book, and to V.K. Ramachandran for playing a catalyst's role in this context. The Introduction, specially written for this edition, owes its origin to M.S. Prabhakara's insistence that I must explain to the twenty-first century scholars how relevant my three-decades-old perception of Assam's past will be to them, when they try to understand the past with new questions in mind. He also wanted me to tell them what difficulties we had to undergo to collect materials and work in the mid-1970s. Many thanks to him for his counsel, and also to P.K. Shukla, Jiten Sharma, Uttam Bathari and my son, Supratik Guha.

January 2006   AMALENDU GUHA

CHAPTER ONE

Under the Umbrella of the Bengal Presidency: 1826–73

British Conquest of Northeast India

It was after the acquisition of the Diwani of Bengal in 1765 that the East India Company came into direct contact with the medieval kingdoms of Manipur, Jaintia, Cachar and Assam, as well as the tribal communities of the adjoining hills. These sparsely populated territories did not yet have enough economic worth or surplus revenue-yielding potential to attract the attention of the British annexationists. They had therefore been left undisturbed, until the Burmese invasion (1817–24) of Manipur, Assam and the Cachar plains brought an end to this policy of indifference. In November 1823, David Scott, the Magistrate of Rangpur and Civil Commissioner for the district of Goalpara and Garo Hills (formed in 1822), was also appointed Agent to the Governor-General on the Northeast Frontier of Bengal. 'We have not come (here) to quench our thirst for the conquest of your kingdom', proclaimed a manifesto published in Bengali on behalf of the interventionist British–Indian troops, 'but to destroy our enemies, interested as we are to protect ourselves.'[1] The Burmese were finally forced to surrender their claim over Assam under the Treaty of Yandabo, 1826.

During the following decade and a half, the kingdoms of Jaintia, Cachar and Assam along with their dependencies, and all the petty, independent tribal states of the Khasi Hills were annexed. Further annexation of the remaining hills was subsequently completed step by step in the face of stiff tribal resistance. The North Cachar Hills were organized into a separate administrative unit, after their subjugation was completed by 1854. A part of the Naga Hills was annexed in 1866, the country of the Lhota Nagas in 1875, of the Angami Nagas in 1878–80, and of the Ao Nagas in 1889. The Garo Hills, long under loose political control, was made a separate district in 1869, but the Garos could not be brought under full control until 1873. The Lushais (Mizo) were brought under control during the years 1871–89, but formation of the Lushai Hills district took place only in 1898. The boundaries of the British power in Northeast India were in fact

---

[1] Quote from *Samachar Darpan* (in Bengali, Serampore), 17 April 1824; translation ours.

always moving, always in a flux, right up to its last days in India.[2] Nevertheless, the British province that came to be known as Assam had more or less taken shape by 1873.

The Raj appeared on the scene in the guise of saviours of the people who were suffering under the chaos, lawlessness and oppression that had persisted since the 1770s, starting with the Moamaria civil war and culminating in the Burmese occupation of the Assam plains (1817–24). But it soon dawned on the people that the Raj had come to stay. Its purpose was to turn Assam into an agricultural estate of tea-drinking Britons and to transform local traditional institutions to suit the colonial pattern of exploitation. The people found out from experience that the new masters' immediate concern was extortion of land revenue, even to the detriment of the welfare of their subjects. After assuming charge of Assam from his predecessor in 1832, Robertson found 'its inhabitants emigrating, its villages decaying and its revenue annually declining'. The Court of Directors was grieved to learn that 'a dreadful extortion had beggared the ryots and rendered a large portion of Assam waste in which up to our conquest such a thing as jungle was hardly to be seen'.[3]

Peoples' Resistance to the Conquerors
The Early Phase of Resistance

The old aristocracy, which had lost its offices of profit, was the first to react violently to the alien rule. The rebellions of Gomdhar Konwar and Rupchand Konwar in 1828 and 1829, respectively, were but attempts at a palace revolution by pretenders to the throne. These were quickly suppressed. For his role in the 1829 rebellion, Peali Barphukan was executed. The Singphos, a tribe on the Burma border, too, raised the banner of revolt during 1830–31. They were in touch with the organizers of the first rebellion and with the Khasi resistance leaders. The British ban on their slave-hunting operations in Assamese territory was one major factor that had actually led the Singphos into this infructuous revolt. The Khasi war of independence (1829–33), led by U. Tirot Singh at the head of an alliance of the petty Khasi republics, was, on the other hand, a protracted resistance movement of the entire people, employing guerrilla tactics of warfare. Together with their people, the Khasi chiefs fought valiantly against the British, but they had to ultimately surrender before superior arms.[4]

---

[2] For details of the annexations, see E.A. Gait, *A History of Assam* (second edition, Calcutta/Simla, 1926), Chapters XIV and XV; S.K. Bhuyan, *Anglo–Assamese Relations 1771–1826* (Gauhati, 1949); R.M. Lahiri, *The Annexation of Assam: 1824–54* (Calcutta, 1954); H. Bareh, *The History and Culture of the Khasi People* (Shillong, 1967); P.C. Kar, *British Annexation of Garo Hills* (Calcutta, 1970); N.K. Barooah, *David Scott in North-East India: A Study in British Paternalism* (New Delhi, 1970).

[3] Quotes are respectively from *Political Proceedings*, 23 July 1832, No. 90 and letter from the Court of Directors, No. 14 of 1834, both cited in Lahiri, *Annexation of Assam*, pp. 225 and 235.

[4] Lahiri, *Annexation of Assam*, Chapter III, particularly pp. 59–60. Also Gait, *History of Assam*, pp. 301–03 and 324.

Captain A. White visited the Khasi country in connection with settling a succession dispute there in 1826. He was very impressed when he witnessed how the Khasi tribal democracy functioned. He saw an assembly of three to four hundred people in session, who 'were entitled to vote on the question'. While narrating this experience three years later, he wrote: 'their debates were conducted with much spirit and animation for 2 days and with an order, decorum and apparent courtesy which I have not seen surpassed in any European Society'. Even as the hostilities started, White recognized in the Khasis

> a people likely to show the same stubborn independence and hatred of foreign domination . . . which the character of their Government was calculated to foster, being apparently founded on an extensive popular basis, the power of the Rajah being apparently checked by an aristocracy of a widely extended nature bordering upon democracy.[5]

The National Revolt of 1857 and Its Impact

The great national upheaval of 1857 did not leave Assam untouched. Wild rumours that the end of the British rule in India was imminent spread all over the province. The Hindustani sepoys stationed at Dibrugarh and Gauhati, as well as some members of the deposed local aristocracy, became restive towards the close of July 1857. Contact was established between soldiers' barracks and followers of the Charing Raja who aspired for restoration. This was done through the efforts of Maniram Dewan (1806–1858), who was then sojourning in Calcutta, and his associate Madhu Mullick, a Bengali Mukhtear. A plan was reportedly agreed upon, and preparations for the uprising went on secretly. The planters and missionaries became panicky; many of them left their posts to take shelter at Gauhati. Marwari traders and moneylenders buried their properties in apprehension of trouble. The Commissioner of Assam, in his dispatch of 29 August 1857, asked the Bengal government to send a European force 'to save the province from the (impending) revolution'.[6] Because of the loyalty of the Gurkha and local tribal sepoys of the Assam Light Infantry, however, the apprehensions were belied. Large-scale arrests were nevertheless made. Many sepoys were courtmartialled for mutiny, and no less than twenty-one civilians were tried and punished for treason. Maniram Dewan and Peali Barua were given death sentences. Madhu Mullick, Bahadur Gaonburha and several others were sentenced to transportation for life or long jail terms. Thus ended the attempt to dislodge the British from power in Assam. With the arrival of three 100-strong units of a British naval brigade from Calcutta, the situation further eased, much to the relief of the local administration and the planters.

---

[5] White to Swinton, Gauhati, 24 April 1829, *Foreign Secret*, 8 May, No. 11–12 (National Archives of India; hereafter NAI).

[6] Cited in H.K. Barpujari, *Assam in the Days of the Company 1826–1858* (Gauhati, 1963), p. 169; see also ibid., pp. 163–79. Gait, *History of Assam*, pp. 326–28.

There can be no doubt about the national character of the attempted uprising. The persons accused of treason belonged to diverse social and ethnic groups. Yet they were able to unite with the common objective of driving out the alien intruder and also of reducing the burden of taxation. The said leader of the 'plot', Maniram Dewan, was a man of ability and vision. His well-argued critique of the British rule, submitted to the authorities in the early 1850s, remains a remarkable political document. The bias of the leaders of the revolt was basically pro-feudal. Yet it was not altogether without popular support. There is evidence that workers of the Assam Company – all of them Assamese villagers working under contractors – struck work to fraternize with the rebels. This is evident from observations made by the planters at the time. On the arrival of the naval brigade at Sibsagar, a reception was given to them by the local planters. The Calcutta Board of Directors of the Assam Company, in this connection, reported as follows on 2 March 1858:

> whilst our private servants were cheerfully obedient to our co-operative proceedings with Government in the maintenance of order, the independent contractors for cultivating our lands, *the indigenous inhabitants of the neighbouring villages held off from the performance of their contracts* on the plea that they were not to be paid, believing that the Europeans 'were to be cut up'; so far from aiding Government in suppressing revolt, they remained utterly passive, many sympathizing with their conspiring Rajah and the disaffected Seepoys. *Had an outbreak occurred, there can be little doubt that they would have sided with the rebels.* (Emphasis ours.)

The planters may have exaggerated their distrust of the natives. But the fact remains that the contractors and their labour gangs struck work and refused to cooperate with the Europeans in the maintenance of order at the crucial hour. Madhuram Koch, the leader of this labour strike, was sentenced to seven years of rigorous imprisonment on 30 January 1858.[7] A few months after the suppression of the revolt, when stories of assaults on respectable persons, of the slaughtering of their cattle, arson and such other incidental outrages committed by British sailors of the naval brigade at Dibrugarh were reported in the press, a correspondent wrote to the editor of the Calcutta-based *Hindoo Patriot* on 25 September 1858 (the letter was published on 21 October 1858): 'It appears from their manners and expressions that they, as if instruments of torture and cruelty, are employed to bend the unbroken spirits of a newly acquired territory to the yoke of subjection.'

---

[7] Quote from an extract in H.A. Antrobus, *A History of Assam Company 1839–1953* (Edinburgh, 1957), p. 96. For information on Madhuram, see B. Sharma, *The Rebellion of 1857 vis-à-vis Assam* (Gauhati, 1957), pp. 40 and 75; also, by the same author, *Maniram Dewan* (in Assamese, Gauhati, 1950), pp. 185–86.

Peasant Struggles of a New Type

Two other uprisings of a local nature took place in the early 1860s – one in the Jaintia Hills and the other in the plains of Nowgong – in the wake of a series of new taxation measures.

In the Jaintia Hills, the people were not accustomed to any kind of money tax. When a house tax and stamp duty were introduced in 1860, they rose in open rebellion. The revolt was put down with an iron hand, but the people lay low only for the time being. A fresh levy of the new income tax of 1860 – insignificant though it was in its incidence locally – made them apprehensive of further imposts. The introduction of the licence tax in January 1862 and attempts at confiscation of even ceremonial weapons by a brutalized police force caused a more serious outburst of revolt in the same month. Led by their traditional chiefs, the Khasi people of the Jaintia Hills stood as one man. Two Sikh regiments and an elephant battery were moved in, but the people, 'though armed with bows and arrows, fought bravely for their independence'.[8] They did not surrender until November 1863.

The increase in land revenue on dry crop lands in 1861 was much resented in Nowgong, as it was in the three other affected districts. However, it was the 1860 ban on poppy cultivation that affected the peasant economy of Nowgong the most, for it was the largest opium-producing district of Assam. The Income Tax Act, as amended in 1861, did not in fact touch a single agriculturist in Assam. Nevertheless, because of an information gap, it created misapprehensions about the government's intentions. People knew that in the adjoining Jaintia Hills, peasants had fought with arms against unfair taxes. At this juncture, the Bengal government called upon its officers in Assam to report on the feasibility of a tax on betel-nut and *paan* cultivation. This led to an agitation in Nowgong, mainly in the Phulaguri area inhabited by tribal people (Lalung).

In September 1861, some 1,500 peasants marched to the district town. They demonstrated peacefully before the Magistrate and presented a petition to him. It referred to the harm that had already been done to them by prohibiting poppy cultivation. It prayed that no further taxes be levied on their betel-nut and *paan* orchards. The District Magistrate treated the demonstrators casually and was callous towards their grievances. It was established through an official enquiry later that the Magistrate always dealt with ryots in a high-handed and provocative manner, and did not allow them to even enter his office compound.[9]

---

[8] Gait, *History of Assam*, pp. 328–29 for the quote, and Bareh, *History and Culture of the Khasi People*, pp. 173 and 177. Also H.K. Barpujari, 'Facts behind the Jaintia Rebellion 1862–64', *Journal of Indian History,* 51, Part I (April 1973), pp. 141–48.

[9] This account is based on the *Bengal Administrative Report,* 1861–62, pp. 65–67; the evidence of J.J.S. Driberg, Commissioner of Excise in Assam, in the *Report of the Royal Commission on Opium,* 1893, Vol. 2 (London, 1894), pp. 300–01, and 'Papers on Phulaguri Ryots', No. 891, Fort William, 31 May 1862, from Secretary to the Government of Bengal to Off. Commissioner of Assam, given as an appendix therein, pp. 459–60.

They were even fined on several occasions for allegedly making noise within the court compound.

A *raij mel* (people's assembly)[10] was thereupon held at Phulaguri in October 1861. The assembly was scheduled to be in session for five days to ensure participation from distant villages. Approximately 1,000 people assembled by 15 October, 500–600 of whom were armed with lathis. A police party that came to disperse the assembly was driven out, save one policeman who was taken into custody by the people. By 17 October, 3,000 to 4,000 people had gathered. The police made yet another attempt to break up the assembly and arrested some of the leaders the same day. However, after all of them were forcibly rescued by the people, the police had to leave the spot. The next day, a British officer, Lieutenant Singer, came with a police party and met the leading members of the assembly. They reiterated, through a spokesman named Jati Kalita, their complaints about the ban on opium cultivation, and their apprehensions about the income and *paan* taxes. They added that, as the District Magistrate had not attended to their grievances, they were contemplating means of carrying their complaints to the higher authorities in the *mel*. Singer ordered them to disperse and tried to seize their bamboo lathis. He got himself inadvertently killed in the scuffle. The police force accompanying him fled in panic.

The news of Singer's death, accompanied by rumours of an intended attack on the town, reached Nowgong the same evening. The panicky District Magistrate entrenched himself at the Treasury and sent a small armed force to the trouble-spot. It fired on the crowd, leading to several deaths. By 23 October all was quiet again with the arrival of fresh military forces from Tezpur and Gauhati. Narsingh Lalung and eight other peasant leaders, mostly tribals, were punished with long-term imprisonment or transportation. This episode of heroic resistance by the people to the increasing tax burden and bureaucratic mindlessness is still very much alive in folk memory as the 'Phulaguri Dhawa'. From this time onwards, the traditionally popular institution of the *raij mel* was increasingly resorted to by the Assamese people for resisting enhancement of the land revenue, which took place periodically. The Phulaguri Dhawa was vilified by colonial scribes as an uprising against the ban on poppy cultivation (see Census of India, *Assam*, Vol. I, 1891, p. 231). But the available evidence reveals that such a characterization was a deliberate distortion. The Secretary to the Government of Bengal concluded that 'the infliction of numerous fines on the people for their importunity in urging their grievances' on the District Magistrate's attention was a major cause of the revolt. The tactless District Magistrate was subsequently demoted to a lower rank, under the Lieutenant-Governor's orders.[11]

---

[10] For the significance of the term *raij mel,* see Chapter Two, footnotes 52 and 54.

[11] Same as footnote 9 above and K.N. Dutt, *Landmarks of the Freedom Struggle in Assam* (Gauhati, 1958), p. 26. See *Arunoday* (in Assamese, Sibsagar), 14 (November 1861), for a comment by N.L. Farwell condemning the uprising as futile adventurism. (We have used a later version of the spelling of the name of the journal.) For a folk

To sum up, the Assamese peasantry, unlike the Khasis, reacted to the new regime at first with mixed feelings. After half a century of chronic political chaos, the British measures towards restoration of law and order appeared to them as a welcome phenomenon. But soon they began to feel the increasing strain of progressive enhancement of land revenue and other taxes. The accompanying monetization process that was suddenly enforced was also somewhat disastrous in its initial impact. The new masters ceased to collect taxes in kind or in the form of labour rent, which had been the erstwhile practice. In the given transitional situation of deficient currency supply and extremely limited facilities for marketing farm products, this policy caused hardship and resentment, for, peasants failed to secure enough cash to pay the land tax. In the interiormost areas, even around 1850, peasants had to walk long distances for two to three days to get their goods converted into cash.[12] Such a situation naturally tended to inhibit any expansion of agricultural acreage.

Planter Raj Strikes Roots
Rob Peasants to Pay Planters
The Assam Company – the first joint-stock company of India to be incorporated with limited liabilities under an Act of Parliament in August 1845 – was started in 1839. It remained virtually the sole planter in the field till 1850. By 1859 the Jorehaut Tea Co. and several individual enterprises were started. The total number of tea estates under distinct proprietors was then 51. The total acreage under tea in Assam proper increased from 2,311 acres in 1841 to about 8,000 acres by 1859, and the output of tea from 29,267 lbs to more than one million lbs. However, the Assam Company still accounted for 60 per cent of this acreage.[13] Faced by an acute labour shortage, the planter community urged the government in 1859 to further enhance the land revenue rates so that poor peasants could be flushed out of their villages to work for wages on the plantations. Another recommendation of theirs was to put a ban on the cultivation and sale of opium, the widespread consumption of which was believed to have made the

---

memory, see Benudhar Kalita, *Phulagurir Dhewa* (in Assamese, Deurigaon, Nowgong, 1961). *Dhawa (Dhewa)* means a battle or chase.

12　Observation by a missionary in *Arunoday*, 9 (January 1854). The scarcity of coins as circulating media of exchange continued till the early 1850s. For a corroboration, see T.K. Agarwala, ed., *Haribilas Agarwala Dangariiyar Atmajiivanii* (in Assamese, Gauhati, 1967), p. 14. An anonymous letter published in *Samachar Darpan*, 18 June 1832, protested against the exorbitant rate of land revenue and unjust assessment. For problems of transition, see A. Guha, 'Colonization of Assam: Years of Transitional Crisis (1825–40)', *Indian Economic and Social History Review* (hereafter *IESHR*) (Delhi), 5 (June 1968), pp. 125–48.

13　A. Guha, 'Colonization of Assam: Second Phase 1840–1859', *IESHR*, 4 (December 1967), pp. 1–2. For the 1859 acreage figures, *Selections from the Records of the Government of Bengal,* Vol. 37 (Calcutta, 1861), pp. 33–35, and Memorandum of Campbell in *Papers Relating to the Tea Industry of Bengal* (Calcutta, 1873), Appendix D, p. 121.

local people apathetic towards work.[14] The cultivation of poppy in Assam proper had almost trebled while the population had increased by 10 per cent or so under British rule between 1826 and 1853.

After some initial hesitation, the government responded favourably. It ordered a 15 to 30 per cent increase in the land revenue rates on the dry crop lands of four districts – Lakhimpur, Sibsagar, Darrang and Nowgong.[15] It also placed a ban on the cultivation of poppy in 1860, but the lucrative monopoly sale of north Indian opium, that had been yielding a profit to the government at least since 1851–52, was not discontinued. The sale price of this opium was increased, however, from Rs 14 per *seer* in 1860 to Rs 20 in 1862 and Rs 23 by 1873.[16] The addicts were thus forced to purchase high-priced government opium instead of growing it themselves. It appears that prohibition of the cultivation of poppy – practically the only crop peasants could readily dispose of for a cash earning – and raising of the opium price were both motivated not so much by humanitarian as by revenue considerations.

The land revenue rates on both dry and wet crops were uniformly and arbitrarily doubled in 1868, throughout Assam proper.[17] As a result of these enhanced rates, which were implemented during 1860–71, the total land revenue demand jumped up from Rs 1,001,773 in 1864–65 to Rs 2,165,157 in 1872–73. In some parts of Assam, people reacted to the new assessment by organizing *raij mels* (people's assemblies). In Lakhimpur district, the people protested in a novel way. They surrendered so much of their land to the government that the revised rates, though about double the previous rates in force, yielded an enhancement of only about 26 per cent in the total land revenue collection. This was at a time when the acreage under foodgrains was failing to increase sufficiently to meet the rising local demand for food. Food prices were higher in Assam than in any part of neighbouring Bengal. Yet the *Administrative Report* for the year 1871–72 commented: 'The whole question whether low rates would lead to increase of cultivation is a difficult and doubtful one.'[18]

---

[14] Antrobus, *History of Assam Company*, p. 99.

[15] Barpujari, *Assam in the Days of the Company*, p. 205. Also letters published in *Friend of India* (Calcutta), as cited in an editorial comment of *Arunoday*, 10 (February 1860), in anticipation of the tax increase.

[16] Barpujari, *Assam in the Days of the Company*, p. 207. Opium prices are from J.J.S. Driberg, 'Appendix XX – Historical Account of the Administration of Opium in Assam', *Report of the Royal Commission on Opium*, 1893, Vol. 2, p. 140.

[17] The erstwhile Ahom territory, that is, the districts (as of 1947) of Sibsagar, Lakhimpur, Nowgong, Darrang and Kamrup, was known as Assam proper.

[18] Commissioner's order, vide letter No. 665, 14 November 1868, as cited in K.C. Bardoloi, ed., *Sadaramiinar Atmajiivanii* (in Assamese, Gauhati, 1960), p. 40. Also *Bengal Administrative Report*, 1872–73, p. 82, and ibid., 1871–72, p. 140. For the reference to Lakhimpur, Mackenzie as cited in L. Barua's speech, 10 September, *Assam Legislative Council Proceedings* (hereafter *ALCP*) (1929), Vol. 9, p. 1069.

Chattel Slaves Become Tenants

One of the few good things the Raj did, and which was appreciated by both the planters and the people, was the abolition of slavery in 1843. As an institution, slavery was of more than mere marginal importance to the labour-short economy of the Brahmaputra valley. An estimated 5 to 9 per cent of its population were apparently slaves and bondsmen, a considerable number of whom worked on agricultural farms. The abolition of slavery almost crippled the old Ahom aristocracy. Brahmin and Mahanta land-owners, who had for long depended on slaves and bondsmen for cultivation of their *devottar, brahmottar* and *dharmottar* lands, were also severely affected. Brahmin slave-holders of the district of Kamrup even held a protest demonstration and submitted to the authorities a bunch of 1,000 petitions seeking permission to retain their slaves and bondsmen. On the other hand, there were enthusiastic men like Radhanath Kataki, a Fauzdari Mohrur, to induce the slaves and bondsmen to address petitions to the government for their liberation, and, then, to expedite action thereupon.[19]

Slavery as an institution was so deep-rooted in the contemporary Assamese way of life that it took decades, in the absence of a rehabilitation programme, to die out. Records do not suggest large-scale opting out of slaves either for employment in the tea gardens or as wage labour in the villages. The bulk of them appear to have emerged, in due course, under the prevailing conditions of land abundance and capital shortage, as poor tenants. The immediate aftermath of the abolition of slavery was therefore a break-up of whatever large-sized farms there had been, if any, for lack of hired labour to take the place of the slaves. In fact, the process of transformation of chattel slaves into serfs and semi-serf tenants had started long before the formal abolition of slavery. Besides, the practice of mortgaging labour to a creditor as a means of settling one's debt was never suppressed. The Workmen's Breach of Contract Act, 1859, was a new step towards strengthening this form of debt slavery.

Jenkins's Colonization Scheme

The Charter granted to the East India Company in 1833 marked the final ascendancy of British industrial interests over mercantile interests and had its full impact on the settlement of newly conquered Assam. The Charter, for the first time, allowed Europeans to hold land outside the Presidency towns on a long-term lease or with freehold rights. This paved the path for a colonial plantation economy.

Even before the feasibility of tea culture in Assam had been firmly established, Francis Jenkins, in a report dated 22 July 1833, advocated the settlement of Englishmen of capital on its waste lands. It appeared to him that a scheme of colonization 'offered a better prospect for the speedy realization of improve-

---

[19] Bardoloi, ed., *Sadaramiinar Atmajiivanii,* p. 40. See also A. Guha, 'Land Rights and Social Classes in Medieval Assam', *IESHR,* 3 (September 1966), pp. 230–35 for the roots of the institution.

ments than any measures that could be adopted in the present ignorant and demoralized state of native inhabitants'. His idea was to attract a class of European planters with capital who would produce sugarcane, indigo and such other plantation crops. 'To obtain the full advantages that could accrue from European settlers, it appears to me', he said, 'that the grants must be altogether freehold, subject to no other condition than the payment of a fixed and unalterable rate of rent and absolutely unencumbered with any stipulations in regard to ryots or sub-tenants.'

Jenkins would not mind even the displacement of local ryots from their lands through the operation of a discriminatory land revenue policy in favour of white colonists. For, such a policy, according to him, would promote the long-run interests of the ryots themselves. He was afraid that 'if the government assessments upon the natives were generalized and not heavy', they would not be available as tenant cultivators under European superintendence, and, therefore, the introduction of commercial agriculture would be inhibited. On the other hand, if the assessment on cultivation was heavy, the ryots would have no alternative other than work for the European capitalist farmers. Any shortfall in the total proceeds of land revenue resulting from the twin policies of squeezing peasant holdings and granting substantial revenue concessions to planters, Jenkins believed, would be more than made up as soon as large quantities of waste land were brought under tillage and other improvements followed. The two premises of this colonization thesis were: (i) that a large number of local peasants had no means to provide ploughs, seeds and cattle for themselves, and (ii) that the colonists would be able to make the necessary advances to the former for growing export crops.[20]

Land to the Planter: A New Slogan

The idea of introducing British enterprise, capital and skill in agriculture caught the imagination of the Board of Revenue and the Lieutenant-Governor of Bengal. Meanwhile, the growing prospects of tea culture in Assam – the formation of the Tea Committee in early 1834, the starting of the Government Experimental Tea Gardens in 1836 and the first successful manufacture of Assam tea in December 1837 – made Jenkins's scheme of colonization all the more acceptable. In 1840, two-thirds of the Government Experimental Gardens were transferred to the Assam Company, rent-free for the initial years. To make the waste lands available for special cultivation on attractive terms, a set of rules were framed. These were known as the Wasteland Rules of 6 March 1838.

Waste land was offered to applicants on a forty-five-year lease on condition that a quarter of the area must be cleared within five years, failing which the land was liable to resumption. Indigenous aspirants were not discriminated against

---

[20] Jenkins to Secretary to the Government at Fort William, 22 July 1833, *Foreign Political Proceedings*, 11 February 1835, No. 90 (NAI).

as such, but the Rules were apparently framed in such a manner as to exclude them from all concessional grants in practice. No grant for agricultural purpose could be made for less than 100 acres at a time and to one who did not possess capital or stock worth at least Rs 3 per acre. Under these conditions, only Europeans could avail themselves of the opportunities.[21] According to the Rules, one-fourth of a grant was to be held revenue-free in perpetuity. The remaining portion of the grant, too, was to remain revenue-free for the initial five to twenty years, the period varying according to the nature of the waste land concerned, as shown below in tabular form.

However, since the 1838 Rules did not go far in attracting European capitalists, these were revised in 1854 providing for a 99-year lease on more liberal terms, as indicated in the table. At the same time, the minimum area of land for which one could apply was raised to 500 acres. Later the limit was reduced to 200 acres and relaxed to even 100 acres in special cases, if native applicants could satisfy the Collectors of their ability to bring ryots from outside Assam. These Rules stimulated a land rush not only in Assam proper, but also in the district of Cachar.

The waste lands settlement policy tempted planters to grab more land than they required or could manage. This was because such waste lands provided them with far greater resources than what land as a factor of production ordinarily denotes. The waste lands contained necessary housing materials including, in most cases, even valuable timber. Being transferable under the 1854 Rules, such lands could be sold later for an unearned profit. Above all, labourers could be settled as tenants on the surplus lands of the plantations, like so many serfs tied to the soil. It was additional bait to lure land-hungry tribals and low-caste peasants from famine-stricken areas outside Assam to come and work at wages that were otherwise unattractive. Yet another motivation behind this perverse land-grab policy was to keep away prospective competitors from the neighbourhood.

To facilitate the land-grabbing, a system of fee simple grants was introduced in 1861, under which land was sold at rates ranging from Rs 2–8 as. to Rs 5 per acre. No clearance condition was attached to the fee simple grants. Leases under the former Rules were made commutable to fee simple at twenty years' purchase payable at the time of commutation. From 1862 onwards, grants were put on auction sale. From 1876, the sale of fee simple land was stopped and a new system of thirty-year leases, also on liberal terms, was introduced.[22]

About 0.7 million acres of land had been settled with the planters in Assam by 1870–71, but the area actually under tea was only 56,000 acres, that

---

21 Revenue and Judicial letters from India and Bengal, 14 March 1837, No. 5, cited by Barpujari, *Assam in the Days of the Company*, p. 212; Gait, *History of Assam*, p. 359.
22 Gait, *History of Assam*, pp. 359–60; Barpujari, *Assam in the Days of the Company*, pp. 212–14. For the 1859 acreage figures, *Selections from the Records of the Government of Bengal*, Vol. 37, pp. 33–35.

Waste Land Settlement Rules: 1838 and 1854

Rules of 6 March 1838 *Three Categories of Waste Land*				Rules of 23 October 1854 *Irrespective of Categories of Waste Land*	
Under grass	*Under reeds and high grass*	*Under forests*	*Land revenue per acre*		*Land revenue per acre*
First 5 yrs Next	First 10 yrs	First 20 yrs	Nil	First 15 yrs	Nil
6–8 yrs Next	11–13 yrs	21–23 yrs	9 as.	16–25 yrs	3 as.
9–30 yrs	14–35 yrs	24–25 yrs	Rs 1–2 as.	26–99 yrs	6 as.
On expiry of leases:			at par with rice lands		at par with rice lands
One-fourth of grant perpetually revenue-free.				One-fourth of grant perpetually revenue-free	

Source: Tabulated from information in B.H. Baden–Powell, *The Land Systems of British India,* Vol. 3 (London, 1895), pp. 410–15.

is, 8 per cent or so thereof.[23] While the peasants annually paid Rs 3 to Rs 1–8 as. per acre of their land-holdings towards land revenue in 1870, the planters paid nothing at all for the major part of their holdings. They paid towards land revenue only a nominal rate of 3 as. to 9 as. and, in rare cases, Re. 1–2 as. per acre, for the remaining part.[24] They were the biggest landlords in the countryside they dominated, but they paid the lowest average rates per acre of holding. Not only did they employ wage workers, but they also settled rice-producing tenant cultivators on their lands, so that the latter could provide them with casual labour in the peak seasons. The planters usurped the grazing fields and encroached upon the *jhum* (slash and burn) rights of the tribal shifting cultivators. They even disrupted inter-village communications by fencing in portions of existing public roads and denying the right of way to villagers. There were cases where cultivators' lands, not yet regularly settled, were sold as waste lands to tea companies over the heads of their occupants.[25]

Wage Slaves on Plantations

The Assam Company in its early years paid its imported Chinese staff – some 70 workers at one stage – four to five times the wage rate paid to the corresponding categories of Assamese labour.[26] After the services of the Chinese workers were dispensed with in 1843, the local people remained practically the

[23] Altogether 6,25,780 acres in Assam were held by the planters under concessional grants and 33,761 acres under ordinary settlement rules. *Report on the Land Revenue Administration of the Lower Province, 1870–71,* pp. 43–44.

[24] Land revenue rates on ordinary cultivation in 1870 are from Gait, *History of Assam,* pp. 342–43. For the concessional rates, see the table in the text above.

[25] *Bengal Administrative Report,* 1867–68, p. 144, and ibid., 1871–72, Part I, pp. 143–44.

[26] Antrobus, *History of Assam Company,* pp. 383 and 388.

sole source of labour for the industry till 1859. The total labour force in the Assam plantations that year hardly exceeded 10,000, although knowledgeable planters put the requirement for the province at 16,000 to 20,000 hands for current cultivation alone.[27] The most important source of recruitment was the Kachari tribe of Darrang district. Besides, peasants of nearby villages in their slack season were also employed through contractors.

The wage rate generally varied between Rs 2.50 and Rs 3.50 per month in the 1840s and early 1850s, and it rose to Rs 4 immediately after the revolt of 1857. In the absence of indentured labour till then and in the given context, these wages, on the whole, were not unfair. This was because the local labour had bargaining power. It is on record that the labour of the Assam Company struck work in 1848 and *gheraoed* the superintendent's office to realize three months' wage arrears. They were able to secure an assurance about no default in payment of wages in the future. Again, in 1859, the Company's Kachari labour struck work for a wage increase. This time, with the help of the District Magistrate, the leaders of the strike were apprehended, tried on the spot and punished on the plea that any stoppage of work before the expiry of their contract was illegal.[28] Twenty-two leaders were arrested and imprisoned for periods up to one year, and twenty others were dismissed from service.[29]

The conditions soon changed after indentured labour began to appear on the scene, and the prices of wage goods went on increasing. The labour policy of the planters and their government was not to encourage a free labour market by offering competitive wages. Unlike the public works department and the railways, the planters made the worst use of semi-feudal methods of reducing the free labourer to a kind of serfdom. In 1864, while a free labourer was able to earn a wage of Rs 7 per month when employed by the public works department, the going rate of wages in the Assam Company's plantations was only Rs 4 to Rs 5. The average wage earned in many tea gardens was even as low as Rs 3.50 per month. The Transport of Native Labourers Act of 1863 did not stipulate a minimum wage but required the wage rate to be stated in the written contract. However, the actual payment was made proportionate to the amount of work done, according to a tariff of task work shown to the recruit in Calcutta.[30] Obviously, the Act was passed merely for licensing recruiters and registering inmigrants – in short, to regularize the recruitment through *arkattis* (agents) that had been going on for some time.

Statutory wages were laid down by the amending Act of 1865. Though

---

[27] *Selections from the Records of the Government of Bengal*, Vol. 37, pp. 63–66 and 69–72.

[28] Antrobus, *History of Assam Company*, pp. 97–98 and 389; P. Griffiths, *The History of the Indian Tea Industry* (London, 1967), pp. 304–06.

[29] 'Proceedings of the Company's Calcutta Board', 28.10.1859, Manuscript No. 9925, Vol. 10 (Guildhall Library, London).

[30] *Bengal Legislative Council Proceedings*, 1865–67, p. 14. Antrobus, *History of Assam Company*, p. 389.

the provision was formally abolished in 1870 by another amendment, it was re-inforced under the Inland Emigration Act of 1882, and the same statutory wages continued in practice up to 1901. The minimum wages so set were Rs 5 and Rs 4, respectively, for men and women workers above the age of 12. Child labour was to be paid Rs 3 per month. The planters had undertaken to supply labour with rice at Re. 1 per maund. The relevant legislation merely provided for the supply of rice at a specified rate, to be included in the terms of the written contract. But once a rate was specified, it had to be maintained. Planters soon began to violate their own undertaking and started charging around Rs 2–8 as. per maund of rice supplied to labour. Thus they could lower the real wage by manipulating the stipulated price of rice. Even the nominal minimum wage could be further lowered by varying the standard task. A commission of enquiry appointed in 1867 found that in most gardens minimum wages were not earned. There were even instances where the wage payment was kept in arrears for as long as six months.[31]

The Act of 1865 prescribed nine hours of work per day and six days per week. It also laid down that a contract must not extend beyond three years. But, for lack of proper inspection, these provisions of the Act were not observed. The same was the case with the provision for a hospital in every garden. The afore-mentioned commission of enquiry found that, generally speaking, the protective clauses had broken down.[32] Desertion on the part of the worker was made crimi-nally punishable under the Act, and even continued 'laziness' on his part was a criminal offence. The planter was empowered in his own district to arrest with-out warrant any worker alleged to have absconded from his tea garden, and this privilege he enjoyed right up to 1908.

Under the Amendment Act of 1870, the *sardari* system of recruitment was recognized, though not allowed to replace forthwith the *arkatti* (licensed recruiter) system. From that time till 1915, both methods of recruitment were in vogue, side by side. Yet another amendment, the Bengal Labour Districts Emi-gration Act, passed in 1873, permitted free recruitment outside the provisions of the Act of 1865, provided that the contract did not extend beyond one year. As the penal clauses could not be imposed on labourers so employed, planters were not at all interested in this mode of recruitment. However, this provision indi-rectly legalized their old practice of inducing time-expired emigrant labourers to enter into fresh contracts under the Workmen's Breach of Contract Act (1859).[33]

By the mid-1860s, the policy of recruitment of labour from other prov-inces was well under way. Available early labour statistics, though imperfect, are adequate to show the change that was going on in the ethnic composition of

[31] Secretary to Government of Bengal to Secretary to Government of India, Home Department, 3 December 1866, and Agent to the G.G. and Commissioner of Assam to Secretary to Government of Bengal, 21 March 1867, *Assam, Proceedings of Leg-islative Department*, Government of Bengal, August 1867, No. 15. *Report of the Commissioners on the Tea Cultivation of Assam*, 1868, p. 50.
[32] Griffiths, *History of the Indian Tea Industry*, pp. 261–71.
[33] Ibid., pp. 272–74.

the labour force. Of a total plantation labour force of 34,433 in Assam proper, as reported by the *Bengal Administrative Report* for 1867–68, 22,800 or two-thirds were imported labour, and only 11,633 or one-third local. The total number of outside recruits, net of all wastages by way of death, desertion, etc., stood at approximately 24,000 in Assam proper and 20,000 in Cachar on 31 December 1872.[34] Living far away from their homes and hearths and contract-bound, these labourers were undoubtedly the most easily exploitable and exploited section of the people.

The conditions of recruitment were inhuman. During the two years from 15 December 1859 to 21 November 1861, the Assam Company brought 2,272 recruits from outside, of whom 250 or 11 per cent died on the way. Of a total of 2,569 recruits who were sent down the Brahmaputra in two batches during the period from 2 April 1861 to 25 February 1862, as many as 135 died, including deaths by drowning, and 103 absconded. Of 84,915 recruits for Assam between 1 May 1863 and 1 May 1866, 30,000 had died by 30 June 1866. This high mortality did cost the planters, for the price charged by contractors per recruit ranged from Rs 12 to Rs 20.[35] Men, women and children were enticed, even kidnapped, and traded like cattle; absconders were hunted down like runaway slaves. Under the Workmen's Breach of Contract Act of 1859, Sections 490 and 492 of the Indian Penal Code (1860), and the Labour Act of 1863 as amended in 1865, 1870 and 1873, runaway workers could be punished by the government alone. Yet the planters themselves generally disciplined such workers, inflicting upon them punitive tortures of all kinds. For labour was too precious to be sent out of their tea gardens to police and jail custody.[36]

Modern Political Consciousness: The Beginnings
Threshold of Modernization

It was in the immediate pre-British period, 1770–1826, that the Assamese people took to the cultivation of poppy and consumption of opium. During that period, their territory was devastated by prolonged civil wars, followed by the Burmese occupation; their population dwindled to less than half of what it had been; and their smiling fields were overtaken by jungles. In the first decade after the British take-over, these conditions worsened under the burden of taxation and mismanagement. In the long run, however, the British rule made an attempt to play a developmental role for some decades, within its colonial limits. Was not the country to be prepared for meaningful economic exploitation?

Although Jenkins's scheme failed to bring in permanent European settlements because of climatic and other reasons, European capital and immigrant

---

[34] *Bengal Administrative Report,* 1867–68, p. 204 and ibid., 1872–73, p. 390.

[35] Note by J.W. Edgar, Off. Junior Secretary to Government of Bengal, 11 September 1873, in *Papers Regarding the Tea Industry in Bengal,* 1873, p. XIX. *Proceedings of Legislative Department,* Government of Bengal, 1863, No. 15–18.

[36] Griffiths, *History of the Indian Tea Industry,* pp. 269–73; D. Chaman Lal, *Coolie: The Story of Labour and Capital in India,* Vol. 2 (Lahore, 1932), p. 5.

Indian labour from other provinces did settle down on the tea estates of Assam. Despite its limited linkage effects, the plantation economy also began to slowly generate a network of secondary economic activities within three decades of its coming into existence. The administration was successfully prevailed upon by the planters to build roads and bridges, and to ply steamer services on the Brahmaputra. Traders and bankers from other Indian provinces flocked to Assam and, in the absence of local business acumen, provided the economy with the necessary, yet exploitative, services of trading and banking. All these factors helped the rapid growth of the population of the Brahmaputra Valley – from an estimated one million in 1826 to about two million by 1872 – and of the economy as well. But the economic growth was almost entirely limited to the foreign-owned and foreign-managed sector. The base of exploitation for British capital was ramified and expanded. Alongside, missionary and administrative activities led to the founding of English schools and printing presses – an infrastructure based on which a colonial hybrid bourgeois culture could now emerge.

Dewan and Dhekial–Phukan: Two Trends

The beginnings of modern political consciousness in the Brahmaputra Valley can be traced from 1853, when Maniram Dewan and Anandaram Dhekial–Phukan (1829–1859) submitted their memorials to A.J. Moffat Mills, who had come to enquire into the conditions of the province and to recommend measures for improvement.[37] Despite his early collaboration with the British, Maniram – the last of the old aristocrats – had turned an extremist and had by then taken an anti-British stance. On the other hand, born into an enlightened Brahmin land-owner family and educated in the Hindu College of Calcutta, Anandaram believed in the regenerative role of British rule and remained a loyal government servant until his death. The memorials thus reveal two opposite trends in the new political consciousness that was emerging. But both reflected certain popular grievances that were going to dominate Assam politics for a century to come. Hence, the thoughts contained in them need careful assessment, in the context of the times.

In one of his two memorials, Maniram Dewan pleaded for restoration of the Rajah's domain in upper Assam as a protectorate, which – once conceded in 1833 – was finally resumed in October 1838 on charges of maladministration. He resented the reduction of the upper and landed classes to the most abject and hopeless state of misery through abolition of their offices, liberation of their slaves and unprecedented subjection to the assessment of land revenue. He protested against the appointment of several 'Bengalees from Sylhet' and Marwaris as *mauzadars* when a number of respectable Assamese were already out of employ. He pointed out that by the introduction of new customs, 'innumerable courts, an unjust system of taxation and the objectionable treatment of the Hill

---

[37] For the full text of the memorials, A.J.M. Mills, *Report on the Province of Assam* (Calcutta, 1854), Appendices.

Tribes, the consequence of which has been a constant state of warfare, . . . neither the British Government nor their subjects have gained any benefit'. He charged that the continued sale of *abkari* opium by the government had made the people unfit for agriculture, and that discontinuation of the puja at *Kamakhya* had invited calamities upon the country.

However, the memorial was not blind to the good aspects of the British rule in Assam. It noted that by stopping such cruel punitive practices as the mutilation of limbs and the forcible abduction of virgins from private homes, by removing all wayside transit duties, and by abolishing the system of forced labour for keeping roads clear for the government, 'the British Government had earned for itself inestimable praise and renown'.

The memorial recommended both an immediate stop to the sale of monopoly opium and a phased programme of gradual prohibition of poppy cultivation within twenty years. A cheaper and simpler system of administering justice through panchayats was also advocated, alongside the restoration of native rule under British protection, at least in a part of Assam.

Dewan's political platform was no doubt a revivalist one, betraying his orthodoxy and basic loyalty to an outmoded social system. Nevertheless, he was not totally blind to the need for change and for opening up of the country for exploitation of its resources. He admitted that the abolition of slavery and the introduction of modern schools would do good to the common people. Even though no concessional land grants were made available to him, he came forward to establish two small proprietory tea gardens of his own, which were confiscated by the state after his execution for treason in 1858. Incidentally, a second notable Assamese tea planter was Rosheswar Barua, who established about half a dozen tea gardens in the 1860s but could not survive the tea crisis of 1866–69. In the same crisis, sixteen Indian tea gardens in Goalpara district alone were literally nipped in the bud.[38]

Dewan did not subscribe to an ideology that was progressive enough even in the context of his times, nor was he a very consistent freedom fighter throughout his career. But because of his role in the revolt of 1857, it is his anti-imperialist image that lives in people's memory – in folk songs and modern patriotic literature. He had an entrepreneurial career that was objectively progressive. He was indeed a bridge between the old and the new.[39]

Anandaram Dhekial–Phukan, on the other hand, was in every respect a product of the modern age of enlightenment. He got his inspiration from the contemporary 'Bengal renaissance', and from what he read about England's material progress and Peter the Great's reforms in medieval Russia. He dreamt of the day when reforms and material progress would surely dawn upon Assam.

[38] A.K. Sharma, 'Asamar cah udyogat bideshii muldhan', *Sadiniia Navayug* (in Assamese, Gauhati), 30 October 1963, p. 27. *Bengal Administrative Report*, 1867–68, p. 207 and ibid., 1868–69, p. 191.

[39] For details, see A. Guha, 'Impact of Bengal Renaissance on Assam 1825–75', *IESHR*, 9 (September 1972), pp. 288–304.

He reportedly wrote to Hemchandra Barua (1835–1896), a confirmed atheist and young social reformer of the day: 'A group of people styled as Young Bengal has emerged in Bengal and some people in Assam are absorbing what is good in them, but not their vices. My mind is full of joy at the sight of this germination.'[40]

One of his publications in Bengali, *Notes on Laws of Bengal*, Vol. I (Calcutta, 1855), was modelled on Blackstone's commentary on the *English Law Digest*; it dealt with such topics as the principles of morality and law, human rights, liberty of the person and master–servant relations. This book and his articles in the Assamese periodical, *Arunoday* (1846–83), reveal his faith in the bourgeois values of life.

The memorial Dhekial–Phukan submitted espoused the cause of the persecuted Assamese language. It had lost its rightful place to Bengali in local schools and courts in 1837, on the false ground that it was a dialect of the latter language. The battle for due recognition of Assamese as a distinct and separate language was carried on through Dhekial–Phukan's long-drawn efforts, alongside those of the American Baptist missionaries. As a result of the agitation, Assamese was finally recognized for use in the courts and schools of Assam proper several years after his death, under the Bengal government order of 19 April 1873. Bengali, of course, continued to exist side by side. Besides, due to the paucity of suitable books in Assamese, textbooks published in Bengali continued to be in use in all high schools in the plains for at least another two decades.

In the same memorial, Dhekial–Phukan also laid bare the existing evils of the administration, and advocated an increase in the number of mofussil courts and native judges with enlarged powers for the latter. Like Dewan, he recommended lightening of the tax burden and simplification of the complicated procedure in the law courts. In his opinion, the Bengal system of permanent settlement of land tenure would not suit the needs of Assam.

As to the opium policy, Dhekial–Phukan warned that the replacement of locally produced opium by *abkari* opium, sold on a monopoly basis by the government, would not at all lead to eradication of the evil. He rather suggested that the sale of government opium be discontinued forthwith and that local poppy cultivation be subjected to heavy taxation – the tax being enhanced progressively from time to time. Thus, the opium policy advocated by him was basically the same as Dewan's. Dhekial–Phukan also advocated compulsory registration of marriages.

New Politics: The Germination[41]

The two memorials discussed above indicate some of the major issues that were churning the minds of the Assamese middle classes and peasants during

---

[40] Quote from Padmanath Gohain–Barua, ed., *Jiivanii-Sangraha* (in Assamese, Gauhati, 1969), p. 22; translation ours.

[41] Guha, 'Impact of Bengal Renaissance on Assam'.

the years 1853–73, by which time the so-called Bengal renaissance had had its impact on Assam. It was precisely because of this that, despite the conflict of interests between the immigrant Bengali babus and the indigenous *dangariyas* for administrative jobs, their mutual relations were not yet embittered to the extent it was to be in later times. Assamese and immigrant Bengali adherents to the Brahmo Samaj had a social impact in the growing administrative townships. Gunabhiram Barua (1834–1894), a pioneer of the new awakening, was attracted towards the Brahmo Samaj even before 1857, but was formally initiated to the new faith at Dhubri in 1869. True to his zeal for social reform, he married a widow in 1870 and got the marriage registered under Act III of 1872 in December the same year. Padmahas Goswami (1829–1879) of Jakhlabandha Satra was another important Assamese Brahmo who wrote several books in Assamese in the early 1870s to popularize the Brahmo movement. Yet another westernizing influence on Assam was that of the resident American Baptist missionaries.

Contemporary Assamese public opinion increasingly focused on three social evils of the day: (i) the plight of the widows of the Brahmin, Kayastha and Daivajna castes, (ii) the prevalent practice of polygamy, and (iii) the widespread addiction to opium. Intellectuals of the day boldly expressed themselves on these issues not only in the local press – there were three such periodicals in Assam proper in 1872 – but also through creative literature. Educated people formed societies and circles for dissemination of scientific knowledge and ideas about social reforms. In the years 1857–59, the *Jnan-Pradayini-Sabha* (society for disseminating knowledge) functioned at Nowgong under the patronage of Dhekial–Phukan. Another society with the same name was formed in upper Assam in 1857, which held regular Sunday study circles. Still earlier, towards the close of 1855, the *Asam Desh Hitaishini Sabha* was formed at Sibsagar, for holding study circles every Saturday. Poornananda Sharma Deka, a Mohrur in the Criminal Court, who was its secretary in September 1856, issued a circular urging the local people to represent their manifold grievances to the Lieutenant-Governor, F.J. Halliday, then camping in the district. It appears that the same Poornananda Mohrur was suspended from service for six months in the 1858 trial of the mutineers, for not reporting certain allegedly seditious proceedings to the government.[42]

In 1872, the Assamese Literary Society was formed in Calcutta at the initiative of its Assamese residents. On behalf of this Society, Jagannath Barooah (1851–1907) and Manik Chandra Barooah (1851–1915), then studying in Presidency College, submitted a memorial on 21 May 1872 to the Viceroy, Lord Northbrook, drawing his attention to the potential resources of Assam. The memorial urged him to connect the province with Bengal by a railway line – a proposal that was already under his consideration.[43] These activities reflected the

---

[42] Ibid., p. 302 and Dutt, *Landmarks of the Freedom Struggle in Assam*, p. 126.

[43] Extract from the memorial reproduced in P. Goswami, *Manikendra Baruva aru teonr yug* (in Assamese, Gauhati, 1970), pp. 12–13.

dawning of a modern political consciousness in the Brahmaputra Valley. The Bengali-speaking districts of Sylhet and Cachar, by that time, were much more involved in the mainstream of Bengal politics. Nevertheless, students therefrom, who were residents in Calcutta, asserted their separate identity by forming the *Shrihatta Sammilani* in 1877.

There was no official recognition of this growing political consciousness of the people even at the local levels of administration. On 11 June 1852, 113 residents of Gauhati submitted a petition to the District Magistrate for introduction of the permissive Bengal Act of 1850 for the establishment of a municipal board. Accordingly, the first statutory municipal board came into being in 1853 – an all-British board, with only three nominated members. No other board in Assam was constituted under the Act. When the question of introducing the Bengal Municipal Act of 1864 came before the Commissioner, he took the stand that Assam's prevailing social conditions did not permit use of the Act. He asserted that Gauhati was nothing but a permanent camp of government officials whose butlers and followers constituted the townspeople, and that Assam's towns were merely glorified villages used as centres for policing the surrounding countryside. Nevertheless, due to the insistence of the higher authorities, the Act was eventually extended to Gauhati in May 1865.

The rudimentary beginnings of local boards had the same history. For example, the ferry fund earmarked for the construction of roads and bridges was administered in every district by a small committee of nominated officials and non-officials. But the majority of the committee members were of course Europeans, excepting in such districts as Goalpara and Kamrup, where tea interests were minimal.[44]

At the Presidency level, Bengal had a Legislative Council formed in 1862 under the Indian Councils Act of 1861. But representation on this Council was limited to the Bengal Divisions alone, to the exclusion of the Assam Division.

A Summing-Up and a Perspective

The period from 1826 to 1873 was one of transition of Assam's precapitalist economy into its colonial phase. British capital penetrated the economy and started building an infrastructure to sustain the exotic capitalistic set-up. Collaborating traders, bankers, lawyers and clerks from other Indian provinces came as camp followers. Bullock-carts, a novelty for the region, were introduced. The economy was monetized. The closed society was exposed to immigration of labour, new skills, new vices and new ideas. Marwari trader-cum-moneylenders monopolized the internal trade as agents of the British trading houses of Calcutta, who in turn worked for their metropolitan counterparts in London. Bengali clerks, doctors and lawyers, with the advantage of their early

---

[44] V. Venkata Rao, *A Hundred Years of Local Self-Government in Assam* (second edition, Gauhati, 1963), pp. 43–44.

initiation in English education and the British–Indian administrative system, monopolized government jobs and professions.

In this context, the newborn, rickety Assamese intelligentsia of the period found itself to be an insignificant minority in the 'urban' sector. Throughout the nineteenth century and early decades of the twentieth century, the so-called towns of Assam were mere permanent camps of government servants and traders, or just glorified villages, where non-indigenous elements constituted the overwhelmingly dominant section. This situation of complete lack of urbanization alongside pre-capitalist production relations was not, and could not be, rapidly altered by the new set-up. (See Appendix 1.) Superimposed as it was on a semi-tribal, semi-feudal society of petty producers, the new plantation economy – subjugated to foreign capital, and linked with immigrant usury and merchant capital – could not bring about a radical transformation *within the local society itself*.[45] The start of modernization was indeed a false one in this respect. It did, no doubt, slowly transform Assamese society, but not radically. It distorted the trajectory of development in a manner that served the imperial British economy best, while Assam's peasant economy underwent deindustrialization and stagnation.

Under the circumstances, the extent of urbanization that was achieved in due course was practically nil. The incipient Assamese middle class was extremely small, weak and unconsolidated as a class. Links between the plantation economy and the surrounding peasant economy – both labour-short – remained tenuous and minimal. Except land, practically all other inputs of production for the expanding modern sector were brought from outside the province: capital and enterprise from the imperial metropolis itself, and labour from other Indian provinces. A dual economy or, more precisely, a multi-structured plural economy, began functioning at different levels.

In such an unenviable and complex situation – where tribalism and elements of feudalism persistently coexisted with new-born capitalist relationships – the early modern political consciousness was bound to be inhibited and get blurred by group rivalries at the court of the colonial masters. But the peasantry – traditionally unaccustomed to any kind of money taxation, and, now, constantly in dread of the enhancement of land revenue and imposition of new taxes – kept up the smouldering fire of protest and hatred against the Raj.

The emergent middle class took its own time, under the circumstances, to identity the root cause of many of the evils of imperialism. How this happened in due course, how the safety-valve of controlled parliamentary activities was built into the political system, how sections of the people got themselves increasingly involved in electoral politics, and, finally, how the freedom struggles fought outside the legislatures made inroads into the latter and *vice versa* – all these will be narrated and discussed in the following chapters.

---

[45] The pattern has been analysed in detail elsewhere. See Guha, 'Colonization of Assam: Years of Transitional Crisis' and 'Colonization of Assam: Second Phase'. Also by the same author, 'Socio-Economic Changes in Agrarian Assam', in M.K. Chaudhuri, ed., *Trends in Socio-Economy Change in India 1871–1901* (Simla, 1967), pp. 569–622.

CHAPTER TWO

A New Province *sans* Legislature: 1874–1905

Strange Bed-Fellows: Assam Proper and Sylhet

The inconvenience of governing the Assam districts as a division of the unwieldy Bengal Presidency had long been recognized. Fairly differing local conditions and the unique position there of British planters warranted the creation of a new province to ensure administrative efficiency. Accordingly, Assam proper, together with Cachar, Goalpara, Garo Hills and the other hills districts, was formed into a Chief Commissioner's province on 6 February 1874. Although vast in area, this new province, with its small population of 2,443,000, had a meagre revenue potential. To make it financially viable, the authorities therefore decided, in September 1874, to incorporate into it the populous Bengali-speaking district of Sylhet, which, historically as well as ethnically, was an integral part of Bengal. Even with the additional 1,720,000 people of Sylhet, the new province was only about half as populous as the Central Provinces, which was then India's next least populous province.

A memorial protesting against the transfer of Sylhet on behalf of both its Hindu and Muslim inhabitants was submitted to the Viceroy on 10 August 1874. The memorialists based their protest on the cultural identity and historical association that Sylhet had with Bengal, and the disadvantages of Sylhet being yoked with a 'backward' region. They further apprehended that the district would have to put up with laws and institutions inferior to what it had been accustomed to in Bengal under the permanent settlement. The Government of India, on 5 September 1874, refused to accede to their prayer. However, the petitioners obtained an assurance of no change whatsoever in either the system of law and judicial procedures they had hitherto lived under, or in the Bengal principles of settlement and collection of land revenue.[1]

Even with this guarantee, the public opinion of Bengal and Sylhet remained unchanged. *Hindoo Patriot* published a series of articles to ventilate the

---

[1] Letter from the Government of Assam, No. Pol-1917–5585, dated 30 October 1924, reproduced in January, *Assam Legislative Council Proceedings* (hereafter *ALCP*), 1924, Vol. 6, pp. 51–52; B.N. Chaudhury's speech, July, *ALCP*, 1924, Vol. 4, pp. 568–75.

public protest (for example, on 7 September 1874). Kristodas Pal, its editor, echoed the sentiments of the Bengalis when he stated that Sylhet was the golden calf that was being sacrificed for the new idol called the province of Assam.[2] Despite the agitation, however, Sylhet was incorporated into the Chief Commissioner's province on 12 September 1874.

The province that emerged was an amalgam of four disparate elements: (i) the preliterate hills districts, speaking diverse tongues; (ii) the five Assamese-speaking districts of the Brahmaputra Valley together known as Assam proper; (iii) Goalpara of the Brahmaputra Valley where the Bengali and Assamese cultures overlapped; and (iv) the two Bengali-speaking districts of the Surma Valley – Sylhet and Cachar.

The hills districts, inhabited by various tribes, had an insignificant population. A tribal middle class competing for jobs and other openings was yet unborn there. The rest of the provincial population was more or less evenly balanced between the two valleys, although the Surma Valley had an edge over the other in this respect until 1911 (see Appendix 2). The population of the district of Sylhet alone matched that of Assam proper as a whole. There was practically no Assamese-speaking element in the Surma Valley, whereas in the Goalpara district of Brahmaputra Valley, the majority, according to the census figures, spoke Bengali. This was because it had formed a constituent part of Bengal continuously for about two hundred years from 1639 to 1822. Besides, the plains tribals of the Tibeto–Burman linguistic group constituted another sizeable element in the population of the valley. Under the circumstances, the Bengali linguistic group rapidly increased in numbers from census to census through immigration. It continued to outnumber the Assamese even in the new province well until the partition of Assam in 1947.

The term 'Assam', which had originally stood for Assam proper – that is, the erstwhile Ahom territory alone – and later for the whole of the Brahmaputra Valley that was under common Commissionership, was now given a wider signification to denote the newly emerged composite province.[3] The population mix of the province was such that, given the limited opportunities of development, the ugly face of valley-ism was bound to arise in due course in Assam politics. Perhaps no better administrative arrangement could have been devised 'to divide and rule' the province than a white Chief Commissioner maintaining the balance of loaves and fishes – not power certainly – between two rival valleys jealous of each other. The Brahmaputra Valley had an overwhelming Hindu majority and the Surma Valley a comfortable Muslim majority. In the overall context of the province, Muslims constituted some one-third of the population.

[2] Pal cited in K. Deb's speech, July, *ALCP*, 1924, Vol. 4, p. 590.
[3] E.A. Gait, *A History of Assam* (second edition, Calcutta/Simla, 1926), p. 337.

Chief Commissioner, Planters and Local Self-Government

Chief Commissioner's Powers

In theory, the Chief Commissioner administered his province as a delegate of the Governor-General who might resume or modify such powers as he had himself conferred. In official terminology, therefore, the Chief Commissionership of Assam was referred to as a local administration rather than as a provincial government. But, in practice, the powers entrusted to the Chief Commissioner were nearly as wide as those of a Lieutenant-Governor. Subject to the control of the Government of India, he was the supreme authority in all matters of legislation, finance and administration. There was no power within the province – not even a small council – that had any legal authority to advise him in such matters.

During the years 1874–1905, Assam had no legislature of its own, and the people there had no opportunity of participating in legislative activities of any kind. The Chief Commissioner was no doubt a powerful autocrat. Even so, he was under constant pressure from the province's British planting interests and he dared not cross swords with them. There was every chance of his losing the job if he did, as happened with Sir Henry Cotton in 1902.

Planters and Local Bodies

As owners of hundreds of square miles of inaccessible sprawling tracts, the planters were keen on development of local communications and the diversion of public funds towards that end. They were therefore the chief body of non-officials who were asked by the government to participate in the local committees set up for the purpose. From 1874 there were, at the district level, road, school and dispensary committees, with one-third *ex-officio* members in each committee. After the promulgation of the Local Rates Regulation in 1879, all these nominated committees were replaced by a single district committee. Each such district committee had no less than six members, of whom one-third were to be resident non-officials. The members of a district committee were appointed by the Chief Commissioner on recommendations from the district officer. Side by side, there was a provision for branch committees, each with at least three members. An analysis of the eight district committees so formed in 1880 in the plains districts clearly indicates the British planters' domination over them. It was therefore but natural that the non-official Indian members lost all interest in these bodies.[4] Particularly, the zamindars of Sylhet and Goalpara were opposed to the Local Rates Regulation. Their plea was that hospitals, schools, lunatic asylums, etc., should be supported out of the general funds of the government, as in Bengal and other parts of the Empire, without special taxation for such purposes.[5]

The Government of India Resolutions of 1881 and 1882, inspired by

---

[4] The account of the evolution of local bodies is based on relevant information from V. Venkata Rao, *A Hundred Years of Local Self-Government in Assam* (second edition, Gauhati, 1963), pp. 39–100 and 182–275.

[5] *The Bengalee* (Calcutta), 2 and 3 April 1880.

Ripon, provided the starting point of a new outlook for local self-government in India. They suggested that non-officials should constitute as much as one-half to two-thirds of the total membership of a local body, and that the district or sub-divisional officer need not be the *ex-officio* chairman of such a body. The Ripon reforms were stiffly opposed in official circles and were much watered down in the course of their implementation through the Government of Assam Resolution of 17 November 1882. It contemplated a non-official chairman, but no bar was put against an official one. For all the nineteen sub-divisions of the plains districts, local boards (called sub-divisional boards) were constituted. Each had eight to twenty-four members – and in a later period, ten to thirty members – of whom three to four were officials.[6] At least half of the non-official resident members were to be elected by the planters in all the important tea districts. All other non-official, that is, Indian, members were to be nominated by the Chief Commissioner, except in Sylhet, Kamrup and Sibsagar. In these three districts they were to be elected. The boards so constituted were continuous bodies, with half the non-official members retiring every year.

Heavily loaded with *ex-officio* and elected planter members, these boards functioned till 1905 and, with some modifications, till 1915. As to their undemocratic composition, the 1883 list is illustrative. In that year, out of 300 members of sixteen sub-divisional boards, 25 per cent were planters' elected representatives and 15 per cent official members. In the tea districts, the planters' representation was, of course, much higher than this average. In most of the local boards, therefore, Britishers, acting in coalition with Indian official and nominated non-official members, constituted the majority. In 1903–04, out of 364 members of nineteen local boards, 133 were elected (most of them by planters), 60 *ex-officio* and 171 nominated members. Of this total membership, 132 or 36.3 per cent were Britons.[7]

Since planters' interests were not directly involved in municipal affairs, one could perhaps expect the municipalities to have been relatively less crowded by Britons and more by elected Indian elements. There were two sets of municipalities constituted under two separate Acts – one set under the Bengal Municipal Act of 1876, adopted also by the Government of Assam in the same year, and another set since 1887, under the provisions of the Bengal Municipal Act of 1884. Both types of municipalities coexisted in Assam till 1923 and did not differ from each other in essential principles. Under both the Acts, municipal commissioners were to be nominated; when specifically so permitted, they could also be elected.

---

[6] Rao, *Hundred Years of Local Self-Government*, p. 188 and *An Account of the Province of Assam and its Administration* (Government of Assam, Shillong, 1903), p. 96. In 1884–85, out of thirty-seven members of the Dibrugarh Local Board, twenty-six were either officials or planters. The same combination dominated eight other local boards. Rao, *Hundred Years of Local Self-Government*, p. 211n and pp. 186–88.

[7] Worked out from data presented in Rao, ibid., p. 188n and *Imperial Gazetteer of India*, Vol. 6, p. 16, p. 96 for the 1883 and 1903–04 figures, respectively. An obvious printing mistake in Rao's figure for Barpeta is corrected. Also, Rao, ibid., p. 189.

Under the first Act, the District Magistrate or the sub-divisional officer was ordinarily to be the chairman, though any other person was also held eligible for such appointment. Despite the accent of the Ripon reforms on an elected chairman, the second Act provided that the board could elect its chairman from amongst the municipal commissioners or, if it so desired, could request the government to appoint a chairman.

The Ripon reforms contemplated slow introduction of the elective principle in small towns. The Government of Assam therefore proceeded cautiously. By 1905–06, election had been introduced only in six municipalities.[8] Even as late as 1913, there was not a single elected member in ten out of the nineteen municipalities. Out of a total of 125 municipal commissioners in 1885–86, only 59, and out of 144 in 1900–01, only 53 were elected members.[9] Thus the ratio of the elected element to the total strength had actually decreased. In both the years, Britishers constituted one-fifth of the total strength. As to having an elected chairman, as admissible under the rules in several municipalities, caution was exercised, under pressure, by the municipal politicians themselves. They would rather forego the honour than offend their ambitious district officers, who were the real makers of Rai Sahibs and Rai Bahadurs. Only Sylhet had a non-official and Indian municipal chairman from 1887. Everywhere else, for about three decades after the Ripon reforms, the District Magistrate or the sub-divisional officer continued to retain chairmanship, at the ostensible request of the boards themselves.

Public Concern for Democratization

British officials reacted adversely to the Ripon reforms. The Commissioner of the Assam Valley Division, W.E. Ward, was of the opinion in 1882 that the soil of the Brahmaputra Valley was not 'fertile enough for local governmental institutions to flourish' because the Assamese were devoid of 'those business-like habits which are so needful to make a person a useful member of any committee to which he may be appointed'.[10] Ward was opposed to elections of any kind – direct or indirect, and, of course, also to the appointment or election of a non-official to chairmanship.

The heavy over-representation given to British planters on the local bodies was rationalized by the Chief Commissioner, C.A. Elliot, in terms of their interest in improved communications. He said:

> No measure could be more fatal to the prosperity of the Province than any which would tend to alienate the powerful and energetic tea interest and to make its representatives unwilling to continue that assistance which they have hitherto freely rendered with great benefit to themselves and to the State.[11]

---

[8] *Report of the Administration of Eastern Bengal and Assam, 1905–06* (Shillong, 1907), p. 40.

[9] Rao, *Hundred Years of Local Self-Government*, pp. 185–86.

[10] No. 1784, Home-A, 2 November 1882, cited by Rao, ibid., p. 84.

[11] No. 1784, General, 2 November 1882, ibid., p. 86.

The reforms in Assam were tailored accordingly. Both the elective principle and the access to chairmanship were practically out of bounds for Indians.

Naturally, these reforms never became popular. In 1882, Gangagovinda Phukan and Indibar Baruah went from village to village explaining the Ripon scheme and succeeded in awakening some interest among the ryots. They held a big meeting at Sibsagar to discuss the scheme and passed a resolution demanding that elected Indian members should constitute five-eighths, British members one-eighth and nominated officials two-eighths of the total strength of a subdivisional board; and that the chairman should be chosen by the board. These proposals, however, were found to be too radical for official acceptance. The Sibsagar Local Board formed in 1883 did not satisfy popular aspirations.[12]

In December 1886, an anonymous comment in *Mau*, an Assamese periodical published from Calcutta, castigated the way the local boards had functioned for three years since their inception. Referring to the bloc of *ex-officio* members, it asked: 'Is self-government taught merely by the officers of another authority tumbling into the public councils and doing work which the public ought to do? Never. . . . What functions can members have if the Government are at once the proposers, the controllers of funds and the executives?'[13]

Proceeds of the local rate, collected mainly from the peasants, were not spent on projects that would primarily benefit them. For example, in 1888–89, when a local board grant was needed for the renovation of the Janji bund to protect thousands of acres of paddy land from inundation, there was no response at all. 'By all means the district officers may keep the tea garden roads in good order, but', warned a correspondent of *The Bengalee* on this occasion, 'they are not at liberty to rob Peter to pay Paul.'[14]

Chief Commissioner Sir Bampfylde Fuller introduced certain changes in 1904, to provide for elected Indian members in all local boards. The officials' and planters' representations were however retained as before. Of the rest, while some members were still to be nominated, one was to be elected by the voters at the headquarter station, another by the mercantile community and some others by the village authorities (Chaukidari Panchayats), or, where the latter did not exist, by the *gaon-burhas* (village headmen who were near-hereditary appointees of the government). The entire scheme, particularly the 'obnoxious principle' of election of rural representatives by *gaon-burhas,* was vehemently opposed by educated men like Manik Chandra Barooah.[15] Nevertheless, elections according to the scheme were held in the year 1905–06, and this mockery of local self-government continued for many years.

<hr>

12 For Sibsagar resolution, ibid., p. 84*n*; *Indian Echo* (Calcutta), 29 November 1883 and also 20 November 1886.

13 Quoted by I.N. Borra, *Bolinarayan Borrah: His Life, Work, and Musings* (Calcutta, 1967), pp. 53–54. Bolinarayan himself was an *ex-officio* member of the Nowgong Local Board in 1889. He caused displeasure among British planter members for hauling it up for irregularities. Ibid., p. 79.

14 *The Bengalee*, 9 March 1889.

15 Rao, *Hundred Years of Local Self-Government*, pp. 95–96.

Economic Growth: Tea Leads the Way

There was a tremendous growth of the tea industry during the last three decades of the nineteenth century. The total land area in possession of the industry doubled and accounted for some one-seventh of the entire settled area in the Assam plains. The land actually under tea in the province increased from a little over 56,000 acres in 1872 to 3,38,000 acres in 1901; and the output of tea increased from about 12 million lbs to 134 million lbs during the same period. The total amount of capital invested in the industry increased from £1 million, or even less than that, in 1872 to an estimated £14 million (Rs 210 million) by 1903. This tremendous growth was in response to the rising British demand for Indian tea, both in absolute and in relative terms. For, whereas in 1866 only 4 per cent of British tea imports were from India, this share increased to 38 per cent in 1886 and 59 per cent by 1903.[16]

The planters needed improved infrastructure, particularly communications. Hence, construction of railways started in 1881. The province's railway mileage was pushed up to 114 miles by 1891 and 715 miles by 1903. At an estimated investment of Rs 1,31,000 per mile, the total railway investment made in Assam till that year appears to have been not less than Rs 95 million (roughly equivalent to £6 million). With the demand from tea factories and the railways rising, the output of coal increased from less than 50 tons in 1872 to more than 2,77,000 tons by 1905–06. The oil fields developed by British capital in the 1890s increased their annual production of crude oil from 8,82,000 gallons in 1900–01 to 2,733,000 gallons in 1905–06. To supply packing boxes and scantlings to the tea industry, as many as fourteen saw mills were functioning in 1901. British investments in coal, petroleum and saw mills amounted to an estimated Rs 5.4 million, Rs 4.6 million and Rs 1 million, respectively, at the close of the century.[17] Steamers plying on the Brahmaputra, telecommunications and metalled roads also represented a considerable amount of private and public investments. But no estimates are available for these investments and, hence, these are not included in our overall estimate.

The total investment in the organized sector of the economy was no less than Rs 315 million (£21 million) or so during the years 1874–1905, even at a conservative estimate. An average investment of a little over Rs 10 million a year for the province's population that rose from 4.2 million to 5.8 million in thirty years was indeed considerable. But the big push in the government and

<hr>

[16] *Statistical Abstract Relating to British India 1891–92 to 1900–01*; Gait, *History of Assam*, pp. 356–57; A. Guha, 'A Big Push without a Take-Off: A Case Study of Assam 1871–1901', *Indian Economic and Social History Review* (hereafter *IESHR*), 5 (September 1968), pp. 202–04; *Bengal Administrative Report*, 1872–73, p. 20, for the 1872 acreage figure.

[17] Guha, 'A Big Push without a Take-Off', pp. 203–04; *Imperial Gazetteer of India* (new edition, Oxford, 1908), Vol. 6, pp. 70–71; *Report of the Administration of Eastern Bengal and Assam, 1905–06*, p. 148; *An Account of the Province of Assam*, pp. 41 and 44; *Bengal Administrative Report*, 1872–73, p. 37.

British private sectors failed to induce a commensurate growth of the indigenous private sector. What was developing with an amazing tempo was the British-managed part of the economy, with labour and middlemen services almost entirely recruited from outside the province.

It may be observed here that only a part of the total British capital invested in tea originated from Britain's own home savings. The major chunk of it apparently was built up from undistributed profits and ploughed-back dividends of older companies operating in this country. Between 1854 and 1901, the Assam Company did not raise any additional capital or long-term loans to augment its initial investment. Nor was it in possession of any idle capital resources. Yet it could treble its tea acreage from 3,313 to 10,762 acres during the period. In other words, the real worth of the Company's investment trebled, despite its distributing an average 15.3 per cent dividend during the years 1872–1901. The total amount so distributed over the years was about five times as big as the initial paid-up capital, of which one-fifth was raised in India. Many British companies were started by retired civil servants, army officers and business executives who earned their initial capital legitimately or otherwise while on service in India but got their companies registered in London. Thus, a considerable part of the British investments actually came out of incomes earned in India.[18]

As to railway investments, the risk-taking by private British capital was partly shared or subsidized by the Indian government. For example, a total subsidy of Rs 1.2 million was paid to the 91-mile Dibru–Sadiya Railways over the period 1884–1903. The 30-mile Jorhat State Railways, which was a project of the Government of Assam itself 'for the convenience of numerous tea gardens in the neighbourhood of Jorhat', involved a state investment of Rs 1 million and a cumulative loss of Rs 0.5 million on the tax-payers' account over the years till 1901. Even local board funds were diverted to the construction of light railways and tramways needed by the tea industry. For example, the 20-mile Tezpur–Balipara Light Railways, in which almost half the share capital was owned by tea companies, was subsidized by the Tezpur Local Board to the tune of Rs 0.1 million – a sum equivalent to one-fourth of the paid-up capital and payable in twenty annual instalments. The Board, however, was not given any shares in lieu of this sacrifice.[19] Besides, the Company received its supply of timber from government forests royalty-free.

The alignment of the railways was done through the thinly populated sub-montane tea-belt with the obvious purpose of serving the planters' interests

---

[18] Guha, 'A Big Push without a Take-Off', pp. 203–09. The average dividend is worked out from statistics in H.A. Antrobus, *A History of the Assam Company 1839–1953* (Edinburgh, 1957), pp. 409–10.

[19] Guha, 'A Big Push without a Take-Off', pp. 203–09. By blocking the outlet of water of the Begijan river, the Jorhat State Railways caused water-logging of a large area under cultivation and thus damaged the ryots' interests. *Indian Echo,* 28 September 1886. The quote in the paragraph is from *History of Indian Railways Constructed and the Progress upto 31ˢᵗ March 1918* (Government of India, Simla, 1919), p. 248.

best. Old trading centres like Goalpara and Barpeta, and towns like Sibsagar were bypassed, allowing them to stagnate and decay. The structure of railway rates was biased in favour of the tea industry. With improved communications and an organized trade in indentured coolie supply, thousands of labourers could now be recruited in remote tribal tracts and forwarded to Assam. By 1905–06, the adult labour force on Assam plantations swelled to a total number of 4,17,262. Of these only a few thousands were local men. The mortality rate in the plantations was very high: during the thirteen years ending 1899, it averaged 53.2 per thousand of adult indentured labour.[20]

Demographic Change and Its Impact

The land-abundant economy of the Brahmaputra Valley failed to grow enough foodgrains to feed its increasing population. The annual import of foodgrains into the valley increased from 0.3 million maunds around 1872 to some 0.7 million maunds during the last five years of the century.[21] Although this deficit was marginal, to the tune of less than 2 per cent of the total requirement, the tendency in the context was a pointer. With 1884–85 as the base year, the index number of total tea acreage in Assam proper, for which alone more or less complete agricultural data are available, steadily increased to 192 in 1900–01. But the comparable index of total gross cropped area exclusive of the area under tea, after having risen to a peak of 129 by 1892–93, went on decreasing from year to year until it fell to 113 in 1900–01. Thus, it more or less just kept pace with the rate of population growth. It was of course the black fever epidemic (discussed below) that caused much of the stagnation. The prices of foodgrains were rising, and many starvation deaths were reported from Nowgong in the bad season of 1896. On 16 October of that year, troops had to be called out there to suppress a riotous outburst against the *banias* who had cornered the grain market.[22] Conditions were further worsened by the great earthquake of 1897 that caused many deaths and havoc over many hundreds of acres of farm land.

Epidemic Tilts the Population Balance

One important cause of the retarded agricultural growth was no doubt the slow population increase in both the valleys from the mid-1880s. The population increased very fast during the years 1872–81 but its rate of growth slowed down over the next twenty years. During 1891–1901, the decadal rate of population growth was 5.7 per cent in the Brahmaputra Valley and a little more than

---

[20] Resolution on Immigrant Labour in the Assam Districts of East Bengal and Assam for the year ending the 30 June 1910 (Shillong, 1910), pp. 1–2. For the mortality rate, Sir Henry Cotton, Indian and Home Memories (London, 1911), p. 167.

[21] Import figures in Bengal Administrative Report, 1871–72, p. 140 and the relevant Assam Administration Reports. For example, as per Assam Administrative Report, 1895–96, App. (82).

[22] The Bengalee, 17 October 1896. For the index used, see Guha, 'A Big Push without a Take-Off', p. 220, Table 5.

6 per cent in the Surma Valley. The situation was in fact more serious in the former than what the total figures revealed. Had there been no continuous immigration, the population would have actually gone down.

The black fever *(kala azar)* epidemic, originating in the Garo Hills, appeared in Goalpara in 1883, entered Assam proper in 1888, and gradually spread throughout its length and breadth. During the decade 1881–91, the population of Goalpara sub-division decreased by 18 per cent and that of Kamrup district by 1.6 per cent. During the next decade, the population of Kamrup decreased by 7.1 per cent, that of the Mangaldai sub-division of Darrang by 9 per cent and of Nowgong by 24.8 per cent. Immigration in these areas was then marginal. The tea districts, however, were the least affected, much to the relief of the planters. The population of Lakhimpur actually increased by 46.1 per cent between 1891 and 1901 – an estimated 16 per cent through natural growth and 30 per cent through immigration. The population of Sibsagar increased by 24.4 per cent – half the increase due to immigration.[23]

It is clear, therefore, that the indigenous population of the Brahmaputra Valley tended to stagnate or even decrease during the two decades before 1901. On the basis of an exercise listing all Hindu indigenous castes and indigenous tribes of Assam proper, and their numbers for the relevant census years, the census authorities came to the conclusion that the indigenous population actually decreased by 5.4 per cent between 1881 and 1891, and 6.4 per cent between 1891 and 1901. Later, the Assam Congress Opium Enquiry Committee re-examined the issue. On the basis of a list of indigenous linguistic groups of the Brahmaputra Valley, they came to the conclusion that the decline was much less, the respective rates being nevertheless 2.9 and 1.9 per cent. On the basis of these latter figures, the cumulative decline of the indigenous population of the Valley may be accepted to have been at least 7.7 per cent over the last two decades of the century. The non-indigenous population of Assam proper increased, meanwhile, from less than 1 lakh in a total population of 15 lakhs in 1872, to an estimated 5 to 6 lakhs in a total population of about 22 lakhs in 1901. The influx of immigrants more than neutralized the decline in the indigenous population.[24] The population mix thus underwent a substantial ethnic redistribution.

Immigration apart, there was also some internal inter-district migration of the Kachari population from Kamrup and Mangaldai to the tea districts. As a result of the combined effect of these population movements and particularly the epidemic havoc in the Mangaldai sub-division, the indigenous component of the

---

[23] Ibid., p. 221; *An Account of the Province of Assam*, pp. 20 and 129–30; *Report of the Administration of Eastern Bengal and Assam, 1905–06*, p. 78; *Census of India, 1901, Vol. 4, Assam-Part I Report* (Shillong, 1902), pp. 16–22.

The increase in Sibsagar district was despite the *kala azar* havoc in its Golaghat sub-division.

[24] *Census of India, 1901, Vol. 4*, pp. 27 and 30; *Assam Congress Opium Enquiry Report* (hereafter *ACOER*), Jorhat, 1925, pp. 14 and 97. The revised figures are derived from the population table given on p. 14 of this *Report*.

population of Darrang district was believed by the census authorities to have decreased by 8 per cent between 1891 and 1901. Thus, two major demographic changes took place during the years 1874–1905: (i) a shift in the ethnic composition of the population and (ii) a change in its spatial distribution over the districts. Non-indigenous elements came to constitute at least one-quarter of the population of Assam proper in 1901. In that year, two-fifths of the population of the district of Lakhimpur were enumerated as born outside the province and only 39 per cent as having Assamese as their mother-tongue. People born outside the province constituted a quarter of the population both in Darrang and Sibsagar, in the same year.[25] Over the years, till 1901, the density of population increased more rapidly in the tea districts than in other areas (Appendix 3).

This major shift in the composition and distribution of the population was bound to affect the peasant economy adversely. Most of the immigrants into nineteenth-century Assam came from the tribal tracts and were absorbed as labour, and sometimes also as tenants, in the tea plantations. Those who took to cultivation of ordinary crops as tenants or ryots were poor cultivators, with backward techniques and serf-like social status. Despite an increasing demand from the plantation sector for grain, the peasant economy of Assam failed to respond adequately because of an acute manpower shortage.

Thus there emerged a serious imbalance between the fast-growing modern sector comprising plantations, coal mines, oil fields and the associated infrastructure, on the one hand, and the near-stagnant, traditional agricultural sector, on the other. The gap between the income stream accrued and the income disbursed within the province increasingly widened. Not only was the extracted surplus remitted to Britain in the form of fabulously high dividends and individual savings from inflated pay packets, but also a part of the hard-earned wage bill was remitted outside the province. For example, by way of money orders alone there was a net outflow of Rs 4.8 million in the year 1904–05 – when the corresponding national income of the province was presumably low.[26] Even otherwise, a good part of the remaining disbursed income stream was spent on services and goods procured from outside, rather than on local supplies. Thus, the indigenous sector of the economy was only marginally benefited – more so till about 1905 – by the characteristically limited spread effects of the colonial development pattern, as was suggested in Chapter One.

Production Relations on Plantations
'Legislative Abetment of Slavery'
The British civil servants, who believed in England's civilizing mission in India, did not ever seem to have a clear conscience over the burning issue of the coolie trade. As President of the Bengal Legislative Council, even Sir George

---

[25] Guha, 'A Big Push without a Take-Off', pp. 211–12.
[26] *Data in Financial and Commercial Statistics of British India, 13th Issue* (1907), pp. 258 and 264, as worked out by Guha, 'A Big Push without a Take-Off', p. 213.

Campbell did not hesitate to describe the recruitment system as one reducing the coolie to the position of a slave. Sir Bampfylde Fuller described the condition of the coolies in an unpublished memorandum as that of 'beasts in a menagerie'. There loomed all the time in the background like a spectre – as Cotton tells us in his autobiography – the larger and independent question of the protection of thousands of helpless labourers, often transmitted over more than a thousand miles by rail and river to work on the tea gardens for inadequate wages and under penal provisions.[27] And yet the corpus of emigrant labour legislation produced by this uneasy conscience turned out to be practically nothing but abetment of the same notorious 'slavery' system.

In 1882, the Indian Emigration Act was passed, despite opposition from Kristodas Pal in the Imperial Legislative Council. Of course, there was the assurance that labour recruitment under penal contracts would soon be abolished. The Secretary of State for India, in his dispatch of 17 July 1886, directed that the working of the Act should be 'narrowly watched' and that a report should be submitted not later than 1889 on the advisability of repealing the Act. On 5 October 1891, he even suggested that, preferably, a contract labour system modelled on the Act of 1882 should not any longer be continued in practice. Yet the amending legislations that followed in 1893 and 1901 differed from each other and from that of 1889 only in the details of their utopian welfare prescriptions. These, in any case, were liable to total evasion by the planters under the given circumstances of poor inspection. The law in existence, meanwhile, continued to validate penal contracts, inadequate wages and the *arkatti* system of recruitment, as before.[28] The Law Member, in course of the debate on the Bill in the Imperial Legislative Council in March 1901, said unblushingly:

> The labour contract authorized by the Bill is a transaction by which, to put it rather bluntly, a man is often committed to Assam before he knows what he is doing, and is thereupon held to his promise for four years, with a threat of arrest and imprisonment, if he fails to perform it. Conditions like these have no place in the ordinary law of master and servant. We made them part of the law of British India at the instance and for the benefit of the planters of Assam . . . the motive power in this legislation is the interest of the planter, not the interest of the coolie.[29]

---

[27] Cotton, *Indian and Home Memories*, pp. 247 and 265.

[28] Speech by J.C. Ghose, *Proceedings of Indian National Congress 17th Session* (Calcutta, 1901), pp. 165–66. Also see editorial comment by Kristodas Pal, *Hindoo Patriot*, 9 January 1882. He called the 1882 Act 'Slave Law' in disguise.

  For the Indian nationalist reaction to coolie legislation in details, see Bipan Chandra, *The Rise and Growth of Economic Nationalism in India* (New Delhi, 1966; reprinted 1969), pp. 360–79.

[29] Quote as reproduced by Ghose, *Proceedings of Indian National Congress 17th Session*, p. 165. For Indian opinion in the legislature, *Imperial (Indian) Legislative Council Proceedings* (hereafter *ILCP*), 1901, Vol. 11, pp. 86–158.

How powerful the Assam planters were as a pressure group at the highest level of administration, was graphically narrated by Cotton in his autobiography. Like his predecessors, he too went far in supporting the conduct of the planters and promoting their interests during his Chief Commissionership (1896–1902). He did not hesitate to strain the law for the purpose of recovering runaway coolies found working for higher wages on the railways, and handing them over to their masters. He spent public funds liberally in the furtherance of tea interests and encouraged the planters to take up lands for ordinary cultivation as well in the vicinity of their gardens. In the initial three or four years, he even concealed the fact of wanton oppression in his routine labour reports to the Government of India.[30]

Towards the close of his tenure, in course of an official assignment to investigate into and report on the statutory wage question, Cotton learnt about the horrifying sufferings of the coolies, which, as simply a Chief Commissioner, he would have never known. He decided 'not to conceal the truth' any more.[31]

Under the mounting pressure of public opinion in India, Curzon had already pledged to support the general principle of an increase in coolies' wages. A Bill was therefore brought before the Imperial Legislative Council in 1899 to alter the time-old statutory wages for men from Rs 5 to Rs 6, and for women from Rs 4 to Rs 5 per month. As a member of the Council, Cotton was shocked to find that even this mild and modest proposal was not acceptable to the British capitalist lobby therein. In spite of his protest, the proposed rates were modified at the committee stage to a graduated scale, with annual increments reaching the full rates only in the fourth and last year of the contract. Curzon announced in the Council a postponement of even this graduated rate for two years, in view of the depression in the tea industry. The Assam Labour and Emigration Bill was enacted on 8 March 1901 by fifteen votes – all British – to four, including the lone British vote of Cotton. The Act was condemned by Indian opinion both inside and outside the legislature. After this showdown, Cotton had to finally go into retirement from service under pressure. In the role of a British liberal, he carried on his persistent campaign against the planter Raj. The Indian National Congress expressed its gratitude by electing him president of its twentieth annual session at Bombay in 1904.[32]

[30] Cotton, *Indian and Home Memories*, p. 258.

[31] Ibid., p. 259.

[32] 8 March, *ILCP*, 1901, p. 158. Cotton, *Indian and Home Memories*, pp. 260–61 and 287; *New India* (Calcutta), 27 August 1901.

The Indian Tea Association's plea was that, in most cases, earnings were low because labour worked 'so few days in the week', and also because there was a crisis in the tea industry during 1901–05. See P. Griffiths, *The History of the Indian Tea Industry* (London, 1967), pp. 145–46. The plea, though upheld by Griffiths, is unconvincing.

'Beasts of a Menagerie'

The harrowing tale of coolie oppression, during the period 1874–1905, by planters and their hirelings – the *arkattis* and the *sardars* – needs to be told in detail, even at the risk of repetition. For, some of its features persisted through the early decades of the twentieth century as well.

The planters used to pay their contractors and agents a sum varying from Rs 120 to Rs 150 for every recruit under a penal contract, at the beginning of the twentieth century. The agents frequently resorted to criminal means such as inducing their victims by misrepresentation or by threats. The records of the criminal courts, as Cotton pointed out, teemed with instances of abduction of married women and children, fraud, wrongful confinement, intimidation, and actual violence. Due to congestion, lack of adequate food and unhygienic conditions, many coolies died like cattle while still on their way to the plantations. The overwhelming majority, of course, survived to be sold to the planters at the prices stated above. At the expiry of the contract period, the coolie was legally free but was repeatedly induced, under duress, to re-engage himself. Thus, having once come to a tea garden, he had practically no hope of returning to his native place.[33]

Although the prices of wage goods were rising, the legal minimum wages remained unaltered during the years 1865–1903. The actual paid-out wages were even lower. During the seventeen years preceding 1901, for example, these remained well below the prescribed rates, as well as what unskilled labour elsewhere in Assam or in the recruiting districts were earning at that time.[34] The wage rate of able-bodied agricultural labourers in Lakhimpur, for example, was Rs 9.37 per month in 1873; and, for most of the subsequent period till 1901, it remained within the range of Rs 7 to Rs 10. In the early 1880s an unskilled railway construction labourer earned Rs 12 to Rs 16 per month.[35] Free-market wages tended to increase during this period but the Act denied the tea garden labourer any such increase. On the contrary, the price he had to pay for concessional rice supply was gradually enhanced from Re. 1 in the early 1860s to Rs 3 by 1900.[36]

Besides, there were various other forms of semi-feudal exploitation. Cotton wrote:

> I knew cases in which coolies in the fourth year of their agreement were not paid the higher rate of salary to which they were entitled. In other cases, rice was not provided at the statutory price and the subsistence allowance prescribed by law was not paid to sick coolies or pregnant women. Advances were often illegally

---

[33] Cotton, *Indian and Home Memories*, pp. 262–63. Sir Bampfylde Fuller, *Some Personal Experiences* (London, 1930), p. 117; *Somprakash* (Changripota), 11 *shravan* 1293 (AD 1886), pp. 461–62 and also 24 *paush* 1273 (AD 1867), pp. 153–54.

[34] Cotton, *Indian and Home Memories*, pp. 261–62.

[35] *Imperial Gazetteer of India*, Vol. 1 (second edition, 1885), p. 361. Guha, 'A Big Push without a Take-Off', pp. 206–07.

[36] Guha, 'A Big Push without a Take-Off', p. 206. Griffiths, *History of the Indian Tea Industry*, pp. 304 and 306.

debited against coolies on account of subsistence allowance or sick diet, as well as on account of rewards paid for the arrest of deserters, and labourers were thus bound hand and foot to the garden service. In some instances only a few annas (or pence) found their way into the hands of a coolie as wages in course of the whole year.[37]

Such miserable conditions could be imposed upon the coolies not only because of their illiteracy and ignorance, but also because of their inability to strike work under the bindings of the penal contract. If they struck work, they were liable to imprisonment. If they fled, the planters had the right to arrest them without warrant. Flogging and other kinds of torture, with the connivance of even courts of justice, were common practice. Fuller refers to the case of a coolie being flogged to death with a stirrup leather by a European assistant. The murderer was sentenced to eighteen months' simple imprisonment by the lower court but was finally acquitted by the high court under the pressure of 'European' agitation. In another case, a tea garden overseer who had stripped and flogged a woman worker was acquitted on the plea that he had acted under his British manager's orders. Such instances of inhuman treatment were many, and the Indian newspapers were full of them.[38]

Naturally, under such conditions, the workers had no freedom of movement. Communication with neighbouring tea gardens and villages was strictly controlled, even prohibited. If a worker's daughter was to be given away in marriage to a resident of another tea garden, the manager's permission was necessary, as it involved a loss to his actual or potential labour force. In many tea gardens, the coolies were virtually prisoners, under guard night and day. 'I came across notices posted at river ferries and railway stations describing runaway coolies and offering rewards for their apprehension,' wrote Lieutenant-Governor Fuller, 'that reminded one of *Uncle Tom's Cabin*. Runaways who were legally arrested were seldom, if ever, made over to the police as the law required.'[39]

Coolie-catching, their transit to tea gardens under conditions of high mortality, the selling of recruits at a market price, the hunt for runaway coolies – all these remind one of slave-running in Africa and the global slave trade. But, once on the plantations, the coolies were rather treated like serfs, tied to the soil by extra-economic means and, in many cases, also by small allotments of land as cottars on the plantations. Deprived of all freedom, they depended on the planter for the necessities of life and other amenities. The estate manager was the only authority, armed with the legal right to arrest and sometimes also with the legal powers of an honourary magistrate. Even otherwise, he arbitrated in all

<hr>

[37] Cotton, *Indian and Home Memories*, p. 265.

[38] Fuller, *Personal Experiences*, pp. 118–19. For reference to select newspaper reports see footnotes 28 and 33. Also, *Madras Mail*, 11 September 1890, containing an article titled 'Legislative Abetment of Slavery'; and *New India* (Calcutta), 26 August 1901 and 11 November 1901, containing Bipin Chandra Pal's articles.

[39] Fuller, *Personal Experiences*, p. 118.

disputes and punished the offender. He built the coolies' houses, supplied rice to them when necessary, established the market and regulated prices.[40] There was no one to challenge him if he chose to have a coolie woman as his concubine. When he went on a *shikar*, he had the labour gangs beat the jungles for him. He tied the workers to bondage by advancing money against the wage account. Such a system, which emerged in response to a condition of acute labour short-age, was more akin to the worst form of serfdom than slavery. The coolies, however, were essentially neither slaves nor serfs; they constituted the newly emerged working class of Assam, bound together by a common interest against capital in its colonial form.

Class Struggle on Plantations

The plantation labour force was a multilingual, heterogenous society. In 1884–85, 44.7 per cent of them were from Chhotanagpur, 27.2 per cent from Bengal, 21.6 per cent from the United Provinces and Bihar, 0.2 per cent from Bombay, 0.7 per cent from Madras, and 5.5 per cent from within Assam. In 1889, half of them were found to have been recruited from Chhotanagpur, about a quarter from Bengal and only about 5 per cent from Assam itself.[41]

Illiterate, ignorant, unorganized and isolated from their homes as they were, the plantation workers were weak and powerless against the planters. On the other hand, the latter were well organized into the Indian Tea Association (ITA), founded in 1881. Nevertheless, the workers fought back at the individual garden level, as is evident from the available official statistics on disputes for the years 1884–93. The forms of struggle varied from absconding and occasional litigation to strikes and violent mass attacks on the planters. For example, in 1884, the manager of Bowalia Tea Estate in Cachar was *gheraoed* in his house for defiantly caning a boy in the presence of assembled coolies. About a dozen men were sentenced to terms of imprisonment varying from three days to one year on this occasion, while the manager was able to escape by paying a fine of Rs 200 only for his folly. In 1899, Cotton noted in his report that

> there is a growing tendency in the Coolie class to resent a blow by striking a blow in return and this soon leads to serious results, as the Coolies act in com-bination among themselves, and armed with formidable weapons – the imple-ments of their industry; but this very tendency exercises a healthy influence in restraining the hot-headed and impetuous European assistant from raising his hand against them.[42]

---

[40] See Griffiths, *History of the Indian Tea Industry*, p. 376. The interpretation is ours. Also Dwarka Nath Ganguli, *Slavery in Indian Dominion*, edited by K.L. Chatto-padhyay (reprint of thirteen articles published in *The Bengalee*, September 1886 to April 1887, Calcutta, 1972), pp. 30–35 and 56.

[41] *Assam Administrative Report*, 1884, p. 168 and also 1889–90, p. 136.

[42] Report by Cotton in 1899, cited by Griffiths, *History of the Indian Tea Industry*, p. 377. Also see Ganguli, *Slavery in Indian Dominion*, pp. 36–37, for labour disputes in 1884.

The public reception given to Chief Commissioner Cotton in the tea district of Cachar was enthusiastically reported in the seventeenth annual session of the Indian National Congress at Calcutta in 1901. When he was passing from Fenchuganj to Silchar, the roads for a distance of fifteen miles were reportedly lined with coolies holding lanterns and crying out 'Cotton Sahib ka Jai!' (Glory to Cotton!). It was reported in the East Bengal newspapers in December 1901 that, during his recent tour, the Chief Commissioner had found every two miles a coolie standing with a banner that read, 'Mr Cotton, the Protector of the Dumb Coolie'.[43] Obviously, such a demonstration could not have been organized without the coolies and sympathetic educated middle-class elements coming together.

Although the figures of collisions during the years 1890–1903 were not numerous, they indicated a steady increase. In 1902–03, 82 plantation workers were imprisoned for illegal assembly and rioting.[44] Admittedly, the conditions in Assam were much worse than those obtaining in the Bengal tea districts. Cases of assault, rioting and unlawful assembly continued to be reported in the *Annual Immigration Reports* even thereafter.

Remembering his experience as the administrator of Assam during the years 1902–06, Fuller wrote: 'there was bound to be some revolt, and on badly managed gardens riots were not very infrequent. They sometimes ended in the burning of the manager's bungalow.'[45]

Thus the plantation workers carried on their struggle against colonial exploitation, and they had the sympathy of the Indian middle classes. So determined was their resistance that at last, in 1906, a committee was appointed by the Government of India to investigate the working of the labour laws.

Peasants Resent Increased Taxation
Evolution of the Land Tenure System
The system of land tenure in British Assam was not uniform. In the hills districts, communal or clan ownership was the usual form. But private property rights in land also existed, wherever terrace cultivation and horticulture had developed. Land-holders in the hills districts did not have to pay towards land revenue; they generally paid house tax instead. Most parts of Sylhet and Goalpara districts were under permanent settlement, involving the prevalence of various forms of tenancy and sub-tenancy. Zamindars – big and small – were numerous in Sylhet, while only six families held all the nineteen zamindari estates in Goalpara. In Sylhet, the East India Company's government did not enter into engagement with the Chaudhuris (land revenue collectors) but made permanent settlement directly with the ryots, that is, the land-holding cultivators. In the rest of the Assam plains, the system that evolved was ryotwari. What is discussed below concerns mainly the ryotwari areas of Assam proper.

<hr>

[43] Speeches by J.C. Ghose and Bipin Chandra Pal, *Proceedings of Indian National Congress 17th Session*, pp. 165 and 167.
[44] R.K. Das, *Plantation Labour in India* (Calcutta, 1931), p. 25.
[45] Fuller, *Personal Experiences*, p. 120.

It was under the Settlement Rules of 1870 that the government, for the first time, categorically and unequivocally recognized the permanent, transferable and heritable rights in *rupit* (wet paddy) and *bari* (homestead) lands in private occupation. A district was divided into *mauzas* or circles, each such unit – from a few square miles to 200 square miles in area – being placed under a *mauzadar* for purposes of revenue collection. For appointment as a *mauzadar*, one had to be an influential and well-to-do resident of the *mauza* itself. He was bound to pay the entire land revenue due from his *mauza* by the end of April. For this obligation, he received a commission of 10 per cent on the first Rs 10,000 and 5 per cent on the balance of the revenue paid by him. He was ordinarily succeeded to the office by one of his family. The system helped the growth of a stable and loyal rural gentry that could be relied upon as a strong ally of the administration. In rural areas, the *mauzadar's* position was next to that of the planter. Each *mauza* was divided into a number of circles, headed by *mandals* or village surveyors. Like the *mauzadar*, the *mandal* too was a considerable landholder. The latter's pay on a monthly basis being nominal, cultivation was his main business.

Under the 1870 Rules, wet paddy and homestead lands were settled for a period not exceeding ten years at fixed rates, subject to a revision at the end of the period. From 1883, however, settlements made for this category of land were invariably decennial. Other categories of land suitable for dry crops continued to be settled on an annual basis, since the relevant cultivation was of a shifting nature. These were not vested with permanent, transferable rights and could be taken back by the government for public purposes without any compensation. The ryot continued to have the option of relinquishing any amount of land under either category, at his own convenience.

The 1870 Rules remained in force until they were replaced by a comprehensive code – the Assam Land and Revenue Regulations, 1886 – that basically retained all the aforesaid features. A cadastral survey, ordered meanwhile, was completed during the years 1882–93. While the land revenue rates remained unchanged for a quarter century till March 1893, the total land revenue demand increased substantially because of new additions to the settled area and the detection of concealed cultivation. The settled area in the Brahmaputra Valley increased, for example, by 15 per cent between 1881–82 and 1891–92.

Economic Conditions Worsen

The conditions of the peasantry in the 1880s cannot be said to have been prosperous, despite the increased demand for farm products from plantations and railway construction activities. Out of 9,801 professional moneylenders in Assam as per the 1891 Census Report, only 1,793 were in the Brahmaputra Valley (1,211 were in Kamrup alone); of the rest, 7,902 moneylenders were in the Surma Valley. The available statistics on land transfers in the province during the years 1884–93 are not adequate to indicate the extent of prevailing indebtedness. The number of land transfers in any year remained within the range of 12,000 to

29,000 cases, and the acreage transferred varied from 40,000 to 85,000 acres, except for the year 1886–87 when 1,52,000 acres changed hands. These figures were not significant in the context of the province's total cultivated acreage of around 3.4 million acres.[46] Even in 1886–87, the amount of land transferred was less than 5 per cent of the total under cultivation. These early imperfect statistics, however, conceal more than they reveal. The fact that the market sector of the peasant economy had been completely in the grip of the well-entrenched Marwari trading capital ever since the advent of the British rule, is beyond dispute. Peasants used to receive cash advances from the Marwari traders against pledged crops, to a considerable extent. The census put these traders and their agents mostly under the category of petty shopkeepers, rather than moneylenders. The numerous shops provided a network for the filtration of necessary credit into the rural areas. Peasants also secured loans through the mortgage of their labour to local landlords and traders.[47]

Enquiries made in 1882–83 suggested that there were only a few under-tenants, except on the partially or wholly revenue-free (*nisfkhiraj* and *lakhiraj*) estates of Kamrup. The extent of tenancy in the latter category of land was widespread, but no estimate is available. The family of Parbatia Goswami had 41,000 acres of land in this category, spread over 31 *mauzas*. It was estimated in 1883 that Parbatia Goswami and Madhav Devalay, between them, accounted for no less than 1,000 tenant ryots. Such tenants did not enjoy occupancy rights anywhere in the Brahmaputra Valley. The settlement statistics of 1893 revealed that in the Kamrup *mauzas* of Bajali, Bangsar, Barbhag and Patidarang, taken together, as much as one-third of the settled area was tenant-cultivated, mostly on a cash-rent basis. In south Kamrup, this proportion was one-fifth. On the other hand, in Sibsagar, only 7 per cent of the settled area was sub-let. There the rent was, by and large, also paid in cash. Frequently, it did not exceed the land revenue rates paid by the land-owners themselves. The latter derived profit from the labour services that the tenant was required to provide by custom. Besides, those tenants who tilled their plots with the owner's bullocks had to work one day out of three on the latter's fields. The number of tenants in Sibsagar increased from 9,900 in 1891 to 21,500 in 1901. The Director of Land Records and Agriculture noted in 1888 a tendency in the most populous pockets towards accumulation of leases in the hands of non-cultivators who had a command over ready

---

[46] *Note on Land Transfer and Agricultural Indebtedness in India* (Government of India, 1895), pp. 66–67.

[47] Detailed information, collected officially in 1888 from forty-two randomly selected poor agricultural households of labouring people in Assam proper, reveals that half of them were indebted. Of the twenty-one indebted households, seven had to sell labour in an attempt to redeem their debts. In five of these seven cases, this took the shape of bonded labour. Traders or moneylenders advanced loans only in a few cases – 'Conditions of the People of Assam', No. 10, pp. 1–92 in Government of India, *Proceedings of the Revenue and Agricultural Department for December 1888, Famine Reports on the Conditions of the Lower Classes of the Population in India, Nos. 1–24* (confidential) (National Archives of India; hereafter NAI).

money. Most of them were government office clerks and pleaders of the district towns.

The same official was puzzled to find that not many of the non-cultivating land-owners were Marwari merchants.[48] Usurious merchant capital was more interested in seizing the crop for settlement of an advance than in seizing the land. Hence, Marwaris did not feature as an important absentee landholding group. By the close of the century, planters also began to settle tenants on their surplus lands as a matter of policy.[49]

The conditions of the peasantry worsened very much in the period 1891–1901 for complex reasons, as already explained in a preceding section, and also due to a further rise in opium prices and land revenue rates. The devastating earthquake of 1897, which caused the deaths of more than 1,500 people, added to their miseries.

'Raij' against the Raj: The 'Mels'

The impending enhancement of land revenue rates under the new settlement, as notified in 1892, led to a widespread dissatisfaction that rocked the rural society. While on a tour of the Brahmaputra valley in the winter of that year, the Chief Commissioner received 'loud and numerous' complaints that 'afforded a strong indication of the temper of the people'. The ryots complained that because they had to pay the government an exorbitant price for opium, they were unable to pay the enhanced land revenue. The Sarvajanik Sabha of Jorhat held a series of meetings from October 1892 to February 1893, to protest against the government policy of an 'excessive increase of revenue'.[50]

Under the new settlement, the population density and the demand for land in each village were the chief considerations in determining the land value and the rate to be fixed. The revised rates in the Brahmaputra Valley initially involved an enhancement of 53 per cent on average; but in many villages it was

[48] Extract from the Report by H.Z. Darrah as reproduced in *Note on Land Transfer and Agricultural Indebtedness,* p. 67; also, ibid., pp. 234–35.

Phatikchandra Barooah, 'Enquiries into the Status of Cultivating Ryots in *Lakhiraj* and *Nifskhiraj* Estates in Kamrup', dated 13 March 1883 to D.C., Kamrup (Department of Historical and Antiquarian Studies, Government of Assam, Gauhati, Transcript No. 244), and its supplement (Department of Historical and Antiquarian Studies, Government of Assam, Gauhati, Transcript No. 255); B.C. Allen, ed., *Assam District Gazetteers,* Vol. 4, Kamrup (1905), p. 166 and Vol. 7, Sibsagar (1906), pp. 169–70.

Darrah wrote on 22 May 1922: 'subletting was not very common in the five valley districts and where most generally practiced, for example, in Kamrup district, the money rents paid by the tenants rarely exceeded the revenue payable to government'. *Assam Valley Re-assessment Report* (Government of Assam, August 1893), Appendix A, p. 44.

[49] Griffiths, *History of the Indian Tea Industry,* pp. 302–03.

[50] Quotes from the evidence of J.J.S. Driberg in *Royal Commission on Opium,* 1893, Vol. 2 (London, 1894), p. 278; the last quote is from Jagannath Barooah's evidence, ibid., p. 299. Draft Rules for the re-assessment of land revenue rates in the Brahmaputra Valley were published in *Assam Gazette,* 8 October 1892, to elicit public opinion.

as high as 70 to 100 per cent. Having at first refused to pay any heed to the public memorials on the issue, on second thought, the Chief Commissioner passed orders to reduce the increase in effect to an average 37 per cent. The ryots demanded a postponement of the collection even at that reduced rate until the final orders of the Government of India on the pending appeals were received. The Chief Commissioner disallowed any such postponement.[51] People in Kamrup and central Assam spontaneously organized themselves once more into specially convened local *mels* to decide upon a no-rent campaign.[52]

In these *mels* the ryots discussed the increasing economic burden on them. They were already paying much higher prices for opium – a government monopoly. Year after year, they had been pledging their crops to Marwari traders to get advances for paying the land revenue. Now the demand for enhanced land revenue would push them further into the grip of usurious capital. Thus, caught in a vicious circle of intensified exploitation, they started agitating not only against the government, but also against the Marwari traders.[53]

On 24 December 1893, Rangiya Bazar was looted by a crowd of 200 to 250 people, mostly Kacharis. This happened immediately after the holding of a *mel* at the neighbouring village of Belagaon. Similar *mels* were held throughout December and January in almost all the *mauzas* in the compact and thickly populated area of north Kamrup. Everywhere the *mels* directed the people not to pay the enhanced rates. Thousands of people demonstrated in and around Rangiya for several days. Armed police and military forces were posted at Rangiya, with instructions to stop the people from demonstrating and to arrest their leaders. But they failed to do so. On 30 December, about 3,000 people demonstrated against the unpopular measure and managed to disperse unscathed.

On 6 January 1894, the District Magistrate himself came down to Rangiya with an additional force. Two days later, when a *mel* in session was reiterating the people's demands, the police were able to arrest fifteen persons.

---

[51] Government's reply to Rashbehari Ghose, *Abstract of the Proceedings of the Council of Governor General of India, 1894*, Vol. 33 (Calcutta, 1895), pp. 317–19; *Hindoo Patriot*, 30 March and also 9 April 1894.

[52] 'The ordinary village panchayat, originally constituted as an authority on social matters, has developed into the *mel* or assembly not only of the members of a village, but of the whole of the inhabitants of even one or more tahsils. The *mels* are governed by the leading Dolois or Gossains and by the principal landholders of the district.' R.B. McCabe, District Magistrate of Kamrup, to Commissioner, Home Department, Progs. Public 1 (A), Assam Riots, No. 2–T, dated camp Rangiya, 12 January 1894 under No. 112-A, April 1894 (NAI).

[53] The account of the peasant unrest as given here and below is mainly from K.N. Dutt, *Landmarks of the Freedom Struggle in Assam* (Gauhati, 1958), pp. 30–35 and P. Raychaudhuri, 'Uttar Kamrup aru Darangar krishak bidroha' (in Assamese), *Pravaha* (Gauhati), 1, Nos. 6–8 (1956), particularly pp. 407–10, unless otherwise stated. Though not properly documented, both sources are obviously based on official records: Home Department Progs. Public (A), Assam Riots, April–December 1894 (NAI); and press reports in *Hindoo Patriot*, 5 February 1894, *Indian Nation* (Calcutta), 12 February 1894, etc. We have checked these primary sources.

On 10 January, representatives of the people met the District Magistrate. They demanded the release of their detained comrades and postponement of the collection of land revenue at the enhanced rates. Later, they decided to forcibly release their comrades the same evening. When some 2,000 to 3,000 lathi-armed people began drawing close to the *thana*, the District Magistrate, after an infructuous attempt to disperse them by persuasion, ordered a firing. However, according to a report published in the *Hindoo Patriot* of 5 February 1894, there was no loss of life. The government found it difficult to collect land revenue in the *tahsils* of Patidarang, Nalbari, Barama and Bajali, and in the *mauzas* of Upar Barbhag and Sarukhetri – all forming a compact block.

Meanwhile a reign of terror was let loose. Notices were served on principal headmen of the area, under Section 17 of Act V of 1861, to act as special constables for the preservation of peace. The ryot was told by the Raj: 'If you do not pay, your property will be attached.' The *raij* told him: 'If you do pay, you will be cursed and ex-communicated.'[54] The people were further directed by the *raij* not to bid for purchase of attached properties put on auction. Disobedience was threatened with social boycott and excommunication, as well as imposition of fines.

After the incident of 10 January at Rangiya, a detachment of the 44th Gurkha Rifles, armed police units and the Volunteer Force were requisitioned to suppress the defiant people. The *kutcherry* of Rangiya was stockaded. All licensed guns in Rangiya, Nalbari, Barama and Bajali *tahsils* – the storm centres – were seized. Respectable citizens over the entire affected area were forced into the special constabulary. On 21 January, a group of ryots assaulted the *mauzadar* and the *mandal* when they tried to collect revenue at Kapla near Lachima in Sarukhetri *mauza*. Seventy-five persons, arrested and detained in a government rest-house in this connection, were forcibly released by a 3,000-strong assembly of people. The next day, the District Magistrate himself arrived on the spot with a force of armed police. By 25 January, 59 principal leaders were arrested and forced to construct a makeshift lock-up for themselves. The same evening, about 6,000 people approached the District Magistrate's camp and presented a mass petition, signed by all of them, for release of those arrested. They finally dispersed after a bayonet charge was ordered.

The most tragic incident took place at Patharughat in Mangaldai subdivision, on 28 January 1894. The District Magistrate of Darrang went there with an armed force to suppress the agitation. Thousands of people who had rallied in anticipation of his arrival, squatted on the field facing the rest-house where he camped. They refused to disperse unless their demands were met. A

---

[54] Same as footnote 53 above.

The word *raij*, in Assamese, means people in general or in the context of a particular locality. It is derived from the word *rajya*, which meant an administrative or fiscal unit in some parts of medieval Assam. An Assamese proverb says: 'The people are (your) sovereign and the clan (your) Ganga' (*raijei raja, jnatiyei ganga*). Hence *raij mel* was much more than what we understand elsewhere by a village panchayat.

bayonet charge and volleys of firing followed, causing the deaths, according to official reports, of fifteen ryots and injury to as many as thirty-six. They had to retreat, of course, before the superiority of arms, but not before they had answered back by throwing clods of earth and bamboo sticks. The District Magistrate later felt qualms of conscience for having been the author of this dreadful butchery.[55] After incidents such as these, the resistance movement could not be kept up for long in the face of naked repression. Villagers were tortured and their properties destroyed or looted. The people were forced to pay the enhanced revenue.

Meanwhile, the Government of India further reduced the initial increase of land revenue to 32.7 per cent of the previous demand at the old rates, under the pressure of the people's struggle. The same authorities also limited such enhancement for an individual holding up to a maximum of about 50 per cent of the previous rental. This was no doubt a partial victory for the people. An echo of the robust voice of the *raij mels* was heard in 1894 in the Imperial Legislative Council itself, through an interpellation by Dr Rashbehari Ghose.[56]

The widespread peasant struggle, based on the unity of the entire peasantry and a section of the non-cultivating land-owners, made an impact on the contemporary Assamese society. The non-cultivating land-owners – Brahmins, Mahantas and Dolois, the traditional rural elite – apparently took the initiative and a leading role in the struggle. But it was the poor peasantry and other sections of the rural poor, including artisans, who lent it a militant character. One of the militant artisans, Pusparam Kanhar, is still remembered, *inter alia*, by the bell-metal workers of Sarukhetri *mauza* as having undergone a term of imprisonment.[57]

It may be noted that in the disturbed *mauzas* and *tahsils*, tenants constituted a large proportion of the population and occupied some one-third of the settled area. The land-owners apprehended that it would be difficult to shift the burden of the enhancement in land revenue rates on to the shoulders of their tenants. They feared that their profits as middlemen would therefore be cut down. This consideration pushed them into the agitation. But, afraid of a loss of prop-

---

[55] For the toll of killed and injured persons, see B.C. Allen, ed., *Assam District Gazetteers*, Darrang. Folk memory, however, puts the toll at a much higher figure.

Also, Dutt, *Freedom Struggle in Assam*, pp. 36–40.

[56] See footnote 51. To commemorate the Patharughat incident, a local village poet composed a ballad in Assamese, *Dalipuran*. For a reference see Dineswar Sharma, *Patharughatar Ran* (in Assamese, Mangaldoi, 1957), pp. 1–28; also *Patharighator Ran ba Dalipuran* by Norottam (Bheraghat Chatrasangha Mangaldoi, 1355 *can*), p. 13.

The land revenue demand in the Brahmaputra Valley increased from Rs 3,264,605 in 1892–93 to Rs 4,350,170 in 1893–94. *Report of the Administration of the Province of Assam for the Year 1893–94* (Shillong, 1894), p. 122.

[57] Information collected by Assam Kanhar Sangha of Sarthebari, which was founded on 5 November 1933 and registered as a cooperative society in 1938–39. On release, however, Pusparam was supposed to have had lost his 'caste' by having gone to jail and was excommunicated by his co-villagers. Another notable leader was Jajnaram Dev Goswami of Vyaskuchi, a landlord.

erty under attachment orders, they did not continue their resistance for long.[58] Indeed, they were the first to retreat.

Opium of the People

As the monopoly sale of opium by the government at an exorbitant price was a continued means to fleece the peasant, it needs detailed discussion. The professed official policy was one of progressive restriction of the opium evil through gradual enhancement of the sale price and a decrease in the number of licensed opium shops. Accordingly, the number of shops in the province was gradually brought down from 5,137 in 1873–74 to 1,397 in 1880–81, 775 in 1901–02 and 728 by 1905–06. The Treasury price was also increased from Rs 26 per *seer* in 1880–81 to Rs 32 in the years 1883–89, and Rs 37 in the years 1890–91 to 1908–09. The resultant decrease in the province's consumption of opium was apparently 23.5 per cent, while the increase in its total opium revenue was 10 per cent between 1880–81 and 1900–01 (Appendix 4).

The achievement was not much. In Assam proper, an exceptionally high per capita rate of opium consumption persisted. As much as 1,557 maunds out of the province's consumption of 1,686 maunds in 1880–81, and 1,201 maunds out of 1,291 maunds in 1900–01, were consumed there alone. The 18 per cent decline in consumption was partly due to a 7.7 per cent decrease in the opium-addicted indigenous population itself. In other words, the actual per capita consumption of opium in Assam proper decreased to the tune of only about 11 per cent in twenty years. One could suspect that the government was guided purely by revenue considerations rather than a welfare outlook. There was a continuous increase of opium consumption again after 1897–98, while the selling price was kept unchanged at Rs 37 per *seer* for nineteen years till 1908–09. The total consumption in Assam proper was at its lowest in 1897–98 (1,128 maunds) and 1901–02 (1,126 maunds), but thereafter it recorded an increasing trend that persisted until the Non-Cooperation movement of 1921–22 (Appendix 4). Opium was the most important source of the province's revenue, next only to land. A maund of opium would have cost the Treasury Rs 290 at the ex-factory cost in 1883–84, but it brought forth a gross revenue of Rs 1,040 when sold at Rs 26 per *seer*.[59] It was a gold mine for the government, not to be lightly surrendered. The government's opium policy was therefore one of maximizing revenue through a system of monopoly pricing.

The policy hit the opium-addicted Assamese peasant hard not only morally, but also economically. During the years 1874–1905, the habit of taking the drug in its most harmful form, that is, smoking, rapidly increased, raising the

---

[58] McCabe to Assam Valley Commissioner, camp Rangiya, 12 January 1894, Government of India, Home Department Progs. Public 1 (A), Assam Riots, No. 2-T.

[59] *Assam Administrative Report*, 1884–85, p. 71. The ex-factory cost price of opium was Rs 7–4 as. per *seer* until 1 June 1895.

Bengal Administrative Report, 1872–73, p. 292*n*, Driberg, p. 454.

proportion of smokers from an initial estimated 5 to 10 per cent to about 50 per cent of the addicts. Opium smoking had become a congregational religious ritual (*kaniya seva*), eating into the very core of the Assamese society.[60] Although there was an enhancement of price from time to time it still kept the drug within the reach of the peasant, as if only to squeeze him more. The government sold the drug to vendors at Rs 37 per *seer* but the retail price was Rs 45 to Rs 50, the margin going to middlemen. Between 1873 and 1893, the retail price increased two to three-fold. According to the evidence of a pleader of Nowgong before the Royal Commission on Opium in 1893, the lower classes generally spent between 10 to 20 per cent of their income on opium.[61] The 12.5 per cent enhancement of opium price in 1890–91, together with the increased land revenue rates were factors that contributed to widespread discontent.

Besides the government, some planters and traders also allured the Assamese peasants with opium to gain economic advantage. For example, S.E. Peal, a planter, told the Royal Commission on Opium that for some ten to twelve years from 1863, he used to regularly issue about 40 lbs. of the drug every month to his labour – and this constituted half of the wage bill – to serve as circulating media over the area of 200 square miles wherefrom his Assamese labour were recruited. Another planter, E.P. Gilman, also told the Commission that he used to sell opium to Assamese villagers. Haribilas Agarwala (1842–1916), an Assamese planter, ran a lucrative opium shop, although he recommended to the government a policy of gradual eradication of the evil.[62] As long as opium was not a contraband commodity and money put into it paid dividends, there was no dearth of distributors for the drug.

Further Growth of Modern Political Consciousness
Modest Growth of a Class

After the restoration of Assamese as a recognized language, the Assamese intelligentsia became increasingly self-confident and sought self-expression through organized literary and political activities. Half a dozen young scholars, who had had their early education at Gauhati High School during the 1860s, startled everybody with the successful careers they achieved for themselves.

Anundoram Barua (1850–1889) was the fifth Indian, and the first and only Assamese ever to be a member of the Indian Civil Service.[63] Like him, Bolinarayan Bora (1852–1927) too competed for the Gilchrist Scholarship in Calcutta in 1872, and, after completing his training in England, joined the Engineering Service. Zalnur Ali Ahmed (1848–1931) and Sibram Bora (1847–1907) joined the Indian Medical Service. Manik Chandra Barooah started his business

---

[60] *ACOER*, p. 40.

[61] Evidence of R.D. Mazumdar, pleader, and J.D. Anderson, D.C. of Darrang, in *Royal Commission on Opium*, 1893 (London, 1894), Vol. 2, pp. 62 and 281, respectively.

[62] Relevant evidences, ibid., pp. 153, 266 and 293.

[63] Gajnafar Ali Khan (1872–1959) and Gurusaday Dutta (1882–1941), both of Sylhet, entered the Indian Civil Service in 1897 and 1905, respectively.

career as a timber and tea merchant, and settled down, after the meteoric rise and fall of his business, as a modest planter. However, such a rich crop was not repeatedly harvested. Opportunities in Assam were extremely limited as compared to Bengal, and aspiring Assamese students had to go all the way to Calcutta for higher education. Of the 938 students who matriculated from Calcutta University in 1872, only four were from schools of the Brahmaputra Valley. In the First Arts Examination the same year, as against 81 from Bengal, eleven from Bihar and one from Orissa, none out of the five candidates from the Brahmaputra Valley schools came out successful.[64]

These results provided a plea for closing down the First Arts classes that were held at the Gauhati School from 1866 to 1875. No opportunity for college education existed any more in the province until a college was founded at Sylhet in 1892 and another at Gauhati in 1901. Even school education made very slow progress. Around 1887, while as much as Rs 18,000 was spent annually on the lone European Inspector heading the education department, a sum of Rs 19,000 only was spent by the provincial government on high schools. With such a frail and narrow educational infrastructure, the annual out-turn of educated personnel was naturally small. In 1881, only fourteen Assamese boys matriculated from the schools in Assam proper. Even as late as 1898 and 1899, students matriculating from the schools of the Brahmaputra Valley numbered only thirty-two and 51, respectively. During the twelve years preceding 1900, altogether twenty-nine residents of the Brahmaputra Valley obtained BA degrees, as against 68 of the Surma Valley. In 1905–06, there were 52 students in Cotton College, Gauhati, as against 63 in the Murarichand College of Sylhet.[65] Out of 1,346 boys and girls who matriculated from the schools of Assam during the years 1882–99, 335 (25 per cent) were natives of the Brahmaputra Valley, 629 (47 per cent) of the Surma Valley and 382 (28 per cent) of other provinces.[66]

The provincial administration was not prepared to build up appropriate educational infrastructure for the simple reason that it could recruit Bengal's surplus-educated personnel to staff its offices at a minimum cost. Hence, the shortage of educated indigenous personnel in the Brahmaputra Valley persisted. The share of people from Surma Valley and outsiders to the province in government jobs remained disproportionately large, and many of the new vacancies continued to be filled every year with recruits from neighbouring Bengal. The handful of educated Assamese youth apparently faced no problem of unemployment as such during the nineteenth century. Even those who lacked sufficient formal education could look forward to clerical and labour supervisory jobs in the expanding tea gardens, the steamer company, the railways, and post and

[64] *Bengal Administrative Report*, 1872–73, pp. 432 and 436.

[65] Bolinarayan Bora, 'Uccashiksha', *Mau*, 1 (January 1887) and (March 1887); *Report of the Administration of Eastern Bengal and Assam, 1905–06*, p. 165; *Friend of India*, 23 January 1882; *Imperial Gazetteer of India*, new edition, Vol. 6, p. 102.

[66] *The Golden Jubilee Volume Cotton College* (Gauhati, 1951–52), App. C II. The available figures do not cover the years 1884 and 1889.

telegraph communications, if they so chose. But the underemployed rural youth made only limited use of these opportunities. Besides, employers often discriminated against them because of their alleged addiction to opium. Appointments to near-hereditary *mauzadarship* were, on the other hand, almost the exclusive reserve of the local rural gentry. Numbering about a thousand, the village *mandals* formed the lower echelons of this rural gentry.

A band of educated young men who were attracted towards modern business in the last quarter of the century no doubt contributed to eventual bourgeois formations in Assamese society, but their stunted progress needs detailed discussion. Medieval Assam had very limited trading activities and hence lacked well-developed trading castes. The only vigorous trading elements in the early nineteenth century were the peasant-traders of Barpeta and Sualkuchi, who plied their boats laden with mustard-seed as far down as Bengal or hawked their handicrafts in Assam villages. Members of the fishermen's caste (Nadial) were engaged in petty trade – for example, the retailing of fish, betel-nuts and betel-leaves, lime, etc.[67]

But such elements were not of much significance. Modern bourgeois formations in Assam did not emerge from them. On the contrary, they lost their independence to Marwari trading capital, in due course. Generally, it was from the higher caste groups with a background of modern education that the first stratum of an Assamese business community was drawn. They were from land-owning and/or service-holders' and lawyers' families. Investments in a tea garden or two particularly suited them, because certain features of tenant exploitation could also be carried over into the realm of tea production. There were, according to Jagannath Barooah, 'two to three dozen native' planters in his valley towards the close of the century.[68] Appendix 5 represents a cross-section of the Assamese middle class of the last quarter of the nineteenth century and their respective backgrounds. Some of them employed wage labour to a considerable extent and their production activities were market-oriented. Others, not necessarily involved in any production activities, were nevertheless precursors of an ideology congenial to accumulation and of new values oriented to capitalism. The bourgeois stratum that was emerging was enlightened as well as enterprising, and it provided leadership, however tenuous, to the Assamese society in every field.

Its existence at the fringe of the vast economic empire that British capital had built in Assam was, however, precarious. More than 97 per cent of the total

---

[67] Capt. Francis Jenkins, 'Journal of a Tour in Upper Assam, 1838' (Department of Historical and Antiquarian Studies, Government of Assam, Gauhati, Trans. Vol. 18, No. 122), pp. 56–57, on Nadial traders. According to the *Imperial Gazetteer of India*, new edition, Vol. 6, p. 76, a considerable share of the trade in mustard-seed also for markets outside the province was still in the hands of a class of traders who were natives of Kamrup, but the rest of the inter-provincial trade and nearly the whole of the import traffic of the Brahmaputra valley were carried on by the Marwari traders. The tea market was almost entirely in British hands.

[68] Evidence of J. Barooah, *Royal Commission on Opium*, 1893, Vol. 2, p. 296.

acreage of the thousand-odd tea gardens belonged to British owners. In terms of capital invested or wage labour employed, the British share up to World War I was even higher. Local capitalists, extremely poor in resources, tried to develop their business activities not in competition but in cooperation with the British and, like many other sections of the Indian bourgeoisie, they had comprador origins to begin with.[69] It was difficult to accumulate and get investment opportunities without cultivating servile contacts with Britishers in administration and business. This explains their basic faith, until the end of World War I, in the benevolence of British rule. Their political vision ranged from blind loyalty to moderate constructive criticism. Even as land-owners they were opposed to the policy of progressive enhancement of land revenue and envied the still bigger British planter–land-owners, who had to pay practically nothing towards land revenue.

Throughout the nineteenth century, the small band of enlightened Assamese businessmen continued to break fresh ground for themselves. Bholanath Barooah (1853–1923), a close relation of Manik, started his career as manager of the latter's timber business and later rose to become an independent millionaire timber merchant of Orissa with his head office in Calcutta. Dinanath Bezbarua (1813–1895) established two small tea gardens. One of his sons left for south America to make his career there and finally settled in Bengal after obtaining higher medical education in Great Britain. The other son, Lakshminath Bezbarua (1864–1938), after graduation and marriage into the famous Tagore family of Calcutta, settled down in the timber business outside Assam, first as a partner of Bholanath and later independently. Of Anandaram Dhekial–Phukan's two sons, one settled abroad; the other, Annadaram, was a partner until his death in 1884 in the business concern of Manik Chandra, styled Barooah Phukan Bros. (1875–84). Hemadhar Barooah (d. 1871) and his graduate son Jagannath Barooah devoted their energies to developing their own tea gardens. Even the devout scholar Anundoram Barua's dream was to purchase a tea garden after his retirement from the Indian Civil Service. He had accumulated not less than Rs 40,000 by the time of his premature death. Gunabhiram Barua left behind a legacy of Rs 50,000. Thus one finds that the newly educated in Assam were not allergic to business or accumulation initially. A few Assamese-owned small printing presses and newspapers were also there, in which leading men like Manik Chandra Barooah, Hemchandra Barua and Radhanath Changkakati (1853–1923) had put their money. Incidentally, Hemchandra, too, left behind a modest legacy (See Appendix 5).

It was the paucity of capital and, even more, of opportunities under the domination of British and comprador Marwari capital in different fields of business that ultimately killed this spirit. For example, one of the early Assamese pioneers in tea, Gangaram Sharma, lost both his gardens to British rivals. One of

---

[69] Many Assamese planters, for example, had no factories to process their tea leaves. They sent their leaves to neighbouring European gardens which had factories.

them had to be sold under duress in 1892–93 to settle a dispute with a neighbouring British garden over right of way. The other was acquired through foul means by the Jhanjee Tea Company, also under British ownership.[70]

Most of these businessmen were closely associated with the literary and political activities of their day, and integrally connected with the rural peasant community at large. Early political organizations were, therefore, broad-based common platforms of the ryots, that is, the assessees of land revenue, even though the leadership was almost entirely limited to the enlightened section. A number of such organizations sprang up, some of them pre-dating even the Indian National Congress.

The example of the Bengal ryots was an obvious influence on the wave of politically oriented ryot meetings that were held all over Assam, even in 'sundry places'.[71] The centres of this new wave, however, were the so-called towns. Around 1878, a branch of the Indian Association was established at Goalpara but it soon went out of existence, allegedly because of the displeasure of the British District Magistrate (*Statesman*, Calcutta, 20 January 1880). The Jorhat Sarvajanik Sabha was reportedly founded in 1875 at the initiative of Jagannath Barooah. He was its vice-president for six consecutive years, from 1887 to 1892, and president from 1893. Devicharan Barua (1864–1926), a lawyer and planter, was its secretary for about seventeen years from about 1890. How skin-deep was the concern of these gentlemen for the welfare of the ryots is indicated by the memorial they submitted on behalf of the Sabha to the Royal Commission on Opium in November 1893. The memorialists were against an immediate prohibition of opium sales on the plea that: 'The people of this province are not able and would not be willing to make up by the contribution of other taxes, any deficit in the revenues of the province caused by such measures.' They dreaded that, as land-owners, they would have to pay a much heavier amount as land revenue if opium was prohibited.[72]

The Tezpur Ryot Sabha was established around 1884, at the initiative of the new elite. Amongst its founders were Haribilas Agarwala (a merchant planter of Assamese birth from his mother's side), Lakshmikanta Barkakati (the manager of his saw-mills) and Lambodar Bora (1860–1892), a lawyer. Organized primarily to protest against the enhancement of land revenue, this Ryot Sabha had a wide base in the villages. It collected small subscriptions from hundreds of peasants and, in 1887, built the Tezpur Town Hall, the first of its kind in Assam. By 1886, the Shillong Association, the Nowgong Ryot Sabha and the Upper Assam

---

[70] Krishnanath Sharma, *Krishna Sharma Diary* (in Assamese, Gauhati, 1972), pp. 7 and 9.

[71] *Mau*, I (January 1887), cited by Borra, *Bolinarayan Borrah*, pp. 53–54.

[72] 'Memorial of Jorhat Sarvajanik Sabha', dated 11 November 1893, reproduced as Appendix 9 in this book. Evidence of J. Barooah in *Royal Commission on Opium*, 1893, Vol. 2, pp. 296–97. There is some confusion about the date of establishment of the Sabha. The year 1875 is suggested by P. Goswami, *Manikchandra Baruva aru teonryug* (in Assamese, Gauhati, 1970), p. 48*n*. The more probable date is 1884.

Associations came into being. The last-mentioned bodies, according to Radhanath Changkakati (1853–1923), who was their secretary at least during the years 1887–93, were composed of ryots of the area to represent popular grievances and protest against any enhancement or fresh imposition of taxes; these coordinated associations sprang up all over the districts of Sibsagar and Lakhimpur.[73]

Thus, by and large, the new elite made a united front with the proprietary peasants against the rulers on all common issues. However, there were some like Bolinarayan Bora who frowned upon this fraternization. Even while sharing the moderate political views of his celebrated father-in-law, R.C. Dutt, Bora had a more conservative and pro-British bent of mind. Although a first-rate intellect who possessed a deep understanding of the basic malady of Assamese society, this first engineer of Assam put his energies into cultivating English ways of life and making expensive trips to Europe. Denied legitimate promotion in service and superseded by a junior of British birth, he finally went into premature retirement and quietly settled down in Bengal. All said, despite his reactionary views on female education and his collaboration with the British rule, Assam owes him a debt, for he was the first person to initiate political discussions on an intellectual plane through his short-lived Assamese periodical, *Mau* (1886–87).

'Those restless Assamese young men who, in quest of celebrity and aping the Bengalees, carry on unintelligible political movements by calling together the peasants, would do real good to the cause of the country', observed *Mau* in an anonymous comment in February 1887, '. . . if they dedicate half of the energy to the promotion of higher education in this province.' In another article published in January the same year, a sarcastic attack was launched on the organizers of such meetings who were described as 'a few unemployed cunning youths, eager to make a name for themselves' by delivering long speeches, adopting a few resolutions and then sending a petition to the Chief Commissioner. As to the outcome of such meetings, the opinion expressed was that:

> The poor peasant remains as wise as he was when he came to the meeting; his gain is the loss of the four ploughing days lost in coming and going and annas two paid towards the sending of the petition. Such as a matter of fact, are the origin and functions of the peasant meetings of Assam.[74]

Although motivated by a pro-government attitude, the above comments had an element of truth in them. The educated middle-class elements had no action-oriented programme of agitation and could not take the popular discontent outside the channel of petition-making. In areas where these modern ryot *sabhas* and associations were in the field, no militant mass struggles on the lines of the *raij mels* (1893–94) ever took place. Nevertheless, even these institutions

---

[73] Dutt, *Freedom Struggle in Assam*, p. 36; our Appendix 6; Radhanath Changkakati's evidence before the *Royal Commission on Opium*, 1893, Vol. 2, p. 305. Omeo Kumar Das, 'Jiivan-Smriti', *Manidiip*, 6, No. 10 (August 1966), p. 688.

[74] Extracts, respectively, from *Mau*, I (February 1887) and I (January 1887) as reproduced in translation by Borra, *Bolinarayan Borrah*, pp. 55 and 60–61.

were useful in their early stage as organized platforms for the spread of a modern political consciousness and the development of nationalism. That is why they attracted attack from conservative quarters.

It was in the wake of these local associations that the Assamese middle class began to act in terms of a valley-wide political organization – the Assam Association. An association with this name was active in 1882 with its headquarters at Sibsagar. It asked the Chief Commissioner in that year for a copy of the proposed Assam Land Tenure Bill with a view to offer comments on it. Public concern in Sibsagar over this Bill was duly reported in the Calcutta press. However, it was in 1903 that the Assam Association was formed afresh on a firm and wider basis, with Manik Chandra Barooah as its secretary, Raja Prabhatchandra Barua (d. 1942) of Gauripur as its president and Jagannath Barooah as its vice-president. Other important personalities like Kamalakanta Bhattacharya (1853–1936), a Brahmo convert, and Radhanath Changkakati, editor and founder of the *Times of Assam* (estd. 1895) were also among its founders. The Assam Association held its first general session at Dibrugarh, under the presidency of Raja Prabhatchandra Barua (d. 1943), in April 1905.[75] A new phase of constitutional agitation in Assam was ushered in thereby.

Impact of the National Congress

At the Congress session in Calcutta in 1886, four Assamese delegates were present. One of them, Kalikanta Barkakati, represented the Shillong Association; Devicharan Barua and Gopinath Bardoloi, both graduates, represented the Upper Assam Associations; and Satyanath Borah (1860–1925), also a graduate, the Nowgong Ryot Association. At the Madras Congress session of 1887, Radhanath Changkakati represented the Upper Assam Associations and Lakshmikanta Barkakati the Tezpur Ryot Sabha. The former attended a Congress session for the second time at Allahabad in 1892, as a delegate alongside Bholanath Barooah and Lakshminath Bezbarua. Bezbarua was also a delegate to the Madras, Bombay and Calcutta sessions in 1903, 1904 and 1906, respectively (Appendix 6).

Other delegates from the Brahmaputra Valley who attended Congress sessions during the years 1888–1905 included Ghanashyam Barua of the Nowgong Ryot Association (1888); H. Singha Chaudhuri, zamindar of Bagribari (1888); Manik Chandra Barooah (1890); Meghnath Banerjee, a medical practitioner of Jaypur (1891); Hariprasad Nath, a Mukhtear of Goalpara (1901); Chandrakamal Bezbarua, a planter of Jorhat (1904); and Bhabanikanta Das, a pleader of Dhubri (1904). Delegates from the Surma Valley also attended many of these sessions during the years 1885–1905. Bipin Chandra Pal (1858–1932), Kamini Kumar

---

[75] *Friend of India*, 28 March 1882 and Goswami, *Manikcandra Baruva*, p. 52. There is some confusion over the exact date of the founding of the new Assam Association. We have followed Goswami. It is possible that Gangagovinda Phukan was the founder of an earlier and lately defunct organization with the same name, as Benudhar Sharma once told this author.

Chanda (1862–1936), Sundarimohan Das (1857–1950) and Ramanimohan Das (1873–1930) were the most prominent among them (see Appendices 6 and 7).

There is evidence that the early Indian National Congress sessions created an enthusiasm among the middle classes throughout Assam. For example, on 16 December 1886, there was a well-attended meeting at Murarichand College of Sylhet that was attended, among others, by Sundarimohan Das and Ramanimohan Das. The meeting resolved that it had become necessary, in the interests of both India and England, to reconstitute the Legislative Councils with no less than two-thirds of the members elected by local bodies and with the right of interpellation. It also demanded that the maximum age of a candidate for the Indian Civil Service examination be raised to 23 years, and that the examination be held simultaneously in India and England. The chairman of a public meeting in Shillong and one Radhikacharan Mitra, *vokeel*, representing the Indian Committee of Dibrugarh, sent greetings telegrams to the 1886 Congress session. The achievement of this session was reviewed in *Mau* in its February 1887 issue with the comment that as too many weighty resolutions were on the agenda, sufficient time had not been devoted to an analysis and examination of each of them. Nevertheless, the assemblage, the expression of friendship therein and the urge for a common object, in spite of differences of race and religion, were highlighted as unique signs of 'India's unity'. The readers were reminded that 'English education and British rule are at the root of the birth of this unity', and also that British rule would be necessary for a long time for the good of India; British officers should continue in the civil service for the present.[76]

The real character of *Mau* came out when it lent support to the planters on the indentured coolie question. Ever since the late 1860s, the Bengal nationalist press had been carrying on an incessant campaign against the oppression of the coolies. In 1879, Ram Kumar Vidyaratna, a Bengali Brahmo missionary, made risky trips to Assam to gather first-hand information on the conditions of the coolies and published a series of telling reports. In 1886, Dwarakanath Ganguli, another Brahmo missionary and assistant secretary of the Indian Association of Calcutta, went to the Brahmaputra Valley and brought back horrifying reports, which were serialized in *Sanjivani* (Calcutta) under the pen-name of 'Son of Legni'. In an article published in *Somprakash* of Calcutta the same year, the Act of 1882 was condemned. 'Oh, residents of Bengal and Assam,' it asked 'can't you crush the vanity of the white planters by killing this Coolie Act?'[77]

It was these press reports that provoked *Mau* to come out with venomous comments against the agitation, in three out of its four issues of 1886–87. In course of a six-page anonymous article, it drew up a list of the benefits that the plantation workers supposedly derived from their British employers. For this

---

[76] Newspapers cited in the *Report of the Second Indian National Congress Held at Calcutta, 1886*, p. 144. Quote from *Mau*, 1 (February 1887) as reproduced by Borra, *Bolinarayan Borrah*, pp. 58–60.

[77] Quote from *Somprakash*, 11 *shravan* 1293 (AD 1886), pp. 461–62.

role, the Calcutta mouthpiece of British capital, the *Englishman*, showered praise on the periodical. However, the reactionary view of *Mau* was not shared by the Assamese middle class in general. The Assamese students in Calcutta whose 'minds had already been turned red in the furnace of the political ideology of the new Congress' – wrote Bezbarua in his autobiography – reacted sharply to its pro-planter stance. Bezbarua got a letter published in *Mau* that vindicated the noble role of the Bengal press and exposed the evils of the labour recruitment system. The editor, of course, disagreed with him.[78]

While opposing a resolution recommending extension of the system of trial by jury all over India, Devicharan Barua, a delegate from Assam at the Calcutta Congress (1886), pointed out that it had already proved injurious in Assam in all cases involving Europeans

> because the majority on the jury list are Europeans, and they are selected from a class of men strong in race prejudices and ignorant of the first principles of jurisprudence – I mean the class of the planters . . . and this very system is one of the reasons why our *poor coolies are so oppressed in Assam.*[79] (Emphasis added)

Despite pressure from the ranks, no resolution could be moved on the question of the Assam coolies in the early annual sessions of the Congress – for example, in the Madras session of 1887 – because of technical jurisdictional difficulties. However, from 1896, the Congress annual sessions started demanding the repeal of all penal labour laws in Assam. While reiterating the same in 1901, the Congress regretted that immediate effect had not been given even to the government's own proposal to enhance the coolies' wages.[80]

Desire for participation in the legislative process was also growing in the minds of the Assamese middle class. While supporting Surendranath Banerjea's resolution containing tentative suggestions for the expansion and Indianization of the Council system, Devicharan Barua, at the same Calcutta Congress session, said that introduction of 'a representative system in some form' was as urgently required in Assam as in other provinces. Claiming to speak on behalf of the entire people of Assam, he said:

> Allowing freely that our rulers, foreigners and strangers as they are to all that most intimately affects us, are actuated by the highest motives and do their best for us, the present state of the country, and the universal feeling that pervades

---

78 '*Cah bagicar* coolie' in *Mau*, 1 (December 1886), pp. 10–16; L. Bezbarua's letter, ibid. (February 1887). L. Bezbarua, *Mor Jiivan Sonvaran* (in Assamese, Jorhat, 1966), pp. 77–78. Quote from the same (translation ours).

79 *Report of the Second Indian National Congress*, p. 84.

80 *Proceedings of the Indian National Congress, 17th Session*, Resolution No. 13, p. 164. No resolution on Assam tea labour was allowed to be moved at the early Indian National Congress sessions, on the plea that it was a provincial, and not a national, issue. However, the Bengal Provincial Conference, meeting annually since 1888, always took a sympathetic interest in the problems of Assam's coolies.

it, sufficiently show that neither the purity of their intentions nor the consciousness of their efforts can compensate for that want of political sympathy with and detailed knowledge of the circumstances of our case, which only our own people, carefully selected by ourselves, can supply. (Loud cheers.)[81]

It is thus clear that the founding of the National Congress in 1885 was not the mere handiwork of a few British and Indian gentlemen at the top. Evidently, it was a response of the Indian middle classes to the new national awakening. The Assamese middle class no exception as they reacted similarly. Progressive Indianization of the civil service, abolition of European racial practices, further democratization of the Legislative Councils and their extension to new areas, repeal of the repugnant penal provisions of the indentured labour Acts – all these demands, and an unflinching faith in the growing unity of India, echoed and re-echoed. Equality with British citizens under a potentially benevolent British rule was what the articulate Indian middle classes aspired towards, for many years to come.

Westernization and Sanskritization

It is significant that, in the nineteenth century, the enlightened section of the Assamese middle class welcomed large-scale immigration of productive labour and skill from other provinces, and did not suffer from the 'xenophobia' of the later periods. It was convinced that no economic progress was feasible unless the then depopulated condition was restored to normalcy.

Gunabhiram Barua estimated that no less than a million people could be immediately settled from outside on the wide acres of Assam. He enumerated three factors that were favourable to such immigration: (i) cheap and fertile land, (ii) attractive earnings for skilled labour and craftsmen in view of the local skilled manpower shortage and (iii) the prevailing conditions of easy matrimony into local families. He wrote a long article in 1885 to discuss, in this perspective, Bengali–Assamese relations, which were already tending to develop into a love-and-hate spectrum. He noted that, whether desirable or not, the Bengali babu or *bhadralok* had become the model for the growing Assamese middle class. The acculturation that was going on, he suggested (though not in so many words), was but a simultaneous process of westernization and sanskritization. Traditional Assamese dress, hair-do, manners, culinary art and even other forms of culture – all had begun to undergo rapid changes in the townships under the Anglo-Bengali influence. People like Gunabhiram and Bolinarayan, on the whole, hailed such changes as inevitable and necessary.[82]

---

[81] *Report of the Second Indian National Congress*, pp. 109–10.

[82] Editorial article, 'Bangali', *Assam Bandhu*, 1, No. 3 (1885), pp. 95–100, and 'Amar manuh', ibid., No. 4 (1885), pp. 133–35. Also see Anonymous, 'Asamiya aru Bangali', *Mau*, 1 (January 1887), pp. 49–52 and 'Tirutar ban ki', *Mau* (December 1886), pp. 1–2. Bolinarayan appears to be the author of these articles in *Mau*. For the concepts of westernization and sanskritization as used by M.N. Srinivas, see his *Social Change in*

But all changes were not considered necessarily beneficial. As early as 1847, Dhekial–Phukan had particularly noted the rigour of the caste system as a hindrance to production in the contemporary Bengali society. The traditional caste system in Assam did not go that far and used to function less rigorously in this respect.[83] But now the aping of the Bengali way of life was tending to introduce this rigour in Assam as well. The Assamese Brahmin's rigidity against widow remarriage was extended further by the example set by the Bengali caste-Hindu elite (traditionally, several non-Brahmin castes in Bengal did not practise widow remarriage). Even the Kalitas – a dominant peasant caste of Assam which had no such traditional prejudice – began to take a stand against widow remarriage. Theories were invented to establish that the Kalita was identical with the Kayastha or even the Kshatriya.[84] Similarly, the simple rites of marriage practised by non-Brahmins at the popular level were being progressively replaced by elaborate *sastric* rituals, presided over by Brahmin priests.

Thus, the social change in nineteenth-century Assam was, more or less, modelled on the immigrant Bengali caste-Hindu society of the time – with all its virtues and vices. The latter society itself was passing through the twin processes of westernization and sanskritization, acting upon and often conflicting with each other. An understanding of these dimensions of social development, and of the intricacies of multiform relationships between the two dominant linguistic groups competing for jobs and positions of influence, is essential for comprehending the struggle for self-government that unfolded in course of the next half-century.

Under the constant shadow of a Bengali–Assamese conflict, the growth of nationalism in nineteenth-century Assam was a two-track process. People were increasingly turning as much to pan-Indian nationalism at the all-India level as to little nationalism at the linguistic–regional level.[85] It was through these twin processes, more often complementary than conflicting, that nationalism in India and, for that matter, also in Assam, projected itself as a viable challenge to imperialism.

Modern India (Berkeley, 1966), *The Cohesive Role of Sanskritization* (mimeographed, University of Delhi, 1966), and 'Note on Sanskritization and Westernization', *Far Eastern Quarterly*, No. 4 (1956).

[83] Anandaram Dhekial–Phukan, 'Inglandar bivaran', *Arunoday*, No. 4 (April 1847), p. 48. Lakshmiram Bora, comp., *Asamar Samkshep Itihas: A Brief History of Assam for Children* (Gauhati, 1875) pp. 67–68.

[84] For example, Dutta Narayan, father of Bolinarayan Bora – though a Kalita – wore 'the sacred thread (*oot-tori*)'. Borra, *Bolinarayan Borrah*, pp. 1–3. '*Oot-tori*' is not exactly the sacred thread but is said to be its legacy – a close substitute.

[85] Broadly speaking, pan-Indian nationalism suited the interests of the still incipient big bourgeoisie of India, while little nationalism was related to the small bourgeoisie – the regional middle classes. Indian nationalism developed through a process of merger between the two. This is further discussed in the last chapter of this book.

CHAPTER THREE

First Taste of Council Government: 1906–20

Eastern Bengal and Assam under a Lieutenant-Governor: 1906–12

Operation Partition and Swadeshi

Towards the close of the nineteenth century, the partition of Bengal was imminent. In 1892, some officials in the foreign department suggested that the Chittagong Division of Bengal be transferred to Assam. When the idea was discussed in detail at the official level during 1896–97, the then Chief Commissioner of Assam further suggested that the districts of Dacca and Mymensingh also be transferred along with the Chittagong Division. The planters, in particular, desired a re-drawing of the boundaries with a view to having the port of Chittagong and the plantations of north Bengal and Assam included in one and the same province. When Viceroy Curzon visited Assam in 1903, they put into his head the idea that if Chittagong was tagged to Assam and developed as an outlet to the sea, the prohibitive transportation costs of tea could be substantially reduced. In the following year, Chief Commissioner Fuller also briefed him as to the administrative necessity of enlarging the size of Assam, without which no experienced senior civilian was likely to opt for it. These considerations were buttressed by the general desire of the British civilians to aim a blow at the Bengali middle class – the mainstay of the rising Congress movement, and to dislocate it in a vital part of its sphere of influence. The creation of a Muslim-majority province on the flank of a truncated Bengal, which could take care of all these considerations, thus became a political necessity. Bengal was partitioned in the face of the fiercest opposition that the government had ever encountered since 1857.[1]

Assam's status as a separate province came to an end on 16 October 1905, and Fuller was promoted as the first Lieutenant-Governor of the new composite province of Eastern Bengal and Assam. Available official and private

---

[1] B.B. Mazumdar, *Indian Political Associations and Reform of Legislature 1818–1917* (Calcutta, 1965), p. 360. A. Tripathi, *The Extremist Challenge in India between 1890–1910* (Calcutta, 1967), pp. 93–103. Sumit Sarkar, *The Swadeshi Movement in Bengal 1903–1908* (New Delhi, 1973), pp. 1–20.

papers leave no doubt that a major objective of the Curzon Plan was 'to split up and thereby weaken a solid body of opponents to our rule'.[2]

The anti-partition agitation, meanwhile, was in full swing in Bengal and the Surma Valley. The call to boycott British goods echoed through all Bengali-speaking areas and inspired the cult of *swadeshi* all over India. A major section of Muslim landlords and middle classes, however, were won over by Curzon in favour of his Operation Partition and Assam's merger with Eastern Bengal. They found the mainstream of nationalism to be heavily loaded with Hindu spiritual content. Bipin Chandra Pal was openly asserting the Hindu might and exhorting young Hindus to take up cudgels. All positions of power, as many as could be reached by Indians under the given colonial set-up, were practically monopolized by caste-Hindus in Bengal. This fact was used to sow seeds of communal distrust. The prospect of Muslims outnumbering the Bengali Hindus in the new province appealed to the former. Fuller openly declared that Muslims would be the favoured community in the new province.[3]

As an offshoot of the boycott movement, national schools sprang up all over Bengal and the Surma Valley. The first Surma Valley Political Conference, held on 11–12 August 1906 at Sylhet under the presidency of K.K. Chanda, was addressed by Bipin Chandra Pal. At a students' rally at Sylhet addressed by him on 16 August 1906, about forty school boys declared their intention to quit the government school. At Silchar, on 21 August, Pal asked the people to learn politics and the 'tactics of war' from resurgent Japan. He was reported to have said:

> The time had come now for the Hindus to prepare themselves. They had opened Swadeshi Schools, and held Swadeshi meetings not only for the purpose of teaching books, but also to teach the art of war, as the day had come when the *Feringhis Raj* would not reign much longer in India. . . . Indian money is taken away by *Feringhis*, while the people starve for want of money. . . . They could not govern India or stay in it if the Indians did not cooperate with them.

Silchar was caught in the whirlwind of the boycott movement in the wake of two more speeches by Pal on 22 and 23 August. Wholesale traders, who happened to be Hindus, warned their retailers that they would not be supplied with tobacco and pulses if they sold foreign salt. Carters boycotted merchants – all Muslims – who stocked Liverpool salt. Even washermen, in their caste meeting, decided not to wash foreign cloth. Pal revisited the town in March 1907, after addressing a meeting at Habiganj in February. The second Surma Valley Political Conference was held at Karimganj in April 1908 and the third at the

---

[2] Sir A. Frazer's note of 6 December 1904, Home Public Progs. A, February 1904, as cited by Sarkar, *Swadeshi Movement in Bengal*, pp. 17–18. In his earlier note of 7 February 1904, Frazer had already pointed out 'that Bengal is very densely populated, that Eastern Bengal is the most densely populated portion, that it needs room for expansion and that it can only expand towards the East. So far from hindering national development we are really giving it greater scope and *enabling Bengal to absorb Assam*' (emphasis ours). Ibid.

[3] Tripathi, *Extremist Challenge in India*, pp. 96–103, 158–59 and 175.

village of Jalsuka, in 1909. Incidentally, Pal – the harbinger of revolutionary nationalism – was imprisoned for six months in Bengal in 1907–08 and soon, after his release, he left for England on a political mission. During his sojourn there (1909–11), he climbed down to a moderate stand and, on return, lost his magic influence on the people.[4] A divided Congress movement during the years 1907–15, the blind alley of terrorism based on militant nationalism and the Hindu religious appeal – all these in effect strengthened the Muslim communal reaction. By 1909, Sylhet had branches of two Bengal terrorist parties – the Suhrid Samiti and the Anushiilan Samiti. The Swadesh Sevak Samiti (estd. 1906) was probably an offshoot of the latter body.[5]

There was no ground for the Assamese to be happy or to gloat over becoming once more an appendage of Bengal – this time of Eastern Bengal. The new province was reportedly going to be called 'North Eastern Province'. Padmanath Gohain–Barua (1871–1946), in an editorial comment in *Asam Banti* on 10 July 1905, raised an alarm at the prospect of the very name of Assam being obliterated forever. He diffidently accepted the proposed new province as a settled fact but, at the same time, made a plea for at least retaining the word 'Assam' in its designation. As the anti-partition Swadeshi movement gathered momentum in Bengal, he further articulated his stand. He urged the Assamese people, in course of another editorial, to stand up in protest against the merger itself. He appealed to the Assam Association and the Jorhat Sarvajanik Sabha to take up the issue.[6]

Neither the newborn Assam Association nor the Jorhat Sarvajanik Sabha led by Assamese planters responded to the call. For, as early as February 1904, both Manik Chandra Barooah and Jagannath Barooah, their respective spokesmen, had extended conditional support to the Curzon Plan. Fuller's skilful, divisive role was the decisive factor in this matter. He believed – mistakenly, if not mischievously – that the inhabitants of the Brahmaputra Valley 'speak a language which is, in fact, a dialect of Bengali'.[7] But, like many other British civilians of his day, he too thought that the spreading tree of Indian nationalism could be cut at its roots only by isolating the Bengali babus. The prevailing situation of

---

[4] H. Mukherjee and U. Mukherjee, *Bipin Chandra Pal and India's Struggle for Swaraj* (Calcutta, 1958), pp. 45–48, 71 and 110–12. Quotes from his speech are as they appear in the *Confidential History Sheet*, cited ibid.

For reference to the second and third Surma Valley (Sylhet–Cachar) Political Conference, *The Bengalee*, 19 April 1909; and R.N. Aditya, *Fight for Freedom in Sylhet* (Karimganj, 1964), pp. 2–3.

[5] Home (Pol.) Progs. Deposit, August 1909, No. 26, Appendix II (National Archives of India; hereafter NAI); and Narendrakumar Gupta Chaudhury, ed., *Shriihatta Pratibha* (Sylhet, 1961), pp. 233–34.

[6] P. Goswami, *Manikchandra Barua aru teonr yug* (in Assamese, Gauhati, 1970), pp. 79–80.

[7] Quote from Bampfylde Fuller, *Some Personal Experiences* (London, 1930), p. 104.

M.C. Barooah, in his note of 27 February 1904, Enclosure 7, Government of Assam to Government of India, 6 April 1904, Home Public A, February 1905, No. 156 (NAI), was prepared to accept the new province provided 80 per cent of the vacancies in government jobs were reserved for local candidates. On behalf of the Jorhat

the Bengali hold over government jobs in Assam, as well as the pitiable public status of the Assamese language, provided a handle. Not much enthusiasm was observed among the Assamese people in favour of *swadeshi*. 'So far as Assam is concerned,' wrote the *Amritabazar Patrika* on 29 December 1905, 'the Swadeshi movement does not seem to have touched even the outer fringe of Manchester trade.'

When he was the Chief Commissioner, Fuller projected himself as a champion of the Assamese cause. The Government Resolution of 17 November 1903 provided that, save with the Chief Commissioner's previous sanction, all appointments were to be henceforth limited to *bonafide* permanent residents of Assam alone. Newcomers who had acquired land or house property, and could prove their intention to live in Assam permanently, were also to be counted as permanent residents. Fuller ordered that so long as candidates possessed the required educational qualifications, preference was to be given to the Assamese.[8]

It was partially through Fuller's efforts that the struggling Assamese language, then in a decadent and moribund condition, was recognized by the Calcutta University in 1903 for purposes of its entrance examination. Incidentally, there was only one Assamese newspaper in 1906, as compared to ten in Hindi, nine in Oriya and eight in Bengali.[9] As the first Lieutenant-Governor of the new province, Fuller found in the Assamese, as well as in the Muslim religious community, a counterpoise to the 'expansionism' of the Bengali Hindus. Seemingly based on a sense of justice, this manoeuvre was sure to bear bitter fruit in the context of the 'divide and rule' policy. Even after Fuller's resignation on 3 August 1906, his policy in this respect was continued by his successors.

The Councils Act of 1892 and Assam

It was only in 1906 that Assam came to belatedly enjoy the right of representation in a provincial Council formed under the Act of 1892. For, now it was an integral part of a Lieutenant-Governor's province endowed with a Legislative Council. This Council was a small body of fifteen members, out of which two quasi-elected seats were allotted to Assam. These members did not come through elections in the ordinary sense of the term, but were merely recommended in rotation by groups of public bodies, such as local boards and munici-

---

Sarvajanik Sabha, Jagannath Barooah, too, expressed an essentially similar view in his note dated 10 February 1904.

Sir Henry Cotton, Chief Commissioner from 1896 to 1902, had noted earlier: 'Every educated Assamese is bound to know Bengali just as every educated Welshman is bound to know English. . . . All efforts to boost up Assamese as a separate language are, I am convinced, doomed to failure.' File No. Home A, December 1897, No. 50–54, cited by M. Kar, 'Assam's Language Question in Retrospect', *Social Scientist*, Vol. 4, No. 2 (September 1975), pp. 21–34.

[8] Fuller, *Some Personal Experiences*, p. 109; Government of Assam Resolution of 17 November 1903, cited in S.M. Lahiri's speech of 31 August, *Assam Legislative Council Proceedings* (hereafter *ALCP*) (1938), pp. 32–33.

[9] Sarkar, *Swadeshi Movement in Bengal*, p. 377.

palities. Thereafter, it rested with the Lieutenant-Governor to accept the recommendations or not, as he thought fit. Even the Lieutenant-Governor in those days had no power to appoint the members of his Council. He could only make a nomination which was subject to the sanction of the Governor-General.[10] Such a small Council could hardly accommodate the top brass of all communities, particularly since two-thirds of its members were in practice always Britishers. It was no surprise, therefore, that the Assamese community went unrepresented on this Council until February 1909.

Saddled as it was with an official majority, the Council hardly enjoyed powers worth mentioning. Estimates of expenditures prepared for the provinces used to be submitted to the Government of India. These were minutely checked and often altered by its finance department, and then incorporated in the consolidated Indian budget. This budget was then discussed in the Imperial Legislative Council; and extracts relating to the provinces, in the respective provincial Councils. However, the latter were not allowed to pass resolutions affecting the budget or, for that matter, anything else. Formal questions could be put if due notice was given but no supplementary questions were allowed. The rules laid down that a member desiring to make any observation on any subject before the Council was to address the president without rising from his chair. 'The old Council was in fact a sort of advisory committee', said a Governor of Assam in 1923, 'and had no pretensions to parliamentary status of any kind'.[11]

Such a Council, naturally, could not attract much public attention in the stormy days of *swadeshi*. There was a genuine desire for wider political participation even then in the minds of the Indian members. Rai Bahadur Sitanath Ray, a zamindar member from East Bengal, timidly pointed out in 1907 that since the budget, having been fixed a long time ahead, was unalterable, and since the non-official minority could not move an amendment on any budgetary item, 'such discussions and debates can have hardly more than an academic interest'. He demanded that all the Councils be reformed and enlarged, and 'a potential and substantive voice allowed to the people in the legislation and in the management of the finances of their own country'. He repeated the same view again next year. Through a letter, Surendranath Banerjea advised K.K. Chanda in 1906 not to stand as an electoral candidate and to also pursuade D. Deb to follow the same course as a mark of protest against the partition.[12]

---

[10] Governor's address, 16 August, *ALCP* (1923), Vol. 3, pp. 694–97. At the time of Curzon's visit to Assam in 1903, the public there demanded a seat in the Imperial Legislative Council, but it was not conceded. *The Bengalee*, 8 September 1905. The Eastern Bengal and Assam Legislative Council held its first meeting on 18 December 1906.

[11] Governor's address, 16 August, *ALCP* (1923), Vol. 3, pp. 694–97. Also see Tripathi, *Extremist Challenge in India*, pp. 207–08.

[12] Speech by S. Ray, *Eastern Bengal and Assam Legislative Council Proceedings* (hereafter *EBALCP*) (1907), No. 4, p. 85 (page numbers refer to relevant *Gazette* issues), and Banerjea to Chanda, 17 May 1906 (transcript in the possession of the Chanda family). Apparently, Chanda obliged.

The proceedings of the newborn Eastern Bengal and Assam Legislative Council during the years 1906–12 amply show how the upper-class leaders of the two linguistic areas entered into petty squabbles and, thus, played into the hands of the rulers. A Bengali zamindar member, in 1907, for example, gave vent to the fear that Eastern Bengal would be starved 'for the benefit of a poorer and much less civilized country'. Making a false claim that Anundorum Barua, Bolinarayan Bora and a host of other distinguished gentlemen had taken pride in calling themselves Bengalis, he said: 'but times are changed and the cries "Behar for Biharis" and "Assam for Assamese" have commenced to bar the passage of the Bengalis into the services of those countries'.

Sitanath Ray, who claimed to be a loyalist 'to the backbone', echoed the same fear in April 1908.[13] We do not know what would have been the immediate reaction of an Assamese member to such statements, for there was none in the Council until February 1909, when Manik Chandra Barooah came in as a representative of the local boards of Assam. As a spokesman for Assamese indigenous middle-class interests, he had already emerged as an important public figure.

The Commissioner of the Assam Valley Division, Lt. Col. P.R.T. Gurdon, publicly warned against the danger of the Assamese language being crushed, and the Ahom and Assamese Hindus being elbowed out of employment by people from Eastern Bengal. Taking the cue from him, Barooah, in his maiden speech in the Council, said that 'the partition in its present shape was a mistake', and that Assam had suffered most under the Curzon Plan. He implored the government to protect the special interests of the Assamese as a minority community. He pointed out that while only 10 per cent of the province's total revenue should have come from Assam on the basis of its relative population strength, it was actually contributing one-third. Thus, contrary to the common belief, it was being taxed more heavily than Eastern Bengal. The same point had been made two years earlier by Rai Bahadur Dulalchandra Deb (1841–1921) of Sylhet, except that his estimate of Assam's contribution to the total revenue then was one-fourth. In his speech, Barooah showered praise on Fuller for having 'officially recorded in unambiguous words the exclusive rights of the children of the soil to the public services of their country'. With reference to the British planters, he said:

> The planting community have been the pioneers of progress and enlightenment in Assam. Their example has stimulated a number of my countrymen to follow an independent and honourable profession, and I am glad and thankful to say that at the present moment, though their number is small, there are some Assamese tea planters who are doing a lucrative business and occupying a much coveted position, and that with the brighter prospects of the Industry, the number is sure to increase.

---

[13] Quotes from speeches respectively by Maharaja Girijanath Ray, *EBALCP* (1907), No. 4, pp. 93–94 and S. Ray on 6 April, *EBALCP* (1908), No. 3, p. 61.

Incidentally, Barooah did not miss his very first opportunity in the Council to declare on behalf of the Assamese people their 'loyal devotion to the British crown', as was the usual ritual in those days.[14]

Assam and Morley–Minto Reforms

Under the Indian Councils Act of 25 May 1909, embodying the Morley–Minto Reforms, the provincial Councils were enlarged and given a non-official majority. But, in practice, there was a British majority, all nominated Indian members forming its trail. The draft budget for each province provided for all obligatory expenditures and also showed a sum of varying amount as 'unallotted expenditure'. After a scrutiny by the Government of India, this was discussed by a small committee of the provincial Council, called the Finance Committee, of which half the members were elected. Having before it all the particulars of the sanctioned schemes, this committee only recommended appropriate financial provisions from the funds earmarked as 'unallotted expenditure'. Its views were considered before the consolidated draft financial statement for the whole country was finally introduced in the Imperial Legislative Council. Changes made through resolutions affecting taxation proposals for grants to the provinces, if any at that level, were communicated to the provincial Councils.

After all these adjustments were over, the provincial Council was allowed to move resolutions on the budget – it was of course presented in a cut-and-dried form – and on other matters. These recommendatory resolutions were generally of little effect in regard to the budget under discussion. They had only an indirect effect on the next budget. Moreover, the budget itself was only an estimate from which the government could depart any time without further reference to the Council. Supplementary questions were, for the first time, allowed under this Act, but they could be put only by the member who had asked the original question.[15]

No nation-building activities could ever be undertaken at the Council's initiative under such a rigid financial system. Hence, the reforms were rightly spurned by the Congress movement of the day. No such dissatisfaction was, however, reflected in the Eastern Bengal and Assam Legislative Council itself. In course of his speech in the Council on 6 April 1909, Manik Chandra Barooah went so far as to hail the reforms scheme. According to him, 'the people considered the reform scheme to be their Magna Carta of rights and privileges'. Perhaps the sole cause for his wonderful perception was the fact that, in response to an address presented at Gauhati on behalf of the Assam Association, Sir Charles Bayley had held out the hope that the Assamese would soon receive their

---

[14] Speech by M.C. Barooah on 6 April, *EBALCP* (1909), No. 3, pp. 57–62. Speech by D. Deb on the budget, *EBALCP* (1907), No. 4, p. 90.

[15] Tripathi, *Extremist Challenge in India*, p. 208.

Governor's inaugural address in 1921, *ALCP* (1921), Vol. 1, p. 25. Governor's address, 16 August, *ALCP* (1923), Vol. 3, pp. 696–97.

representation on a sure footing in the reformed legislature.[16] In a way, perhaps, Barooah's analogy was quite pertinent, since the Magna Carta, too, came as a small concession to the upper classes, and its meaning was expanded in due course only under the pressure of popular struggles.

Regulations framed for East Bengal and Assam under the Indian Councils Act of 1909 came into force on 15 November 1909. They provided for a maximum of forty-two Council members and a non-official majority. The representation of Assam in this body increased, as a result of the reforms, from two to five. The local boards of the two Valleys elected one each. The municipalities of Assam elected one member. One member of the Mohammedan constituency was alternately elected by the Surma and Assam Valleys, with the former getting the first chance. Besides, one additional member representing the Surma Valley was likely to be elected alternately either from the land-holders' or from another municipal constituency. For the province's tea interests, there was a provision for two seats. The enlarged provincial Council that emerged had forty members, and its first meeting was held on 4 January 1910. An examination of its membership list, as of 14 March 1910, shows that out of the thirty-nine members present on that day, excluding the Lieutenant-Governor who presided, as many as twenty-one were Britishers, sixteen Bengalis and only two Assamese – Manik Chandra Barooah and Rai Bahadur Bhubanram Das (1856–1916).[17] The latter two were elected from the Brahmaputra Valley.

It is very clear from the Council proceedings that, due to a lack of rapport between Eastern Bengal and Assam, the handful of members from the latter region had practically no role to play. They had to look to the administration for support, rather than to the body of non-official Indian members, whenever they wanted to bring into focus such subjects as the opium question or the unfair community-wise distribution of government jobs. Limited job opportunities provided the main reason for discord between the Assamese and Bengali middle classes.

More about the Swadeshi Movement

The Swadeshi and boycott movement of Bengal and Sylhet sent ripples across the Brahmaputra Valley. On 12 November 1905, a big meeting was held at Bagribari under the patronage of S.N. Sinha Chaudhuri, local zamindar and proprietor of the Bengal Soap Factory of Howrah, to protest against the partition. The extremist challenge in the form of terrorism, too, found a few adherents in lower Assam. At Gauhati, a Bengali employee of the Assam Valley Trading

---

[16] Barooah's speech on 6 April, *EBALCP* (1909), No. 3, p. 58.

[17] *East Bengal and Assam Administrative Report 1909–10*, p. 11. Mazumdar, *Indian Political Associations*, p. 422. Membership list of the enlarged Council on 14 March 1910, *Eastern Bengal and Assam Gazette,* Part VI, 20 April 1910.

Raja Prabhatchandra Barua, a son of the soil, more at home with Bengali than with Assamese, was the only nominated Indian member from the Brahmaputra Valley. But he was not present in the house.

Company, Govinda Lahiri, and Ambikagiri Raychaudhury (1885–1967) tried to organize the local students in the spirit of *swadeshi*. A group of Assamese students decided to work for two days a week at the steamer and railway stations, and to donate their earnings towards the *swadeshi* cause. According to the Gauhati correspondent of the *Bengalee* (21 December 1905), the priests of *Kamakhya* ceased using beet sugar and Liverpool salt. Marwari traders were induced to indent *swadeshi* salt and sugar, but their response was obviously not very encouraging. Young Raychaudhury and a few of his comrades were attracted towards the cult of terrorism. The manuscript of his patriotic drama, *Bandinii Bharat*, was intercepted by the police in 1906, and he was under police vigilance at Barpeta during the years 1907–15. This was, in any case, an isolated instance of extremism, not emerging out of any mass unrest in the Valley.[18]

Even the little agitation that was experienced was out of tune with the collaborationist outlook of the Assam Association, both inside and outside the Council. A list of *swadeshi* volunteers enrolled up to June 1907 in East Bengal and Assam districts revealed that out of a total of 8,485 such volunteers, 59 were from Sylhet, eighteen from Cachar and none from Darrang, Nowgong and Lakhimpur. The number of volunteers from Goalpara and Kamrup was not given.[19] Nevertheless, the *swadeshi* agitation made a deep impression on the young generation of the day, as we know from several published memoirs. The *swadeshi* songs and drama of Mukunda Das, who visited Gauhati with his troupe in 1905 (and again in 1920), left a permanent mark on the cultural milieu of Assam.

Extremism was relatively more widespread and deep-rooted in the Surma Valley, inspired as it was by Pal, a native of Sylhet. Mahendranath De (d. 1912), who was a delegate from Sylhet to the historic Calcutta Congress of 1906, was a professor for some time in Calcutta National College. Back in his home district as a teacher at the Habiganj National School, he started a monthly called *Maitri* in April 1909 and, the next year, he began editing *Prajashakti*. The latter was an anti-government organ run by the same school and printed in De's own Maitri Press. His extremist politics, however, was soon obscured by a religious cult he subscribed to, as a disciple of Dayananda Swami *alias* Gurudas Chaudhuri (1882–1937), a former government servant and political suspect.

The Arunachal Ashram, founded by Swami Dayananda at Silchar in 1908, was under police vigilance. On 28 April 1910, the Ashram was searched and several copies of *Karmayogin* and *Dharma* were seized. In July, the District Magistrate took action against *Prajashakti* under the Press Act of 1910, and the

---

[18] Atulchandra Barua *et al.*, *Sharatcandra Goswamiir Camu Jiivanii* (in Assamese, Gauhati, n.d.), pp. 11–12. M. Tayyebulla, *Karagarar Cithi* (in Assamese, Gauhati, 1962), p. 23. Ambikagiri Raychaudhury, *Mor Jiivan Dhumuhar Echhati* (in Assamese, Gauhati, 1973), pp. 16–26 and 'Bharatar swadhiinata yuddhat deshatma-bodhak sangiitar bhumika' in Harendranath Barua *et al.*, eds, *Bharatar Mukti Yunjat Asam* (in Assamese, Gauhati, 1972), pp. 320–22. *The Bengalee*, 7 and 21 December 1905.
[19] Sarkar, *Swadeshi Movement in Bengal*, p. 356.

paper ceased publication. In August the same year, government servants were directed to sever all connections with the Ashram. A defiant Dayananda issued a statement challenging official interference in matters of religion. The Ashram branch founded at the village of Jagatshi by Mahendranath De was raided by the police. In course of a police firing there in July 1912, De was fatally injured; Dayananda and several others were convicted, thereafter, to jail terms. Subsequent events, for example, the Maulvibazar bomb case of 27 March 1913, suggest that a small group or two of terrorists continued to function in Sylhet.[20]

The Curzon Plan could not be sustained for long in the face of the rising forces of nationalism in Bengal. In July 1911, Lord Hardinge observed in his correspondence with the Secretary of State for India, that the political power of the Bengalis – born agitators as they were – had not been broken and that they would never cease to agitate 'until they have attained a modification of the partition'.[21] So, at the Delhi Durbar on 12 December 1911, the partition was annulled by a royal declaration. Assam, Sylhet inclusive, was formally reverted to its old status as a Chief Commissioner's province with effect from 1 April 1912.

Assam Legislative Council 1912–20
A Glorified Debating Society

The apprehension that reconstitution of Assam again as a Chief Commissionership might mean a retrograde step, a reversion to the old one-man rule, somewhat disappeared following the creation of the Assam Legislative Council in November 1912. The composition of this Council, under the Act of 1909, was as follows:

Composition of the Assam Legislative Council 1912–20

Chief Commissioner	(*Ex-officio* President)	1
Nominated Members	(including not more than 9 officials)	13
Constituencies for Elected Members	*No. of Electors:*	
Municipalities	119 Commissioners	2
Local boards	217 local board members	2
Land-holders	192 land-holders	2
Muslims	1,188 electors	2
Tea planters		3
Total strength of the Council		25

Note: One expert member might be added, if found necessary.

---

[20] Home (Pol.), May 1912, No. 3 (NAI), Confidential Home (Pol.) 1913, Part-B-Proc., August 1913, Nos. 7–11 (NAI). For details on the two Ashrams, see Aditya, *Fight for Freedom in Sylhet*, pp. 6–7 and Gupta Chaudhury, ed., *Shriihatta Pratibha*, pp. 68 and 124.

[21] Hardinge to Crewe, 13, July 1911, *Crewe Papers*, cited by Tripathi, *Extremist Challenge in India*, p. 102.

The Assam Legislative Council, so formed, held its first sitting on 2 January 1913. Technically, it had a non-official majority, but certainly not a non-official Indian majority as such. The officials nominated on the body were invariably British by race, with the exception of one or, at the most, two. All the three elected planter members were also British. Even the non-official nominee to represent labour was, in the initial years, a Britisher. One of the Indian members being elected to the Imperial Legislative Council, his seat in the early years continued to remain vacant. A close examination of the composition of the first Council shows that the British members, together with one or two Indian official members, always had an assured majority in the house. It was not ordinarily so in the second Council. But there, too, in a full house of twenty-five, there were thirteen Britishers, including the president, as against twelve Indian members, on 13 March 1918. Of the latter, one was a Muslim or Parsi official, as could be guessed from his surname (Banatwala), six were Bengalis and five Assamese. The rules saw to it that the Assamese and Bengali members had numerical parity in the house. The elective seats were evenly distributed between the two Valleys with a view to achieve this purpose. Besides, the nomination of Indian members was skilfully manipulated, if necessary, to maintain the parity.[22]

Thus counterpoised in the legislature, the Bengali and Assamese middle-class elements often tended to act as rival groups. In the absence of a common political platform outside the Council, their narrow group interests, cleverly posed as their respective community interests, dominated the proceedings. Yet, on such common questions as further democratization of the administration, non-official Indian members often forged a united stand, although they did not necessarily think in terms of a stable opposition bloc.

The Indian members considered the house to be a sort of debating society where certain issues of public importance could be focused. But even this opportunity was, under the procedural rules of the Council Manual, more limited in practice than was originally intended by the Morley–Minto Reforms. The procedure required full five days' notice if a member wanted to raise a discussion on the budget. At least until 1917, not a single resolution was moved – and hence no specific discussion could follow – on particular budget items. Not that the Council members lacked the acumen to do that. It was because of official failure to present the draft financial statement to the members in time that they failed to give the required notice for raising a discussion. Castigating the government for its impracticable procedure, Saiyid Muhammad Saadulla (1886–1955) said:

> We consoled ourselves with the thought that we could not be authors of the budget, yet we had the valuable right of discussing the budget and try to pursuade Government by moving resolutions to modify it according to popular view . . .

---

[22] East India (Constitutional Reforms) Lord Southborough's Committee, Vol. I, *The Franchise Committee 1918–19* (London, 1919), p. 76; Padmanath Gohain–Barua, *Mor Jiivan Sonwaranii* (in Assamese, Gauhati, 1971), pp. 199–204; and the list of members present on 13 March, *ALCP* (1918).

by an impracticable procedure and on the strength of a rule in the Council
Manual, this cherished right of real discussion of the budget is being snatched
away, and the right of the people to influence the main heads of the budget
turned into a sham.

But his arguments fell on deaf ears. Members were advised to present
themselves at Shillong a week or so before the session so that they could collect
the relevant papers in advance and notify the government about their proposed
motions on the budget. Thus, the procedural handicap continued to be there till
the end of the Council's life.[23]

The British declaration of 1917 promising further constitutional reforms
and the countrywide restlessness about the political future brought about a firm
shift in the attitude of the Council members to this debating society towards the
close of World War I.

Radha Binod Das (1857–1938), a lawyer of Sylhet, gave vent to the
general feeling when he said in the Council on 6 April 1918, in an exasperated
mood:

> Sir, we have met today in this Council with the avowed object of talking, and of
> doing little besides. I fail to appreciate the usefulness of such talk, and I sincerely
> hope that the reform scheme will sound the death-knell of such solemn talk. We
> shall then be spared of the necessity of participating in the discussion of the
> Budget without having the power to control it, and of offering suggestions
> which there is no obligation to carry out.[24]

Thus, what was termed as the Magna Carta by M.C. Barooah in 1909 was
increasingly put under ridicule from about 1917.

Elections to the Council were held in 1912 and again in 1916. Thereafter its life was extended twice by an executive order in anticipation of the
reforms. Public interest in it, if any at all, was ebbing fast. So uninteresting and
useless were the proceedings that Radha Binod Das and Tarun Ram Phookan
(1877–1939), both busy lawyers, wisely resigned from the body in early 1919,
after a prolonged absence.[25] So did Phanidhar Chaliha (1854–1923), in protest
against a derogatory remark made from the chair. About this time, his son
Kuladhar Chaliha (1888–1963), too, resigned from government service.

Tame Performance of Indian Councillors

During the years 1912–20, altogether twenty Indian members, including
two officials, served on the Legislative Council for a part or whole of the period
(see Appendix 8). Almost all the members came from the educated top social

---

23 Speech by S.M. Saadulla on budget, 25 April 1917 and Botham's reply thereto, *ALCP*
(1917), No. 2, pp. 124–25.

24 Speech by R.B. Das on 6 April, *ALCP* (1918), No. 3, p. 130.

25 Chief Commissioner's comment from the chair on 5 April, *ALCP* (1919), No. 2, p. 90.

stratum, with considerable landed property, tea gardens or a lucrative legal profession as their mainstay of political influence. This explains why they were moderates and/or loyalists. At least thirteen of them were already, or in due course to be, government title-holders. The social background of two important Councillors of the period may be discussed here to prove the point.

Manik Chandra Barooah, son of a government servant, was undoubtedly the doyen of politicians of the Brahmaputra Valley of his time. An honorary magistrate since 1884 and general secretary of the Assam Association since its inception in 1903, Barooah was also the first non-official and Indian chairman (26 March 1913–24 July 1915) of the Gauhati Municipality. His meteoric rise and fall as a businessman was referred to in Chapter Two. About his faith in 'benign British rule' and his expressed gratitude to the British planters, too, enough has already been said. With facts and figures at his fingertips, Barooah utilized almost every Council session he attended to show that the educated Assamese were not getting a fair share of jobs in their own land. However, one should also note that during the last four years of his office he took a leading part in exposing the planters' grip over the local boards, and in demanding their partial democratization (to be discussed later). As early as 13 March 1915, he alleged that large-scale immigration of East Bengal Muslim peasants belonging to 'a notoriously turbulent class of people' had been going on for several years and asked the government to 'take precautions that they may not come into conflict with the local villagers'. Barooah also pressed on the government that the time had come to amend the Land and Revenue Regulations, 1886, and make a rent law for Assam, since the rights of tenants and sub-tenants of *lakheraj/nisfkheraj/devottar* and *brahmottar* lands had not yet been properly defined. 'The "dolois" or managers of the temples', he said, 'indiscriminately lease out temple lands for their own benefit.'[26]

It remains a puzzle why he was not made a Rai Bahadur. Perhaps he was considered too big for that title and yet, as a mere provincial (or Valley) politician, not big enough for a knighthood. Under the compulsion of unenviable local circumstances, he could not afford to aspire for the all-India stature he deserved and, in fact, attended only one session of the Indian National Congress (1890). He failed or refused to see that Assam's miseries followed from a system of colonialism. However, it was he 'who for the first time showed to Assam', as Saadulla said in a condolence speech, 'what bright prospects lay behind trade and commerce'.[27] Indeed, it was his chequered career, again, that showed how such prospects could also end in a disaster in the given colonial situation.

Ghanashyam Barua (1867–1923), too, belonged to the same loyalist–

---

[26] Speeches by Barooah on 13 March, *ALCP* (1915), No. 2, p. 38 and *EBALCP* (1911), No. 3, p. 110, respectively.

[27] Homage paid to late Barooah on 5 November, *ALCP* (1915), No. 4, pp. 141–43. Incidentally, Saadulla was the only Assamese to receive a late knighthood which he relinquished immediately before independence.

moderate tradition. He and Abdul Majid (1867–1924),[28] the lone Assamese official later nominated as a Councillor and made a high court judge, matriculated in the same year, studied together for two years in Presidency College of Calcutta, and served together as joint secretaries of the Assamese Students' Literary Club (Calcutta). Elected from the local boards' constituency to the Assam Legislative Council, Barua represented it in the Imperial Legislative Council for the term 1913–16. Himself a planter, he pleaded for exemption of tea from income taxation on the ground that it was an agricultural rather than manufactured produce. In this respect, he lent full support to the British planters' lobby in the Imperial Legislative Council.[29]

Barua almost emerged as the unofficial opposition leader in the second Assam Legislative Council. He was general secretary of the Assam Association for three consecutive years until he was replaced by T.R. Phookan at its Goalpara session (December 1918). Incidentally, the latter relinquished his office prematurely and the mantle fell on Nabin Chandra Bardaloi (1875–1936). Barua was not only a successful lawyer, but also the promoter and owner of a small tea garden in his own district. After 1917, as a counterpoise to the tide of the national movement, he was increasingly favoured by the colonial rulers. He was made a Rai Bahadur and appointed vice-president of the Assam Legislative Council in September 1919. Indeed, he was the first non-official vice-president in the annals of Indian Legislative Councils. While a few of his erstwhile colleagues chose to be non-cooperators, he got himself elected into the Reformed Council. A minister under the dyarchy, he died in harness on 26 March 1923, unsung and unwept. On the question of the opium evil, grazing tax and sham local bodies, Barua's sharp exposés, inside and outside the Council, did show up the mettle of his leadership. But with the eclipse of moderate politics, his hold even on the middle classes was rapidly relegated to obsolescence.

Opium Policy and Grazing Fees under Attack: 1906–20
The Fact-Sheet on Opium
The thread of our discussion on the opium evil may be picked up from where it was left in Chapter Two. We had observed that after a gradual fall in the last quarter of the nineteenth century, the total opium consumption once more recorded a rising trend after 1897–98. The Treasury price of opium, which was kept fixed at Rs 37 per *seer* during the entire period from 1890–91 to 1908–09, was revised to Rs 40 for the period 1909–13 and then gradually raised to Rs 57 by 1920–21. The number of licensed opium shops was, at the same time, cut down from 728 in 1905–06 to 315 in 1920–21. By 1914, the ceiling on the quantity allowed for private possession, as well as on the retail one-time sale of opium, was reduced from three to two *tolas*, and on individual possession of

---

[28] Majid's father, Mohammad Shah of Jorhat, was a *mauzadar*.
[29] 5 April, *ALCP* (1923), Vol. 3, pp. 260–64 and G.S. Barua's speech on budget, *Imperial (Indian) Legislative Council Proceedings (hereafter ILCP)*, 1916–17, pp. 513–14.

Annual Consumption of Opium per 10,000 People (seers)

Year	Assam Province	Brahmaputra Valley	Indigenous Assamese population only
1881	123.4	255.9	313.4
1891	95.5	188.7	267.2
1901	84.3	177.7	274.9
1911	85.5	172.7	277.1
1921	81.1	151.9	286.9

Source: *Assam Congress Opium Enquiry Report* (Jorhat, 1925), p. 97. Though not strictly accurate in calculation, these estimates are acceptable as fair approximations.

smoking preparation from one to half a *tola*.[30] These were but half-hearted, petty measures – obviously not equal to the task. The provincial consumption of opium went on increasing by leaps and bounds, alongside an increase in the excise revenue – the real purpose behind the policy. Opium consumption and the corresponding government revenue of the province increased from 1,415 maunds and Rs 1,982,000, respectively, in 1905–06, to 1615 *maunds* and Rs 4,412,000 by 1920–21 (see Appendix 4). The statistics of annual opium consumption in *seers* per 10,000 people are also available and are reproduced in the table above.

Thus, while the official policy was claimed to be 'maximum of revenue with minimum of consumption', its real aim turned out in practice to be an increase in both revenue and consumption, so far as the vitally affected segment of the society was concerned. As against the internationally accepted norm of 6 *seers* per 10,000 people,[31] which could be safely allowed to the concerned population, the consumption was as high as 267 *seers* in 1891 for the indigenous Assamese population; and it gradually increased to 287 *seers* by 1921. This was the net outcome of the colonial taxation policy in operation and that too in the name of containment of opium!

For the Assamese people, this situation involved a life-and-death question. Yet the anti-opium agitation took time to gather momentum. The dependent educated middle class, with their vested interests in tea plantations and in the bureaucratic distributive system, appears to have been unfit for the task. Even the most outspoken critics of the policy would not, until the days of Non-Co-operation, raise such demands as direct taxation of planters' incomes as an alternative revenue source to relieve the over-taxed peasantry. On the contrary, some of those middle-class leaders, like Jagannath Barooah, Devicharan Barua and their Jorhat Sarvajanik Sabha, lent support to the official opium excise policy towards the close of the last century (see Appendix 9). In that context alone, the anti-opium agitation of the subsequent years was significant.

---

[30] *Assam Congress Opium Enquiry Report* (hereafter *ACOER*) (Jorhat, 1925), Appendix X, pp. 90–91 and 138–39. *Report of the Committee Appointed to Enquire into Certain Aspects of Opium and Ganja Consumption* (Botham Committee, submitted on 18 April 1913 and said to be published on 5 December 1913), pp. 1–23.

[31] C.F. Andrews, *The Opium Evil in India* (London, 1926), p. 22.

Opium Issue Inside and Outside the Council

In 1907, an anti-opium conference was held at Dibrugarh with official blessings and at the initiative of local social workers. Apart from submitting a memorial to the government urging upon it to check the opium menace, it also gave out a call for the formation of an Assam Temperance Association, with permanent committees functioning at the sub-divisional level in all towns of the Brahmaputra Valley. The organizational plan was not, however, carried out. There was again an anti-opium conference at Dibrugarh again in 1912, with the *satradhikar* of Dinjay Satra (the abbot of Dinjay monastery) in the chair, where a temperance society was formed. It recommended the opening of a public register of opium-eaters, as had been successfully done in Burma, with a view to check further progress of the habit.[32]

Simultaneously, there was the pressure of international public opinion. In the wake of the Shanghai International Opium Commission (1910), the Government of India examined the question of prohibition of opium-smoking – the most injurious form of taking the drug – but considered the task to be impracticable. Under the Hague Convention of 1912, India was formally committed to suppressing opium-smoking in all its provinces. Accordingly, it advised the Assam administration to impose necessary restrictions. Within the provincial Council, too, Assamese members were increasingly expressing their anxiety over the opium situation. Government members invariably tried to explain away the rising trend in opium consumption in terms of rapid population growth and of increasing purchasing power under the resurgent conditions of prosperity. They argued that a more severe restrictive policy would drive the addicts to other intoxicants. Nevertheless, under pressure from all quarters, the Government of Assam appointed a committee on 10 December 1912 to go into the question and submit a report. The committee was formed with A.W. Botham as chairman, and Kaliprasad Chaliha (1862–1914), Kutubuddin Ahmed (d. 1948) and Radhanath Phukan (1875–1964) as members.[33]

In his maiden speech in the Council on 10 April 1913, Padmanath Gohain–Barua thanked the Chief Commissioner for appointing the committee. He said that the steps hitherto taken with a view to reduce opium consumption, namely, the enhancement of its price and the reduction in the number of its vendors, had failed to produce the desired effect. He was strongly in favour of the Dibrugarh proposal for opening an opium-eaters' register.[34]

The Botham Committee's Report submitted on 18 April 1913 was no doubt revealing, but its recommendations were disappointing. It concluded that

---

[32] *ACOER*, p. 142. Dilip Chaudhuri, *Nilmani Phukanar Cintadhara* (in Assamese, Gauhati, 1972), p. 16. Gohain–Barua's speech on 10 April 1913, *ALCP* (1913), No. 5, p. 72.

[33] Speech by P.G. Melitus, a government member, on 5 April, *EBALCP* (1910), No. 3, p. 95; Major Kennedy's speech on 10 April, *ALCP* (1913), No. 5, p. 106. Revised Financial Statement for 1914–15, 13 March, *ALCP* (1914), No. 11 (*sic*) pp. 34–35.

[34] Gohain–Barua's speech on 10 April 1913, *ALCP* (1913), No. 5.

a severe restriction on opium without similar restrictions on *ganja* (hashish) would only divert consumption from one drug to the other. It refused to recommend a system of personal registration of opium-eaters. Instead of a total ban on opium-smoking, which accounted for about half the consumption, it merely prescribed 'prohibition of smoking in company' as a deterrent. The government did not implement even this mild recommendation. It only increased the retail price to 12 annas per *tola* and accepted some minor suggestions with effect from 1 April 1914.[35] The opium statistics of the subsequent years as cited above amply show that, even as an eyewash, these measures were a total failure. The Report was withheld from the public until 1925, when it was made available under Congress pressure.

The wordy battle over opium in the second Council reached its climax in the last two years of its existence. On 5 April 1919, in course of a speech on the budget, Rai Bahadur Phanidhar Chaliha, a retired government servant of whom mention has already been made, warned: 'If the opium trade is retained, the Assamese race will be almost extinct within about two hundred years hence.' Pointing to the increase in smuggling, he emphasized that nothing short of a total ban on the opium trade would really and materially benefit the people. Angry at his remark that opium revenue was 'tainted money', Chief Commissioner Beatson Bell tauntingly remarked from his presidential chair that every bit out of that tainted revenue earned by Chaliha as a government servant and pensioner, should then be returned.[36] Chaliha thereafter resigned.

Swansong of the Debating Society

The annual conference of the Assam Association at Barpeta in December 1919 recommended gradual eradication of the opium trade within a period of ten years. The matter was forcefully brought before the house on 13 March 1920 by Ghanashyam Barua in the form of a resolution. He moved that, in order to eradicate the opium habit or bring it down to an unavoidable minimum, the government should introduce a system of personal registration of opium-eaters, at least in the Brahmaputra Valley, and that a careful count of opium-eaters should be taken at the next population census. He said that, at the time of the Botham Committee, the average annual consumption of opium was 141 grains per head in the province as a whole, but as high as 357 grains per head in the Brahmaputra Valley as against 91 grains in Berar and 14–47 grains in other Indian provinces. Barua submitted that per capita consumption in the Brahmaputra Valley had since increased to 554 grains. And this was so when the bare medicinal need of opium in any country was estimated by the League of Nations to be about 7 grains per head of population per year. According to official circles, the

---

[35] *ACOER,* pp. 136–39. Chief Commissioner's Resolution of 22 April 1914 on Botham Committee's Report, No. 2444 M. in Municipal Department, Government of Assam.
[36] Chaliha's speech on the budget on 5 April and Chief Commissioner Bell's comment from the chair, *ALCP* (1919), No. 2, pp. 64–66 and 90.

number of adult opium-eaters 'probably' amounted to a lakh in Assam.[37]

The discussion on the resolution was resumed on 8 April. To enhance its chances of acceptance, Barua remodelled it to restrict its scope to Assam proper alone, where the evil was mostly concentrated. But of the twelve Indian members present in a full house of twenty-four, only four – Saadulla, Krishnakumar Barua (d. 1951), Chandradhar Barua (1874–1961) and Ghanashyam Barua – voted for the resolution. The fifth and lone British vote in favour was Playfair's. The three Hindu and three Muslim members from the Surma Valley, Rajendranarayan Chaudhuri – a Goalpara zamindar, and four Britishers voted against it. The rest remained neutral. The dying legislature had one more session in October 1920.[38] But by that time everybody had probably forgotten its existence in the excitement of a new kind of politics outside the Council that had meanwhile gripped the country.

Discontent over Grazing Fees

In land-abundant Assam, peasants had enjoyed, from time immemorial, the traditional right to graze their cattle freely on the village commons and neighbouring forests. Hence, they were not in the habit of growing fodder crops on their own private lands. Under the British regime, this right was gradually encroached upon to bring forth additional revenue to the exchequer. A grazing fee per head of horned animals was introduced. In 1888, this fee was 8 annas per annum per head of buffaloes and 4 annas per head of cows.[39]

As early as 1 July 1903, the ryots of about thirty *mauzas* of Golaghat sub-division sent a memorial to the Chief Commissioner protesting against the grazing fee on buffaloes, but the government upheld it. The fee was raised to Re. 1 per buffalo in 1907 and still higher in 1912. The Grazing Rules, which were framed in 1911, were somewhat modified after an official enquiry in 1915, under the pressure of public opinion. Thereafter, this grazing fee continued to be Rs 3 per buffalo and 6 annas per cow. In the hills districts, a rate ranging from Rs 4 to Rs 6 per buffalo was in force since 1917. Incidentally, milch buffaloes in the vicinity of towns were taxed at the concessional rate of Re. 1 per head until 1916 and Rs 2 thereafter. Though initially an insignificant source of government revenue, these grazing fees were indeed an expanding source because of the steady rise in the immigration of Nepali and other graziers along with their cattle. The total number of buffaloes taxed in the Brahmaputra Valley increased from year to year as follows:

Year	1895	1900	1905	1910	1915	1920
No.	15,640	18,735	24,346	40,000	42,000	86,325

---

[37] Dalim Bora's interpellation on 23 February, *ALCP* (1921), Vol. I, p. 9. Also G.S. Barua's speech, *ALCP* (1920), p. 41.

[38] 8 April, *ALCP* (1920), No. 2, pp. 92–100.

[39] Reid's reply, 23 September, *ALCP* (1921), Vol. I, pp. 708–10.

As a result of the increase in the number of buffaloes and in the rates payable, and the tightening up of the collection machinery, the revenue from this source doubled between 1916–17 and 1920–21, as can be seen from the relevant figures given below:

Year	1916–17	1917–18	1919–20	1920–21
Rs (1,000)	183	342	277	341

The people resented not only the increased fees, but also the arbitrary and harassing methods of collection, against which there was no relief in civil courts of law under the rules. The burden was practically limited to the Brahmaputra Valley which abounded in grazing grounds. For example, as against the total collection of Rs 2,77,356 as grazing fees from this Valley in 1919–20, only Rs 25,841 were collected from the Surma Valley and the hills districts. The assessees were divided into two classes: (i) professional graziers and (ii) agriculturists. While the latter were allowed exemption under the revised rules of up to ten heads of cattle, the former had to pay for the whole herd.[40] It was over the definition of a professional grazier and the anomalies in assessment that disputes arose between agriculturists and the government.

The revamping of the grazing fees and tightening of the collection machinery during the years 1912–17 raised a storm of protest in the Brahmaputra Valley. An analysis of the relevant statistics clearly shows that the bulk of the agriculturists were not touched by this tax. In 1917–18, only 622 cattle-owners of local domicile were treated as professional graziers. The total revenue of Rs 2,77,000 collected in 1919–20 from grazing fees was accounted for by only 1,25,000 heads of cattle actually assessed in that year under the rules. The overwhelming bulk of these cattle again belonged to 6,319 professional graziers of whom, excepting a few hundred, all were Nepali migrants.[41]

A question then arises as to why the then resentment was so widespread and persistent. Obviously, the rich peasants and town-dwelling, absentee landholders used to invest in a small way in herds of cattle left under professional graziers' care. They were powerful enough to launch an agitation through the revitalization of the Assam Association from around 1914. One argument put forward by them was that the tax would raise the price of milk products to the detriment of the consumers, particularly in urban areas. Although by and large it represented sectional interests, the agitation had mass support because of the traditional background explained earlier.

The Assam Association took the lead in this persistent agitation during 1914–20. Anxiety over the assessment of cattle-owning Assamese peasants and

---

[40] Ibid., pp. 708–12; Dalim Bora's speech, ibid., pp. 703–08; Reply to Saadulla, 13 March, *ALCP* (1917), No. 1, p. 26; Speeches by Barua and Botham, 5 October, *ALCP* (1918), No. 4, pp. 186–93.

[41] Webster's reply to Barua, 12 January, *ALCP* (1918) No. 1, pp. 7–8.
Government's statement in reply to Mahadev Sharma in September 1927, cited in *ALCP* (1928), Vol. 8, pp. 84–89 (App. A).

land-holders, and their harassment was raised in the Council, again and again. No subject had come so frequently before the house in the form of questions and resolutions as the grazing tax issue, said an official member in 1921. Opinions expressed in the Council were but a reflection of the public opinion outside. The public of Dibrugarh submitted a protest memorial on 20 July 1914. The Assam Association expressed its concern over the issue in its meeting at Gauhati on 9 October 1914, and in its annual sessions at Gauhati in 1916 and at Sibsagar in 1917. In the latter session, a resolution was passed for the first time firmly demanding total abolition of the grazing tax.[42]

The demand for its abolition was raised by Phanidhar Chaliha in the Council on 6 April 1918. On 5 October the same year, Ghanashyam Barua formally moved that the tax on so-called professional graziers in the Brahmaputra Valley be entirely abolished or at least reduced to the level that had prevailed before 1912. He described the measure as 'oppressive, hateful and abominable'. Faced with official opposition, Barua pleaded in a conceding mood that at least *bonafide* native and domiciled cultivator should have the free allowance of ten cattle 'now supposed to be made to him, whether he makes a profit from cattle-breeding or not'. Chaliha and Saadulla lent support to him in the animated debate. However, the fate of the motion was predestined; it was lost, as usual, for lack of official support.[43]

Barua, the unofficial leader of the opposition, later compromised his stand. But the agitation was sustained and it led to many animated debates subsequently in the Reformed Council.[44]

Struggle for Democratization of Local Bodies
On the Municipal Front

It was noted in Chapter Two that the municipalities of Assam, except the one at Sylhet, always had *ex-officio* British chairmen right up to 1912. With the election of Parasuram Khaund, an honorary Magistrate, as the first non-official chairman of the Dibrugarh Municipality on 11 April 1912, a beginning was made in Assam towards Indianization of this office. However, Khaund was forced to resign from chairmanship within a month or so under pressure. It was not until 15 February 1915 that this Municipality once more had a non-official and Indian

---

[42] Reid's reply, 22 September, *ALCP* (1912), Vol. 1, p. 708. Gohain–Barua's questions, 10 November, *ALCP* (1914), No. 4.

Questions by Barooah, 13 March, *ALCP* (1915), No. 1, p. 38 and Botham's reply thereto.

T.R. Phookan's speech, 6 April, *ALCP* (1916), No. 2, p. 39. Questions by Saadulla and Chaliha, 13 March, *ALCP* (1917), No. 1, pp. 13 and 26. It was Chaliha who referred to the Assam Association's stand. Government's reply to Saadulla, 5 October, *ALCP* (1918), No. 4, p. 175.

The Mussalman, 4 January 1918.

[43] 5 October, *ALCP* (1918), No. 4, pp. 186–90 and 193.

[44] Speech by G.S. Barua, 23 September, *ALCP* (1921), Vol. 1, pp. 719–22.

chairman in the person of Radhanath Changkakati. The Silchar Municipality had a non-official Indian chairman from 1913 onwards. The Gauhati Municipality – which had so far refused to avail itself of the permission granted as far back as 1888 to elect a non-official as chairman – now followed suit. It elected Manik Chandra Barooah as chairman on 24 March 1913. Barooah was succeeded – he died on 7 September 1915 – by Bhubanram Das, an ex-member of the Eastern Bengal and Assam Legislative Council. Manmohan Lahiri (1866–1938), a Bengali lawyer and small capitalist, was elected chairman of the Tezpur Municipality on 4 December 1916.[45]

In 1916, the government proposed to convert the Sibsagar Station Committee into a municipality, with an appointed chairman to begin with. The citizens welcomed the municipalization but not the proposed appointment of its chairman. The demand of the Sibsagar Ratepayers' Association for an elected chairman was also voiced on the Council floor. The government had to concede to this demand. Elected chairmen for all municipalities was an issue raised again and again in the Council by such members as K.K. Chanda, Muhammad Bakht Mazumdar (1861–1936) and others.[46]

When the Assam Municipal Bill, 1917, came up before the house, Ramanimohan Das and the Karimganj Bar Association wanted its postponement until the much-awaited British declaration on India's Constitutional Reforms. This was the general opinion in both the Valleys, despite the fact that the Bill provided for an elective chairmanship. The Chief Commissioner called an informal conference of all non-official Council members and asked for their opinion, since such a step would delay the proposed change. Out of the ten present, four members favoured a postponement *sine die*, three wanted postponement till March and three opposed any postponement. The Chief Commissioner decided to take up the Bill in March.[47]

The Indian members offered stiff opposition when the Bill was referred to a Select Committee on 13 March 1918. 'By this time we all know', said Radha Binod Das, 'that the Bill has not been approved and accepted by the general public as a liberal measure.' T.R. Phookan found that there was 'a great deal of extra-official control provided for in matters of vital importance, which is quite opposed to the accepted principles of self-government,' Das's amendment to postpone consideration of the Bill *sine die* was accepted by the house by eight votes to six, the officials remaining neutral.[48]

Thus the government was already yielding to public pressure on the

---

[45] V. Venkata Rao, *A Hundred Years of Local Self-Government in Assam* (second edition, Gauhati, 1965), pp. 144–46 and 149–50.

[46] Ibid., pp. 146–47; Chaliha's question, 23 October, *ACLP* (1916), No. 4. Bakht Mazumdar's speech, 6 April, *ALCP* (1918), No. 2, pp. 155–56. Citations by Rao, *Hundred Years of Local Self-Government*, p. 158n.

[47] Chief Commissioner's speech from the chair, 12 January, *ALCP* (1918), No. 1, pp. 17–18.

[48] 13 March, *ALCP* (1918), No. 2, p. 90.

question of municipal reforms. By 1918–19, thirteen out of the twenty-three municipal boards had elected non-official chairmen.[49]

Local Boards in Planters' Clutches

Planters' domination over fifteen out of the nineteen local boards continued to persist. This domination was quite out of proportion to both their numerical strength as a community and their contribution towards the local rates. In 1912, for example, they paid altogether Rs 92,669 only as local rates whereas the rest of the rate-payers paid as much as Rs 5,39,401. Nevertheless, there were 82 elected planter members on these boards, while only 57 represented the rural rate-payers. If the relative shares in the total contribution was to be the criterion for allocation of seats, then the planters were undoubtedly favoured with a disproportionately large number of seats. They had twenty-one times their due share of local board seats in north Lakhimpur; twenty-seven times in Mangaldai; five to six times in Jorhat, Golaghat, Sibsagar and Tezpur; about three times in Dibrugarh and Silchar; twenty-five times in Nowgong; and forty times in Gauhati. In each of these fifteen local boards, excepting the one for Gauhati, planter members outnumbered the so-called rural rate-payers' representatives.[50]

British planters tried to justify this discriminatory and disproportionate distribution of local board seats by claiming to also represent the tea labour population. They pointed out that in 1914–15, on the 7,65,298 acres of plantation enclaves in the Brahmaputra Valley alone, there were 5,70,000 resident labourers whose interests were looked after by the planters. They also linked their claim to the £16 million British investment in the tea industry without which Assam would not have developed at all.[51]

Clearly, the planters were not ready to contribute towards the local rates in proportion to the control they enjoyed over them. Such control was deemed necessary as they wanted their own local interests to be served first and best, at public expense. For this, they could go to any length. A typical example is the case of the Sibsagar Local Board. On 19 March 1913, M.C. Barooah complained that almost all its proceeds from local rates were being spent for metalling two particular roads and constructing a bridge – almost entirely to benefit the planters. So sure were the planters of their grip over this Local Board that even its formal meetings, instead of being convened at its office premises, were sometimes held at the Assam Company's workshop town – Nazira, much to the disadvantage of Indian members.[52]

Indian Councillors like M.C. Barooah used the Council floor to expose

[49] Rao, *Hundred Years of Local Self-Government*, p. 152.

[50] Ibid., p. 205. Speech by Ghanashyam Barua, 12 January, *ALCP* (1918), No. 1, pp. 28–30.

[51] Speeches by Playfair and Kennedy, 15 March, *ALCP* (1915), No. 1, pp. 87 ff. Speech by Miller, 12 January, *ALCP* (1918), No. 1, p. 31.

[52] Barooah's questions on 19 March and government's reply thereto, *ALCP* (1913), No. 4 and again on 13 March, *ALCP* (1914), No. 11 (*sic.*), pp. 22–23.

the planters' stranglehold over the so-called 'rural self-government', and pressed for a change in favour of an elective system. They also demanded legislation for regularization of the local boards which were, till then, functioning by virtue of an executive order. The government introduced the much-awaited Local Self-Government Bill in 1914.

The Local Self-Government (LSG) Act 1915:
Old Wine in a New Bottle

Democratization of local self-government with a broad-based franchise was obviously not amongst the ostensible purposes of the Act of 1915. Nor was the political movement of the day committed to such a principle. The articulated demand was for elected representation of only the educated and propertied classes on all local bodies so that they could – within certain limits – influence the decision-making process at the local level. As a member of the Select Committee on the Bill, M.C. Barooah agreed with the government that the boards 'need not be necessarily a representative body of all sections and interests'. The Assam Association, of which he was the general secretary, was 'decidedly of opinion that property qualification is the only qualification which should be recognized in forming the electorates'.[53] Even so, he found the relevant provisions of the Bill unsatisfactory. 'There ought to be a well-understood principle of allotment of seats', he said, *inter alia*, in a note of dissent, 'according to the amount of payment of Local Rates'.[54]

Another reactionary feature of the Bill was the continued provision for appointed chairmen, except in a few special cases permitted by the Chief Commissioner. The *Eastern Chronicle* (Sylhet) spoke up in favour of modification of this provision and deplored the fact of too much official interference.[55] K.K. Chanda moved an amendment to provide for an elected chairman invariably for all the boards, and was supported by T.R. Phookan and Saadulla. However, it had to be withdrawn in the face of stiff opposition from the planters.[56]

From 1905–06 onwards, the rural population had indirectly elected representation on all local boards, but in a perverse manner. Government-appointed village headmen, called *gaon-burhas*, continued to elect the rural representatives, despite an increasing public protest. The government's intention was to provide a system under which rate-payers would elect their own representatives to the village authorities, village authorities to the local boards, and local boards to the provincial Legislative Council. But as there were no such village authori-

---

[53] Articles on the Bill in *Eastern Chronicle* (Sylhet), 5 December 1914 and 19 December 1914, cited in *L-S-G. A – June 1915*, Nos. 43–44, pp. 11–13 (Assam Secretariat Files; hereafter AS). The quote is from a memorandum submitted by M.C. Barooah, general secretary of the Assam Association, to the secretary of the ALC, dated 1 March 1915, ibid.

[54] Note of dissent by Barooah, cited in 13 March, *ALCP* (1914), No. 2, p. 161.

[55] *Eastern Chronicle*, 5 December and also 19 December 1914.

[56] 13 March, *ALCP* (1915), No. 2, pp. 61–67.

ties in existence in Assam proper other than *gaon-burhas,* the provisions of the Bill were self-defeating. The Bill provided that 'the village authority shall consist of a member or members appointed or elected in accordance with such rules as may be prescribed' in the future. This clause was clearly permissive of the continuity of *gaon-burhas* in Assam proper, and of the Chaukidari Panchayats (formed under the Act of 1870) in Goalpara and the Surma Valley, as the sole rural electors for an indefinite period. Chanda moved an amendment that such a village authority be plural and elected. This motion, too, had to be withdrawn to avoid a miserable defeat in terms of votes.

Amendments moved by Chanda and Gohain–Barua to make the representation of various sectional interests proportionate to their respective contributions towards land revenue and/or local rates, as far as practicable, were also defeated. The fate of other amendments, except a few of minor significance, was similar. Some were withdrawn to avoid voting. Chanda, a lawyer of eminence, virtually emerged as the informal opposition leader during this debate. It had begun with spirit and earnestness but sagged towards the end. Chanda pathetically said on 15 March 1915: 'as our proceedings commenced and as the discussions which were placed before the Council by us were taken up one by one, the process of evaporation of our hope commenced and by the time the voting on clause 37 was taken, it reached almost a vanishing point.'[57] Yet he decided to go through the rest of the ritual and moved the amendments still standing in his name, one by one.

The Bill was enacted almost in its original form, without any division at its final stage. Gohain–Barua did not miss the opportunity at the end of the debate to express his gratitude to the Chief Commissioner and president of the Council, 'for having succeeded in giving a legal basis to our local boards – the first seminaries of political education for us in this country'. All, however, did not agree with him in considering the LSG Act as 'a great boon conferred upon this poor province'.[58] The debate opened the eyes of several moderates who, in subsequent years, were to take an increasingly bolder stand.

Continued Struggle for Local Board Reforms

The Assam Association, in its annual session at Dibrugarh in December 1915, as well as at Gauhati in December 1916, passed resolutions expressing its concern over the continuation of *gaon-burhas* as the rural electors for the local boards. The government admitted the unsatisfactoriness of the situation and hoped to replace them soon by duly constituted village authorities. Ghanashyam Barua, on 17 October 1917, again expressed concern over the delay in the formation of the village authorities. On 25 April 1917, both Phanidhar Chaliha and Barua reiterated that the distribution of local board seats between different sections should be related to their respective contributions towards direct taxes. They also

---

[57] K.K. Chanda's speech on 15 March, *ALCP* (1915), No. 2, p. 84.
[58] Gohain–Barua's speech on 9 April, *ALCP* (1915), No. 3, p. 116.

said that non-officials should be made chairmen at least in some select local boards.[59]

A resolution in the Council to abridge the over-representation of planters on the local boards was moved by Ghanashyam Barua on 12 January 1918. His speech on this occasion was one of the best in the Council's annals. He sharply pointed out that the planters were wanting in local knowledge and, except in the matter of communications, also in local interests. 'The claim of tea planters . . . is intrinsically based on their being agriculturists and payers of local rates and my point is that', said Barua, 'their representation should be proportionate to the local rates paid by them'. He was supported by Ramanimohan Das of Karimganj, Saadulla and others. Bakht Mazumdar made the point that, besides the elected seats, the planters also had a share of the nominated seats. The government spokesmen bluntly dismissed all these arguments on the plea that Assam owed its prosperity and development to the planter community. In a division forced upon the house, all the nine British members (excluding the president and the vice-president) voted against, and seven out of the eight Indian members for the defeated resolution.[60]

Chief Commissioner Archdale Earle proposed an experiment in early 1918: a non-official chairman in one selected local board in each Valley. In the Surma Valley, the proposal was carried through. But in the Brahmaputra Valley, it had to be finally dropped because of alleged opposition from the concerned local board itself. By 1920, however, the government permitted five local boards – north Sylhet, Sunamganj, Dhubri, Goalpara and Barpeta – to each elect a non-official chairman. The permission was extended to all by 1921.[61]

The composition of local boards under the 1915 Act was not at all popular. The actual position of local boards in 1918 was exemplary. In that year, besides the *ex-officio* members, there were altogether 323 members in the nineteen local boards. Of them, 121 members were nominated, 82 elected by the planters, 82 elected by *gaon-burhas*, and the rest elected by voters of the headquarters town and the mercantile constituencies. *Ex-officio*, nominated and elected planter members together accounted for no less than two-thirds of the consolidated membership of all the nineteen local boards. In fifteen of them, this concentration was still higher.[62]

In a sense, the local boards were 'political seminaries' indeed! Through

---

[59] Chaliha's question on 13 March, *ALCP* (1917), No. 2, pp. 13–16 and the replies thereto; reply to Gohain–Barua, 13 March, *ALCP* (1916), No. 2, pp. 2–5; Barua's questions, 17 October, *ALCP* (1917), No. 3, *ALCP* (1917), No. 2, pp. 118 and 120.

[60] 12 January, *ALCP* (1918), No. 1, pp. 26–34.

[61] Edward's speech, 6 April, *ALCP* (1918), No. 3, pp. 155–56. Rao, *Hundred Years of Local Self-Government*, pp. 161–62.

[62] Ibid., p. 190.
    In this context, a provision of the Act authorizing local boards to levy a special tax on the land-holders for construction of light railways by a two-thirds majority was particularly significant, since planters were interested in the construction of such light railways.

their very way of functioning in Assam under close public watch in every sub-division, these boards laid bare the direct links of British monopoly capital with its colonial political system, and thus helped to raise the popular anti-imperialist consciousness to a higher level.

Assam's Growing Economy and Post-War Unrest
Economic Growth in the Province: 1905–20

After the short-term crisis in the tea industry was over by 1905, there was steady and continuous growth of the province's economy almost till the end of World War I. By then, one-fourth of the total acreage settled with planters had come under actual cultivation. The rate of growth of acreage under tea – as compared to the nineteenth-century record – had of course slowed down under the restrictive, monopolistic policy of the Indian Tea Association. Despite the introduction of fine plucking, however, both the quantity and total value of output went on increasing fast as a result of the rising crop yield per acre and the rising price trend in the world market. The total output of manufactured tea in Assam increased from 134 million lbs in 1901 to 200 million lbs in 1913, and to 234 million lbs by 1920. At the end of a decade of unbroken prosperity, the tea industry was found 'well-equipped to stand the shock of the war'. The summary of rupee company results published in the Indian Tea Association's Report for 1915 showed an average dividend of 24 per cent in Assam. Fairly high dividends persisted through the remaining war years.[63] About 12,00,000 coolie recruits were brought into Assam – the majority of them for Assam proper – between 1911 and 1931. Despite repatriation and other leakages warranting continuous replenishment of the labour force, a considerable number stayed back (see Appendix 10).

Railway investments were of even greater importance during this period. Assam acquired 439 miles of new tracks during the decade 1901–11. There was also expansion of ordinary peasant cultivation side by side. Ex-tea garden coolies were taking up waste lands for cultivation, mainly in the neighbourhood of tea gardens.[64] The extent of government lands taken up by such coolies for cultivation increased from 1,12,000 acres in 1906 to 2,62,000 acres by 1921. This was in addition to their tenant cultivation on tea garden lands. Even coolies on the tea garden muster rolls carried on some cultivation of ordinary crops. For example, in 1920–21 they held 1,00,728 acres of tea garden lands as tenants, 10,376 acres as tenants of other landlords and 15,847 acres as direct settlement-holders under the government, according to official sources. At the same time,

---

[63] P. Griffiths, *The History of the Indian Tea Industry* (London, 1967), pp. 170–71 and 144. E.A. Gait, *A History of Assam* (second edition, Calcutta/Simla, 1926), p. 356. A. Guha, 'Socio-Economic Change in Agrarian Assam', in M.K. Chaudhuri, ed., *Trends in Socio-Economic Change in India 1871–1961* (Simla, 1967), pp. 583 and 615–16.

[64] In Assam proper, 55,929 acres were settled with contract-expired plantation workers by the government till 1897–98. H. Cotton, *Colonization of Wastelands in the Province of Assam* (1899), p. 41.

land-hungry immigrant peasants from East Bengal, of whom an estimated 85 per cent were Muslims, started settling down in their thousands from about 1905 on the uninhabited riverine tracts. According to the birthplace data of the 1911 Census, immigrants from adjacent Bengal districts numbered only 51,000 in Goalpara district and 3,000 in Assam proper in that year. By 1921, altogether 1,41,000 East Bengal immigrants had settled down in Goalpara and 1,17,000 in Assam proper. The number of East Bengal settlers together with their children in the Brahmaputra Valley were estimated at 3,00,000 by the census authorities in 1921.[65]

Marwari traders and even Assamese moneylenders of Barpeta provided a substantial part of the necessary finance to enable the immigrant peasants to bring virgin soil under the plough. With their superior techniques of cultivation, these East Bengal peasants taught Assam how to grow jute, *mung* (a kind of pulse) and several other crops. For example, the acreage under jute in the Brahmaputra Valley increased, as a result of this great population movement, from a little less than 30,000 acres in 1905–06 to more than 1,06,000 acres in 1919–20.[66] A steady influx of Nepali graziers into the Brahmaputra Valley led to an increased cattle population and milk production. The number of Nepal-born persons in Assam increased from 21,000 in 1901 to 88,000 by 1931. All these factors were conducive to overall economic growth. Between 1900–01 and 1920–21, the population of Assam proper increased by 41 per cent. The comparable gross cropped acreage under ordinary cultivation increased 54 per cent and the acreage under tea 29 per cent.[67]

Besides, the belated impact of tea garden markets for farm products was found somewhat favourable to the local peasant economy. Under the changed conditions, ex-tea garden and immigrant Bengali wage labour were now available to an increasing extent in the neighbourhood of labour-short Assamese villages. This relative prosperity was not necessarily shared by all, and it was once more threatened by the post-war depression in the tea industry around 1920. Economic and political struggles broke out in both the Surma and Brahmaputra Valleys in the wake of World War I.

Conditions of the Peasantry

Nearly 4,000 Manipuri tenants of a zamindar of Pargana Bhanugachh (Bhanubil) in Sylhet rose in revolt and killed two of his employees in 1900. The Manipuri peasantry of the district, numbering some 20,000, raised a fund to defend the accused in the court and got them released.[68] Nothing more is known about the peasant struggles of the period under review here. Perhaps the peasant

---

[65] Ibid., pp. 582–84. Griffiths, *History of the Indian Tea Industry*, p. 304.
    Assam Labour Enquiry Committee Report (hereafter *ALECR) 1921–22* (Government of Assam, Arbuthnott Committee), p. 23.
[66] Guha, 'Socio-Economic Change in Agrarian Assam', Table 8, pp. 600–01.
[67] Ibid., p. 584 and Table 7a on p. 610.
[68] Gupta Chaudhury, ed., *Shriihatta Pratibha*, p. 19.

movement was not sufficiently widespread as to attract the attention of administrative reports and the press. At the time of resettlement in Assam proper in 1905, lessons of the 1892–93 land settlement were not forgotten by the administration. Hence the revised rates of assessment were, on the whole, relatively light and did not lead to any peasant unrest. The average rates were reportedly decreased by 2 per cent in Kamrup and increased by 6 per cent in Sibsagar, although the prices of farm products had considerably increased meanwhile.[69] In the absence of any specific tenancy legislation for the ryotwari areas, landlord–tenant relations there were being regulated by contract, local custom and the principles of natural justice.[70]

Under the circumstances, tenants' discontent was already becoming a cause for concern for the government, as well as for the enlightened middle class. During 1897–1917, a large number of memorials and petitions were presented to the Government of Assam by the zamindari tenants of Goalpara. These were occasionally supported by an agitation in the local press. On 15 November 1915, the Garo ryots of the Raja of Bijni sent a memorial to the government against acts of zamindari oppression. Both M.C. Barooah and Phanidhar Chaliha suggested that the Bengal Rent Law of 1869, in force then in the district of Goalpara under Government Notification No. 2080 of 9 May 1892, be suitably amended to ameliorate the conditions of the zamindari tenants.[71] Sonaram Sangma, a Garo headman, emerged as a leader of the tenants' struggle against the Bijni Raj, which was at its peak during 1907–16. There were simultaneous agitations in the zamindari estates of Gauripur, Mechpara and Parbatjoar as well. The tenants' agitation in Parbatjoar was led by Kalicharan Brahmo.[72]

The official concern for tenants' rights appeared to be conspicuously deeper than that of the Legislative Council itself, packed as it was with landholders. When the Bengal Tenancy Act, 1869, was being modified in Bengal in the early 1880s, a similar amending Bill was actually drafted in Assam. But as there was allegedly no articulated demand for it in the areas where sub-letting was rampant, the Bill was dropped. As early as 1913, a Bill on tenancy rights was again prepared for the district of Cachar, but it was also dropped in the absence of any organized public opinion there in its favour. So, it was under an

---

[69] R.K. Chaudhuri's speech on 19 September, *ALCP* (1928), Vol. 8, pp. 873–74.

[70] Reply to Chanda's question, 7 March, *ILCP* (1917), cited on 25 April, *ALCP* (1917), No. 2.

[71] Barooah's speech on the budget on 5 April 1911, *EBALCP* (1911), No. 3, p. 110. Chaliha's question on 13 March, *ALCP* (1916), No. 1. Editorial comment on the Bijni Raj, *Times of Assam* (Dibrugarh), 6 November 1915, cited by Chaliha, ibid. Also A.J. Laine, D.C. of Goalpara on Special Duty, *An Account of the Land Revenue System of Goalpara: with Criticisms of the Existing Rent Law and Suggestions for Its Amendments* (Shillong, 15 March 1917), pp. 1–35.

[72] Peasant agitation in Goalpara was directed both against zamindars and *jotdars*. Demands were raised for the issue of proper rent receipts, abolition of illegal cesses, grant of occupancy and transfer rights, and protection against rent enhancements. Ibid., pp. 4 and 21–25.

executive order that Sections 93–100 of the Bengal Tenancy Act, 1885, were extended to the district of Goalpara on 14 June 1916.[73] In 1916, the District Magistrate of Goalpara was appointed on special duty to report on the defects of the 1869 rent law, then in force in his district. His report, based on intensive local enquiries, was submitted in 1917 and accepted by the government. But the contemplated legislation was postponed pending a regular resurvey and resettlement. It appears from later discussions in the Reformed Council that the pressing need for a suitable rent law was cold-storaged. The government did not like antagonizing the zamindars and landlords.[74]

Conditions of Plantation Workers

As a result of the recommendations of the *Assam Labour Enquiry Report* of 1906, certain changes were introduced in the legal position of the plantation workers. The planter's private power to arrest his workers was abolished in 1908. The labour districts of Surma Valley and Lower Assam from 1908, and the remaining districts from 1915, ceased to be subjected to certain repugnant provisions of the Assam Labour and Emigration Act of 1901. A time-expired labourer, while still in Assam, could no longer be asked to sign another periodic contract under the Act of 1901. Under the Assam Labour and Emigration Act of 1915, further recruitment of tea labour through contractors and *arkattis* was made unlawful, and the tea garden *sardars* were made the sole recruiting agents. In response to the new situation, the organized tea interests came forward and formed the Tea Districts Labour Supply Association in 1917, to control and coordinate recruitment under the *sardari* system. By 1920 it had complete monopoly over the supply of labour to the tea industry.

But this could not put a stop to the practice of enticing time-expired labourers to a fresh contract under the Workmen's Breach of Contract Act, 1859. This, too, provided for imprisonment for a breach of contract. In fact this Act had already, to a large extent, replaced the Act of 1901, even before the latter's repeal by the Assam Labour and Emigration Act of 1915. Penal labour contracts therefore continued very much as before. It was not till 12 March 1920 that the 1859 Act was modified to eliminate the penal provision.[75]

The official reports regarding workers' conditions on the plantations were revealing. An example is the report for the year 1917–18. The estimated number of children of school-going age on the plantations was 2,00,000, but not even 2 per cent of them went to any kind of primary school. Wrote a European DPI of Assam in his report for the year:

> Education steadily goes back in the tea gardens. The number of schools has
> fallen from 149 with an enrolment of 3,615 to 142 with an enrolment of 2,888

---

[73] Ibid., p. 16.
[74] Speech by Laine on 21 March, *ALCP* (1933), Vol. 13, pp. 736–37.
[75] Griffiths, *History of the Indian Tea Industry*, pp. 281–92 and *ALECR*, 1921–22, p. 102.

(these are only lower primary schools). The decline is in the number of 'C' class schools – that is, schools maintained by the planters themselves.[76]

Apparently, the average monthly wage earnings of Rs 8.09 per man and Rs 7.59 per woman in 1917–18, including diet rations, subsistence allowance and bonus, showed a slight improvement as compared to 1905–06.[77] But in real terms much of it was eroded by the rising prices.

In many tea gardens, even the above rates were not available to the workers, as will be discussed later. Although the period from 1905–06 to the end of the war was, on the whole, one of prosperity for the planters, troubles did nevertheless take place in the gardens. Even during the war years, the semi-slave or semi-serf status of plantation workers remained essentially as deplorable as in the days of Cotton and Fuller. Himself a petty planter, besides being a lawyer–politician, N.C. Bardaloi reported in 1919:

> A tea garden is like a small town by itself, with the barracks for labourers and the stately bungalows of the managers and their assistants. Nobody, not even the policemen can enter this kingdom without the manager's permission. A manager may assault a labourer, insult him, and take girl after girl from the lines as his mistress, yet there will be none to dispute his action or authority. It is only at sometime when the manager's cruelty surpasses all bounds that the labourers set upon him and assault him. Had it not been for the fear of Britishers and the guns and pistols they possess, and the fact that at their beck and call all the constabulary and magistracy of the district would come over there and punish the labourer, rioting would have occurred pretty frequently in these small dominions.[78]

Economic Struggle: Intensification under War Strains

The period from 1905–06 to the end of World War I was one of high dividends, rising prices and relatively low wages. As the economic conditions of the labouring people tended to worsen, they were spontaneously drawn into partial struggles from time to time. According to official sources, out of 210 reported disputes between planters and their workers during the period from 1904–05 to 1920–21, as many as 141 were cases of 'rioting' and 'unlawful assembly'.[79] These often ended in violence. In 1917–18, planters or their assistants were directly assaulted by labourers in as many as six disputes. Moreover, 172 contract-bound workers deserted their jobs. Warrants of arrest were issued against forty-seven plantation workers in that year, but of them only twenty-six could be arrested.[80]

---

[76] DPI of Assam, *Report for 1917–18*, p. 21, quoted by N.C. Bardaloi in 'Condition of Labour in the Tea Gardens of Assam', *India* (London), 14 November 1919, p. 188.
[77] Official figures cited by Bardaloi, ibid., p. 187.
[78] Ibid., p. 187.
[79] *ALECR*, 1921–22, p. 89.
[80] Bardaloi, 'Condition of Labour', p. 187.

For a million-strong plantation labour population, these figures no doubt appear insignificant; but since relevant official reporting was deficient, these need not be taken at their face value. As the war was approaching its end, the discontent against rising prices culminated in an outburst of economic struggles and attacks on the established order in the plantations and elsewhere. It commenced with the queer phenomenon of a wave of *haat*-looting.

In early 1918, the forbidding price of even the 'standard cloth' on sale caused widespread resentment and spurred a wave of looting of rural *haats*. Having started in Bengal, the wave spread eastward, reached Sylhet and, finally, the western border of the Hailakandi sub-division of Cachar. S.P. Desai of the Indian Civil Service, then in charge of the sub-division, thought it to be the handiwork of anti-social elements and took stern measures, such as exemplary flogging of the culprits, to stop its further advance. Although he claimed success in dealing with the trouble, it was too complex a social phenomenon and far beyond the understanding of a young civilian. The same phenomenon manifested in Assam proper with equal vehemence in reaction to high prices of salt, cloth and foodstuff. Several persons were sentenced to long-term imprisonment there in this connection.[81]

A month-long strike at the Government Press in Shillong in August 1918 forced the *Assam Gazette* to cease its publication temporarily.[82] The next important strike was by the workers of the Dibru–Sadiya Railways in July 1920, on the demand for a 50 per cent wage increase. The ten-day-old strike was withdrawn only after a 30–35 per cent increase in all wages below Rs 100 per month was agreed upon. This led to a wave of lightning strikes in the neighbouring plantation area. Successive one-day strikes took place in three gardens of the British-owned Doomdooma Tea Company in Sibsagar, on 6, 15 and 25 September, in protest against bad and inadequate rice supplies. On the last-mentioned day, three Marwari shops were also looted by the strikers. Workers in two tea gardens of the Pabhojan Tea Company, also British-owned, struck work on 21 and 22 September, respectively. Their demand was an increase in their cash wages, from Rs 6 to Rs 8 per month, and also in the cheap grain supply, from 6 *seers* to 8 *seers* per week. The workers of Hookanguri garden of the British-owned Assam Frontier Company struck work on 27 September and raided a nearby weekly *haat* at Borhapjan for cloth and rice. In October there were swift and sudden strikes in three more British-owned tea gardens – Diamali, Monabari and Katonibari.[83]

The basic cause behind these strikes of 1920 was the failure of wages to

<hr>

81 S.P. Desai, 'My Thirty-Five Years in Assam', in K.L. Panjabi, ed., *The Civil Servant in India* (Bombay, 1965), p. 62. Author's interview with Desai at Poona on 4 April 1973. Speech by R.B. Das, 6 April, *ALCP* (1918), No. 4; Chaliha's speech, 13 March, *ALCP* (1919), No. 1, pp. 35–36.

82 *Times of Assam,* 18 August 1918 and also 31 August 1918, cited on 5 October, *ALCP* (1918), No. 4, p. 162.

83 Royal Commission on Labour of India, *Written Evidence, Vol. VI , Part I, Assam and Dooars* (London, 1930), p. 25. *ALECR, 1921–22*, pp. 6–8.

Declared Dividends of Select Tea Companies: 1918–20

Name of the Company	Dividends Declared		
	1918	*1919*	*1920*
Pabhojan Tea Co.	35%	35%	25%
Doomdooma Tea Co.	15%	15%	10%
Assam Co.	25%	25%	15%
Jorehaut Tea Co.	30%	15%	15%

Note: Declared dividends include also bonus to share-holders in the form of additional shares, if any.

Source: *Report of the Assam Labour Enquiry Committee, 1921–22*, pp. 6–7. H.A. Antrobus, *A History of the Assam Company, 1839–1953* (Edinburgh, 1957), p. 411; and *A History of the Jorehaut Tea Co. Ltd. 1859–1946* (London, 1948), p. 48.

respond to the enormous wartime rise in prices and profits. The declared dividends of British tea companies continued to be high, as can be seen from the examples given in the table above. Working conditions were still inhuman and primitive not only in the small tea gardens, but also in such big British-owned concerns as Monabari and Katonibari tea estates, which were under the managing agency of Mcleod and Co. The monthly rates of wages there remained basically unchanged for about a quarter of a century till 1920. In course of the year ending September 1920, there was a decline in the average earnings to the tune of Rs 2 in the case of men and Rs 4 in the case of women. Monthly cash wages were Rs 5 per man, Rs 4 per woman and Rs 2 to Rs 3 per working child in the month of October. Even these wages were frozen by the planters in settlement of rice advances made by them. New coolies were enticed into 939-day agreements for a petty cash advance of Rs 9 per head. Thus labour was reduced practically to a condition of servitude. It was but natural for the 2,857-strong labour force of Monabari to rise in revolt. Together with the workers of Katonibari, they struck work on 16 October, looted the tea garden shops and assaulted the supervisory Indian staff.[84]

The province-wide political upheaval that followed was an integral part of the national upsurge triggered by the call for Non-Cooperation. In the following and last section of this chapter, therefore, it is proposed to recapitulate the national political background and to show how the people of Assam responded to the situation. Up to 1920, the Congress had no branch or formally affiliated body in the Brahmaputra Valley, nor was there any organized trade union in either Valley. Delegates from both Valleys to the annual Congress sessions used to form a part of the Bengal delegation, as was required by the then Congress constitution.

[84] Ibid.

Towards a New Consciousness against Imperialism
Political Situation: India and Assam

The Indian middle classes showed a general desire to cooperate with the British cause in World War I rather than hamper it; and their aspirations were limited to what, in Bipin Chandra Pal's words, was 'an equal co-partnership with Great Britain and her colonies in the present association called the British Empire'.[85] The Indian attitude was one of bargaining for political reforms as a price for loyalty to the British Crown. Muslims in general resented Great Britain's unhelpful attitude towards Turkey which was constantly in trouble since 1911. And their younger sections, particularly those of the middle classes, were positively with the mainstream of Indian nationalism.

Economic unrest amongst the masses – the unrest in Assam has already been noted – spurred the all-India political leaders to forge a united stand for constitutional reforms. The Congress–League Pact of 1916, the reunion of the Moderates and Extremists within the Congress the same year, and the joint memorial submitted to the Viceroy in September 1916 by nineteen Imperial Legislative Councillors including M.A. Jinnah and K.K. Chanda – these created the preconditions of mounting pressure on the British government for post-war political concessions. Referring to the growing Hindu–Muslim unity on the demand for self-government, Ramanimohan Das, in his speech of 25 April 1917 in the Assam Legislative Council, said: 'India of today, having rendered such valuable services both in men and money during this disastrous war in Europe, reasonably deserves a recognition of all these and that in the shape of raised status in the British Empire like her sister colonies.'[86]

The spread of the Home Rule movement all over India, Gandhiji's appearance on the political scene in 1915 and his successful experiment of a peasant *satyagraha* in Champaran against British indigo planters, the irrepressible vitality of dedicated bands of terrorists in some provinces, President Wilson's general advocacy of the right of self-determination of nations and, above all, the far-reaching impact of the Russian Revolution – all these combined in 1917 to highlight India's demand for self-government.

To meet this rising tempo, the Government of India adopted a double-edged policy of appeasement and repression. On the one hand, increasing association of Indians in every branch of the administration as well as 'progressive realization of responsible government in India as an integral part of the British Empire' was declared, on 20 August 1917, as the goal of the British policy.[87] On the other hand, the notorious Sedition Committee, presided over by Justice Rowlatt, was appointed on 10 December 1917 to enquire into the revolutionary movement and make recommendations to deal with it effectively.

---

[85] Quoted by Mukherjee and Mukherjee, *Bipin Chandra Pal*, p. 111. The quotation is from Pal's speech on the eve of his return from England in 1911.

[86] Speech by Das, 25 April, *ALCP* (1917), No. 2, p. 123.

[87] Quoted by M. Jha, *Role of Central Legislature in the Freedom Struggle* (New Delhi, 1972), p. 38.

Montagu–Chelmsford Reforms and Rowlatt Acts

In such a political situation, alongside the people's increasing concern over rising prices, the middle-class leaders of the national movement vacillated between acceptance of the anticipated reforms and their total rejection. The *Joint Report on the Constitutional Reforms*, published on 8 July 1918, was called 'disappointing and unsatisfactory' by the Special Congress session at Bombay in August. Speaking on a resolution on the Reforms proposals in the Imperial Legislative Council on 6 September 1918, K.K. Chanda expressed his dissatisfaction with the *Report*, and pleaded for the appointment of a committee to examine and modify the scheme. He stressed that nothing short of executive responsibility to the Legislative Council would satisfy the Indian public.[88]

There was also a sharp reaction to the Rowlatt Committee's Report and the two Bills introduced in the legislature on the basis of its recommendations. Representative public meetings were held on 16, 19 and 23 February at Gauhati, Sylhet and Dibrugarh, respectively, demanding withdrawal of the Rowlatt Bills. While opposing the Criminal Law (Emergency Powers) Bill in the Imperial Legislative Council, Chanda said on 6 February 1919:

> Now my Lord, you are going to give us reforms and side by side with them, and in fact, even before them, you are going to give us this repressive law. Will that pave the ground for the reforms in this country? If this measure is passed it is bound to create considerable agitation.[89]

Almost all the 185 amendments moved by the opposition fell through. The Bill was passed into an Act, with all the thirty-five votes in its favour being cast by non-Indians and all the twenty votes against it by Indians.[90]

Gandhiji's initial favourable response to the Reforms turned into determined hostility to the Raj in the wake of the Rowlatt Report. After the passage of the Rowlatt Bills, he started an all-India *satyagraha* on 30 March 1919, in order to prepare the country for resistance to these lawless laws. A general *hartal* was called on 6 April, and this was to be followed by civil disobedience. Thus the 'considerable agitation' Chanda had warned against gathered momentum. The massacre of Jallianwala Bagh in its wake on 13 April 1919 raised the national anti-imperialist movement to a higher pitch. The Amritsar Congress of December 1919, however, still debated the tactics to be adopted vis-à-vis the Reforms. Tilak was in favour of responsive cooperation. Gandhiji proposed that the Congress should accept and not boycott the new Legislative Councils that were being established. The Congress finally ended with a compromise resolution in favour of giving a fair trial to the Reforms, as and when they were introduced.[91]

The Government of India Act, passed by the British Parliament on 23

[88] Speech by Chanda on 6 September, *ILCP*, April 1918–March 1919, pp. 113–15.
[89] Speech by Chanda on 6 February, ibid., p. 81.
[90] Ibid., p. 1192.
[91] Jha, *Role of Central Legislature*, p. 43.

December 1919, however, fell short of the Indian aspirations. On the international plane, the peace treaties of 1919 belied the war aims of the Allies and the 'fourteen points' of President Wilson. The dismemberment of Turkey roused hatred amongst the Muslim masses of India against British imperialism. In November 1919, Gandhiji was an active participant in the first Khilafat Conference. It was from this platform that he was soon to declare Non-Cooperation. The Moderates thought it wise to split from the National Congress so that they could pursue a softer line, and they set up the National Liberal Federation of India in 1920. Within this frame of all-India political developments, Assam politics were undergoing a rapid change.

Assam Demands Major Province Status

Edwin Montagu, Secretary of State for India, came to this country to ascertain the Indian opinion in November 1917. A delegation of the Assam Association pleaded before him in Calcutta on 6 December for the political advancement of Assam on par with the major provinces. A similar delegation from the Surma Valley, representing both Hindus and Muslims and led by Abdul Karim (1863–1943), a member of the Bengal Legislative Council by virtue of his domicile there, urged upon Montagu not only for constitutional advancement but also for the transfer of Sylhet to Bengal. In December 1917, the Sylhet Peoples' Association submitted a memorandum to the Viceroy and the Secretary of State for India for incorporation of their district into Bengal. The question was also brought up in the Imperial Legislative Council early in 1918 by Chanda, in the form of a general resolution recommending the constitution of linguistic provinces. It was, however, negatived.[92]

The re-emergence of the Sylhet question on the eve of the Montagu–Chelmsford Reforms was inevitable. At this time, the theory of self-determination of distinct nationalities was gaining ground not only abroad, but also in India – particularly Assam. The Calcutta Congress session of 1917 was attended by a thirteen-member delegation from the Brahmaputra Valley – all representing the Assam Association – and nearly forty delegates from the Surma Valley. It was at this session that the Congress, for the first time, conceded the principle of linguistic provinces for purposes of its own organization – in Andhra and Sind to begin with. The old demand for the transfer of Sylhet to Bengal attained new significance in this context. Chanda and others issued a public appeal in 1918 to renew the demand. The demand for a reconstituted Bengal on the basis of the linguistic principle was also voiced at the Bengal Provincial Conference in 1918.[93]

---

[92] Bardaloi's speech, 17 September, *ALCP* (1928), Vol. 8, pp. 802–03; Questions and Replies, 13 March, *ALCP* (1918), No. 2; Letter from Government of Assam, No. Pol. – 1917–5587, dated 30 October 1924, cited in January, *ALCP* (1926), Vol. 6, pp. 51–52; Chanda's speech, *ILCP*, April 1917 to March 1918, Vol. 56, pp. 492–95.

[93] Speech by B.N. Chaudhury, July, *ALCP* (1924), Vol. 4, pp. 568–70; and speech by K. Deb, ibid., p. 588.

Public opinion in the Brahmaputra Valley was no less in favour of the separation of Sylhet. But there were other aspects to this question. Would Assam, minus Sylhet, achieve major province status with a Governor heading it? The government gave it to understand that it would not, if Sylhet's demands had to be conceded. Besides, the separation of Sylhet would trigger off a similar agitation in Cachar and Goalpara for merger with Bengal. In fact, Raja Prabhatchandra Barua, one of the founders of the Assam Association, and other zamindars of Goalpara had by then already raised the demand.[94] Thus, a feeling of uncertainty and inter-Valley jealousy was cleverly brought into the situation by those at the helm of affairs. The Sylhet Reunion League was formed in 1920.

Fires Underground

The War Resolution that was passed by the Assam Legislative Council on 10 November 1914, pledging help to Britain, had unanimous support from all members – Indian as well as British. However, outside the Council, a handful of terrorists in the Surma Valley continued to pursue their secret, anti-imperialist activities.

Some of the political suspects of Sylhet were arrested and placed under internment or detention, but the grounds of such action by the government were not disclosed in most cases. Mukunda Das, Bengal's great exponent of *swadeshi* people's theatre, was served a notice in 1918 at Karimganj to leave Assam within twenty-four hours. Questions were raised on the floor of the Council about all such cases of curtailment of individual freedom.[95]

The continued repressive policy and the nervousness on the part of the rulers were but recognition of the fact that the fire of militant nationalism was still smouldering. However, the Assamese middle class, at least its dominant section that had access to the Council, had no sympathy for the creed of revolutionary violence. In December 1917, seven revolutionaries of Bengal were encircled on a hill near Gauhati in connection with the lone terrorist action in the Brahmaputra Valley. While five of them were arrested by the police on the spot, two escaped. Of the latter, Satish Pakrashi was later apprehended in Bengal, in February 1918. T.R. Phookan sided with the government while taking part in the tribunal set up to try the arrested persons. 'The citizens and the public of Gauhati cooperated in the arrest', gloated R.K. Chaudhuri (1889–1955) years later in the Reformed Council, 'and captured all the revolutionary party.'[96] Chaudhuri's com-

---

[94] Speech by B.N. Chaudhury, ibid., pp. 575–76. Speech by Bipin Chandra Ghosh, 7 January, *ALCP* (1926), Vol. 6, pp. 105–06.

[95] Anilchandra Datta, a school boy arrested at Calcutta in November 1916, Mohinimohan Ray-Burman of Habiganj, Bipinbehari De of north Sylhet, and others like Hemchandra Sen of Habiganj and his brother, were detained under orders of internment, outside their own home districts. R.B. Das's interpellation, 13 March, *ALCP* (1918), No. 1; interpellation by both, 6 April, *ALCP* (1918), No. 3; R.M. Das's interpellation, 5 October, *ALCP* (1918), No. 4. p. 10.

[96] Speech by R.K. Chaudhuri on the Assam Criminal Law Amendment Bill on 19 March, *ALCP* (1934), Vol. 14, pp. 683–84; and N.K. Guha, *Banglay Biplabvad* (in Bengali,

ment was perfectly in tune with the general attitude of the Council, as reflected earlier also in the speeches of Ramanimohan Das and Saadulla following the Maulvibazar bomb attack on a British officer on 27 March 1913.[97]

Post-War Radicalization: Towards Non-Cooperation

The talk of forthcoming reforms, under the pressure of multiform struggles of the people, roused political expectations in all quarters. In the Assam Legislative Council, Phanidhar Chaliha said on 6 April 1918: 'The proposed reform, when announced, will be found to be substantive and conceived in a liberal and generous spirit.'[98] However, with the publication on 8 July of the *Joint Report on the Indian Constitutional Reforms*, all these expectations were belied. Even the prospect of Assam being brought within the scope of the Reforms scheme with major province status appeared doubtful, in view of the opposition from the Chief Commissioner and the Surma Valley Branch of the ITA. At this critical juncture, in November 1918, the Assam Association took the bold step to send a hurried mission to London to plead for the case before the House of Lords' Selbourne Committee, which was then working out specific details of the principles laid down in the *Report*.[99]

Almost the same age, on the wrong side of forty, and in the same lucrative legal profession, T.R. Phookan was certainly a more colourful personality than N.C. Bardaloi. The latter had never been on the Council nor had he visited England until then. Phookan, on the other hand, had represented the land-holders of his Valley on the Assam Legislative Council ever since 1912, and was an eminent England-returned barrister. Even his family background was more impressive. He was the grandson of Juggoram Khargharia Phukan (1805–1838), a close associate of Raja Rammohan Ray and the first Assamese to learn English. Phookan's father-in-law, Parasuram Khaund, was also a man of influence. Nevertheless, it was Bardaloi, and not Phookan, who was chosen by the Assam Association to carry out its political mission in England. Prasannakumar Barua, Bardaloi's brother-in-law and a tea planter, accompanied him. The choice was no doubt significant. According to confidential police reports, Phookan – 'an undistinguished and moderate member' of the Assam Legislative Council – was losing ground to a fellow politician.[100] Bardaloi too was well-connected. He was the son of a high-ranking government servant, Rai Bahadur Madhavchandra

---

fourth edition, Calcutta, 1376 BS), p. 259. Also see Satish Pakrashi, *Agnidiner Katha* (in Bengali, Calcutta, ?), p. 78.

[97] Speeches by Das and Saadulla on 10 April, *ALCP* (1913), No. 5, pp. 74 and 80.

[98] Chaliha's speech, 6 April, *ALCP* (1918), No. 3, pp. 133–36.

[99] K.N. Dutt, *Landmarks of the Freedom Struggle in Assam* (Gauhati, 1958), pp. 42–43. 'Note by Sir N.D. Beatson Bell, dated 24 October 1918' in East India (Constitutional Reforms) – *Letter from the Government of India dated 5th March 1919 and Enclosures on the Questions Raised in the Report on Indian Constitutional Reforms* (Parliamentary Papers, London, 1919), p. 299.

[100] Confidential, Home (Pol.) 1924 – K.W., X to File No. 66 (NAI).

Bardaloi, and was married to the daughter of a pioneer Assamese planter – Malbhog Barua. N.C. Bardaloi presided over the annual conference of the Assam Association at Dibrugarh in 1915.

Phookan attended the Calcutta Congress of 1906, but for many years thereafter was not very active in politics outside the Council. Presiding over the annual conference of the Assam Association at Goalpara in December 1918, he, however, struck a note of radicalism in his speech. He said:

> The Government is bad and bureaucratic. . . . The English officers and English traders and also a section of Indians do not advocate popular government, and Lord Sydenham and others say that India is not fit for self-government. . . . If India is not fit for self-government even after a century and a half of British rule, who is responsible for this? It was the British rule which is to blame.[101]

The replacement of Ghanashyam Barua by Phookan as the new general secretary and the election of Chandranath Sharma (1889–1922) as one of the assistant secretaries at this session indicated the trend of radicalization within the Assamese middle class. Phookan ceased to attend the Council and resigned from its membership early in 1919. The fourth annual session of the Assam Chhatra Sanmilan at Tezpur the same year resolved to sponsor the use of *swadeshi* in place of foreign goods.[102] The same year also saw the publication of a new periodical, *Chetana*, giving vent to the new mood.

Bardaloi presented the case for Assam before the Joint Committee of the House of Lords on 25 August 1919 in a manner consistent with the Congress stand. This was noted by Congressmen like S. Satyamurti and Bipin Chandra Pal.[103] The Bardaloi mission to England was crowned with success and Assam eventually emerged as a full-fledged Governor's province under the Government of India Act of 23 December 1919. Sylhet, of course, remained with Assam as before. The Assam Legislative Council unanimously adopted Ghanashyam Barua's motion on 13 March 1920 to tender 'dutiful homage', 'loyal devotion' and 'profound gratefulness' for the Gracious Royal Proclamation on the Reforms.[104]

People outside the Council – even N.C. Bardaloi himself – were not so

---

[101] Quoted by Dutt, *Landmarks of the Freedom Struggle in Assam*, pp. 38–39. The Goalpara session was attended by some 600 people, according to 'Assam Police Abstract of Intelligence 1917', in the Office of the Editor of the History of Freedom Movement (hereafter OEHFM) Government of Assam (Gauhati).

[102] Dutt, *Landmarks of the Freedom Struggle in Assam*, pp. 40 and 47.

[103] Bipin Chandra Pal's letter dated London, 23 October 1919, was published in the *Amrita Bazar Patrika*. In his letter of 28 October 1919 from London to *Asam Bilasinii*, an Assamese student, Bidyananda Duara, also suggested that the separate representation made by the Assam Mission in no way weakened the overall Congress stand, since it had little affinity with the approach of the moderates.

For details and the citations, see O.K. Das, '*Karmabiir* Bardaloi's Sowanranat', in C. Saikia, comp., *Smritigrantha: Nabiincandra Bardaloi* (in Assamese, Gauhati, 1975), pp. 87–89.

[104] 13 March, *ALCP* (1920), No. 1, pp. 51–54.

happy with the offer of dyarchy, particularly over the issue of communal representation. There was country-wide indignation against the Raj after the Punjab atrocities and the massacre at Jallianwala Bagh. On his return from London, Bardaloi got himself increasingly involved in the thick of politics and was elected general secretary of the Assam Association at its Barpeta session (1919). The careers of both Phookan and Bardaloi, eventful as they were after World War I, are illustrative of the vacillating, yet, on the whole, democratic role of the Assamese middle class in the inter-war period.

Bardaloi's father attained notoriety in the nineteenth century as a faithful government servant for putting down the *raij mels* of 1893–94 with a strong hand, and for giving evidence in support of the official opium policy before the Royal Commission on Opium in (1893).[105] N.C. Bardaloi had to make ample amends in due course for all those indiscreet actions of his father. While practising in the Calcutta High Court during World War I, he got himself enrolled in the Bengal Light Horse with a view, in his own words, 'to defend my home and die fighting for the glorious British Empire'. He presided over the annual session of the Assam Association in 1915 and attended the Calcutta Congress of 1917 as a delegate. Since then he was active as a moderate politician. During his few months' sojourn in England, he addressed several labour meetings and published an article exposing the inhuman treatment of labour by British planters in Assam. This he did in order to rouse the British public opinion against the evil. Years later he narrated in a memorable speech in the Assam Legislative Council, how he was transformed into an anti-imperialist agitator. He said:

> After I went to get Reforms, after I fought hard for the Reforms and after I had contributed something to get the Reforms for Assam, I returned to India only to see the blood-stained field of Jalliana Bagh and the callous indifference of our rulers. I travelled to that place – I walked on the field and while there I knelt down and said 'Oh, God! If this is what has come out of our being partners of the same Empire then save me from this Empire.' A man who was a faithful ally and a faithful and loyal subject of this British Government, on that day his heart was torn to pieces and his feelings were outraged. Then an agitation was set afoot throughout the country.[106]

The process of disillusionment of Bardaloi and, for that matter, of Phookan, was not exactly as sudden and dramatic in real life as depicted above. The local leadership of Assam came under the spell of Gandhiji's influence through a hard and fairly prolonged experience. Gandhi's stand on linguistic provinces, particularly, appears to have been a factor that attracted them.

The political struggle started with an organized attempt for Hindu–Muslim

---

[105] Evidence of M. Bardaloi on 29 December 1893, *Royal Commission on Opium*, 1893, Vol. 2 (London, 1894), pp. 302–05. R.K. Chaudhuri's speech on 19 September, *ALCP* (1928), Vol. 8, pp. 873–74.

[106] N.C. Bardaloi's speech on 3 April, *ALCP* (1928), Vol. 8, pp. 259–60.

unity. Bardaloi, Phookan and others called a Khilafat meeting at Gauhati on 19 March 1920. After Tilak's death, the condolence meeting of the Gauhati public on 5 August 1920 passed a resolution urging the people to boycott the daily *Statesman* (Calcutta) – a mouthpiece of British capital – for its insulting comment on the departed.[107] The programme of Council Boycott was first adopted by the Central Khilafat Committee and Gandhiji as early as March 1920. In May, however, Gandhiji envisaged people voting in the elections for candidates who supported *swadeshi*, the use of vernacular languages in the administration, the formation of linguistic provinces and Hindu–Muslim unity. He did not come out clearly in favour of an active poll boycott until the end of June 1920. It was in the same month that an all-party conference met at Allahabad and approved of a boycott of schools, colleges and law courts. On 31 August 1920, the All-India Khilafat Committee launched its Non-Cooperation movement.[108] By September, many Assam Association leaders were participating in activities preparatory to the Non-Cooperation movement, although they had differences over the issue of its proper scope and jurisdiction.

Assam was thus slowly drawn into the orbit of the new, action-oriented, all-India political agitation. At the Special Congress at Calcutta during 4–9 September 1920, the entire Assam Association delegation was, according to Bardaloi, opposed to Gandhiji's draft resolution on the Non-Cooperation issue.[109] However, the biographer of Chandranath Sharma states that only a minority of the Assam delegates led by Bardaloi were opposed to the draft resolution as such, and that Sharma, together with a majority of the Assam delegates – mostly young people like him, sided with Gandhiji.[110]

In any case, the Assam delegation abstained from voting on the issue at Calcutta.[111] On return to Assam, the old guard slowly gave way to Sharma's tactful persuasion in favour of complete Non-Cooperation. On 4 October 1920, the Gauhati Municipality dropped its proposal to present an address to the Viceroy, as a majority of the rate-payers and municipal commissioners, under Phookan's leadership, opposed it. A special session of the Assam Association was held at Gauhati on 11 October 1920 to discuss the Congress programme of Non-Cooperation, with Faiznur Ali (1877–1962) in the chair. Three of the objectives highlighted in the programme – an organized boycott of the sale of all excisable

---

107 'History Sheet of Tarun Ram Phookan', pp. 1–6 in Confidential Home (Pol.), 1924.
108 Judith M. Brown, *Gandhiji's Rise to Power: Indian Politics 1915–1922* (Cambridge, 1972), p. 221.
109 N.C. Bardaloi's statement appended to *ACOER*, (Jorhat, 1925), pp. 54–57.
110 Dandinath Kalita, *Karmmabir Candranath* (in Assamese, Tezpur, 1846 *saka*), p. 59. It appears clearly from police reports that until a decision was firmly taken on the matter by the Assam Association on 11 October 1920, Chandranath Sharma was in favour of Council entry. *Assam Police Abstract of Intelligence 1920*, No. 722: Assam S.B., 30 October 1920 (transcript in OEHFM, Government of Assam, Gauhati).
111 Extract from 'My Reminiscences' by Prasanna Kumar Barua in OEHFM, Government of Assam (Gauhati).

goods, an active promotion of handspun yarn and other *swadeshi* goods, and a boycott of the forthcoming elections to the Councils – were to be given effect to immediately. The action on the withdrawal of boys and girls from government-supported schools and colleges, and the suspension of practice in law courts by lawyers, was to be gradual. The entire programme was adopted by a majority decision in the face of opposition from the Moderates. Chandranath Sharma and a few others favoured the idea of entering the Councils with a view to obstruct their proceedings. But no modification was made in the resolution to accommodate their views. Sharma, Ambikagiri Raychaudhury and Trigunacharan Barua were of the opinion that the boycott of schools, colleges and law courts should also start immediately. But Bardaloi, Phookan and other leaders did not agree. A resolution calling for an immediate boycott of schools and colleges, when pressed by Trigunacharan Barua, was in fact defeated.[112]

Unlike the question of Council entry, the matter did not end there. After a couple of months, when the Association met for its annual conference at Tezpur in December, it had to appoint a sub-committee to find out those behind the boycott of the Mangaldai Government High School, where the students were already on strike.[113]

Bardaloi delivered his first Non-Cooperation lecture at the village of Belsor in November 1920, before a gathering of about 500 people. After that, a band of volunteers, under the leadership of Bardaloi and Phookan, rapidly organized meetings all over Kamrup; within a month, foreign cigarettes reportedly disappeared from the areas. The seventeenth annual conference of the Assam Association, which met at Tezpur in December 1920 with Prasannakumar Barua in the chair, ratified the Gauhati decision on Non-Cooperation. Moderates and loyalists like Gangagovinda Phukan, Ghanashyam Barua and Kamakhyaram Barua (1883–1965) had by then left the Association and its branches. The Tezpur session was virtually converted into a Congress forum; its *pandal* gates were named after national leaders like Tilak, Gandhi and Shaukat Ali. Nationalization of the Assam Association was thus complete by the end of 1920.[114] The Assam Valley Moslem Association, which met at Jorhat with Debeswar Sharma in the chair on 26 October 1920, also unanimously passed a resolution recommending gradual implementation of the Non-Cooperation programme and

---

[112] Confidential, Home (Pol.) 1924, and *Assam Police Abstract of Intelligence 1920*, No. 722, supplemented by Bardaloi's statement in *ACOER* (Jorhat, 1925).

[113] *Assam Police Abstract of Intelligence 1921*, No. 58: Darrang, 8 January 1921.

The schoolboys' strike at Mangaldai was soon followed up by the resignation of their teacher, Dinanath Sharma, from government service, and by the founding of a national school. Thus it was Mangaldai, more a village than a town, that triggered large-scale student participation in the Non-Cooperation movement of Assam. For details, see Tankeswar Sharma's *Swadhiinata Samgramat Mangaldai* in Barua *et al.*, eds, *Sharatcandra Goswamür Camu Jüvanü*, pp. 360–61.

[114] Same as footnotes 112 and 113. Also Dutt, *Landmarks of the Freedom Struggle in Assam*, pp. 47–49.

boycott of the Councils, after Tafazzal Hossain, a tea planter, and two others had walked out.[115]

Meanwhile, a delegation representing the Assam Association and led by Bardaloi attended the Nagpur Congress. It was there that Bardaloi, like C.R. Das, changed his view and gave support to the Non-Cooperation Resolution. At Nagpur, it was also decided to organize the Congress henceforth on the basis of linguistic provinces. The Congress entrusted Bardaloi, among others, to take part in drafting its new constitution. A number of college students of Gauhati simultaneously attended the All-India Students' Conference, also held at Nagpur. Inspired by the new action-oriented mass politics of Gandhiji, they returned to Assam, ahead of Bardaloi, and put their college in ferment in January 1921. They found in Chandranath Sharma a new leader of a different type. This young Brahmin lawyer, hailing from a poor rural family of Tezpur, had no pretence of any upper-class background but for his caste. 'Circumstances compelled me', said Bardaloi later, with hindsight, 'to call out boys from the college, only those who would work for the country and go to jail.'[116] Thus started the Non-Co-operation movement in the Brahmaputra Valley.

Only a brief mention may be made here to the course of developments in the Surma Valley. K.K. Chanda presided over the politically tense Special Session of the Bengal Provincial Conference in 1919, in which a large delegation from the Surma Valley participated. The Khilafatists were already active in the Valley. An armed dacoity in the house of a big moneylender at Patabuka in Sylhet on 20 October 1920 was suspected by the government to have been committed by some fanatic Muslims connected with this movement.[117]

On 19–20 September 1920, the fifth Surma Valley Political Conference, with Abdul Karim in the chair, passed *inter alia* a long resolution moved by Khirodechandra Deb (1893–1937). It was clearly directed against the British planters and merchants, in view of their systematic opposition to national aspirations, their tyranny over Indian employees and their complete identification with the administration. As a first step towards complete, non-violent Non-Cooperation with British planters and merchants, the conference recommended the following programme of action:

   (i) refusal to serve under British planters and merchants;
   (ii) gradual withdrawal of those who are already in such service;
   (iii) non-acceptance of briefs by lawyers from aforesaid non-official Britishers;
   (iv) refusal on the part of the people to grant or renew leases of land to them;
   (v) immediate withdrawal from any kind of association with them, and abstention from all gatherings to which they are invited.

---

[115] *Assam Police Abstract of Intelligence 1920*, No. 759: Sibsagar, 30–10–20 in the OEHFM, Government of Assam (Gauhati).

[116] Bardaloi's statement, *ACOER*, (Jorhat, 1925), pp. 54–57; *Assam Police Abstract of Intelligence 1921*, No. 34: Gauhati, 4 January 1921 and No. 97: Assam S.B., 29 January 1921 (transcripts in the OEHFM, Government of Assam, Gauhati).

[117] Patabuka dacoity case, cited in 6 February, *ALCP* (1922), Vol. 2, pp. 48–49, 83–84.

This resolution, as will be seen in the next chapter, apparently made a deep impression on the plantation labour of the Valley, but not before February 1921. The conference also decided against presenting any address to the Viceroy on the issue of Sylhet's reunion with Bengal. The Sylhet Reunion League, formed for this purpose in 1920, was dissolved.[118]

With the province in political ferment, the general election held for the Reformed Council in November 1920 proved to be an anti-climax. All the hills areas, except for the urban constituency in Shillong, had been excluded from the 1919 Reforms. The registered voters, numbering 203,191, constituted less than 3 per cent of the province's 7 million population in its enfranchised districts. All those who paid a land tax of Rs 15 in Assam proper or a Chaukidari tax of Re. 1 in Goalpara and the Surma Valley were entitled to vote. At first, the nationalists were of a mind to seriously go to the polls. In a private letter to a friend, even a radical like Chandranath Sharma wrote on 7 May 1920:

> My honest and sincere opinion is that if I can't go to the Reformed Council much harm will be done to Assam, particularly its peasant community. . . . Something has to be done by the Government regarding the foreign settlers. Otherwise, the country will have to face very bad days and a miserable situation; our national identity will disappear.[119]

The Assam Association was rather late in arriving at a firm decision on the issue of boycotting the elections. Nevertheless, when the decision was taken, the response was spectacular. Kaliram Barman withdrew his nomination paper after scrutiny. Kumudram Bora, although already elected from Mangaldai, never attended the Council, and either resigned or allowed his membership to lapse. Everywhere, Congressmen and other nationalists carried on a peaceful poll boycott campaign. As a result, only 33,352 votes, or less than a quarter of the voters in the twenty-one contested constituencies, participated in the poll. A further breakdown of the figures suggests that urban Hindus polled nearly 50 per cent, while their rural counterparts polled 24.7 per cent. The response of the voters for the Indian Legislative Assembly was even poorer, for lack of a keen contest. Out of 19,503 registered voters for the Assembly, only 2,308 or less than 12 per cent actually voted. The elections appeared to be a big joke. Devicharan Barua, Girishchandra Nag, Amjad Ali and one Britisher represented Assam on India's first Legislative Assembly. Another Britisher had the honour of being the first and sole representative of the people of this province in the Indian Council of State.[120]

---

118 Resolution quoted in full, 27 September, *ALCP* (1921) Vol. 1, pp. 881–84; *ALECR*, 1921–22, p. 19.

119 Sharma's letter to Lochan Barua, as reproduced by Kalita, *Karmmabir Condranath*, Appendix. Translation ours. The reference to 'foreign settlers' is obviously to the large-scale immigration from Bengal into the province.

120 22 February, *ALCP* (1921), Vol. I, pp. 11–13. *India in 1920: A Report Prepared for Presentation to Parliament* (Calcutta, 1921), Appendix III, p. 48; *Return Showing the Results of Election in India*, PP. cmd 1261 (London, 1921), p. 2.

CHAPTER FOUR

Non-Cooperation and Dyarchy on Trial: 1921–23

Gathering of the Storm

Flag Unfurled: Students Join Lawyers

On return from Nagpur, Kanakchandra Sharma (1883–1951) addressed a series of meetings in the district of Nowgong, and others in the districts of Lakhimpur and Kamrup, during the early months of 1921. The agitation centred round the propagation of *swadeshi*, temperance, Khilafat and the exposure of colonial misrule. Within a single fortnight in February, more than thirty mass meetings attended by thousands of people were held in Kamrup alone. These were addressed by local leaders of the movement. T.R. Phookan spoke at Maroa (Kamrup) on 26 February on the British ill-treatment of the Turkish Sultan. He spoke again on 27 February at Hajo. In a five-hour-long meeting held at Gauhati on 24 February, presided over by M. Tayyebulla (1894–1966), a number of sweepers, cobblers, washermen, carters and labourers swore to abstain from liquor before a reported gathering of 4,000 people. The Provincial Khilafat Committee was formed at Gauhati on 10 April 1921. In the same month, with the aid of Phookan's casting vote from the chair, the Gauhati Municipal Board threw out the proposal to present a civic address to the Governor.[1]

Started in the last quarter of 1920, the movement made a great leap forward and underwent a qualitative change when the student community was roused to action in January 1921. At a public meeting in Gauhati on 2 January 1921 chaired by Phookan, student delegates returning from Nagpur and the young lawyer Chandranath Sharma implored students to come out of their schools and colleges to work for the country. Sharma himself suspended his legal practice with effect from 7 January to respond actively to Gandhiji's call. Lakshmidhar Sharma (1899–1934), then a post-graduate and law student at Calcutta, as well as other student leaders like Bidyadhar Sharma who had been to Nagpur, played

---

[1] Collated from the following sources: N.C. Bardaloi's statement appended to *Assam Congress Opium Enquiry Report* (hereafter *ACOER*) (Jorhat, 1925), pp. 54–57; *The Mussalman* (Calcutta), 25 February 1921; Confidential Home Department (Pol.), 1924, K.W., X to File No. 66 (National Archives of India; hereafter NAI). The last-mentioned source, a dossier, also contains a six-page printed 'History-Sheet on Tarun Ram Phookan'.

a significant role in drawing students into the fold of Non-Cooperation. Under the circumstances, T.R. Phookan, N.C. Bardaloi and Kuladhar Chaliha – the three top leaders who had earlier opposed the student participation – reluctantly conceded that those who were determined to work for the country and go to jails could boycott their classes, but strikes *en masse* in schools and colleges should be avoided.[2] Students of Cotton College decided in favour of the boycott call on 17 January and went on strike for an indefinite period with effect from 20 January 1921.[3]

Students came out on the streets all over Assam in large numbers, in that first flush of enthusiasm. After a month or so, however, most of them returned to their classes. In the two colleges of the Brahmaputra Valley, only thirty-eight students were in fact found deliberately absent from their classes on 16 February. The involvement of school children continued, however, on a larger scale. It was reported in the press that half of the student population of Kamrup was still out of class towards the end of February. According to the Education Minister, the number of students who withdrew from colleges and government-controlled high schools was between 9 and 10 per cent of the enrolment at the height of the movement.[4] The Director of Public Instruction later estimated that, of those who had joined the movement, some 15,000 never returned to their classes.[5] Thus there emerged a sizeable core of dedicated student volunteers who moved out to spread Gandhiji's message of '*swaraj* in a year'.

The principle of linguistic provinces for the future Congress organization had been firmly adopted at Nagpur in 1920 and N.C. Bardaloi was elected there as the first Assamese member of the All India Congress Committee (AICC). But under the old Congress constitution, his seat on this body was still from the Bengal quota. The new Congress constitution provided for the formation of the Assam Provincial Congress Committee (APCC) for the Assamese-speaking area, that is, the Brahmaputra Valley, with its headquarters at Gauhati. The Surma Valley was to remain, as before, under the jurisdiction of the Bengal Provincial Congress. In January 1921, the Congress Working Committee (CWC) passed a resolution allocating five AICC seats to the Assam Provincial Congress.[6]

---

[2] Collated from: Bardaloi's statement, *ACOER*, pp. 54–57; M. Tayyebulla, *Karagarar Cithi* (in Assamese, Gauhati, 1962), pp. 269–70; extract from 'Bidyadhar Sharma's Diary' appended to B. Sharma, *Congressar Kanchiali Ra'dat* (in Assamese, Gauhati, 1959), pp. 295–97.

[3] For details of the agitation among Cotton College students, see *Assam Police Abstract of Intelligence 1921*, No. 34: Gauhati, 4 January, No. 56: Assam S.B., 15 January and No. 97: Assam S.B., 29 January (transcripts in the Office of the Editor of the History of Freedom Movement [hereafter OEHFM], Government of Assam, Gauhati).

[4] *The Mussalman*, 25 February 1921; Minister's replies to R.N. Chaudhuri, 24 March, *Assam Legislative Council Proceedings* (hereafter *ALCP*) (1921), Vol. 1, p. 77 and to Munawar Ali, 29 March, ibid., pp. 117–18; 'Bidyadhar Sharma's Diary', pp. 295–97.

[5] Speech by J. Cunningham, 10 September, *ALCP* (1930), Vol. 10, p. 743.

[6] Anonymous, comp., *Indian National Congress 1920–23* (Allahabad, 1924), p. 41; J.S. Sharma, *India's Struggle for Freedom: Select Documents and Sources* (Delhi, 1965),

The Assam Association, which had changed its name and had been virtually turned into a Congress platform at its Tezpur session,[7] had a special and its last meeting at Jorhat, with Chhabilal Upadhyay in the chair, in April 1921. Besides condemning the recent evictions of Nepali graziers from the Kaziranga Forest Reserves and the police atrocities on them, the meeting also discussed the Non-Cooperation programme and organizational matters.[8] This was followed by a representative provincial meeting of all Congress supporters at Gauhati on 5 June 1921, to elect the first office-bearers of the Assam Provincial Congress. Barring a few, none of the lawyer leaders, not even Bardaloi and Phookan, had yet suspended their legal practice and, hence, could not be strictly termed as Non-Cooperators. As the consensus of the meeting was not in favour of electing a practising lawyer as president of the APCC, Phookan had to step down from the contest. He had already resigned his part-time lectureship in the Law College in April, but was not yet prepared to leave his profession. Kuladhar Chaliha, the other aspirant for presidentship, established his *bonafides* by declaring that he had suspended his practice the day before. He was therefore unanimously elected president.[9] Son of Rai Bahadur Phanidhar Chaliha, he had plantation and landed interests to fall back upon for an income. Continuance of legal practice, however, did not come in the way of N.C. Bardaloi's unanimous election as the general secretary.

Gandhiji Ignites

Prominent Congressmen of Assam thereafter attended the Bombay session of the AICC (July 1921). Invited by them to visit Assam, Gandhiji, along with Shaukat Ali and Mohammed Ali, arrived at Gauhati on 18 August on a ten-day provincial tour. In meetings held at Gauhati, Tezpur, Nowgong, Jorhat, Dibrugarh, Silchar and Sylhet, bonfires were made of heaps of foreign cloth in a demonstrative manner before thousands of onlookers. These had a great impact on the sellers of foreign cloth and yarn. At Silchar, for example, all the cloth merchants, with the exception of three, met Gandhiji and signed the pledge for boycott of foreign cloth. The cloth merchants of Lakhipur, in the neighbourhood,

---

Vol. 3, p. 870; *Report of the Thirty fifth Session of the Indian National Congress, 26–31 December 1920* (Nagpur, n. d.), Appendix B, p. 2.

[7] The name of the association was changed to 'Assam National Assembly' and its declared object now was to work for the attainment of *swaraj* by all legitimate means and to adopt such measures as to effectively educate the people to that end. *Assam Police Abstract of Intelligence 1921*, No. 58: Darrang, 8 January.

[8] Krishnanath Sharma, *Krishna Sharmar Diary* (in Assamese, Gauhati, 1972), p. 78. The political conference, as mentioned by Sharma, was indeed the special session of the Assam Association held at Jorhat in April 1921. Also see 'Bidyadhar Sharma's Diary', p. 296. A mention of the same meeting was made by O.K. Das in an interview at Gauhati on 10 July 1973, followed by correspondence.

[9] Confidential Home (Pol.), 1924; P. Barthakur, *Swadhiinata Ranar Samsparshat* (in Assamese, Dibrugarh, 1968), pp. 32–34; 'Bidyadhar Sharma's diary', p. 297.

According to the police sources, Phookan's income from landed interests then hardly exceeded Rs 700 or so per annum.

did not come in person, but they too sent in their pledge. Gandhiji's second Tezpur meeting on 22 August – the first having been held on the preceding day – was attended by a large number of tea garden coolies who came from the Rangapara circle by a special train.[10]

It was on Gandhiji's advice that the agitation in the Brahmaputra Valley was given a primarily anti-opium orientation. Full of enthusiasm, hundreds of young men took up the cause of temperance and preached against opium, liquor, *ganja* and other drug habits. They held meetings and stood outside excise shops, imploring people not to buy drugs. The movement gathered momentum during the three months after Gandhiji's departure. Gandhiji was later happy to note that by the end of September, out of the 78 Assamese lawyers in the province, fifteen, including N.C. Bardaloi and M. Tayyebullah, had suspended their practice. A majority of the Assamese pleaders and their clerks, according to a police intelligence report, also suspended their practice in course of the movement. On 2 September 1921, the Gauhati Town Congress Committee was formed with Phookan as president. On 31 October, Phookan, Kuladhar Chaliha, Faiznur Ali and Rajanikanta Barua (1880–1942) left for Delhi to attend the AICC meeting; they returned on 13 November. Meanwhile, thousands of spinning wheels were distributed and peaceful picketing of opium and liquor shops was continued. The Congress struck its organizational roots by setting up offices in every sub-division all over the Assam plains. In the Surma Valley, two of the earliest to suspend law practice were K.K. Chanda and Shyamacharan Dev of Cachar.[11] In June 1921, while on a tour of his home district, Sylhet, one of the ministers, Syed Abdul Mazid (1872–1922), was immensely impressed by the sweep and grip of the movement.[12]

Until November 1921, the government put no great hindrance to restrict the peaceful activities of Congress volunteers except that they were watched by the police wherever they went. The officials tried to counteract the Congress efforts by organizing leagues against Non-Cooperation and counter-propaganda. On 24 September, Phookan addressed a meeting at Dhubri on the Khilafat issue which was attended by 800 people, according to a police confidential report. The next day, he was served with an order under Section 144 of the Indian Penal Code (IPC), not to hold meetings within seven miles of the towns of Dhubri, Gauripur, Goalpara and Sapatgram. Towards the end of November, however, there was a sudden turn in this situation of peaceful coexistence.[13] A severe and brutal policy

---

[10] 'History-Sheet of Tarun Ram Phookan'; C. Saikia, ed., *Asamat Mahatma* (in Assamese, Gauhati, 1969), p. 50; Silchar news in *The Mussalman*, 2 September 1921.

[11] *ACOER*, pp. 27–28; M.K. Gandhi, 'Lovely Assam', *Young India*, 1 September 1921, cited in Saikia, ed., *Asamat Mahatma*, p. 65; 'History-Sheet of Tarun Ram Phookan'; Tayyebulla, *Karagarar Cithi*, pp. 48–49.

[12] See Judith M. Brown, *Gandhiji's Rise to Power: Indian Politics 1915–1922* (Cambridge, 1972), p. 322.

[13] T. Chaliha's speech, September, *ALCP* (1924), Vol. 4, pp. 471–72; *ACOER*, pp. 27–28; Confidential Home (Pol.), 1924.

of repression, as in the case of the labour struggles, was let loose upon the Congress agitators.

Awakening of Toilers

Storm in the Tea Pot

Even as the Non-Cooperation movement was progressing, the export economy of Assam was caught in a deep crisis because of a slump in the tea industry and an unfavourable rate of exchange. There was a sharp fall in labour earnings and an increase in unemployment. Sporadic lightning strikes, not necessarily non-violent in character, were breaking out here and there against the planters' 'labour squeeze' policy throughout the latter half of 1920 and the year 1921.

It was in September 1920 that the Surma Valley Political Conference had declared total, non-violent Non-Cooperation against the British merchants and planters as one of the goals of the movement, and advised people to withdraw gradually from service under them. What Congressmen meant by gradual withdrawal from service was not, of course, 'strikes' as understood by labour. Nothing therefore came out of this resolution, although individual Congressmen here and there tried to act in this spirit. For example, Abdul Matin Chaudhury (1895–1948), a young lawyer and Congressman (later a Muslim League leader), organized a Khansama Union at Shillong, reportedly with the motive of causing inconvenience to the British residents. On 6 June 1921 he was expelled from the district concerned and thus ended the earliest attempt in Assam to form a trade union.[14]

In Sylhet and Cachar, the tea garden workers became restive once more from the beginning of 1921, because of persistent economic hardships. Their frequent contacts with the Congress/Khilafat volunteers at *haats* and bazaars encouraged them to come out in action in their own way against the common enemy. In February, three Hindi-speaking emissaries of the Non-Cooperation movement arrived at Srimangal and addressed meetings attended *inter alia* by groups of labour from the surrounding tea gardens. Similar meetings were held in Longai Valley in March and April. According to the official thinking, these meetings made a deep impression on the labour and resulted in a prolonged strike in the Lungla Tea Estate.[15]

During the first half of 1921, the sensational Khoreal shooting case laid bare the racist character of the planter Raj. A white planter who wanted to live with a coolie girl, on being refused, shot her father with a revolver, and he was

---

[14] Khaleque Chaudhuri's question, *ALCP* (1921), Vol. 1, pp. 847–48.

   Son of a police sub-inspector, Chaudhury – an Aligarh graduate – had his law degree from Calcutta. He sat for the ICS examination, but was not accepted. Pol. B, November 1921, No. 262–269 (Chief Secretary, Assam to Government of India, 23 August 1921). Chaudhury underwent a term of imprisonment as a Khilafatist.

[15] *Assam Labour Enquiry Committee Report* (hereafter *ALECR*) *1921–22*, pp. 9, 14 and 19.

acquitted by the lower court. The Calcutta High Court set aside the proceedings and ordered a retrial. However, the accused was once again acquitted by the jury on a verdict of eight to one. What was striking was that out of the nine jurors, eight were Europeans. The wide publicity given to this case during the months March to June might have been an additional factor contributing to the growing labour unrest in the Surma Valley.[16] In any case, there was a strike in the Khoreal Tea Estate in or soon after April 1921.[17]

On 1 May 1921, the demand for an enhanced daily wage of eight annas for men and six annas for women was raised in a meeting held at Adampur in Dholai Valley. On the same and the following day, Non-Cooperators held meetings at Ratabari in Chargola Valley. These meetings were reportedly attended by tea garden labourers. The main theme of these meetings was no doubt *swaraj* and Khilafat. Yet, according to police reports, one of the speakers from Silchar, Radhakrishna Pande, advocated not only the cause of *swaraj*, but also a wage increase in the plantations. He cited the examples of Khoreal and several other gardens around Lakhipur in Cachar where the labour had struck work for increased pay. In Cachar, tea workers' strikes which began in April 1921 intermittently persisted throughout the year.[18]

The Chargola Exodus[19]

Strikes broke out in the Dholai Valley in south Sylhet in the first week of May. On 2 May, tea garden labourers in Chargola Valley struck work demanding a pay increase. Section 144 of the IPC was promulgated in the entire area within seven miles of the town of Sylhet and in several other sensitive areas, so that the tea garden labour might not be contaminated by political agitations. Meanwhile, however, the historic mass labour exodus from the Chargola and Longai Valleys in Karimganj sub-division had started, with the homeward departure of 750 men, women and children from Anipur Tea Estate on 3 May. Those simple folk had demanded a wage increase that was denied. They had lately heard the name of Gandhiji and put their faith in myths concerning his powers of doing good to the oppressed. They themselves indulged in all sorts of myth-making and accepted Gandhiji as a messiah – an *avatar*. Their sufferings ultimately goaded them to follow Gandhi's path – to go back to their villages and live a simple and plain life.[20]

Thousands of labourers, particularly from the tea gardens of the Chargola and Longai Valleys, left their gardens and trekked to the nearest railway stations, many shouting '*Gandhi Maharaj ki Jai*' as they walked. Determined to quit their jobs, they sold their cattle and other properties at ridiculously low

---

[16] *The Mussalman*, 5 March 1921 and also 1 July 1921.
[17] *ALECR 1921–22*, p. 10.
[18] Ibid., pp. 9 and 19.
[19] Ibid., and sources to be further mentioned.
[20] N.K. Mitra, ed., *Indian Annual Register* (hereafter *IAR*) (1922), pp. 1168 ff., 193–95 and 205.

prices. The government feared that the exodus would be a blow to the plantation economy and tried to make the coolies return by persuasion and threats, but failed. Denied the facilities of free travel on trains, turned destitute in the course of several days' journey, and falling prey to epidemics and police atrocities, the hapless workers assembled at Chandpur and other railway heads and began to subsist on relief. By 19 May their number had swollen to 4,000 at Chandpur alone. On the night of 20 May they were fiercely chased out of the station yard by armed police. They attracted the sympathy of the Congress and the people at large. The sufferings of the stranded labourers continued to persist until the middle of June, by when all the coolies were on their way home. Adequate public funds were raised to meet their transport costs.[21]

In protest against the brutal armed police assault of 20 May on the tea garden workers, the railwaymen at Chandpur and Laksam junctions spontaneously struck work on 24 May. The local steamer workers joined the strike in sympathy after four days. The entire country was charged with indignation, and the strikes paralysed the railways and the inland steamer navigation service – the two arteries of communications in Assam and East Bengal. According to police reports, Phookan was largely responsible for the spread of the May strike to the Brahmaputra Valley section of the Assam Bengal Railways.[22] At a meeting of the Bar Association on 3 June, the pleaders of Gauhati decided by a majority to suspend practice for three days in protest against the inhuman action of the authorities against the coolies at Chandpur. A Gauhati public meeting, while echoing the protest, also applauded the admirable solidarity action of the railwaymen.[23]

Following an ultimatum to the strikers on 7 June and an acute dislocation of food supply, the strike had almost petered out at Lumding and other places when Phookan and Bardaloi intervened. They addressed the railway workers of Lumding on 19 June and successfully induced them to resume the strike. The same result was not, however, achieved with the Gauhati station staff. The historic Assam–Bengal railway strike lasted for about two-and-a-half months, involving at its peak some 11,000 employees of whom around 4,500 lost their jobs altogether.[24] The steamer workers' strike that had lingered for some time was, however, settled earlier on a no-victimization basis.

The objective of the strike was repatriation of the stranded coolies at planters' or government's expense to their respective homes. It was a politically oriented solidarity action, with the general backing of the Non-Cooperators. Not

<hr>

[21] Ibid.; J.H. Broomfield, *Elite Conflict in a Plural Society: Twentieth Century Bengal* (Bombay, 1968), pp. 214–18.

[22] Ibid.; Confidential Home (Pol.), 1924.

[23] *The Mussalman*, 3 June 1921.

[24] Mitra, ed., *IAR*, p. 205; 'History-Sheet on Tarun Ram Phookan'; *India in 1921–22: A Report Prepared for Presentation to Parliament* (Government of India, Home Department, Calcutta, 1922), p. 204. At the initiative of the local Congress leaders, 100 bags of rice were sent from Gauhati as relief to the Lumding strikers through a Marwari trader.

all Congressmen, however, were sympathetic to this form of struggle. Many of them contended, like Gandhiji himself, that labour strikes were outside the Congress programme.[25] Others – a section of the nationalist press – took up the issue of the exodus and strikes for exposing the oppressive planters and the bureaucracy in league with them, rather than for a quick solution through a constructive welfare approach. It was this political aspect of the movement that evoked bitter criticism from a philanthropist activist like C.F. Andrews.[26] But he, too, did not fail to condemn the outrages committed on the coolies in glaring terms.

The Chargola exodus, though a well-known historical episode, awaits further analysis as a social phenomenon. Generated by a deep-rooted economic malady, the unrest in the Chargola and Longai Valley groups of tea gardens first took the form of a strike for an increase in wages. It later developed into a spontaneous mass exodus of workers in a pathetic endeavour to reach their village homes, hundreds of miles away. Relevant statistics are available for thirteen out of the nineteen tea gardens in the Chargola Valley and for six tea gardens in the Longai Valley. Out of a total labour population of 20,250 in these plantations, 8,799 or 43 per cent left their gardens. In the case of the Chargola Valley alone, this proportion was as high as 52 per cent (8,112 out of 15,618). Contract-bound labour, in most cases entitled to repatriation at the employer's cost, constituted about two-thirds of the labour force concerned. They, as well as the free wage labour, were more or less equally involved in the exodus.[27]

Why was it that an exodus on such a mass scale occurred only in the sub-division of Karimganj, particularly in the Chargola Valley, and not elsewhere? Relevant official statistics throw some light on this. It appears that a considerable proportion of plantation labour there were Hindi-speaking non-tribals (mainly Chamar by caste) who came from the districts of Uttar Pradesh. In fact, more than 4,000 people, that is, half of those who left the Chargola Valley, returned home to the two U.P. districts of Basti and Gorakhpur in June. Their rehabilitation was not a problem since the wage rates there were more attractive than in the Chargola Valley. Recruited as they were from a relatively more politically advanced area and social segment, the Chargola labour were

<hr>

[25] *The Mussalman*, 24 June 1921.

[26] For a distorted view, see Broomfield, *Elite Conflict*, pp. 216–19.

Broomfield holds *bhadralok* Congressmen responsible, at least equally with the Government of Bengal, for deliberately prolonging the avoidable transport strike and thus enhancing the sufferings of the trekkers. He passes judgements on men and their motivations, rather than on the resultant event that emerged as an integral part of the mounting anti-imperialist struggle. His pointer to the exaggerated reports in the Bengal nationalist press on the 'Gurkha outrage' at Chandpur is hardly relevant. He should have noted that the railwaymen of Chandpur who struck work did not have to depend on the press to know what happened locally. Broomfield accepts his facts blindly from Bengal government sources. He even distorts the views of Andrews. On this point, see also L.A. Gordon, *Bengal: The Nationalist Movement 1876–1970* (Delhi, 1974), p. 343*n*.

[27] Statistics contained in Government statement, 27 September, *ALCP* (1921), Vol. 1, pp. 885 and 894.

naturally very sensitive to the challenging political and economic situation. The other important factor relevant to their behaviour pattern was that 42 per cent of those who joined the exodus had been in the tea gardens for less than four years. They were probably not yet fully broken in for industrial discipline. These were some of the plausible official explanations of the exodus.[28]

However, it was too complex a phenomenon to be understood in such simplistic terms. A majority of the workers – both tribal and non-tribal – were bound down to their ill-paid jobs by agreements under the Act of 1859 and other Acts. They were heavily indebted to the planters through a system of advances. An economic struggle at the beginning, the sporadic strikes culminated into a mass political action in the form of a collective escape from the bonded labour system. The exodus was an open revolt, a primitive rebel action against the legitimized conditions of serfdom. It was the product of an interaction between the Gandhian impact on primitive minds and the incipient class militancy.

Strike Wave in the Brahmaputra Valley

The plantation labour had slightly higher earnings in the Brahmaputra Valley than in the other Valley. Nevertheless, labourers there were in no less a discontented and angry mood. There were strikes in April and May in the Dibrugarh and Panitola groups of tea gardens, and, on 22 June, at the Suntak Tea Estate, purely due to economic reasons. A large body of labourers of the last-mentioned garden, led by recruits from Ranchi district, looted several Marwari shops and manhandled the garden *sardars*. The British managerial and other supervisory staff fled from the scene to save their skin. Some 60 workers were jailed on charges of rioting. The other tea estate in Sibsagar where a labour strike turned violent was Suffrey. Otherwise, most of the numerous strikes that took place in Sibsagar from April 1921 were peaceful in character. The coolies demanded higher wages and struck work, but generally returned to work after two or three days. A considerable number of workers in Upper Assam left the tea gardens for their homes in Madras. They set out in small batches and, by rail and steamer, eventually reached their destinations.[29]

Darrang was the other seriously affected district besides Sibsagar. On 21 March 1921, there was a strike at the Halem Tea Estate. The supervisory staff was beaten up by the labourers. Then followed many tea garden strikes, one after another. In September and early October 1921, several peaceful strikes flared up in the Thakurbari group of tea gardens. The main demand raised was for a minimum daily wage of eight annas for men and six annas for women. These strikes were short-lived. But as they spread to the north, they took a serious

<hr>

[28] Ibid., pp. 889–93; extract from 'Report on the Revenue Administration of the United Provinces for the year ending 30th September 1921', cited in *ALECR, 1921–22*, pp. 12 and 15.

[29] Barthakur, *Swadhīnata Ranar Samsparshat*, pp. 83–84 and 96; *ALECR 1921–22*, pp. 15–20; H.A. Antrobus, *A History of the Assam Company 1839–1953* (Edinburgh, 1957), p. 209.

turn. The strikers of the Sonajuli Tea Estate on 9 October and of the Kacharigaon Tea Estate on 10 October manhandled their British bosses. The coolies raised general complaints about low wages, excessive work load, inadequate leave facilities, high prices of food and cloth, and also about the withholding of wage payments to those suspected of helping absconders. The most serious outbreak was at the Dhendai Tea Estate where the intervening superintendent of police was manhandled. In all these cases, the police and the bureaucracy helped the planters to suppress the agitation through large-scale arrests and terrorization of militant labourers.[30] Unfortunately, no sympathetic first-hand accounts of these heroic struggles are available today.

Congressmen, Planters and Coolies

The Non-Cooperation movement could not avoid an offensive directed against the British planter domination in Assam. The Raj in Assam essentially meant the planter Raj. No such well-defined line of action as the one embodied in the fourth resolution of the Surma Valley Political Conference (September 1920) existed in the Brahmaputra Valley. Nonetheless, there too, British planters' domination over rural marts became the target of direct political action.[31]

In most tea gardens, there were weekly bazaars and *haats* where the villagers used to bring their farm products for sale to the labour. These market places were under the planters' exclusive control, often to the detriment of villagers' interests. The villagers therefore had a legitimate grievance about the location of the markets. The other popular grievance was over the right of way through the sprawling tea gardens. Over the decades, the planters had usurped portions of many village paths and ancient public roads by bringing them within their enclosures. For example, such ancient roads as the Rajghar Ali in north Lakhimpur, Lahdoi Garh and Kharikatia Ali in Sibsagar, and the Raja Ali (Na-Halia Road) were encroached upon by the neighbouring tea gardens. In many areas, villagers had to walk circuitously for several miles around a group of tea gardens to reach a destination that was actually within a walking distance of a mile or two. Public roads passing through the tea gardens were of course still

---

[30] *ALECR 1921–22*, pp. 9–10 and 15–20.

About a thousand strikers from the Kacharigaon tea estate marched to the district town of Tezpur. Anticipating a police order of firing, local Congress leaders wired the District Magistrate offering their cooperation in peacefully dispersing the crowd. This offer was accepted. Congressmen stopped the strikers at the outskirts of the town and finally persuaded them to go back peacefully to their work. See O.K. Das, 'Lakshmidhar–Smriti', *Banhiir Pratiddhani*, Vol. 2 (a collection of articles in Assamese, Dhekiajuli, 1968), pp. 36–37.

[31] Historians of the imperialist school refuse to see any idealist element of nationalism in the Congress programme of boycott, particularly that of planter-dominated local markets in Assam. One of them upholds the government view that a vague millenarian hope was sufficient to involve many 'illiterate Assamese' in the market boycott, although 'the few educated Congressmen of the province' intended this as a means of cutting off government revenue. Brown, *Gandhiji's Rise to Power*, p. 324.

See the editorial, *Asamiiya*, 10 December 1922.

used by the villagers, but under sufferance. For example, there were cases when the planters would not allow bullock-carts to ply along the trunk roads, lest the roads be damaged and turned unfit for motor traffic.

Planters had also established, over the years, certain racial and feudal practices in uncouth demonstration of their power. No Indian, certainly not a common villager, was allowed to pass through a tea estate on cycle or horseback, or with his umbrella unfurled, in the presence of the *sahib*.[32] Similarly, in the Non-Cooperation days, the presence of khadi-capped Congress volunteers and villagers was not tolerated within a planter's jurisdiction. In short, there was absolutely no freedom of movement in and across the plantations, despite the fact that villages and plantations had inseparable market links with each other.

The resident plantation labourers were habitual liquor-consumers. They also accounted for a sizeable consumption of the foreign salt and cloth imported into Assam. Hence, free entry of the Congress volunteers into plantations was necessary for the boycott movement. But the planters would not allow the Non-Cooperators to propagate *swadeshi* and temperance in the coolie lines or even in the tea garden bazaars. Under the circumstances, a direct clash between Non-Cooperators and planters was unavoidable. The only alternative for the Non-Cooperators was to boycott the tea garden *haats* and bazaars, and to establish new market places under popular control in their vicinity. This they did with great enthusiasm from April 1921.

In the districts of Darrang, Sibsagar, Sylhet and Cachar, one of the main planks of the Non-Cooperation movement was to boycott market places located in British tea estates, and to establish rival bazaars and *haats*. Although there was nothing unlawful about this activity, prohibitive orders were issued by the government in most cases to nip them in the bud. For example, the Non-Cooperators at Behali in the district of Darrang attempted to force a boycott of the *haat* of the Bedeti Tea Estate on 13 April 1921, and successfully turned back a number of carters and others. On the next *haat* day, prominent Non-Cooperators attended the *haat* and, suspected of fomenting trouble, were turned out of the tea estate. They started a rival *haat* on the same day at about a mile's distance. The District Magistrate thereafter issued an injunction under Section 144, IPC, prohibiting any rival *haat* within four miles of the Bedeti *haat*. It was only rarely that such attempts did not invite official wrath. The successful establishment of the rival Bakata *haat* in the vicinity of the Mahkhuti Tea Estate in the district of Sibsagar deserves mention in this respect.[33]

A couple of questions yet remain to be answered. With so many meeting

---

[32] For instances of racist and feudal practices of planters, see *Indian Echo* (Calcutta), 1 March and 23 August 1886; *The Mussalman*, 14 September, 1926; speeches by R.K. Hatibarua, N. C. Bardaloi, S. Barua and L. Barua, 13 September, *ALCP* (1927), Vol. 7, Part 11, pp. 1249–69; 'Gaonlia ali aru cah khetiyak' (in Assamese), *Asamiiya*, 1 May 1927, cited ibid., pp. 1041–44.

[33] Reply to Dalim Bora, 21 September, *ALCP* (1922), Vol. 2; Barthakur, *Swaddünata Ranar Samsparshat*, p. 96; *ALECR* 1921–22, pp. 19–20.

points between villagers and plantation workers, how did the Congress and labour interact with each other? What was the attitude of the Congress towards the strikers in the plantations, and vice versa?

Congress circles were as much alarmed as the administration itself at the growing number of plantation strikes. Congressmen did not want to get involved in these and persistently tried to disown them. When there was a strike in the Halem Tea Estate in March 1921, the government suspected that it might have been inspired by the Congress agitation that was going on in the neighbouring villages. Chandranath Sharma had addressed a Non-Cooperation meeting at Ghahigaon, not far from Halem, and, according to police sources, it was attended by numerous tea garden labourers. However, the suspicion was not well-founded. Years later, Omeo Kumar Das (1895–1975), a Congress leader who was present at this meeting, confirmed that Sharma had scrupulously avoided in his speech any criticism of the planters in relation to their labour. When there was yet another wave of labour troubles in Sonajuli, Kacharigaon, Dhendai and a few more tea gardens in the Rangapara Circle in October, the Tezpur District Congress Committee even offered its cooperation to the District Magistrate for pacification of the striking labourers.[34]

The general attitude of Congressmen towards plantation strikes in those days is best illustrated by the reminiscences of Padmanath Barthakur – a Non-Cooperator. He writes of his memorable experience in one instance, as follows:

> A group of workers met me at night. Aggrieved with the Barasahib, they wanted to stop work, and I was approached to show them the way. On hearing this, my heart was almost frozen. It was not long ago that some 60 coolies were thrown into the jails, because of a strike in the Suntak Tea Estate of the same Assam Company. It turned out to be a terrible sort of development as a result of which all the white Sahibs and the entire supervisory staff, who had grayed their hairs on the garden service, managed somehow to flee the garden alive. . . . That is why it was but natural that the very mention of a strike would send a shiver down my body, and my mind was indeed filled with a surfeit of repentance. Why, at all, did I enter amidst the tea garden workers, without having considered the *pros* and *cons*?[35]

Barthakur explained to the workers the inevitable, violent consequences of a strike and advised them to adopt softer means like a deputation to the management for redressing their grievances. In this particular case, their grievance was that they were not being allowed to purchase foodstuff from the newly

---

[34] Interview with O.K. Das, 10 July 1973.
    'After arrest of some labourers on charges of rioting and assaults, all the labourers of a few gardens in Rangapara area marched to Tezpur town when we offered cooperation with the Government in persuading them to return to the gardens.' O.K. Das to A. Guha, n.d., in reply to the latter's letter of 5 September 1973. See also footnote 30.

[35] Quote and citation from Barthakur, *Swadhünata Ranar Samsparshat*, pp. 83–84 and 96. Translation ours.

established Bakata *haat*. Eventually, the management yielded to the peaceful pressure. Barthakur was thus able to avoid an inconvenient situation for himself.

Rural Congress volunteers who came into daily contact with the sprawling labour population in course of their temperance and *swadeshi* propagation could not but sympathize with the strikes. Despite ideological reservations and vacillations, occasionally they even made common cause with them in the fight for the freedom of movement and human dignity. In January 1922, there was a short-lived movement in Cachar to enlist tea garden coolies as Congress volunteers.[36] The attempted boycott of tea garden bazaars by villagers in the Brahmaputra Valley was a spontaneous reaction to the insulting behaviour of British planters towards the Gandhi-capped volunteers.

There is sufficient evidence from both the Valleys to suggest that the oppressed labourers were deeply impressed by the nationalist movement and looked to the Congress for help in their cause. On one occasion, a number of coolies of the Belsiri Tea Estate who had come to Tezpur to file their complaints with the district authorities, also paid a visit to the local Congress camp. Ex-coolies-turned-cultivators often provided the link between Congressmen and tea garden workers. For example, Arjun Ghatowar, an ex-coolie of the Dibru–Darrang Tea Estate, used to come to the Congress office at Dhekiajuli, and he attended several Non-Cooperation meetings held in the surrounding villages. Never was he encouraged by the local Congress to hold any meeting in the said garden or to tell his fellow labourers to come out of their garden. Yet, at his own initiative, he held a meeting and, according to the District Magistrate of Darrang, 'was found inciting the garden labour force, nominally to eschew opium and liquor, but in reality to strike work'. He was arrested and convicted to six months' rigorous imprisonment. Both at the time of his trial and after the expiry of his prison term, he was openly acclaimed as a Congress volunteer.[37]

In many cases, local Congressmen reciprocated the workers' urge for united action against the common enemy. This was all too obvious not only in the case of the Chargola upheaval, but also elsewhere. 'Though there is no evidence that the major outbreaks were instigated by political agitators', wrote the District Magistrate of Darrang,

> there is evidence that one or two subsequent incidents connected with tea gardens have received encouragement from the Congress Party . . . and there is no doubt that the activities of the volunteers in the villages created an atmosphere

---

[36] *ALECR 1921–22*, p. 19.

After a wave of lightning strikes in three gardens of the Doomdooma Tea Company in September 1920, there were rumours, according to the police, that the Dibrugarh bar 'intend defending the coolies arrested in connection with the disturbances at Doomdooma free of cost'. *Assam Police Abstract of Intelligence 1920*, No. 663, Assam S.B., 9 October 1920, in OEHFM, Government of Assam, Gauhati.

[37] Written evidence of the District Magistrate of Darrang, cited in *ALECR 1921–22*, p. 15. Also, O.K. Das to the author, see footnote 34.

which was favourable to the occurrence of strikes and outbreaks among ignorant coolies.[38]

Omeo Kumar Das, however, writes in a defensive tone:

> My statement is that there had been no instruction to encourage exodus of labour from the gardens. I had been the Secretary of the Tezpur District Congress. . . . Of course, we cannot deny that the tea garden labourers were affected by the surrounding Indian situation. A spirit of militancy had been roused by the N.C.O. movement. . . . For myself, as a worker and an office-bearer of the Congress, I can say that there was no instruction to call out the labourers from the tea gardens.[39]

The reservations of the Congress were understandable. Several of its local leaders – Kuladhar Chaliha, Jadavprasad Chaliha (1897–1964), even N.C. Bardaloi – were planters themselves. Many were socially and matrimonially related to planter families. Besides, strikes – a working-class form of struggle – were not on the Congress agenda. Ideological reservations prevented the well-organized Non-Cooperation movement and the spontaneous strike wave from being welded into a single unified movement. What happened came closest to such a development only in the Surma Valley. Even there what was achieved was far from a conscious multi-class, anti-imperialist front.

It was *hartals* – not strikes – that suited the Congress ideology and its organization best. As a non-class form of mass struggle, *hartals* had an appeal for everybody, particularly for the tradition-bound artisans and other petty-bourgeois sections, as well as broad chunks of the backward working classes who still maintained their village nexus and had no class organization of their own. Such a *hartal*, when called nation-wide on 17 November – the day the Prince of Wales landed in India – was a remarkable success at Gauhati. A police eyewitness account of the Gauhati *hartal* brings out the inner strength and popular base of the Congress, as follows:

> The non-cooperators succeeded in organizing somewhat effective *hartal* today. The carters, garhiwallas, barbers, sweepers, coolies, milkmen etc., all joined in the hartal. Most of the railway, steamer and motor coolies did not attend to their works today, and the works had to be managed with difficulty. At the end of the day 300 working people assembled at Phookan's compound and wanted him to explain to them Gandhiji's message.[40]

It is also interesting to note that T.R. Phookan, as president of the Gauhati Town Congress Committee, addressed a meeting of the town's prostitutes on 5 September 1921 to explain the objectives of *swaraj*.[41] Thus the Congress had its

---

[38] Evidence of District Magistrate of Darrang, cited in *ALECR 1921–22*, p. 15.
[39] Letter from O.K. Das to A. Guha, footnote 34.
[40] Quote from CID sub-inspector's report, cited in Confidential Home (Pol.), 1924.
[41] 'History-Sheet of Tarun Ram Phookan'.

own ways of reaching the masses with its message of *swaraj* – a message of hope and love for the depressed and the downtrodden. In this mission, it did not hesitate to take advantage of social and religious gatherings. It even encouraged non-secular, obscurantist traits in the movement, such as the communal concern for Khilafat. Nevertheless, through the Non-Cooperation movement of 1920–22, the Congress opened the floodgates of mass politics as much in Assam as in the rest of India.

Non-Cooperators Face Mounting Repression
Two Facets of the Movement

As the spirit of defiance spread like wild fire to every segment of society, particularly to the urban and rural poor, the government could no longer remain complacent with its heretofore soft policy. Control of the movement even by frequent promulgation of Section 144, IPC and action under the Press Act (1910) was becoming increasingly difficult.

The Non-Cooperation aspect of the movement as such was not so visibly prominent in the Surma Valley, overshadowed as it was by the Khilafat movement since the middle of 1921. The Congress and Khilafat Committees had the same office-bearers in most cases. Nevertheless, it was the fanatically religious *ulema* (Islamic jurists) who provided the basic inspiration. The Jamiat-ul-Ulema of the Surma Valley held its third annual conference at Karimganj on 13–14 November 1921, with Maulana Abdul Munaweir, president of the Assam Provincial Khilafat Committee, in the chair. There, in the presence of an estimated gathering of 8,000 visitors, some 259 *ulema* jointly presented a unanimous *fatwa* lending support to and offering service for the cause of the Khilafat. In Sylhet and Karimganj, Muslim tailors held meetings in mosques and pledged that they would no longer sew foreign cloth for their customers.[42] The plight of the Turkish Sultan in the distant Middle East often appeared to be a matter of greater concern for Muslim politicians than the battle for *swaraj* as such. Nevertheless, the 'holy' alliance between the Congress and Khilafatists worked towards a common anti-British front that temporarily outwitted the colonial 'divide and rule' policy.

In the Brahmaputra Valley, however, it was the Congress Non-Cooperators who dominated the field. Their concentrated attack on the official excise policy was also a matter of concern for the government. For, due to the temperance propaganda, effective picketing and modifications forced upon the official excise policy, both the consumption of opium and the excise revenue of the province had recorded a sharp fall (see table below). Because of the agitation the share of excise in the total provincial revenue decreased from about 40 per cent in

---

[42] *The Mussalman*, 25 November 1921.

Mohammad Abdulla (1895–1955), a lawyer of Sylhet, was the secretary of the provincial Khilafat Committee. He remained a nationalist throughout our period and was elected to the East Pakistan Legislative Assembly in 1954. N. Gupta Chaudhury, ed., *Shriihatta Pratibha* (Sylhet, 1961), pp. 15–16.

Provincial Excise Statistics: 1920–24 (includes Manipur 1921–22)

Total	1920–21	1921–22	1922–23	1923–24
Excise Revenue (Rs 1000)*	7,535	6,158	5,681	6,225
Opium Revenue (Rs 1000)	4,412	3,917	3,586	3,810
Opium Consumption (maunds)	1,615	1,048	998	884
Index No.	(100)	(65)	(62)	(55)
Price of opium (per *seer*) (Rs)	57	65	68	75

Note: * Includes opium revenue.
Source: *Excise Statistical Tables for the Province of Assam* (Shillong, 1927), pp. 96–97 and relevant annual reports of the Excise Department, Government of Assam. The consumption figure for 1923–24 is from *ACOER*, p. 45.

1920–21 to less than 30 per cent by 1923–24.[43] Besides, the Non-Cooperators continued to do useful work by bringing into existence village panchayats to take suits out of the law courts.

Repression Let Loose

The Government of Assam became somewhat nervous after the National Congress adopted the deferred programme of Civil Disobedience on 4 November 1921. In the absence of the preconditions as laid down by Gandhiji in the province, the Pradesh Congress Committee decided against any Civil Disobedience involving refusal to pay the land revenue in Assam. Not prepared to take any risk, the government nevertheless resorted to a policy of ruthless oppression. The Criminal Law Amendment Act, kept long in abeyance, was promulgated in Assam on 21 November 1921, making picketing practically illegal. Several organizations like the Congress Volunteer Corps and the Khilafat Volunteer Corps were also declared unlawful under this Act.

N.C. Bardaloi and T.R. Phookan, among others, were arrested on 30 November, and Kuladhar Chaliha on 11 December. Many more arrests followed. On 18 December 1921, the Chief Secretary to the Government of Assam, in a telegram to the Government of India, reported that the Khilafat meetings had a pernicious effect on the fanatic rural masses and that Section 144, IPC was inadequate for tackling the situation. The Prevention of Seditious Meetings Act (1911) was therefore introduced in Sylhet district on 23 December, and in the whole of the Brahmaputra Valley excluding the district of Nowgong, on 31 January 1922. Declared a disturbed area on 23 December, Boko was subjected to a punitive levy. A platoon of the Assam Rifles was stationed there. The districts of Cachar and Nowgong were also soon brought under the operation of the Act. Tabarak Ali and Shyamacharan Dev (1870–1961) of Cachar were sentenced to rigorous imprisonment in March 1922.[44]

---

[43] *ACOER*, p. 45.
[44] Chaliha's speech, September, *ALCP* (1924), Vol. 4, pp. 471–72; Government of India, Home (Pol.), File No. 533, serials 1–7 and 11, 1922 (NAI); *ALCP* (1922), Vol. 2,

The people, however, were not to be easily cowed down. In several areas, they even thought of taking the movement to a higher phase by refusing to pay the land revenue rates in the ryotwari areas and *chaukidari* taxes in the zamindari areas. For example, in the *mauzas* of Haleswar and Mahabhairab in Darrang, an action in the form of refusal to pay land revenue rates was discussed by some ryots. This was not on the agenda of the Pradesh Congress and, hence, nothing perhaps would come out of this flutter. At least that was what the local Congress leaders believed. However, the *mauzadars* concerned came to Tezpur and raised a hue and cry, merely to exhibit their anti-Non-Cooperation zeal. They returned to their respective *mauzas* on 21 January 1922 with an escort of batches of armed police.[45] Preparations for refusal to pay land revenue were also made by Congressmen at some places like Boko in south Kamrup.[46]

Between 23 December 1921 and 8 May 1922, as many as three dozen select areas (*mauza*/police station/town ward) in the plains districts were declared disturbed. The inhabitants of these places were subjected to collective fines (about Rs 0.2 million in all) to pay for the deployment of additional police forces, which included nine-and-a-half platoons of the Assam Rifles (see Appendix 11). Loyal citizens were of course exempted from this levy. Flag marches of the Assam Rifles were conducted in the districts of Sylhet and Sibsagar. In Goalpara, the Assam Rifles was called in by the Forest Department to eject politically undesirable persons from some forest villages of Kochugaon. In Kamrup, too, the Assam Rifles marched through some villages.[47]

These measures were deemed necessary principally to check such activities as 'seditious' meetings, fund collections in aid of unlawful associations, intimidation of villagers willing to attend tea garden *haats* and the influx of 'trouble-shooting' rural volunteers to the towns. The people did not always remain non-violent. A collaborating *mauzadar's* house was reportedly burnt down in a village of Sibsagar. One police inspector and two sub-inspectors of the same district were assaulted. The government reacted fiercely. The police forcibly dispersed a youth procession at Jorhat on 3 January 1922, for singing revolution-

---

pp. 86 and 790–98; Confidential Home Department (Pol.), 1924; *The Mussalman*, 3 March 1922.

[45] *The Mussalman*, 3 February 1922, supplemented by O.K. Das in an interview at Gauhati on 10 July 1973, followed by correspondence.

[46] K.N. Dutt, *Landmarks of the Freedom Struggle in Assam* (Gauhati, 1958; reprinted, 1969), p. 57.

[47] *ALCP* (1922), Vol. 2, pp. 790–91; speech by Kuladhar Chaliha, 12 March, *ALCP* (1925), Vol. 5, p. 404; *The Mussalman*, 23 June 1922; reply to Dalim Bora, *ALCP* (1922), Vol. 2, p. 300.

In all forest villages, the villagers were expected to provide the forest department with *begar* or unpaid labour. In 1921 the ryots of the Kochugaon forest in Dhubri subdivision stopped supplying *begar*, under the leadership of Pratapchandra Brahma, a Boro–Kachari peasant. They were all served with eviction notices, and a unit of the Assam Rifles was called in to push them out. The *begar* system finally had to go. 'A Note on His Reminiscences by Pramathanath Chakravarti to Mahadev Sharma', in OEHFM, Government of Assam, Gauhati.

ary songs 'noisily'. The Congress office premises in many places in Sibsagar district were either burnt down or demolished under official orders. Even a big *pandal* constructed for a religious performance was burnt down on 23 January on the plea of forestalling a seditious meeting.[48]

There were signs of agitation even amongst the beneficiaries of the government. Out of the province's 118 title-holders, two had relinquished their titles by September 1921. Several police constables and many government employees resigned their jobs. Two government pensioners, Nilkanta Barua and Krishnakanta Bhattacharyya, were penalized for actively supporting the movement. Bhattacharyya was the editor of *Assam Bilasini* (Jorhat) which had ceased publication following a security demand of Rs 2,000 in April 1921. Similarly victimized under the Press Act (1910) were the *Janashakti* (Sylhet) and *Surma* (Silchar). The weekly *Asamiiya* (Dibrugarh) was fined on a defamation charge. The most serious and tragic police action, however, took place at Kanairghat in the Surma Valley. In a police firing on an angry crowd there on 15 February 1922, six people were killed and twenty-two wounded – all Muslims. One Hindu police constable was also found dead from an accidental gun shot. The Kanairghat tragedy, and the subsequent police atrocities in the area, aroused province-wise indignation.[49]

Even as the people were boldly facing repression, the Congress Working Committee – following the tragic Chaurichaura incident – called off the mass Civil Disobedience movement by its resolution of 12 February 1922 at Bardoli. Although the provincial Congress Committees were later permitted to carry on individual civil disobedience on a limited scale, the surging movement soon subsided in Assam and elsewhere. A constructive programme that included popularization of the *charkha*, the setting up of national schools and the eradication of untouchability was put forward before the people. In March 1922, Omeo Kumar Das placed before the All India Congress Committee (AICC) an account of the unprecedented police repression in Assam. Thereupon, Rajendra Prasad and M.M. Malaviya visited Assam – Boko in particular – in May the same year.[50]

Thousands participated in the upheaval of 1921–22. Statistics relating to militant plantation workers who underwent jail terms or were put under arrest are not available. Estimates are, however, available for the total number of persons who went to jail in connection with the Non-Cooperation movement. It was officially stated that, between 24 November 1921 and 31 January 1922, 477 Non-Cooperators in the Brahmaputra Valley and twenty in the Surma Valley were sentenced to various terms of imprisonment. According to one estimate,

---

[48] Reply from Government bench, *ALCP* (1922), Vol. 2, pp. 93–94, 556–62, 793 and 798; speech by R.K. Hatibarua, 4 April, *ALCP* (1924), Vol. 4, pp. 462–63; *ALCP* (1921), Vol. 1, pp. 428 and 523; Dutt, *Landmarks of Freedom Struggle in Assam*, pp. 61 and 63*n*.

[49] Same as footnote 48.

[50] Dutt, *Landmarks of Freedom Struggle in Assam*, p. 65.

996 persons including twenty-two lawyers of the Brahmaputra Valley were convicted under the Criminal Law Amendment Act alone up to 30 March 1922. According to the *Assam Congress Opium Enquiry Report*, about 1,100 persons of the same Valley had gone to jail in connection with the movement. K.N. Dutt estimates that more than 4,000 people in the province as a whole had entered jail precincts in response to the Non-Cooperation call.[51]

Statistics available on the daily average of the jail population of Assam, including convicts, under-trials and civil prisoners, show that the number increased from 2,656 in 1921 to 2,915 in 1922 and then came down gradually to 2,357 – a normal level – in 1924. The increase in 1922 was chiefly due to the Non-Cooperation movement.[52] There were thirty-eight national schools in Assam with 1,908 scholars in 1921–22.[53]

Local Reaction to the Bardoli Retreat

The sudden withdrawal of the movement did not go unprotested in Assam. Chandranath Sharma, the real founder of the Congress movement in the Brahmaputra Valley, was then on his death-bed, suffering as he was from consumption. He was shocked to find Gandhiji developing a 'religious mania' from November 1921 and mixing up political issues with those of religious morality. Neither the Calcutta resolution on Non-Cooperation nor its Nagpur variant had been loaded with any such moral or religious values. These resolutions simply laid down that *swaraj* was to be attained by all legitimate and peaceful means. How was it then that Gandhiji later defined Non-Cooperation as a process of purification? In anguish, Sharma wrote to a friend on 22 February 1922, bringing out the irrelevance and emptiness of the Bardoli decision and the Gandhian tactics. Expressing the desire that his letter be published in one of the Congress organs, he wrote:

> I am stunned after receiving the Congress Working Committee Resolutions of Bardoli. . . . The fact that the Congress is not a religious body is known pretty well by Mahatma Gandhi. . . . If this Non-Cooperation movement is entirely a religious and spiritual movement, then why did he not say so at the very outset? In fact in order to purify Indian people and initiate them to the religion of non-violence, there was no need of non-cooperation with the British Government. Nor was there any need of fighting with that Government to achieve the sort of independence he now wants to give Indians.

Sharma did not at all relish Gandhiji giving top priority to the untouchability programme; rather, he wanted the political movement to continue in a

---

[51] *ALCP* (1922), Vol. 2, p. 507; T. Chaliha's estimate, *ALCP* (1924), Vol. 4, pp. 471–72; *ACOER*, p. 29; Dutt, *Landmarks of Freedom Struggle in Assam*, p. 61.

[52] Government of India, Reforms Department, File No. 76/27 – special notes on jail population in Assam (1921–26) (NAI).

[53] P.C. Bamford, *Histories of the Non-Cooperation and Khilafat Movements* (Delhi, 1925), p. 104.

do-or-die spirit, in the face of all consequences.[54] After the collapse of the move-ment, the Government of India found it opportune to put Gandhiji under arrest on 10 March. Broken-hearted, Sharma died on 20 July 1922, at the age of about thirty-three. Assam was meanwhile completely submerged under a prolonged spell of Gandhism.

T.R. Phookan was released from jail on 25 November 1922. 'We could not complete our *sadhana* for *swaraj*,' said Phookan at a Gauhati meeting imme-diately after his release, 'and that is why we could not obtain it.' Bardaloi was released a few months later. Both devoted themselves to constructive work. Rel-eased on 1 July 1922, M. Tayyebulla and about forty Non-Cooperating college students – mostly Hindus – joined the teaching staff of Jamia Millia, Aligarh, on receiving an invitation from Maulana Mohamed Ali in September.[55] By the end of 1922, all was quiet. With the revolutionary overthrow of the Turkish Sultan from his throne and consequently also from the altar of Khilafat, the Khilafat movement as such came to an end.

Reforms as By-products of the Movement

The short-sighted policy of bringing religious issues into politics did not pay any dividend in the long run. The way the agitation was suspended laid bare the ideological weakness of the movement, besides setting in demoralization among the ranks of freedom fighters.

The Non-Cooperation movement was nevertheless able to create a revolu-tion in expectations by turning the Congress into a mass political platform. In Assam, the movement achieved success at least in one respect. It forced the alien government to modify its opium policy. Even as the Non-Cooperationists agitat-ed, the government introduced such measures as would eventually lead to a decline of opium consumption in Assam, with a watchdog legislature never allowing it to forget its commitment.

Another by-product of the movement was perhaps the immediate official action to expedite reformation of the local bodies. For this purpose, a revised set of rules under the Local Self-Government Act of 1915 was introduced on 3 Jan-uary 1921, and the Assam Municipal Act was passed in 1923. The franchise related to the local boards was extended and made identical with that of the Assam Legislative Council. Thereby, however, the principle of separate elector-ates on a communal basis for election to the local boards was also, for the first time, adopted through the backdoor of the government's rule-making author-ity.[56] Thus Muslim middle-class elements, who claimed to champion Muslim

---

[54] Dandinath Kalita, *Karmmabiir Chandranath* (in Assamese, Tezpur, 1846 *saka*), p. 92; quote from Chandranath to Durganath Barua, dated Puri, 22 February 1922, repro-duced, ibid., pp. 93–97; translation ours.

[55] Confidential Home Deparment (Pol.), 1924; *ACOER*, pp. 56–57. M. Tayyebulla, *Between the Symbol and the Idol at Last* (New Delhi, 1964), p. 46.

[56] V. Venkata Rao, *A Hundred Years of Local Self-Government in Assam* (second edi-tion, Gauhati, 1965), pp. 206–07.

interests, were able to achieve for themselves a political gain that the hard-pressed alien government was all too ready to concede for tactical advantages.

The proportion of elected to total members in the local boards considerably increased after the reform. For example, out of the province's 380 local board members in 1922–23, 47 were *ex-officio*, 69 nominated and the remaining 264 (69.5 per cent) elected members. Besides, the local boards were now allowed to elect their own chairmen. Whereas all but one local board chairman were officials in 1920–21, thirteen out of nineteen local boards had elected non-official chairmen in 1922–23.[57]

The government of course continued to exercise considerable external control through its nominees on these boards, as well as through its rule-making powers, audit and inspection. The Non-Cooperation movement had little effect on these bodies, except for the fact that several individuals were removed from membership on conviction. So was the case with the municipalities in general. In the case of one municipal board alone, all the non-official members resigned in a body following a disagreement between its chairman and the District Magistrate in connection with Gandhiji's visit to the town.[58] Thus, through extended institutional opportunities, the Raj was able to win over, or at least neutralize, a section of the local elite that was itching for a fringe share in the power structure. Even Non-Cooperators thought it expedient not to boycott local bodies as a matter of general policy.

Role of the First Reformed Council: 1921–23

An Anatomy of the House

The Reformed Council came into its existence in the face of an organized poll boycott (1920) and, as such, comprised only of loyal and opportunist elements who were hardly representative of even the educated classes. Amongst its 53 members, there were a dozen planters of whom five were British. Besides, there were quite a few zamindars and *mauzadars* among the elected representatives. The Governor had questioned the eligibility of *mauzadars* for election, since they had a quasi-official status. However, his opinion was over-ruled by the Secretary of State for India and by the British Parliament, in the process of constitution-making.

Of the 53 Councillors, only thirty-three were elected from the general Muslim and non-Muslim constituencies – sixteen from each valley, and one from the Shillong urban constituency. Another six elected members represented such special interests as tea, commerce and industry. The Governor nominated twelve members, including not more than seven officials. Apparently, the Reformed Council had a safe non-official and Indian majority. However, since at least twenty-seven members were required to form a majority party – undoubtedly a

---

[57] Reply to S. Barua, *ALCP* (1924), Vol. 4, p. 151.
[58] *Indian Constitutional Reforms: Views of Local Governments on the Working of the Reforms dated 1927* (London, 1928), pp. 495 and 521.

difficult proposition – the elected British planters, together with official and nomi-nated members in their trail, continued to exercise substantial influence in the house.[59] With vested economic interests and a stake in the administration, the British and nominated Indian members together formed the government party, and lent their support to the otherwise shaky 'popular' ministers.

The legislature's functions expanded under the Act of 1919. Budget pro-posals were henceforth placed before the house with full details for an item-wise discussion. An item of expenditure, if refused by the Council, could no more be incurred by the executive government. In exceptional circumstances alone, the Governor could restore the cut at his discretion by way of certification. Besides, certain items of expenditure were withheld by the Act itself from the vote of the Council. These items amounted to about 25 per cent of the total provincial expen-diture.[60]

A Public Accounts Committee (PAC) was set up to see, with the aid of the Audit Department, that the voted grants were spent as intended by the Council. Supplementary questions could now be put by any member. The right to move adjournments was also conceded, but this right was not exercised before the for-mation of the second Reformed Council. The first president of the Council to be appointed was, of course, a Britisher. After his premature retirement in 1923, Rai Bahadur Nalinikanta Dastidar (1875–1945), a Sylhet zamindar, was appointed president. The legislature had an elected president only from 1925 onwards.[61]

As in other provinces, the dyarchy in operation in Assam had two wings of its executive government: (i) the administration of transferred subjects and (ii) the administration of reserved subjects. Two ministers, supposedly responsible to the legislature, were to advise the Governor on the administration of transferred subjects. The reserved subjects were entrusted to two executive Councillors who were not responsible to the legislature. In administering these reserved subjects, the provincial government was responsible only to the Government of India. The area of transferred subjects was more limited in Assam, to begin with, than in other provinces. The Departments of Public Works, Excise and Fishery were gradually transferred there only after 1925–26; Excise, as late as in 1926–27. Transferred departments accounted for only 30.2 per cent of the total budgeted expenditure of 1927–28 and 36.7 per cent of that of 1935–36.[62]

The position of a minister under the system was unenviable. He was appointed and dismissed by the Governor, but his pay was fixed by the Council. There was an embarrassing convention that he would not speak his mind in the

---

59 Governor's address, 22 February, *ALCP* (1921), Vol. 1, pp. 1–6; for composition of the first Reformed Council, ibid., pp. 11–13; Governor's address, 16 August, *ALCP* (1923), Vol. 3, pp. 696–704.

The Reformed Council had its first meeting on 22 February 1921.

60 Governor's address, 16 August, *ALCP* (1923), Vol. 3, pp. 696–704.

61 Ibid.

62 Speech by Sadananda Dowerah, 26 March, *ALCP* (1924), Vol. 4, pp. 123–24; A.J. Laine's reply to R.K. Chaudhuri, 1 March, *ALCP* (1935), Vol. 15, p. 287.

Council on points of difference with his colleagues in the government. Besides, executive Councillors had precedence of rank over ministers. The Governor, executive Councillors and ministers usually met together once a week. This arrangement worked rather too well. The *Statesman* (Calcutta), the mouthpiece of British capital in eastern India, editorially commented on 5 June 1929:

> In Assam's happy hills there is no doubt that Dyarchy has succeeded, for the delightful reason that it has never been tried. There, if nowhere else, the Government has been really one, not a collocation of two committees, in one row of chairs. Assam's Legislative Council has seen no distinction of Right and Left on the Government bench. Immediately on appointment, Executive Members and Ministers forget their difference of origin; and with the Governor they form a *panchayat* working the Government as a matter of mutual arrangement.

If the dyarchy functioned like this in Assam till 1929, it was more so during the years 1930–36, with a Council without the Congress–Swarajists.

Timid Performance

Working within the constraints of a sham constitutional framework and lacking a popular base, the first Reformed Council could not but play a colourless and subservient role. It even assumed an anti-national role when it passed unanimous resolutions in September 1921 welcoming the Prince of Wales to India, and conveying a message of loyalty, homage and profound gratefulness to the King-Emperor.[63] A few of the Council members, like Gohain–Barua, Nilmoni Phukan, Dalim Bora and Krishnasundar Dam, no doubt eloquently condemned in their speeches the police excesses let loose upon the Non-Cooperators. However, they considered it safe to do so only after recording their disapproval of Non-Cooperation. 'Sir, it is needless to say that we fundamentally differ from the non-cooperation in our political opinions,' said Gohain–Barua on 14 March 1922, 'or we should not have been here.'[64] Nilmoni Phukan, then an elected member, generally voted with the government on all vital political issues. He said in the same budget session the next day:[65]

> What we want most at this moment is larger sympathy and recognition of people's aspiration for higher and freer life. I do not consider British connection a necessary evil, nor the sole outcome of 'merchant adventurers'. This connection has come to stay for the good of both Englishmen and Indians.

The first Council failed to pass even a perfunctory resolution recommending the release of political prisoners and the withdrawal of repressive laws,

---

[63] *ALCP* (1921), Vol. 1, pp. 479–80. There were *hartals* in Assam's towns on the day the Prince of Wales landed in India. To make amends for this 'sin' of his countrymen, Bholanath Barooah – the millionaire timber merchant – donated funds to establish a technical institute at Jorhat to be named after the said prince.

[64] *ALCP* (1922), Vol. 2, p. 109.

[65] Phukan's speech, 15 March, *ALCP* (1922), Vol. 2, p. 226.

despite the fact that such resolutions had been passed by other provincial Councils after the suspension of the movement. Dalim Bora moved such a resolution on 28 March 1922, but he had to withdraw it for lack of support. He took pains to explain that his object in moving the resolution was not to create unpleasantness but to pray for the release of political prisoners under the changed circumstances. On more than one occasion, Dalim delivered inspired speeches condemning colonialism and upholding the Non-Cooperation movement. One could, however, legitimately suspect that he was playing to the gallery, with an eye on the next election.[66]

Thus, the flutter that was created in the Council through interpellation and speeches on the issue of repression was rather marginal. 'The fact that we eventually had no option but to take action is recognized by this Council's vote of yesterday,' the Governor gleefully told the Council on 14 September 1922, 'when you, gentlemen, gave us the money which we asked for the exceptional expenditure incurred on the movement of the Military Police which were required to reassure law-abiding people and to restore respect for authority in the perturbed areas.'[67]

The first Reformed Council's record of legislative output was conspicuously poor. The only measure of importance was the Municipal Act, 1923, containing provisions for separate electorates on a communal basis in municipal elections as well. Notices were given for as many as 186 resolutions. While 164 of these were admitted and moved, as many as 83 were withdrawn, thirty-nine lost through a voice vote or division, and only forty-two carried. Again, out of a total of 1,608 questions put in the Council, 1,442 were admitted; of these, 1,400 were answered.[68]

Interpellation and cut motions generally related to such issues as primary education, the need for a university, the burden of grazing taxes and the excise policy. For example, despite government opposition, J.J.M. Nichols–Roy's (1884–1959) resolution recommending the introduction of opium rationing and personal registration of opium-eaters, with a view to eradicate the evil from Assam within ten years, was passed by the Council on 22 March 1921. The government refused to implement the time-bound programme, but agreed to take 'such steps as are immediately possible and practicable' to give effect to the Council's wishes. It further agreed to open a register of opium-eaters.[69] The first Reformed Council also forced twelve cuts in budget demands. However, two of these cuts were restored fully and one partially, under the Governor's certificates.[70]

The Council deliberations reflected a disagreement between the majority of its members and the government on the issue of land revenue resettlement

---

[66] Speeches by Bora and Dam, 28 March, *ALCP* (1922), Vol. 2, pp. 534–44.

[67] Governor's address, 14 September, *ALCP* (1922), Vol. 2, pp. 817–19.

[68] *Indian Constitutional Reforms*, p. 509.

[69] *ALCP* (1921), Vol. 1, pp. 71–72.

[70] *Indian Constitutional Reforms*, pp. 522–25.

in the temporarily settled areas. The land revenue demand used to be periodically revised every ten years or so till the early years of the twentieth century. A resettlement had been made during 1905–12, for a period of twenty years. As this settlement was now about to expire, the government decided to commence another resettlement operation in the districts of Kamrup and Sibsagar, to start with. But, scared of increased taxation, the Reformed Council opposed resettlement and, on 14 August 1923, refused to vote the required funds for these operations. The Governor restored the funds.[71]

The government was convinced of the urgency of tenancy legislation in Sylhet, but wanted it to be preceded by preparation of records-of-right. With that end in view, a Bill was introduced in September 1921. However, because of determined opposition from the landlord lobby, its consideration was postponed *sine die* on the vote of the Council. In Goalpara, some spadework was done in the form of local enquiries into tenancy conditions by A.J. Laine, who was appointed Special Officer on Duty in 1916.[72] On the basis of his report in 1917, there was talk of extending the Bengal Tenancy Act, 1885, to Goalpara. Because of local zamindars' opposition, the idea was however eventually dropped. The Governor then proposed to go on with the preparation of records-of-right in Goalpara; but this idea, too, was abandoned due to financial stringency. The only reform so far carried out by the executive was the extension of Sections 150, 151 and 152 of the aforesaid Bengal Tenancy Act, 1885, to the district.[73]

Official attention was drawn also to the unsatisfactory conditions of tenants in the temporarily settled district of Cachar. In 1913, a Bill had been prepared for this district and then dropped, as mentioned in Chapter Three. J.E. Webster, an official, submitted another draft tenancy Bill for Cachar on 9 January 1922. The government decided to slightly remodel his Bill so as to make its provisions applicable to all temporarily settled areas of the province. The remodelled Bill was published on 30 May 1922, but it was also finally dropped on the plea of chill reception by the so-called 'public'.[74]

In Goalpara, some tenants refused to pay their rents under the inspiration of the Non-Cooperation movement. The tenants in Ghurla Pargana, for example, stopped paying rent to the Raja of Gauripur in 1921, until an amicable settlement was reached over the disputed rent enhancement.[75] The Assam Land-

---

71 Governor's address, 16 August, *ALCP* (1923), Vol. 3, pp. 703–04; *ALCP* (1924), Vol. 4, p. 88; *ALCP* (1925), Vol. 5, p. 988.

Under Section 72 D (2) (a) of the Act of 1919, a total amount of Rs 1,52,656 was certified by the Governor as necessary expenditure for resettlement operations.

72 On the question of rent claimed by zamindars for forest produce, the tenants of the Bijni and Parbatjoar zamindars carried on a struggle in 1915 and 1916. 'A Note on His Reminiscences by Pramathanath Chakravarti'.

73 Reply to A.M. Ziaosshams, 29 July, *ALCP* (1924), Vol. 4, p. 552.

74 Speech by R.K. Chaudhuri, 21 March, *ALCP* (1933), Vol. 13, p. 732; speech by Laine, ibid., p. 737.

75 H. Neog, *Pramathanath Cakravarti* (in Assamese, Jorhat, 1968), pp. 18–19 and 'A Note on His Reminiscences by Pramathanath Chakravarti'.

lord and Tenant Procedure (Amendment) Bill 1922 was officially sponsored as an emergency measure to help the zamindars. It was to be applied in case of necessity only to select areas of Sylhet and Goalpara, after due notification in advance. The Bill aimed at giving District Magistrates the power to decide rent refusal cases in a summary fashion. Sylhet zamindars gave their full support to the Bill. But many Councillors, including P.C. Datta (1869–1950), opposed it on grounds of principle as well as procedural technicalities. One member even pointed out that tenants were not at all represented on the Council. On 29 March 1922, a private motion recommending circulation of the Bill for eliciting public opinion was adopted. Officials, together with British and zamindar members, could muster only seventeen votes as against twenty-one non-official Indian votes in favour of this motion. The Bill was thereafter dropped as the emergency situation passed.[76]

Birth of the Swaraj Party

After the formation of the all-India Swaraj Party on 1 January 1923, a process of rethinking started in Assam too, in favour of Council entry. In July, T.R. Phookan founded the party's Assam branch with its headquarters at Gauhati, and he resumed his legal practice in August. Reprimanded severely for his new stand at a Congress organizational meeting, Phookan resigned from presidentship of the local Congress. In September 1923, he issued his party's election manifesto. According to this document, the objects of his Council entry programme were two-fold:

(i) to prevent people with a bad record of repressive, anti-people activities from entry into the legislature; and

(ii) to protest strongly against all legislation that was harmful to the people.

It was further stated that Swarajists would refuse office and offer wholesale obstruction to all measures brought before the Council.[77] A sizeable section in the Assam Congress, including Gopinath Bardoloi, leaned towards the Swaraj Party. In the 1923 election, Phookan was returned to the Indian Legislative Assembly, and several Swarajists to the Assam Legislative Council. Out of the thirty-nine elected members of the latter body, only thirteen or one-third were re-elected members. One of the significant Swarajist victories involved the defeat of Shivaprasad Barua (1880–1938), the richest Assamese planter. R.K. Hatibarua (1895–1929) – a Non-Cooperator who had undergone a term of imprisonment – was the successful candidate. Another important event was Nilmoni Phukan's failure to win the Dibrugarh seat. Both Phukan and Shivaprasad Barua, however, got their Council berths through the backdoor of nomination. It was no surprise, therefore, that Phukan later eloquently defended the principle of nomination in the Council

---

76 *ALCP* (1922), Vol. 2, pp. 566–75.
77 Confidential Home Department (Pol.) 1924; 'History-Sheet of Tarun Ram Phookan'. The dossier on Phookan contains a typed English version of the Swarajya Party's brief election manifesto of 1923, printed as a single-page leaflet at Aruna Press, Gauhati.

debate on local bodies, on considerations of electors' ignorance and illiteracy.[78]

Thus, the politics of effective opposition inside the Council triumphed not only over the no-changers' politics of Non-Cooperation, but also over that of responsivist cooperation. Only 33,352 or less than 25 per cent of the voters in the contested constituencies had participated in the poll of 1920. The comparable figure for the 1923 poll was 83,320 or slightly above 42 per cent; and for 1926, 88,709 or above 43 per cent. The number of candidates also increased from 81 in 1920 to 89 in 1923 and 88 in 1926.[79]

A review of the general elections since 1920 clearly shows that Congress participation in the poll did make a difference. From 1923 the enfranchised section of the people showed relatively wider and sustained electoral interest. This is revealed by the figures in the table given below.

Elections to the Assam Legislatures: 1920–37

	1920	1923	1926	1929	1937
Total number of candidates	81	89	88	n.a.	277
Returned unopposed	18	10	12	19	20
Contested seats	21	29	27	20	88
No. of registered voters	2,02,400	2,24,063	2,50,751	2,88,832	8,15,341
Votes polled	33,352	83,320	88,707		5,22,273
Percentage of votes polled for contested seats	25	42	43.5		71.3
Votes polled as percentage of the province's electorate	16.4	37.2	35.3		64.0

Source: As mentioned in footnote 79. For the last column, East India (Constitutional Reforms – Elections), *Return Showing the Results of Elections in India 1937* (New Delhi, 1937), p. 5.

[78] Dutt, *Landmarks of Freedom Struggle in Assam*, p. 66; ALCP (1926), Vol. 6, p. 869. In 1924 Nilmoni Phukan and Amarnath Roy, a Sylhet zamindar, were complimented as the best two parliamentarians in the house by its leader, William Reid. Speech by S. Dowerah, 27 September, *ALCP* (1924), Vol. 4, p. 1366.

[79] *ALCP* (1924), Vol. 4, p. 3; *ALCP* (1927), Vol. 7, pp. 10–13; *Return Showing the Results of Election in India 1923* (presented to Parliament, London, 1924), pp. 1–18 and 78–83; *India in 1920: A Report Prepared for Presentation to Parliament* (Calcutta, 1921), Appendix 3, p. 48; East India (Constitutional Reforms – Elections), *Return Showing the Results of Elections in India 1925 and 1926* (pp. cmd 2923, London, 1927); East India (Constitutional Reforms) Indian Franchise Committee, Vol. 1, *Report of the Indian Franchise Committee, 1932* (London, 1932), p. 76.

CHAPTER FIVE

Flexible Congress Tactics: 1924–36

About-turn to Swarajism

The Second Reformed Council: 1924–26

After the withdrawal of the Non-Cooperation movement, its constructive programme alone could no longer sustain the morale of the Congress rank
and file. They had so far believed that *swaraj* was attainable within a year but
now began to realize that the government machinery, particularly its legislative
organ, constituted a powerful instrument of propaganda and influence. Was it
not then expedient to enter the Council in order to blunt its harmful operations?
The Swarajist slogan of wrecking the constitution from within became increasingly acceptable in the Congress circles. By the end of 1924, the initial Congress
opposition to the Swarajists totally disappeared.[1] The latter again fully identified themselves with the Congress in Assam as in the rest of India.

With some eight of its members elected to the Assam legislature, the
Swaraj Party was not yet in a position to wreck the constitution. Evidently,
attacks on the government inside the Council were likely to succeed only if the
party could win the support of some independents and responsivists. Hence, it
formed a coalition with other nationalists of varying shades to carry on an
obstructive role in the Council. Saadulla, like Taraprasad Chaliha (1890–1948),
had been elected as an independent candidate with Swarajist support. However,
the expectation that, like the latter, he too would join the coalition was soon belied.[2] He preferred to work under the dyarchy as a minister, alongside P.C. Datta
from the Surma Valley.

The Swarajist–Nationalist–Independent Coalition Party was formed with
Faiznur Ali from the Brahmaputra Valley as its leader and Brojendra Narayan
Chaudhury (1882–1972), an independent member from the other Valley, as the
deputy leader. The first success of the party was achieved on 25 March 1924,

---

[1] Tarachand, *History of the Freedom Movement in India*, Vol. 4 (New Delhi, 1972),
p. 1.

[2] P. Barthakur, *Swadhiinata Ranar Samsparshat* (in Assamese, Dibrugarh, 1968),
p. 198.

when Gopendralal Das Chaudhury was elected deputy president, defeating his rival, Shivaprasad Barua, a nominated member. During its first four years, the Reformed Council had a government-appointed president, as per the requirements of the Act of 1919. The Coalition Party was able to get Abdul Hamid elected as president of the Council on 2 March 1925, immediately after the expiry of the initial four-year period.

The Swarajist strategy was to formulate a national demand for constitutional reform in the legislature and, if the government did not respond satisfactorily, to pursue a policy of obstruction and refusal of supplies. Accordingly, Faiznur Ali moved a resolution on 25 March 1924 demanding a full responsible government. In their speeches, the Swarajists viewed the dyarchy as a total failure. Basanta Kumar Das (1883–1965) defined a full responsible government as complete Indianization of every branch of administration along with complete development of the self-governing institutions. Not all the Coalition members thought that the dyarchy had failed. Even while supporting the resolution, Sadananda Dowerah, for example, felt that 'dyarchy has succeeded in Assam beyond all measures of success'. Nevertheless, in this first round of contest on policy matters, the opposition motion was adopted by twenty-nine to seventeen votes. Amongst the non-official Indian members present, only three, including Nilmoni Phukan, voted against the resolution.[3]

By another resolution moved by Dowerah on 27 September 1924, the house voted, twenty-six to nil, for immediate replacement of the dyarchy by full provincial autonomy and transfer of all reserved subjects to popular control in Assam. Faiznur Ali's resolution recommending the abolition of divisional commissionerships as an economy measure was also adopted by the house on 18 September. The attempts of the opposition to get a committee appointed to probe into the executive measures against the Non-Cooperation movement, however, ended in failure in the March and September sessions of 1924.[4]

Cut motions to reduce the ministerial pay had earlier ended in failure in the first Council. However, in April 1924, the Council was able to reduce it from Rs 3,500 to Rs 1,500 per month, by a single-vote majority. The Governor accepted this verdict. Official attempts to restore the original pay and to introduce the Assam Stamp (Amendment) and Assam Court Fees (Amendment) Bills were successfully blocked by the opposition in September. Kuladhar Chaliha's resolution recommending immediate legislation to prohibit the consumption and sale of opium in Assam, except for medical and scientific purposes, was passed on 3 March 1925. However, soon there was a turn in this anti-government tide. The Swarajist Coalition could no longer command a majority on several vital issues. The aforesaid two Bills, related to stamp and court fees, were passed on 7 March;

---

[3] *Assam Legislative Council Proceedings* (hereafter *ALCP*) (1924), Vol. 4, pp. 44–85.
[4] Ibid., pp. 471–79, 1287–1305, 1338–43 and 1365–69; *Indian Quarterly Register* (July–December 1924), p. 232 (c).

and the ministerial pay was also fully restored.[5] In response to the AICC's call, the Swarajists staged a walk-out from the house on 8 March 1926, as a mark of protest against non-fulfilment of the national demands put forward by the legislatures.[6] The government had smooth sailing in the last budget session of the house in their absence.

An official report on the working of the Act of 1919 revealed that a majority of the elected members considered constructive criticism of the executive government their most important function, the tendency to obstruct being on the decline. Even the Swarajists were willing to offer advice on important policy matters. The attitude of the second Reformed Council towards its legislative function was reasonable, on the whole, and, except in the first year, the government found little difficulty in obtaining supplies from it. A matter of greater concern was the general apathy outside the house. Its proceedings evoked little interest in the constituencies, partially because of the virtual absence of the media in Assam.[7]

For the first time in the Council's history, adjournments were moved in 1925 to force a discussion on matters of public importance. The *Report of the Reforms Enquiry Committee* (Muddiman Committee) was published on 9 March 1925. While the majority viewed the dyarchy as a success, the *Minority Report* noted its breakdown in the Central Provinces and Bengal, and was highly critical of the reforms. Even the Government of Assam, in its note to the Committee, had observed that ministers had no convincing answer to their opponents' cry that 'the reforms have bestowed no benefits on the electors'. An adjournment was moved by Faiznur Ali on 19 March 1925 to discuss the *Report*. The deliberations, in which no official participated, went fully in favour of the *Minority Report*. The house finally condemned the *Majority Report* as 'retrograde, disappointing and calculated to delay the attainment of full responsible government'. It recommended the adoption of such steps as would lead to the appointment of a Royal Commission or a Round Table Conference for devising a suitable constitution.[8]

The second Reformed Council forced as many as twenty-four cuts affecting the budget proposals, as against twelve by the first one. As the cuts were of marginal order in most cases, the government generally accepted the Council's verdict. In seven cases affecting grazing fees and land revenue collections, the cuts were however restored under the Governor's certification. For example, when the 1924–25 budget estimates were reduced by an amount of about Rs 3.5 lakh by the Council, a major part thereof under the heads of land settlement opera-

---

[5] *ALCP* (1924), Vol. 4, pp. 529–32 and 1197 ff.; *Indian Constitutional Reforms: Views of Local Governments on the Working of the Reforms dated 1927* (London, 1928), p. 507; *ALCP* (1925), Vol. 5, pp. 32–64 and 266–323.

[6] *ALCP* (1926), Vol. 6, pp. 553–54.

[7] *Indian Quarterly Register* (January–June 1928), p. 160 (a)–(b). This is the same as the *Indian Annual Register* (hereafter *IAR*).

[8] Ibid. (January–June 1925), p. 257; *ALCP* (1925), Vol. 5, pp. 731, 763–72.

tions, police and excise was restored through such means. On the whole, the second Reformed Council's performance was more impressive than that of the first. It also handled more business in respect of interpellation and resolutions.[9]

The Third Reformed Council: 1927–29

The forty-first session of the Indian National Congress, held at Pandu (Gauhati) in December 1926, was a big event. Despite poor financial resources, Assam was able to demonstrate that the national movement had struck deep roots in its territories. The Congress reiterated that its policy in various legislatures should be one of self-reliant activities for healthy national growth, and of determined resistance to whatever might impede the nation's progress towards *swaraj*. It enjoined upon all Congress legislators not to accept ministries and to oppose their acceptance by other parties.[10]

In the 1926 elections, Congressmen of Assam were able to win more seats than the Swarajists had gained in 1923. Even otherwise there was an infusion of new blood, since more than half of the house consisted of new faces. No less than twenty-two elected members of the first Reformed Council lost their seats to new members. Five of the nominated Councillors were also new. Saadulla was re-elected, but Rai Bahadur P.C. Datta – the other minister since late 1922 – was routed. Yet another blow to the government circles was the defeat of Nilmoni Phukan at the hands of Lakheswar Barua (1893–1964), a Congressman, in the bypoll for the Dibrugarh seat in March 1927. Though backed by officials and British planters, Phukan got only 1,400 votes, while his rival secured 2,268 votes.[11]

The exit of Phukan and Datta from the legislature made the task of ministry-making difficult for the Governor. For, to retain Saadulla in the ministry, the other minister had to be preferably a Surma Valley Hindu. None was, however, readily available, since the suitable elected members held their allegiance to the Congress. No suitable Hindu minister was available from the Brahmaputra Valley either, to have Saadulla replaced by a Muslim member from the Surma Valley constituencies. Under the circumstances, Rev. Nichols–Roy, a Christian Khasi who represented the Shillong general (urban) constituency and was equidistant from both the Valleys, was chosen as Saadulla's colleague.[12] This meant that there was no Hindu minister in the cabinet, nor any

---

[9] *Indian Constitutional Reforms*, pp. 506–09 and 522–25; Governor's address, *ALCP* (1924), Vol. 4, p. 530.

Out of 365 notified resolutions, as many as 327 were admitted but only 123 could be moved. Out of these again, only 56 were carried; 44 were withdrawn and 23 lost. As many as 1,814 out of 1,962 questions were admitted, but only 1,755 were answered.

[10] K.N. Dutt, *Landmarks of Freedom Struggle in Assam* (reprint, Gauhati, 1969), pp. 70–71; *ALCP* (1927), Vol. 7, pt. 1, p. 182.

[11] *The Mussalman*, 13 January 1927; Governor's address on 22 February, *ALCP* (1927), Vol. 7, pt. 1, p. 12; ibid., pt. 2, pp. 869–70.

[12] Governor's address on 22 February, *ALCP* (1927), Vol. 7, pt. 1; *The Mussalman*, 12 February 1927; ibid., 15 February 1927.

minister from the Surma Valley. The situation was awkward for the government, and provided much elbow room for the Congress to foment discontent.

T.R. Phookan was re-elected to the Legislative Assembly for India. Incidentally, Phookan had been chosen a member of the Working Committee of the AICC for 1927, but he never attended its meetings.[13] N.C. Bardaloi, an erstwhile 'no-changer', was chosen by the Swarajist–Nationalist Coalition Party as its leader and B.N. Chaudhury as its deputy leader. By now the latter was a full-fledged Congressman. Abdul Hamid was re-elected president of the Council and G. Das Chaudhury, deputy president.

When the Council met in February 1927, not more than fourteen of its members had any kind of Congress affiliation.[14] But many more independent members were keen on ministry-breaking in order to get the vacant berths for themselves. One such aspirant, Bepinchandra Ghosh of Goalpara, moved a no-confidence on 28 February against both the ministers, on the plea that they had taken an anti-people stand in all vital issues in the previous Council. This no-confidence motion, the first ever in the Assam Legislative Council, was made possible by the new rules of 27 October 1926, introduced as per the recommendations of the Muddiman Committee. Munawwar Ali – another ministerial aspirant from the Surma Valley – directed his venom particularly against Saadulla. He said that Saadulla did not enjoy the confidence of the Surma Valley Muslims, as he devoted himself 'exclusively, or almost exclusively, to doing good to the handful of Mussalmans of the valley from which he comes'. Surma Valley Muslims were particularly disgruntled because there had been no Muslim minister or executive Councillor from that Valley for the last five years. Congress–Swarajists were not interested in the personnel of the ministry as such, but were nonetheless eager to break it. They decided to vote for the motion but not to take part in the debate. The Council voted twenty-eight to twenty-two to reject the motion.[15] The solid British bloc (officials and non-officials) that constituted nearly a fourth of the house was obviously the mainstay of the ministers.

Although defeated in this first trial of their strength, Congress–Swarajists continued their dogged opposition. The number of censure motions carried during the February–March session of the Council left no doubt about their effectiveness. Censures affecting the reserved sphere of administration apart, about half a dozen motions were carried against the policy of the ministers.[16]

Speaking on the budget on 1 March 1927, R.K. Hatibarua told the house that his three-year experience with Assam budgets was about to convert him

---

James Joy Mohan Nichols–Roy graduated from Calcutta and floated a joint-stock fruit-processing company in 1918, of which he was the managing director for several years. A pastor to the Church of God and married to an American lady, he was a widely travelled man.

[13] Krishnanath Sharma, *Krishna Sharmar Diary* (in Assamese, Gauhati, 1972), p. 243.

[14] *The Mussalman,* 18 January 1927.

[15] *ALCP* (1927), Vol. 7, pt. 1, pp. 156–97; *The Mussalman,* 12 February 1927.

[16] *The Mussalman,* 12 March 1927.

'from the position of a non-violent non-cooperator to that of a rabid revolution-ary'. He expressed concern over the rumoured employment of the Assam Rifles beyond India's northeastern frontiers to disturb the integrity of the Republic of China. 'If this be a fact, Sir,' he said, '. . .such bureaucratic action will tempt young men like myself to go there though unwillingly and to engineer a mutiny in the ranks of the Assam Rifles which consist of Assamese people, who should never be employed to enslave others, being slaves themselves.'[17]

A man of the people and appointed secretary of the APCC in 1924, Hati-barua was one of the few leaders of Assam who used to take a wide view of dev-elopments. At one stage he wanted to go abroad to make a first-hand study of the institutions of self-government in Switzerland and other European countries.[18] However, his proposed visit did not materialize. He died prematurely in 1929, even before his disillusionment with the politics of non-violence was complete.

Congress–Swarajist attacks on the government were sustained through cut motions and refusal of grants, particularly under the budget heads of land revenue and excise. On 29 March 1928, the Council refused to take into consi-deration the Assam Stamp (Amendment) and Assam Court Fees (Amendment) Bills. However, when B.K. Das moved a no-confidence against Nichols–Roy questioning his British–Indian citizenship status – the latter hailed from a native state – it was defeated by twenty-seven to twenty-one votes on 3 April. On the same day, the government proposed the formation of a seven-member committee for purposes of cooperation with the Statutory Commission on Constitutional Reforms (Simon Commission, 1927) that had landed in India on 3 February 1928. N.C. Bardaloi delivered one of his finest orations while opposing this motion in the Council. To him, the reformed system was nothing but a sham and, hence, there was no point in cooperating with the Commission.[19]

The communal problem once more came to the fore in the wake of the Simon Commission. The National Congress and a section of the All-India Mus-lim League led by M.A. Jinnah boycotted it.[20] The other section of the League led by Sir Muhammed Shafi decided to cooperate. It was the latter Muslim League that thrived in Assam. A forty-member Assam Provincial Muslim League Council, which included all the Muslim legislators of the province except the Council's president, was formed early in 1928. It pleaded before the Commission for separate communal electorates.[21] Rising to speak after Bardaloi, Sayidur

---

[17] *ALCP* (1927), Vol. 7, pt. 1, pp. 234–35.

[18] D.O. No. 670 C, dated Shillong, 12 September 1925, to the Secretary to Government of India on Hatibarua's application for an international passport in Home (Political): 1925, File No. 94/IX (National Archives of India; hereafter NAI). K. Sharma adds that Hatibarua was invited by Horace Alexander to lecture at Birmingham on the evils of opium in Assam, after the publication of the *Assam Congress Opium Enquiry Report* (hereafter *ACOER*) (1925). See *Krishna Sharmar Diary*, p. 170.

[19] *ALCP* (1928), Vol. 8, pp. 99–114, 256–75, 275, 300 and 435.

[20] Tarachand, *History of the Freedom Movement in India*, p. 100.

[21] Speeches by Saadulla and Munawwar Ali, 17 September, *ALCP* (1928), Vol. 8, pp. 718–19 and 785–86.

Rahman, an Assamese Muslim planter, told the Council on 3 April 1928: 'It is the sincerest desire of our community at the present moment despite what hon. members like Mr Jinnah may say that this separate electorate is absolutely vital to our existence. The separate electorate has been enforced in Kenya, Palestine, Cyprus, Austria, Hungary and other countries.'[22]

The Council voted thirty-one to fifteen to form a seven-member committee to assist the Simon Commission. Of the votes in favour, thirteen were solid British votes. This was a major Congress defeat in the Council. On 9 April, the committee was duly formed with W.D. Smiles, an Irish planter, as the chairman and six members including Sadananda Dowerah.[23] A still bigger defeat on the Sylhet transfer question followed in September 1928. We shall discuss this in detail in a subsequent section.

The all-white Simon Commission arrived in Shillong on 2 January 1929. It conferred for six days with various representations, visited several outlying places and left the province on 11 January. Although boycotted by the Congress and other nationalists, nowhere in the province did the Commission meet with any hostile demonstration. Nor was it welcomed. One point of great importance discussed at length by the conference was the future composition of the provincial legislature. The Assam government proposed to retain communal representation and even to extend the principle of separate representation to such comparatively small groups as Ahoms, Marwaris, land-holders and the like. It was officially held that communal representation did not create friction, it only recognized existing differences. The Government of Assam was also opposed to adult suffrage. The committee appointed by the Assam Legislative Council, however, recommended universal adult suffrage, or at least suffrage for all heads of households aged twenty-five and above. It was of the strong view that the dyarchy should go. The Commission received twenty-seven memoranda altogether – many of them officially inspired – from various groups and organizations of Assam. These were concerned more with sectional than with national interests.[24]

After the Simon Commission's departure, the Council had a stormy budget session. On its closing day, 27 March 1929, Munawwar Ali selected Nichols–Roy, Minister of Local Self-Government, as his target for the third no-confidence motion in the Council. The Congress–Swarajists were only too ready not to miss this grand opportunity to put the government into disarray. The motion was carried by seventeen to fourteen votes. The prorogued Council was later prematurely dissolved without any reason being assigned for the action.[25]

The general election that followed was held in May 1929, in an atmosphere of mounting political discontent in the country. Nichols–Roy, who had

<hr>

[22] 17 September, *ALCP* (1928), Vol. 8, p. 271.

[23] Ibid., pp. 275 and 435.

[24] *Indian Quarterly Register* (July–December 1929), pp. 53 and 117; 'Note by C.K. Rhodes', Confidential A, March 1929, No. 111, File No. 33 C (Assam Secretariat Files; hereafter AS); *The Statesman*, 5, 6 and 8 January 1929.

[25] *ALCP* (1929), Vol. 9, pp. 940–41, 967 and 1170.

represented Shillong for three consecutive terms, found his nomination paper rejected on technical grounds. Nilmoni Phukan failed for the third time to win a seat, much to the regret of the government. All prominent Congressmen of the third Reformed Council, however, came back to the house with flying colours. Both the leader and deputy leader of the Congress–Swarajist Party were re-elected.[26]

The Sylhet Question in the Reformed Council

The Swarajists stood firmly united on the question of redrawing the provincial boundaries on a linguistic basis. B.N. Chaudhury had moved a resolution on the floor of the third Reformed Council in July 1924 for the transfer of Sylhet to Bengal. R.K. Hatibarua said in support of the resolution: 'As we all know, the Indian National Congress is committed to a policy of self-determination. . . . I believe the present is an opportune moment when the wishes of the people of Sylhet should be recorded.' Difficulty arose, however, from the side of Bengali-speaking Cachar which was not keen on vivisection of the province. If Sylhet was transferred to Bengal, there was no point – it was argued – in retaining Cachar. Under the circumstances, the original resolution was modified by the mover to include Cachar within its scope, so that the Cachar votes could be turned in his favour. Of the three Cachar members, two lent their support to the amended resolution but the third still opposed it. The Council voted twenty-two to eighteen to pass the amended motion. Incidentally, Nilmoni Phukan voted for the resolution. The Government of Assam was committed not to stand in the way, provided that Assam's status as a Governor's province remained unimpaired. In its letter of October 1925, the Government of India, however, made it sufficiently clear that Assam's future status was an independent and separate question, not to be linked with that of Sylhet.[27]

The issue, therefore, continued to remain controversial. There was neither a clear-cut consensus on the Cachar question nor an *a priori* official assurance about Assam's continuity as a Governor's province, following its loss of territory. A special session of the Council in January 1926 voted, twenty-six to twelve, to recommend only Sylhet's transfer to Bengal. A second resolution recommended that in no case should Assam lose its major province status. Official members refrained from voting on the first motion. All the Sylhet members, except two Muslims, and all the Indian members from the Brahmaputra Valley, except Saadulla and two other Muslim members, voted for the motion. All the three Cachar members – two Hindus and one Muslim – voted against. They

---

[26] Political B, September 1929, Nos. 314–365 (AS). 'I am sorry Sjt. Nilmoni Phukan has not been returned.' – (Sd.) L. Hammond, 29 December 1929. *The Bengalee,* 7 September 1929, reported that, on being moved by Nichols–Roy, the Election Commission declared the election of Rai Bahadur Nagendranath Chaudhury from Shillong as void. The latter was further ordered to pay costs to the former. A fresh election followed.

[27] *ALCP* (1924), Vol. 4, pp. 568–621; Governor's address on 13 July, *ALCP* (1925), Vol. 5, p. 1589; *ALCP* (1926), Vol. 6, pp. 660–63.

were opposed to Sylhet's transfer to Bengal unless Cachar also was transferred. Another motion recommending the transfer of Cachar also was, however, defeated.[28]

None of the Sylhet leaders was apparently keen on appending Cachar to Sylhet. They conceded to the general Assamese opinion that Cachar was historically, if not linguistically, an integral part of Assam. In the Surma Valley Political Conference held on 1 July 1928, a resolution recommending the inclusion of both Sylhet and Cachar in Bengal was defeated by an overwhelming majority. The Conference voted for the transfer of Sylhet alone.[29] Thus, public opinion in both the Valleys emerged united on the transfer question. As the voting in the Council suggested, a majority of the Surma Valley Muslim members were also behind the move.

Divisive communal politics, however, gained a new dimension after the appointment of the Simon Commission. Throughout his legislative career, Saadulla had opposed all proposals to transfer Sylhet. He explained the logic of his opposition in the clearest of terms as early as 1926. He argued, then, that as long as Sylhet remained in Assam, Muslims, who constituted one-third of the provincial population, would remain a respectable minority and hold the balance of Assam's electoral politics. But with the Muslim-majority district of Sylhet gone to Bengal, they would lose that position in Assam forever. On the other hand, the change would enhance the proportion of Muslims in Bengal's population not even by 1 per cent. He thus built a case for an undivided Assam in the larger political interests of Muslims in India.[30]

This theory had many champions, like Abdul Matin Chaudhury in the other Valley. In fact, the provincial Muslim League Council was formed in 1928 precisely to counter the move to transfer Sylhet. In September 1928, the Sylhet question was reopened in the Council with official backing, in an attempt to revise *volte-face* its earlier stand. Haji Muhammad Bakht Mazumdar, scion of an ancient Sylhet zamindar family and a Khan Bahadur, moved a resolution on 17 September asserting that the people of both Sylhet and Cachar were opposed to their transfer to Bengal. It was a direct affront to the Congress stand on linguistic provinces, an 'inspired resolution' in the words of B.K. Das. In an aggrieved and sarcastic tone, N.C. Bardaloi told the string-pullers behind it:

> . . . you want to have the resolution carried because you want to place it before the Simon Commission. Place this thing before any reasonable man, say to him that the Assam Council has decided the desire of the people by means of the votes of the European planters who forsooth know the desire of the people of Sylhet and Cachar, and by the votes of the European members of the Government, what will he say? Can there be anything more ridiculous than this?

---

[28] Ibid., pp. 126 and 194; Kutubuddin Ahmed's speech, *ALCP* (1928), Vol. 8, p. 715.
[29] B.N. Chaudhury's speech, ibid., p. 738.
[30] Saadulla's speech on 6 January, *ALCP* (1926), Vol. 6, pp. 42–43.

Analysing the structure of the Council, Bardaloi pointed out that in a 52-member house (excluding the president), seven officials, eight British planters and five nominated members, together with the two ministers, constituted a solid bloc of twenty-two who were always moving in one direction. 'So I think it would be better to go to Bengal,' he said, 'if we could go as a whole. It is useless to continue in a province with such a Council.'[31] On the other side, Saadulla would also prefer Assam's merger with Bengal with adequate safeguards rather than part with Sylhet.[32]

In a frantic attempt to stop the resolution, B.K. Das moved an amendment that a referendum be arranged to ascertain the views of all *chaukidari* and municipal rate-payers of Sylhet and Cachar regarding the transfer question. Nothing short of a referendum on the basis of universal adult suffrage would, however, have proportionately reflected the voice of the Muslims. But neither side was keen on this, although such a measure was suggested in his speech by Dowerah. Das's amendment was rejected by twenty-nine to twelve votes. All the thirteen Muslim votes were solidly against the amendment. The original resolution was thereafter passed without a division.[33] The debate rang the death-knell of the heretofore cleverly contrived Swarajist hegemony in the Council. Never again was the demand for transfer of Sylhet to Bengal raised in the legislature in the form of a resolution. For, Muslim members from both the Valleys were henceforth solidly opposed to this idea.

Civil Disobedience and Its Aftermath

Resignation of Congress Legislators

The fourth and last Reformed Council had its first meeting on 7 September 1929. Much to their chagrin, the Congress–Swarajists found that Abdul Hamid, president of the last Council and one-time Non-Cooperator, had meanwhile accepted ministership. The other minister was Rai Bahadur Kanak Lal Barua (1873–1940), who had managed to get himself elected from the special constituency for commerce and industry group – a pocket borough with a few dozen effective voters, mostly Marwaris. Barua was appointed minister in August 1929. After his retirement from government service in 1927, the Rai Bahadur had joined the National Liberal Federation and was elected to its national council at its Allahabad session in 1928. He had also participated in the All Parties' National Convention held in Calcutta.[34] Khan Bahadur Kutubuddin Ahmed, an executive Councillor during the years 1924–29, retired. In his place, Saadulla, who was knighted in

---

[31] *ALCP* (1928), Vol. 8, pp. 711–46; N.C. Bardaloi's speech, ibid., pp. 800–02.

[32] Notings by Saadulla on 20 and 27 July 1925 appended to letter from the officiating Chief Secretary No. 1573 – Pol – 3860 A.P., dated Shillong, 11 August 1925, submitted by the Government of Assam to the Simon Commission, 1929, as reproduced in *ALCP* (1929), Vol. 9.

[33] *ALCP* (1928), Vol. 8, pp. 784 and 811–12.

[34] Speeches by R.K. Chaudhuri and K.L. Barua on 12 September, *ALCP* (1929), Vol. 9, pp. 1169 and 1176.

1928, was taken in. The other executive Councillor was A.W. Botham. Faiznur Ali was elected president of the Council, defeating Keramat Ali (1882–1969). G. Das Chaudhury was unanimously re-elected deputy president. Thus, the business of the new Council started with a victory for the Congress–Swarajists.[35]

On 12 September, R.K. Chaudhuri's (1889–1955) resolution recommending a ministerial salary cut was, however, lost by thirty to seventeen votes. There was not even a single Muslim vote for the resolution. B.N. Chaudhury's motion to present the Governor with an address regretting the latter's failure to show cause for the premature dissolution of the previous Council and to take notice of a starvation death in his speech, was disallowed as *ultra vires* of the constitution. His notice for a no-confidence motion also had to be withdrawn on the last day of the session, 14 September, as the expected support from the so-called Nationalist Party was not forthcoming.[36] The house met again in March 1930 for the budget session; meanwhile, the country was engulfed in the Civil Disobedience movement.

The call of the Lahore Congress (December 1929) to fight for complete independence set the whole country astir. The new Congress Working Committee met on 2 January 1930 and urged the electorate to bring pressure on legislators to resign from their respective legislatures in response to the Lahore call. Many Congress legislators were at first hesitant to resign, as much in Assam as elsewhere. A leading Assamese periodical editorially commented on their procrastination.[37] Finally, eleven Congress–Swarajists from the Assam Legislative Council and T.R. Phookan from the Indian Legislative Assembly resigned. Unlike V.J. Patel, president of the above Assembly, Faiznur Ali clung to his presidential chair till the last day of his tenure. Phookan and two others who had resigned from the Assam Council – R.K. Chaudhuri and Sarveswar Barua (1886–1975) – came back through by-elections to their respective houses quite in time for the next budget sessions. N.C. Bardaloi, too, contested a by-election from Mangaldai to stage a comeback, but failed. Responsivists and stooges filled in the other Council vacancies, except in south Sylhet and Sunamganj. From these two constituencies, two illiterate cobblers – Chiratan Muchi and Kalicharan Muchi – were elected with the connivance of the Congress. Their candidatures were sponsored by *bhadralok* politicians, obviously in an attempt to put the Council to ridicule.[38] Their subsequent role as opposition members in the Council, however, revealed that they had been underestimated.

The Council met without the Congress–Swarajists on 10 March 1930 to

---

[35] *ALCP* (1929), Vol. 9, pp. 680–991, 1097 and 1326.

    N.C. Bardaloi was re-elected leader and B.N. Chaudhury deputy leader of the party. Independent Muslim members of the house, led by Munawwar Ali, formed the Nationalist Party on a makeshift basis.

[36] Ibid., pp. 1165–70, 1183 and 1326.

[37] Editorial, *Tinidiniia Asamiiya* (in Assamese), 1 February 1930, cited by Lakshminath Phukan, *Mahatmarpara Rupkonwaralai* (in Assamese, Calcutta, 1969), p. 4.

[38] Saadulla's reply to R.K. Chaudhuri on 12 September, *ALCP* (1930), Vol. 10, p. 847; Dutt, *Landmarks of Freedom Struggle in Assam*, p. 81.

discuss the budget. The stand that would have been taken by the Congress–Swarajist Party was continued with no less vehemence by the two erstwhile Swarajists and their friends, who now formed a pro-Congress opposition bloc in the Council. Nevertheless, the initiative had definitely passed to more reactionary and loyalist elements.

The First Phase of Civil Disobedience

On 26 January 1930, the national independence pledge was solemnly taken in gatherings all over the province. People pledged to prepare themselves for Civil Disobedience and eventual non-payment of taxes by gradually severing all voluntary association with the British. Gandhiji's 241-mile Dandi March from 12 March to 6 April was the signal for country-wide Civil Disobedience. A national week of 'war against the salt tax' was observed from 6 to 12 April, and the law-breaking movement spread. Abdul Gaffar Khan's arrest in Peshawar was followed by demonstrations and firings in which hundreds were killed and wounded in that part of the country. Platoons of the Garhwali Rifles who had disobeyed the order to shoot were courtmartialled. Peshawar was virtually in the hands of the people for ten days from 25 April to 4 May. Small revolutionary groups inside and outside the Congress, who had no faith in the creed of non-violence, were inspired by the militant mood of the people. The Chittagong armoury raid by a band of such revolutionaries in Bengal on 18 April stirred the youth.

Of the five Assamese AICC members, at least three – Tarun Ram Phookan, R.K. Chaudhuri and Gopinath Bardoloi (1890–1950) – were openly opposed to the idea of boycotting the Councils. Under the circumstance, Assam was failing to keep pace with the fast-moving events. The Pradesh Congress organization was in a doldrum because of dissensions over the policy of Council boycott. The triumvirate who had led the Non-Cooperation movement of the 1920s in the Brahmaputra Valley were unwilling to give the lead once more. Phookan had turned a responsivist and was opposed to the militant Congress programme. Kuladhar Chaliha and N.C. Bardaloi, too, were not prepared to lead the agitation to the stage of Civil Disobedience. On 27 January 1930, the old leaders of the APCC resigned. Bishnu Ram Medhi (1888–1980) was elected its president and Tayyebulla its secretary, with a view to take Assam on to the path of struggle.[39]

The struggle in Assam took the form of boycott of foreign cloth and excisable drugs, and of shops selling such goods. Picketing was resorted to. Until the end of April, the movement could make little headway in the Brahmaputra Valley, except in Gauripur–Dhubri, where a number of public meetings were held from 13 April. A *hartal* was organized there on 19 April leading to an almost complete strike in the Dhubri Government High School.[40] From Sylhet,

[39] O.K. Das, '1930–32 Sanar Swadhiinata Andolanar Smriti', in Harendranath Barua *et al.*, eds, *Bharatar Mukti Yunjat Asam* (in Assamese, Gauhati, 1972), pp. 26–28. Also see *Asamiiya*, 12 January 1930.

[40] Barua *et al.*, eds, *Bharatar Mukti Yunjat Asam*, pp. 72–74; Sharma, *Krishna Sharmar Diary*, pp. 243–44; information supplied by the Government, 10 September, *ALCP*

the first batch of *satyagrahis* commenced their journey on 6 April to break the salt law on the Bengal sea coast. The Sylhet volunteers camped for a month in three places at Noakhali to manufacture salt. Contraband Bengal salt was hawked all over Sylhet and at Dhubri by roving volunteer groups.[41] Mahendra Hazarika (1904–1990) of Nowgong helped organize peasants for the salt *satyagraha* in Midnapore, Bengal.

The organizational weakness and inactivity of the Congress Committees in the Brahmaputra Valley were conspicuous throughout the first quarter of 1930. In May 1930 there was a spell of *hartals*, passive disobedience and picketing at government-controlled schools, colleges, law courts and shops selling foreign cloth and excise goods. The district of Sylhet was rocked by innumerable processions led by Congressmen of two rival factions – the Congress Sangha and the Congress Committee. Out of about 200 pleaders, only twenty-six attended Mr Edgley's courts in Sylhet on 3 May. *Hartals* were declared following the arrest of B.N. Chaudhury on the same day. The *satyagrahi* volunteers were mainly recruited from various youth associations under such names as Tarun Sangha, Yubak Sangha, Sabuj Sangha, Chhatra Sanmilan, Brati Balak Samiti, etc., most of which had revolutionary affiliations or sympathies. The situation took a serious turn in the town of Sylhet on 7 May when the police lathi-charged a procession and injured no less than sixteen persons. According to non-official estimates, the number of those injured were as many as forty-one. Important Congress leaders and many volunteers were arrested all over Sylhet in May.[42]

The Brahmaputra Valley also became restive after Gandhiji's arrest on 5 May 1930. On receipt of the news, all shops in Gauhati spontaneously closed business for the day on 7 May. T.R. Phookan, speaking at a protest meeting at the local park, said that school and college boys need not resort to *hartals*. But between 6 and 15 May, the high schools of north Lakhimpur, Dibrugarh, Golaghat, Sibsagar, Nazira, Jorhat, Nowgong, Tezpur, Gauhati, Nalbari, Palasbari and Dhubri went on a strike or *hartal* for varying periods, followed by passive disobedience. These actions were invariably accompanied by vigorous picketing. As a result, the government schools of Dhubri, Nowgong and Tezpur, and also the Sibsagar Bezbarua School, were closed down for a long vacation in the mid-

---

(1930), Vol. 10, pp. 725–26 and R.K. Chaudhuri's speech, 13 September, ibid., p. 936. Cunningham, DPI, told the house: 'Dhubri had set the lead with hartals, strikes, ultimatum to the headmaster, meetings, processions, passive resistance and all the parapharnelia of disorder . . . Clemency had been tried and failed'; 13 September, ibid., p. 743.

41 'Banglay Swadhiinata Sangram', *Ananda Bazar Patrika* (in Bengali, Calcutta, Autumn special issue, 1338 *Sal*/AD 1931), pp. 102–06; 'A Short Review of the Congress Activities in Assam since it started up to Truce (March 5, 1931)', comp. 5 June 1931, Gauhati by the Secretary, APCC (typed) in the APCC archives, Congress Bhavan, Gauhati.

42 Confidential – A, June 1930, Nos 26–33, File No. 102 C of 1930 A – December 1930, Nos: 27–36, File No. 138 C of 1930 (AS). *Ananda Bazar Patrika*, (Autumn special issue, 1338 *Sal*/AD 1931), pp. 102–06.

dle of May. On 11 May, there was a house-to-house search at Dhubri, starting with the District Magistrate's bungalow. It was carried out under his own orders, on a false alarm that half-a-dozen Chittagong insurgents were hiding in the town. The public of Dhubri–Gauripur held a protest meeting on 12 May, with Abdul Mazid Ziaosshams, MLC in the chair, and resolved upon a more strenuous boycott of foreign goods. On hearing the news of Abbas Tyabji's arrest, a 500-strong procession, largely of school children, attempted to hold a meeting on 14 May in violation of Section 144. It was broken up by a lathi-charge, causing injury to some. The Assam Pradesh Congress Committee set up a public enquiry committee to probe into the Dhubri incident. Its report was published in July 1930. In the same month, a special session of the Assam Chhatra Sanmilan was held at Gauhati, with O.K. Das in the chair, to protest against the Cunningham Circular. It now decided in favour of boycotting government schools and colleges.[43]

Cunningham Circular, Repression and Truce

The May upsurge would have perhaps subsided, at least in Kamrup, but for the government's vindictive policy. R.K. Chaudhuri and T.R. Phookan tried to persuade Gauhati students to give up picketing and the latter were reportedly in a mood to listen. The situation worsened, however, when the Director of Public Instruction, Cunningham, came out with his notorious Circular of 19 May, demanding an undertaking from the strikers and/or their guardians for good behaviour as a condition for their readmission. There was widespread resentment against this move when Cotton College reopened after a long vacation. The anti-Circular agitation drew thousands of students into the movement in both the Valleys. Under pressure from all quarters, the Circular was substantially modified by 20 June. 'The Congress in Assam Valley Division, as far as I know,' Chaudhuri told the Council, 'was poor of funds. They were unable to provide for volunteers. But this Cunningham Circular enabled them to find some volunteers to help the Congress movement.' By 1 September, as per official claims, 85 per cent of the pupils of government-controlled schools of the province had signed the undertaking and were attending their classes. According to another official estimate, out of 15,186 pupils on the rolls before the vacation, 3,117 opted out as a result of the agitation. Several national schools were set up to accommodate the drop-outs.[44]

The Simon Commission Report of June 1930 was universally condemned because of its deliberate failure to mention even 'dominion status' as the goal of Britain's India policy. Inaugurated on 12 November in London, the Round Table Conference met without Congress participation even as the movement was going

[43] *ALCP* (1930), Vol. 10, pp. 725–26; R.K. Chaudhuri's speeches, ibid., pp. 735–43 and 934–37. Mahendramohan Chaudhury, 'Ami swadhiinata samgramalai kenekoi ahilo', in Barua *et al.*, eds, *Bharatar Mukti Yunjat Asam*, pp. 78–79.

[44] *ALCP* (1930), Vol. 10, pp. 703–04, 710–17 and 730–43; quote from Chaudhuri, ibid., p. 740; Governor's speech, 8 September, ibid., p. 566.

on. Assam was represented there by Chandradhar Barua – poet, planter and a member of the Council of State.

At the peak of the 1930 movement, the two leading organs of Assamese public opinion – the *Asamiiya* and the *Sylhet Chronicle* – were forced to stop publication for some time under government orders. By 18 August, altogether 671 participants in the Civil Disobedience movement, including students, had been imprisoned. No less than 100 of them were juvenile law-breakers. In the same month, the government decided to intensify its repressive measures. B.R. Medhi, APCC president, along with several other leaders, was arrested. The motor cars of B.R. Medhi and Bairam Singh (1893–1973), the latter from Dibrugarh, were publicly auctioned. The Working Committee of the APCC was declared unlawful in the last week of August 1930. On 8 September, the Council was told by the Governor that Assam had 'undoubtedly weathered the storm so far better than other Provinces'. But there was no ground yet for such complacency. A procession in Nowgong town had to be forcibly dispersed by the police on 12 November. The next day eighteen volunteers, all women, were arrested at the school gate to make room for the District Magistrate's entry. The police even seized a copy of Edmund Burke's *French Revolution* in the course of house searches in the town. Parallel people's courts were established at Chaparmukh to try civil and criminal cases. The APCC meeting held at Sibsagar on 22 November 1930 expressed its gratitude to the people of Assam for their 'wonderful response to the present India-wide movement'. It congratulated the village women, in particular, for the invaluable help they were rendering to the cause of the freedom struggle. Guneswari Devi of Nowgong was mentioned as one of Assam's first two women to be jailed in connection with the movement. The meeting ratified the replacement of Tayyebulla by Sonaram Datta (d. 1943) as the general secretary of the APCC, for, in the thick of the struggle, Tayyebulla had resigned from his office for personal and domestic reasons.[45]

The APCC and allied associations having the same objects were declared unlawful by a notification on 23 December. In January 1931, the Assam Rifles marched through some interior parts of north Kamrup, with the ostensible purpose of disparaging poaching in reserved forests, but actually to strike terror in the hearts of the pro-Congress village people. In many places, tea garden managers were appointed as special police.[46] After Medhi's arrest, the APCC president's

---

[45] Quote from Governor's speech, 8 September, ibid., p. 565; R.K. Chaudhuri's speech, 10 September, ibid., p. 737; Government's reply to a question, ibid., p. 702; Government communiqué of 27 August 1930, in Confidential A, March 1931, No. 127, File No. 58–C of 1931 (AS); Saadulla's reply to R.K. Chaudhuri on 19 March, *ALCP* (1931), Vol. 11, pp. 472–78; Dutt, *Landmarks of Freedom Struggle in Assam*, pp. 76–77; Confidential A – September 1930, No. 77, File No. 230 of 1930 containing 'Notification by the Government of Assam, General and Judicial Departments' (AS); Confidential A – December 1930, No. 35, File No. 138 C of 1930 (AS).

[46] 'A short review of Congress Activities in Assam', comp. 5 June 1931. This report also reveals that non-payment of *chowkidari* tax and breach of forest law in Goalpara, as methods of struggle, were suggested but did not find favour with the APCC.

office remained vacant for some time because of Gopinath Bardoloi's reluctance to step in, until Jadavprasad Chaliha came forward to officiate in that capacity. This indicated organizational weakness. Nevertheless, the boycott movement continued until it was temporarily suspended by Gandhiji after his historic meeting with the Governor-General on 5 March. In June 1931, the first Assam Provincial Political Conference, under the auspices of the Congress, was held at Jorhat.[47] Subhas Chandra Bose visited Sylhet on 9 May 1931 and succeeded in bringing about a formal merger between the district's two rival factions – the Congress Sangha and the Congress Committee.[48]

The extent and intensity of the Civil Disobedience movement in its first phase, till 5 March 1931, is fairly indicated by two sets of official figures available on convictions and arrests, as given in the table below. More than one-third of the arrested and half of those convicted were from the district of Sylhet. There was a successful campaign against the *chaukidari* tax in several villages, particularly Beheli and Paligaon in the Sunamganj sub-division. As a result, many *chaukidars* resigned. It was in course of the struggle at Beheli that Karunasindhu Ray emerged as a local peasant leader.[49] He contested the 1920 election from Sunamganj and, as it appears, was miserably defeated by the local zamindar, Amarnath Ray. Karunasindhu was elected to the Provincial Assembly in 1937, as a Congress candidate. He was also one of the early communists of Sylhet. However, it appears from the table given below that the intensity and sweep of the

No. of Persons Arrested and Convicted for Civil Disobedience

	Year ending 31 March 1931			1 April 1930–15 February 1931	
District	Arrested under Ordinances	Arrested under Penal Law	Total Arrested	Total Arrested	Total Convicted
Sylhet	467	312	779	892	616
Cachar	8	15	23	22	18
Goalpara	91	3	94	160	67
Kamrup	252	47	299	522	277
Darrang	11	20	31	50	14
Nowgong	96	222	318	555	130
Sibsagar	58	–	58	98	60
Lakhimpur	46	3	49	74	37
	1,029	622	1,651	2,373	1,219

Sources: Saadulla's statement, *ALCP* (1932) Vol. 12, p. 1079; Saadulla's reply to R.K. Chaudhuri, 19 March, *ALCP* (1931), Vol. 11, p. 475.

---

[47] Confidential A – December 1930, No. 36, ibid., and *ALCP* (1931), Vol. 11, p. 478; Dutt, *Landmarks of Freedom Struggle in Assam*, p. 74; Sharma, *Krishna Sharmar Diary*, p. 186. See also Das, '1930–32 Sanar Swadhiinata Andolanar Smriti', p. 39.

[48] Nikunjabihari Goswami, *Shriihatter Swadhiinata Sangramer Sankshipta Itihas* (manuscript in Bengali, Karmibhavan, Kulaura, n.d.), in the Office of the Editor of the History of Freedom Movement (hereafter OEHFM), Government of Assam, Gauhati.

[49] 'Banglay Swadhiinata Sangram', p. 105.

movement was no less in Kamrup and Nowgong than in Sylhet, given their respective populations.

As per the terms of the Gandhi–Irwin Pact signed on March 5, all Civil Disobedience prisoners, other than those committed on charges of violence, were released. This Pact was later ratified by the Karachi Congress. The National Congress took part in the second Round Table Conference, but it ended in a failure in December 1931.

Civil Disobedience: Second Phase

Under the impact of the Great Depression, the ryots in Assam, as elsewhere, were in a pitiable condition in the first half of the 1930s. In the temporarily settled areas of Assam, the cumulative arrears of land revenue went on mounting from year to year as follows:

Land Revenue in Arrears (outstanding)

On 1 July:	1928	1929	1930	1931	1932	1933
Rs (lakhs):	2	3	7	21	36	37

The outstanding arrears of land revenue as of 1 July 1932 amounted to about 37 per cent of the current land revenue demand.[50] Processes issued for the attachment of defaulters' moveable properties increased in number from 81,958 in 1932–33 to 98,122 in 1933–34. In the latter year, distress warrants were issued in as many as 1,60,000 cases. The number of defaulting estates put on sale by the government in an attempt to realize the dues also increased from 41,734 to 59,215 in these years. Eight small tea gardens of the Brahmaputra Valley, similarly put on sale for default of land revenue, had to be purchased by the government at Re. 1 each, for lack of bidders. In 1933–34, the ratio of realized land revenue to the total demand in Assam was only 63.7 per cent. Altogether 3,394 annual and periodic *pattas* of revenue defaulters were annulled in that year in the Brahmaputra Valley alone. Because of the Depression, there was a year-to-year heavy fall in revenue collection, particularly from such sources as land, excise and forests. The provincial excise revenue gradually slid from Rs 6.5 million in 1929–30 to Rs 3.4 million by 1933–34.[51]

It was in such an acute economic situation that the Civil Disobedience movement was again launched in Assam, in response to the Congress Working

---

[50] Governor's address, 12 September, *ALCP* (1932), Vol. 12, p. 761, for the years 1928–32; *ALCP* (1933), Vol. 13, p. 1216, for the year 1933.

[51] A.J. Laine's reply to S. Barua on 6 and 7 June, *ALCP* (1935), Vol. 15, pp. 1127 and 1173; speech by Prichard on 26 February, ibid., p. 130; Abdul Hamid's reply to Keramat Ali on 5 June, ibid., p. 1063; Memorandum of Assam Legislative Council to the Chairman of Joint Select Committee of Parliament, dated 14 September 1933, *ALCP* (1933), Vol. 13, p. 1184.

The Council was informed of the sale of tea gardens on 10 March 1934 – *ALCP* (1934), Vol. 14, pp. 278–79.

Committee's call to the nation on 1 January 1932. Determined to suppress the movement brutally, the Government of Assam promulgated the Prevention of Molestation and Boycott Ordinance of 9 January. The APCC was then constituted of B.R. Medhi, J. Chaliha, Dhaniram Talukdar (1888–1971), Hemchandra Baruah (1893–1945), Omeo Kumar Das and Beliram Das – most of them lawyers by training.[52]

On 26 January, meetings to take the independence pledge and processions were held all over the two Valleys. In Sylhet, seventeen persons sustained injuries from police attacks. Twenty-four persons in all were arrested on that day and jailed for terms varying from six months to two years. Sylhet and Goalpara were declared notified areas under the Unlawful Association Ordinance on 1 and 23 February, respectively. The said Ordinance was progressively brought into force in Sylhet, Kamrup and Goalpara during the span of 5–12 February. Important leaders in both the Valleys were imprisoned. Processions were forcibly dispersed in many places throughout the month of February.[53] Even N.C. Bardaloi, who had kept himself aloof from the first phase of the movement, was arrested on 13 April for hoisting a national flag in his compound and for violating Section 144. Released the same day, he was rearrested on 26 April and thrown into jail. Several thatched huts belonging to him were taken possession of by the police to prevent their use for the Congress cause, and his motor car was publicly auctioned. Bhubaneswar Barua (1893–1956) was also arrested, among others. In the midst of this turmoil, the second Assam Provincial Political Conference was held in June 1932 at Jorhat, presided over by the *satradhikar* of Garmur.[54] The Surma Valley Political Conference held its ninth session at Sylhet on 27 June 1932.[55]

According to official sources, altogether 1,494 persons were arrested up to 31 August in Assam in connection with the 1932 movement. Of them, 1,076 persons, including 80 women, were convicted till mid-August. The APCC's estimate was that no less than 1,700 persons were arrested. Amongst those convicted and imprisoned, to mention only some, were Chandraprava Saikiani (1901–1972), Gahanchandra Goswami (1900–1979), Purnachandra Sharma (b. 1900), Hemchandra Baruah, Mahendramohan Chaudhury (1908–1982), Bejoy Chandra Bhagavati (b. 1907), B.N. Chaudhury, B.K. Das, Rabin Navis, Bimalaprasad Chaliha (1912–1971), Sudhansu Banerjee, and three young poets – Jyotiprasad Agarwala (1903–1951), Hemanga Biswas (1912–1987) and Dhirendrachandra Datta (1912–1972). More than one-third of those arrested or convicted in Assam

---

[52] 'APCC Report, 1933 on the C.D. Movement of 1932', *APCC Papers*, Packet No. 35; Saadulla's statement, *ALCP* (1932), Vol. 12, pp. 690–94.

Hemchandra Baruah was the most dynamic organizer of the Assam Pradesh Congress ever since its inception. Though he had a degree in law in 1925, he never practised.

[53] Saadulla's statement, *ALCP* (1932), Vol. 12, pp. 690–94.

[54] *ALCP* (1932), Vol. 12, pp. 1075–78; 'APCC Report, 1933 on the C.D. Movement of 1932'; M. Chaudhury in H. Barua *et al.*, eds, *Bharatar Mukti Yunjat Asam*, pp. 82–84.

[55] N. Gupta Chaudhury, comp., *Shriihatta Pratibha* (Sylhet, 1961), pp. 235–36.

were from the district of Sylhet. In terms of arrests and convictions, the sub-divisions of Tezpur, Golaghat and Gauhati were also badly affected. In Tezpur and Gauhati, the police force had to be deployed to protect persons engaged in land revenue collection. The north Lakhimpur and Cachar sub-divisions were only marginally touched by the movement. An APCC report on the Civil Disobedience movement of 1932 later stated:[56] 'True it is that Assam has not been able to take up no-tax campaign. But the incapacity of the Rayats to pay up their taxes forced Government into an automatic no-tax campaign. The attachment and auction of property went on everywhere.'

Collapse of Civil Disobedience

In the wake of the Communal Award of 10 August 1932 and the third Round Table Conference (17 November to 24 December 1932, London) came the White Paper of 15 March 1933. It, more or less, endorsed the Simon Commission's recommendations, but also contained a deferred scheme of a federal government, to be implemented only after a requisite number of native states had accepted it. A Joint Parliamentary Committee was formed in April 1933 to consider those proposals. Drafted on the basis of the Committee's report (October 1934), the Government of India Act of 1935 was passed by the British Parliament on 4 August.

The Communal Award was based on the theory that India was not a nation but a heterogeneity of unintegrated communities. The award made the Hindus immediately apprehensive of British motivations in driving a wedge between the depressed classes and other Hindus. Gandhiji's protest fast unto death in September forced the leaders of the two sections to reach an agreement in favour of joint electorates, with more than proportionate seats reserved for the depressed classes, and this settlement was accepted by the British government. Released on 8 May 1933, Gandhiji temporarily suspended the mass Civil Disobedience, to the utter dismay of his followers. In a joint statement, V.J. Patel and Subhas Chandra Bose referred to Gandhiji's failure as a political leader. 'The time, therefore, has come', they said, 'for a radical reorganization of the Congress on a new principle with a new method, for which a new leader is essential.'[57]

In the face of such criticism as well as the adamant British attitude, the movement was revived in the form of individual civil resistance from August 1933 to March 1934. However, on 7 April Gandhiji finally advised Congressmen to suspend their individual resistance. His ten-day tour of Assam that ended on 20 April passed off quietly. In Assam, the Civil Disobedience movement had already petered out long before that date. Congressmen were divided among

---

[56] Two statements of Saadulla on political arrests and convictions, *ALCP* (1932), Vol. 12, pp. 1079 and 1091; for information on prisoners mentioned, *ALCP* (1933), Vol. 13, pp. 301, 404, 557 and 692–93; 'APCC Report, 1933, on the C.D. Movement of 1932'. Sudhansu Banerjee came from Bengal and settled as a trader in Nowgong in 1908.

[57] Cited by Tarachand, *History of the Freedom Movement in India*, p. 186.

themselves as to the next course. Some felt that participation in Councils was warranted by the situation. Others, like B.N. Chaudhury, publicly stated that the cause of independence could not be served through Councils any more. The AICC meeting at Patna in late May finally decided to contest the ensuing national elections. In the autumn of 1934, Gandhiji resigned his Congress membership but yet remained the most powerful behind-the-scenes influence, ready to act whenever needed. Trienniel elections to the municipal and local boards in Assam passed off peacefully in May 1934. In some districts Congressmen contested but with no marked success. The ban on the Congress in Assam was lifted on 13 June.[58]

G. Das Chaudhury, who had resigned his seat in 1930, won a by-election and was sworn in as a Council member on 11 September 1934. In November 1934, N.C. Bardaloi scored a victory over T.R. Phookan in the election to the Indian Legislative Assembly from the Brahmaputra Valley. Similarly, B.K. Das was elected from the other Valley. The Muslim seat was bagged by Abdul Matin Chaudhury, a Muslim Leaguer. Thus, once more the Congress came back into the fold of parliamentary politics, with the intention of opposing the British policy from within the legislatures. In view of the impending constitutional change, no fresh election to the Assam Legislative Council was held, however, till the end of 1936. The fourth Provincial Political Conference, held on 6 December 1936 at Becheria (near Tezpur), gave out a call for capturing the legislature in order to wreck the constitution from inside. Presiding over the open session attended by about 1,100 people, Bhulabhai Desai explained the strategy of poll participation without accepting the constitution as such.[59]

New Dimensions of Struggle
Birth of a Peasant Movement
The economic depression of the 1930s was so widespread that the phased Civil Disobedience movement tended to grow into an anti-imperialist mass revolt. Gandhiji was determined to keep it non-violent and, therefore, halted it twice before its final suspension. Nevertheless, the movement channelized social and political activities in new directions. The eleven-point charter of demands that Gandhiji had raised in the 1930s included the demand for a 50 per cent reduction in land revenue rates. This caught the imagination of the people of Assam.[60]

A number of local peasant organizations were either newly started or re-activized during this period with such demands as reduction and remission of land revenue, distribution of agricultural loans and abolition of cart tax. These organizations at the grassroots level were not necessarily politically oriented.

---

[58] M. Jha, *Role of Central Legislature in the Freedom Struggle* (New Delhi, 1972), pp. 198–200; 'Fortnightly Reports on the Political Situation', April 1934 onwards, Home Political – Files No. 18–4–34 to 18–8–34 (NAI).

[59] Police Department, Shillong: Special Branch, File No. B–2 (17) 36 of 1936.

[60] Sharma, *Krishna Sharmar Diary*, p. 186.

For instance, in 1931, the Konwarpur (Mauza) Hitasadhini Sabha raised a demand for remission of land revenue. The Cachar Zilla Krishak Sanmilani, which held its third annual conference on 1 February 1931, was also a non-political gathering. It was chaired by Khan Sahib Rashid Ali Laskar, MLC, a pleader who owned 60 *bighas* of land and five ploughs. It was attended by some 3,000 people.

Ryot Sabhas all over Assam proper, on the other hand, had close links with the Congress, particularly in Tezpur, Sibsagar and Jorhat sub-divisions. The first session of the Chhayduar Rayat Sanmilani was held at old Gomori on 13–14 June, with the *satradhikar* of Garmur in the chair and the attendance of nearly 600 people. During its discussions, the conference protested against the execution of Bhagat Singh, the stoppage of pension of Harikrishna Das – a retired nationalist civil surgeon, and the enhancement of land revenue rates. The All-Assam Ryot Sabha was formed in 1933 to consolidate the movement. About two to three hundred local Ryot Sabhas, organized on the basis of *mauza*, district, etc., were federated into this All-Assam Ryot Sabha. Its first two annual conferences were held at Tilikiam (near Jorhat) and Dergaon in 1933 and 1934, respectively. The Sabha included both Congressmen and others. It adopted a formal constitution, fixed a membership fee of 1 anna per year and held annual conferences. The proverbial saying – 'the ryots themselves are the sovereign' (*raijei raja*) – now assumed a new meaning and became a popular slogan. The main demand of the Ryot Sabha was a 50 per cent reduction in the land revenue rates.[61]

There was also a Krishak Sanmilani (or Samiti) in Goalpara sub-division since 1933 which used to represent local grievances, particularly those of the tenants of the Mechpara zamindari estate, from time to time. This Krishak Sanmilani was reorganized as an allied Congress body in 1935.[62] Abaruddin Munsi, Khagendranath Nath, Ripunjay Sinha, etc., were among the leaders of this peasant organization of Goalpara. Its first sitting, attended by 15,000 people and presided over by Omeo Kumar Das, was held at Balbala. Its second sitting was held at Dudhnai the next year, with Gopinath Bardoloi in the chair.[63] Ryot Sabha movement came to an end after the Defence of India Rules were promulgated in 1939.

In 1932–33, the unorganized tenant cultivators of Kamrup peacefully agitated for the grant of occupancy rights through suitable legislation. Out of some 1,89,000 acres of *nisfkhiraj* (half revenue-paying) land in the province,

---

[61] Ibid., pp. 203–04 and 249–52; *ALCP* (1931), Vol. 11, pp. 537, 562 and 954; *ALCP* (1933), Vol. 13, pp. 951–52;
    Assam Police Abstract of Intelligence 1931, No. 1079, Assam S.B., 27 June 1931 and *Assam Police Abstract of Intelligence 1936*, No. 339, Sibsagar, 25 March 1916, OEHFM, Government of Assam, Gauhati.
[62] The so-called 'Nikhil Goalpara Krishak Samiti', in its address to J. Nehru on 29 November 1937, claimed to be three years old. *APCC Papers*, Packet No. 35.
[63] An anonymous note on Goalpara, in the OEHFM, Government of Assam, Gauhati. The relevant information contained therein has been confirmed by O.K. Das.

about 1,35,000 acres were concentrated in that district. Besides, some 18 per cent of the *khiraj* (full revenue-paying) lands there were also sub-let. There was so far no legislation for regulating landlord–tenant relations. For want of occupancy rights in land, the tenants often failed to secure agricultural credit in times of need. They were subjected to various illegal cesses by their landlords under such pretences as *seva* (payment as a token of homage to landlords), *mati-pura* (payable on each marriage), *bahakharach* (landlord's touring expenses) and *puja kharach* (*puja* expenses of the landlord).[64]

A petition signed by some 2,000 tenants of Kamrup was addressed to the Governor-in-Council for legislative redress of their grievances. Public meetings were held in support of the tenants' demands. The local press, for example, the *Asamiiya*, came out with articles and editorials to highlight the need for legislative action in this field. Even the landlords were not totally opposed to the movement. This was because the tenants were agreeable to certain provisions, on the same lines as those prescribed in the Goalpara Tenancy Act (I of 1929), to ensure speedy realization of rents in arrear. In response to the agitation, the Council recommended tenancy legislation for all temporarily settled areas on 21 March 1933.[65]

The most politicized peasant movement, however, developed in Sylhet, particularly among the Manipuri tenants of the Bhanubil area. The zamindari *mahal* of Bhanubil in the Pithimpasha estate of Maulvibazar was a cluster of nine villages, with a population of some 9,000 and arable lands amounting to about 1,500 acres. Between 1885 and 1922, the zamindari rent per *kear* (one-third of an acre) there had been gradually enhanced from 10 annas to a rupee-and-a-half. Besides, an *abwub* and fines for failure to pay rent on the due date were also added. The measurement of land by a shorter pole in 1923 resulted in an increased rent burden that the peasants refused to accept.

In 1927 a notice was served, enhancing the rent further to Rs 2–8 as. per *kear*. The estate managed to obtain some decrees at that rate by 1931. While executing the decrees by force, the zamindars demolished hundreds of tenants' homes, seized their cattle and destroyed their granaries in the face of a no-rent campaign. Peasants, helped by a section of Congressmen, offered stiff resistance. Khirodechandra Deb, Purnendukishore Sengupta (1895–1978), Saralabala Deb, and many peasant leaders and Congressmen, including women, were convicted to imprisonment in the Bhanubil case during the years 1931–34. Some, like Baikunthanath Sarma, a leader of the Manipuri peasant community, were convicted for a second term in January 1934.[66]

---

[64] Speech by R.K. Chaudhuri on 21 March, *ALCP* (1933), Vol. 13, p. 732. Chaudhuri read out long extracts from the mass petition.

[65] Chaudhuri's speech, ibid.; *Asamiiya*, 25 *Agrahayana* (24 November 1932) as well as 5, 12 and 23 February 1933, cited in the same source, p. 743.

[66] *ALCP* (1933), Vol. 13, p. 1251; Scott to Dawson, Confidential 349 C, Silchar, 19 June 1934 in Confidential B, March 1935, Nos. 23–44, File No. 98–C of 1934 (AS); a note on the background of the dispute in 'J. Nehru's Assam Tour File', *AICC Files*, No. p. 4 (i), 1937 (Nehru Memorial Museum and Library [hereafter NMML], New Delhi).

The fierce class struggle at Bhanubil, at a time when a workers' and peasants' party was in the process of consolidation in neighbouring Bengal, helped the spreading of nebulous socialist ideas in Sylhet. An association, reportedly styled 'Samyavadi Samiti' (Socialist Association), was formed there in 1931, and its inaugural meeting in July was presided over by Bipinbihari Ganguli from Bengal. Resolutions were passed in that meeting to rouse the ryots against their landlords. Members of the association took up the cause of the Manipuri tenants of Bhanubil and tried to build up a tenants' movement in other places as well.[67]

Not only British rule, but also landlordism and capitalism came under fire from the emergent leftist youth. Dwarakanath Goswami (d. 1939) had to go to prison for a short term as a *satyagraha* volunteer in 1930. Rearrested in 1931, he was convicted by the high court in 1932 to a three-year jail term, on charges of instigating young men of Sylhet to commit murder. After Goswami's arrest, Harendrachandra Chaudhury tried to induce the Manipuri tenants of the British-managed Dhemai Tea Estate not to pay rent to their landlord. According to police reports, he belonged 'to the advanced socialist party'.[68]

A new wind was blowing in Sylhet through other windows as well. Muslim seamen returning from various ports to their native villages in Sylhet brought back with them stories about the Soviet Union and workers' struggles in distant lands. Aftab Ali, secretary of the Seamen's Union of Calcutta, who belonged to Sylhet (Balaganj), addressed a couple of meetings in the district in October 1933. In these, he talked of socialism and the urgency of the abolition of zamindaris. A peasants' and workers' conference was held at Bhartakhala village on 24 December 1932, with Abdul Karim in the chair. A principal organizer of the peasants' and ryots' associations in the district was Muhammed Mortuza Gabutaki.[69] It was the Muslim rich and middle peasants and *jotdars* who were behind this peasant and ryot (*krishak praja*) movement.

Local revolutionary youth groups were also exposed to the influence of socialist thought. They had participated in the non-violent Civil Disobedience but, having seen its futility, moved towards the terrorist path. Finally, their equally

---

R.N. Aditya, *Fight for Freedom in Sylhet* (Karimganj, 1964), pp. 14–15, suggests that Manipuri peasants involved in the struggle numbered more than 50,000. A British delegation came to Bhanubil for a first-hand report of the movement, and the atrocities committed on peasants were discussed in the House of Commons. Also see Ajay Bhattacharya, *Nankar Vidroha*, Vol. 1 (in Bengali, Dacca, 1973), pp. 67–73. He informs that Bankim Mukherjee, a Calcutta communist, also visited Bhanubil for fact-finding.

[67] Saadulla's reply to Nagendranath Chaudhury, a big zamindar, on 15 September, *ALCP* (1932), Vol. 12, pp. 937–38.

[68] Ibid.; Hezlett to Lawrie, Sylhet, 9 January, in Confidential A, March 1932, Nos. 21 – III, File No. 199 C of 1932 (AS); Confidential – A, June 1930, No. 31, File No. 102 C of 1930 (AS); Government's reply to Chiratan Muchi on 16 September, *ALCP* (1933), Vol. 13, p. 1255; Dutt, *Landmarks of Freedom Struggle in Assam*, p. 76.

[69] Gunning to Chief Secretary, Confidential A, September 1934, No. 24 and 26, File No. 42–C (AS); *Shriihatta Pratibha*, p. 11.

frustrating experience and disillusionment with the terrorist path pushed many of them to the creed of Marxism–Leninism. This transition of Sylhet's Hindu middle-class youth from terrorism to early socialist consciousness in the mid-1930s is worth examining.

Appeal of Revolutionary Terrorism

Several Bengal terrorist groups, particularly the Yugantar group, renewed their contacts in Sylhet around 1928. By 1930, the Tarun Sangha emerged as the most important revolutionary youth organization. Openly functioning as a youth wing of the Congress to train its volunteers, the Sangha was a camouflage for terrorist activists. The Vidyasram, with several branches in the district, on the other hand, organized youth on the basis of non-violence and constructive activities. On 25 July 1931, the Surma Valley Youth Conference met at Maulvibazar, presided over by Jnananjan Neogi. It called upon the youth to be inspired by the martyrs. Several local terrorist groups apparently merged into the Tarun Sangha which was banned *inter alia* on 5 February 1932.[70]

Altogether 182 pieces of fire-arms were reportedly stolen during the four years from 1930 to 1933. A series of terrorist actions started with the attempted mail robbery between Haraspur and Govindapur on 6 January 1931. The most daring cases among these were the Itakhola and Tinsukia mail robberies. The latter robbery took place on 11 June 1934 when the Down Assam Mail was stopped near Tinsukia in the Brahmaputra Valley by a band of Surma Valley and East Bengal terrorists. A government communique took note of the existence of a terrorist party in the Surma Valley. A large number of young men were arrested between 13 March 1933 and 12 June 1934. The trial of the revolutionaries involved in these three cases began in Sylhet before a special tribunal in July 1934. Ten revolutionaries were sentenced to transportation for life or long prison terms. Ajitkumar Chakravarty, Bipulananda Kar Chaudhury and Gopendranath Ray (1914–1984) were convicted to jail terms varying from six to seven years, and deported to the Andamans. Asit Bhattacharyya (1915–1934), of the Itakhola case, was executed on 2 July 1934. As an emergency measure to suppress terrorism, the Assam Criminal Law Amendment Act, 1934, was enforced in Sylhet and Cachar with effect from 14 May. It was further amended in 1935 and 1936. Achintyakumar Bhattacharya was one of the seven detenus held under this Act as a suspected terrorist. He was detained in December 1933 for two years and kept home-interned after his release till about the end of 1936.[71]

---

[70] J.A. Dawson's note of 26 May 1934 in Confidential B, March 1935, Nos. 23–44, File No. 98 – C of 1934 (AS); Letter from Addl. Superintendent of Police, Sylhet, to D.C., Sylhet, 6 June 1930, cited in Confidential A, December 1930, Nos. 27–36, File No. 138 C of 1930 (AS); Written testimony of Sibendranath Dam Roy, 79 Umpling, Shillong, 7 August 1972 (interviewed).

[71] Saadulla's speech, 19 March, *ALCP* (1934), Vol. 14, pp. 669–72; Aditya, *Fight for Freedom in Sylhet*, p. 9; *ALCP* (1935), Vol. 15, p. 167; *ALCP* (1939), Vol. 19, pp. 13 and 158; Interview with Achintyakumar Bhattacharya at Gauhati on 1 July 1973. Many of the terrorists later became communists.

The death-defying revolutionary terrorists made a deep impression in the Brahmaputra Valley, too. The execution of Bhagat Singh on 23 March 1931 was followed by a series of protest meetings and mourning processions in many districts of Assam. Though not to the same extent as in Sylhet, the youth of Dhubri were also in close contact with the Bengal terrorists. Two young men of Gauhati – Rajen Kalita and Khargeswar Sharma – were arrested at Dhubri with arms and imprisoned. Hiranyakumar Basu of the Dhubri Khadi Pratisthan was a secret organizer of the Anushilan Samiti. He was later detained under the Assam Criminal Law Amendment Act, 1934.[72] Terrorist activities thrived during 1931–33 in Sylhet but waned thereafter. So was the case with peasants' associations.

The Spectre of Communism

In the wake of the Meerut Conspiracy Case (1929–33), the district authorities were alerted and asked to report on the communist menace in their respective jurisdictions. The District Magistrate of Sylhet wrote on 23 February 1934 to the Chief Secretary:

> The various Raiyats' and Peasants' Societies, whose activities in this district gave cause to a good deal of anxiety some two years ago, at the time of the revival of the Civil Disobedience Movement, suggested that communist agitators might be at the back of the movement. Possibly this suggestion was unjustifiable. But the connection between these societies and other similar societies in the district of Tippera, which were responsible for serious disturbances was established. . . . The activities of these Peasants' and Workers' societies have of course considerably diminished since that time and have now apparently dwindled down to the holding of one or two conferences during the year in the various subdivisions. These bodies however offer communist agitators a convenient focus for the propagation of their principles.

After obtaining reports from all the districts, the Chief Secretary to the Government of Assam concluded on 10 March 1934 that the province was heretofore free from communist propaganda. He had nothing to advise in particular for containing a menace that did not exist.[73]

There was not much ground for his complacency. For, in December 1935, a six-member Sylhet District Organizing Committee was formed in Calcutta, with a view to propagate communism in Sylhet. The Surma Valley Provincial Committee of the All-India Kisan Sabha (AIKS) was formed in 1936. A district branch of the Congress Socialist Party (CSP) had also been formed by then in

---

[72] For reference to Basu, *APCC Papers*: Gen. Secretary's report, 1937, in file no. 5, Packet 6; and Chanchalkumar Sharma, *Shrihatte Biplabvad o Communist Andolan: Smritikatha* (in Bengali, Calcutta, 1984) pp. 38, 85 and 113–15. For reference to Kalita (elder brother of Haren Kalita) and Sharma, written testimony of Haridas Deka, J.C. Das Road, Gauhati 1, 27 February 1974 (interviewed). Dutt, *Landmarks of Freedom Struggle in Assam*, p. 77.

[73] Confidential A, September 1934, Nos. 24 and 33, File No. 42–C (AS).

Sylhet. As the Communist Party of India was under a ban since 1934, the communists carried on their open activities under the banner of the CSP.[74] Jagannath Bhattacharya (1910–1997), an Assamese student at Banaras, joined the CSP and also a communist group functioning within it. He was the lone Assamese participant in the first All-India Kisan Sabha Conference held at Lucknow in 1936.[75] Communist propaganda through the Labour Party of Bengal reached Dhubri, the gateway of the Brahmaputra Valley, by 1936. Articles on revolutionary Russia and its ideology that appeared in the Assamese periodicals in the early 1930s also made an impact on the student intellegentsia.

Working Class Struggles: 1927–36

In December 1927, a two-member delegation of the British Trade Union Congress was assisted by local Congressmen to get first-hand knowledge of the deplorable working conditions in Assam's tea gardens. Later, the All India Trade Union Congress (AITUC) sent Hari Krishna Sahu to organize the tea garden labour in Assam. In May 1928, he visited Dibrugarh and formed a trade union committee with Kedarnath Goswami as secretary and several citizens as members. He was arrested and imprisoned for a month.[76] The stoppage of work as a means to better working conditions came into prominence in 1926–27 when tea garden workers gained concessions through lightning strikes. A series of such strikes took place in the districts of Sibsagar, Lakhimpur and Nowgong. Cases of collision were more numerous the next year when plantation labour turned violent against the management in at least seven cases. In 1928–29, violence had to be prevented by the Assam police on five or six such occasions. A seventeen-day strike in the Dibru–Sadiya Railways in 1928 involved about 430 working men and ended in a wage increase for them. In 1929, about 800 men in the Digboi oil fields struck work on Sundays and won their demand of compensatory payment for extra work. In the same year, there were short-lived strikes in both the Valleys in a number of tea gardens such as Paloi, Silcooria, Allenpur, Salona–Barghat, Messa, Tarajuli, etc., involving no less than 2,500 workers.[77]

Unlike the Non-Cooperation movement of 1921, the political upheaval

---

[74] Bhattacharyya, *Narkar Vidroha*, pp. 78 and 95 and Sharma, *Shrihatte Biplabvad o Communist Andolan*, pp. 156–57.

[75] Jagannath Bhattacharyya to Guha, Calcutta, 23 August 1974; also interviewed on 20 August 1974.

[76] In course of his judgement, the trying magistrate, Benudhar Rajkhowa, commented: 'A criminal trespass into the coolie line of a tea garden in circumstances like those which are found in this case requires, in my opinion, for obvious reasons an exemplary punishment.' Quoted by Hemchandra Baruah in 'Banuvar durdasha', *Tinidiniia Asamiya* (1930) and reproduced in S. Sharma, ed., *Tyagabiir Hemchandra Barua Smritigrantha* (Gauhati, 1971) pp. 282–92.

[77] Royal Commission on Labour in India, *Written Evidence, Vol. 6 – Part I Assam and the Dooars* (London, 1930), pp. 24–25; *Annual Reports on the Immigrant Labour*, separately for each Valley for the year ending 30 June 1929; the same for 1928, cited in D. Chamanlall, *Coolie: the Story of Labour and Capital in India*, Vol. 2 (Lahore, 1932), p. 32; *India in 1928–29: A Report Preferred for Presentation to Parliament*

of the 1930s failed to rouse the workers of Assam into action. Not that they did not suffer from economic depression. But their resentment took the usual path of sporadic and self-contained strikes on economic demands. There were no meeting-points between these economic struggles and the contemporaneous political movement. The number of tea gardens and their workers involved in strikes on record were as follows:

Plantation Workers' Strikes: 1930–36

Year	Gardens Involved	Workers Involved	Man-days Lost
1930	3	1,900	–
1931	12	3,200	–
1932	8	3,200	–
1933	11	5,500	–
1934–35	8	4,071	11,850
1935–36	13	7,016	20,360

Source: Reply of A.K. Das Chanda on 1 March, *Assam Legislative Assembly Proceedings (ALAP)*, (1938), pp. 583–86; Labour Investigation Committee, *Report on an Enquiry into Conditions of Labour in Plantations in India* (Delhi, 1946), p. 72.

The above summary figures suggest that plantation workers' strikes were not correlated with the rise and ebb of the Civil Disobedience movement. They were clearly ebullient all along, although they had neither a trade union organization of their own nor any contact with politics outside.

The only instance of a politicized labour struggle was that of the Dhubri Match Factory workers. The factory, owned by Swedish capital, started production in 1925 with about 500 workers. In 1928 its workers struck work for about a week, but failed to achieve anything. Retrenchment and wage cuts went on unrestrained. In 1935–36, all the 350 workers of the factory were again on a 57-day strike, in protest against retrenchment. Unionized and led by Bipinchandra Chakravarty, a veteran trade unionist from Bengal, this time the workers won almost all their demands. The strike was inspired by the Labour Party of Bengal, of which Chakrabarty was a member. Resolutions passed at the Dhubri Labourers' Conference under his guidance clearly reflected the influence of the new communist ideology. On 14 December 1936, the Dhubri Match Factory workers were again on strike and faced an unusually prolonged lock-out. This episode will be discussed in the next chapter.[78]

. . . (Home Department, Calcutta, 1929), p. 307. Also see A.A. Purcell, M.P. and J. Hallsworth, *Report on Labour Conditions in India* (Trade Union Congress General Council, London, 1928), pp. 35–36.

[78] Confidential D.O. No. 481–C, Godfrey to Gunning, Goalpara, 28 November 1936 (Police Department Special Branch, Government of Assam, Shillong); Fakhruddin Ali Ahmed's speech on 4 August, *Assam Legislative Assembly Proceedings* (hereafter *ALAP*) (1937), pp. 188–90; Reply of A.K. Das to A.K. Chanda, 1 March, *ALAP* (1938), pp. 583–86.

Fourth Reformed Council without Swarajists: 1929–36

The Carrot and the Councillors

The Council, by its resolution of 12 March 1930, welcomed the Governor-General's announcement on the proposed Round Table Conference in London and his declaration regarding the dominion status. Kumar Gopikaraman Roy, a new member who held allegiance to the All-India Landholders' Association, characterized the proposed Round Table Conference rather as a gift 'that we should welcome with gratefulness'.[79] After the Swarajists' exit, several cut motions fell through in March. The Council voted twenty-seven to twelve to defeat R.K. Chaudhuri's motion recommending the withdrawal of the Cunningham Circular. A token cut motion affecting the demand for supplementary grants to the police was also defeated.[80] Friends of the Congress nevertheless managed to expose the government's repressive policy through animated interpellation and critical speeches in September.

Brindabanchandra Goswami, a Hindu Mahasabhaite from Nowgong, tabled a motion on 15 September expressing dissatisfaction with the Simon Commission's recommendations and suggesting substantial modification. He denounced not only separate electorates, but also the provisions permitting the induction of non-elected members into the provincial cabinets.[81]

Munawwar Ali's amendment to this motion was practically a substantive motion by itself. He moved:

> . . . in the opinion of this Council the report of the Simon Commission is unacceptable and that this Council is of opinion that Dominion Status with autonomous provinces forming into a federation, with full responsibility of the provincial as well as of the central Governments to their respective legislatures, be immediately established in India with adequate safeguards of the interests of the Muslim and other minority communities.

Munawwar Ali was dissatisfied because nowhere did the Commission commit itself to the goal of dominion status. Besides, the control of the Indian army by the Governor-General and the provision of a separate budget for it would mean a strong centre that would jeopardize provincial autonomy. He regretted his being a member of the committee that had been set up to assist the Commission. It was his resolution that was finally carried without a division, after he had assured the house of his opposition to both secession from the Empire and repudiation of national debt.[82]

The critical mood of the house changed soon after the Gandhi–Irwin meeting of 5 March 1931. On 14 March, two resolutions were adopted, *nem con.* One of these welcomed the British Prime Minister's policy regarding India's constitutional development, which was declared in his concluding speech at the first

[79] *ALCP* (1930), Vol. 10, pp. 49–52.
[80] Debate on the Cunningham Circular, 10 September, ibid., pp. 735–78.
[81] Ibid., pp. 1051–54.
[82] Ibid., 1059–61 and 1091–92.

Round Table Conference. The resolution noted that the principles enunciated 'should afford a satisfactory basis for further discussion' and eventually provide India with a constitution acceptable to all sections of the community. Equally optimistic, Munawwar Ali's resolution appreciated not only the steps taken by the Government of India but also those by the Congress Working Committee towards creating a favourable atmosphere. It further recorded the Council's gratefulness to Lord Irwin and Mahatma Gandhi 'for the untiring zeal and energy and far-sighted statesmanship displayed by them in bringing about the aforesaid happy state of things'.[83]

When the White Paper of 18 March 1933 came up before the Council, Saadulla, leader of the house, left the entire discussion to non-official members. However, R.K. Chaudhuri moved an adjournment till April, since the House of Commons was going to discuss the White Paper on 28 March. Others joined him in not castigating the proposed reforms until the matter was talked out.[84]

On 9 March 1935, Chaudhuri again opposed the consideration of both the Joint Parliamentary Committee's Report and the Government of India Bill, on the ground that no fruitful discussion on them could be held at that stage. Somewhat surprised at this reluctance of a fellow Indian member to seize one more opportunity to launch a wordy battle against the forthcoming Act of 1935, the British members enthusiastically supported him in order to avoid a debate. The official motion for consideration was put to vote and lost.[85]

The idea of a second chamber was initially favoured neither by the Government of Assam nor by the public at large, though on different considerations. The Assam Provincial Muslim League Council's memorandum to the Simon Commission was unequivocally opposed to it. So was the Council Committee set up to assist the Commission. However, the British planters were keen on having an upper house to act as a check on the lower house. Indian propertied sections were also interested in this. As a result, the Assam Franchise Committee voted nine to five in March 1932 to recommend a bicameral system. When B. Goswami moved a resolution in the Council on 17 September recommending a second chamber, the officials abstained from voting, and the non-official members present were equally divided – six on each side. The motion was rejected by a casting vote. In view of adverse public opinion and financial constraints, neither the White Paper nor the Joint Parliamentary Committee's Report nor the original draft of the Government of India Bill provided for a bicameral system in the case of Assam.[86]

A lot of wire-pulling by Assam planters in India and London, meanwhile, unsettled the settled fact. In the House of Commons on 22 March 1935, Sir

[83] *ALCP* (1931), Vol. 11, pp. 255–76.

[84] Debate on White Paper, 23 March, *ALCP* (1933), Vol. 13, pp. 815–60.

[85] *ALCP* (1935), Vol. 15, 692–95.

[86] *Report from the Committee of the Assam Legislative Council Appointed to Cooperate with the Indian Statutory Commission* (W.D. Smiles Committee, Shillong, 12 May 1929), pp. 1–14; debate on 17 September, *ALCP* (1932), Vol. 12, pp. 1127–57.

W.D. Smiles, an ex-member of the Assam Legislative Council, was told that Assam would get a second chamber if a substantial section of its public really wanted it. The Government of Assam assured the Secretary of State in April – contrary to its earlier advice – that a substantial body was indeed in favour of such a chamber. The Council voted twenty-six to thirteen to reject the adjournment moved by Abdur Rashid Chaudhury on 31 May 1935, to discuss this official *volte-face*. Almost at the last stage of the making of the Act of 1935 in London, Assam was thus saddled with a bicameral legislature.[87]

The Stick to Beat Terrorists

The fight against the forthcoming Act of 1935 inside the fourth Reformed Council was not only weak, but also halting and sterile. The Councillors were both tantalized by the carrot of constitutional advance and goaded by the stick. Time and again, Governors reminded them of their limitations. One Governor told them bluntly that, unlike in Great Britain, membership of a legislature in India was conditional to one's loyalty to the constitution. 'You may and you do aim at amending this constitution, but your presence here means first of all that', he said, 'you are opposed to those who would overthrow the Government by revolution, whether violent or non-violent. Otherwise you are here on false pretence. The corollary of this should be that you will not hesitate to carry out in your action your pledged opposition to revolution.'[88] This piece of advice did not fall flat in the Council. Even the tiny opposition bloc led by R.K. Chaudhuri dared not, or desired not, to go beyond these limits, despite their sympathy for the persecuted revolutionaries on humanitarian and compassionate grounds.

Anti-terrorist law had been part of Bengal's statute books since 1925. Because of Saadulla's resistance, it had gone by default so long in Assam, although police and district authorities had been pressing the Department of Law and Order since 1929 for such legislation. Later, when the Governor wanted the legislature to pass the Assam Criminal Law Amendment Bill, 1934, as an anti-terrorist measure, it had to oblige him readily. The Bill was gazetted on 9 March, introduced in the Council by Saadulla on 12 March and taken up for consideration on 19 March 1934. Bar Associations all over the province demanded withdrawal of this 'black' Bill, on grounds that the situation did not warrant such an extraordinary measure.[89] While opposing the Bill in the Council, R.K. Chaudhuri and others went out of their way to condemn 'revolutionary crimes'. 'I would sooner have a bullet run through my head,' declared Chaudhuri amidst cheers, 'than see the fair name of Assam slurred by any revolutionary crime.' The Council voted thirty-three to fourteen to refuse circulation of the Bill for eliciting public opinion. It voted twenty-eight to nineteen to refer it to a Select Committee,

<hr>

[87] Debate on 31 May, *ALCP* (1935), Vol. 15, pp. 894–99 and 903–22; Official Reports Fifth Series: *Parliamentary Debates Commons 1934–35*, Vol. 299, 11 March to 29 March, pp. 1507–08 and 1512.

[88] Quotes from Governor's address on 5 March, *ALCP* (1934), Vol. 14, p. 3.

[89] Governor's address, ibid., pp. 3–4; 19 March, ibid., pp. 672–79 and 700–01.

and also voted twenty-seven to thirteen to postpone its further consideration in view of an important member's serious illness.[90]

A dogged and losing battle was carried on thereafter, clause by clause. As many as ten amendments were put to division on 21 March 1934 but only two of them were carried. The next day, none of the three divisions forced on the house was favourable to the Opposition. On the whole, the House faced no less than twenty-seven amendments and fourteen divisions on the issue. The substantive motion, marginally amended, was finally carried without even a formal division. Under the provisions of the Act, the police could henceforth arrest citizens without any warrant, commit them to jail custody on mere suspicion and proceed with their trial *in camera*, even in the absence of the accused. Special rules of evidence and the procedure of recording such evidence were also framed. The Act was enforced on 14 May 1934 in Sylhet and Cachar. An amendment in March 1936 extended the operation of some of its sections to the Brahmaputra Valley.[91]

Opium and Agrarian Issues in the Reformed Council

The ceaseless struggle against the official opium policy and the grazing tax, carried on in the second, third and fourth Reformed Councils, attained considerable success. Protests against the resettlement operations in the temporarily settled areas and the demand for reduced land revenue rates were also repeatedly and forcefully registered. On such agrarian issues as landlord–tenant relations and usurious moneylending, the legislative performance, on the other hand, was rather poor. Several Sylhet Councillors were themselves zamindars-cum-moneylenders and, hence, were opposed to such legislation. Even Congress–Swarajists were not all enthusiastic about legislation in these fields. Hindu members from the Surma Valley were certainly less enthusiastic than Muslim legislators in general. Attempts at such legislation often originated from the official quarters.

The Council's performance on the issues of opium, grazing tax, land revenue resettlement and other agrarian issues are summarized later under separate heads. It may be noted here that, although workers' struggles were not infrequent, their cause was hardly touched upon by the legislative deliberations. The almost total lack of primary education facilities for workers' children in the plantations was the only matter concerning them that received the occasional attention of some Councillors.[92]

Council's Battle against Opium

The avowed official policy in the years from 1920–21 to 1927–28 was to grapple with the opium evil through rationing of shops, enforced registration of consumers and gradual raising of the treasury price of opium. This policy,

---

[90] 19 and 21 March, *ALCP* (1934), Vol. 14, pp. 684–87, 706 and 789.
[91] 22 March, *ALCP* (1934), Vol. 14, pp. 861–88; *ALCP* (1936), Vol. 16, pp. 383–90.
[92] For example, Kuladhar Chaliha's resolution adopted by the Council on 31 July 1924.

thrust upon the government by popular agitation, would have remained luke-warm but for the intensive, action-oriented Congress campaign and the continued vigilance of the Council. On 3 March 1925, the Council resolved to recommend prohibition of the sale and consumption of opium in Assam, except for medicinal and scientific uses, through immediate and suitable legislation. The *Assam Congress Opium Enquiry Report* (1925) made a thorough exposure of the yet uncommitted government policy. The number of registered opium consumers in the Assam plains was about 90,000 in 1925–26. The battle was kept alive through the moving of cut motions on the excise budget, year after year. Treasury issues of opium decreased from 838 maunds in 1925–26 to 722 maunds in 1927–28. A Bill prohibiting the preparation of opium for smoking was adopted in 1927. But the biggest policy change came the next year, when the government agreed to implement the Council resolution of 18 July 1927 recommending total prohibition within ten years. The ration of registered opium-eaters aged below 50 was to be reduced by 10 per cent each year until the province was free from the evil. The Council also voted the necessary maintenance funds for the preventive staff required to deal with smuggling. As a result, the recorded opium consumption gradually came down to 356 maunds by 1932–33 and to 294 maunds by 1934–35. The Civil Disobedience movement contributed significantly to this reduction.[93]

On 6 March 1933, the Council voted twenty-six to seven to institute a seven-member committee for reviewing the government's opium policy in the light of the conclusions of a global enquiry made by the League of Nations. R.K. Chaudhuri and Sanatkumar Das (Cachar) said that they would welcome a committee to prohibit rather than to preserve opium. The committee was formed on 7 March with Nichols–Roy as its chairman. Its findings were revealing. Immediately prior to the implementation of the 10 per cent annual cut, that is, on 31 March 1928, there were altogether 85,976 registered opium consumers. Their number decreased to 69,605 at the end of 1932–33, and half of them were aged above 50 years. Their per capita consumption of opium meanwhile decreased from 2.2 *tolas* to 1.36 *tolas* a month. The retail consumer price was Rs 160 per *seer* in 1932–33. The economics of opium as a state monopoly worked out as follows in the same year:[94]

---

[93] *ALCP* (1925), Vol. 5, pp. 32–53; *ALCP* (1926), Vol. 6, p. 950; Governor's address on 4 March, *ALCP* (1929), Vol. 9, p. 4; Government of Assam Resolution on the Excise Ad. Rep., 1918–19, cited by Abdul Hamid, Minister, 22 March, *ALCP* (1930), Vol. 10, pp. 383–84; Governor's address, 6 March, *ALCP* (1933), Vol. 13, pp. 5–6; M. Tayyebulla, *Between the Symbol and the Idol at Last* (Bombay, 1964), p. 56; *Report of the Assam Opium Enquiry Committee* (Nichols–Roy Committee, Shillong, 1933), pp. 10–15. See also Appendix 4.

[94] *Nichols–Roy Committee Report*, pp. 10–16, 20 and 40; *ALCP* (1933), Vol. 13, pp. 49–56 and 81.

Economics of Opium Monopoly: 1932–33

Gross provincial opium revenue	Rs 21,20,944 (100)
Less price paid out to Ghazipur factory	Rs 2,74,686 (13)
Less maintenance cost of excise staff	Rs 1,08,118 (5)
Net provincial opium revenue	Rs 17,38,140 (82)

Grazing Fees and the Council

Revised grazing rules were enforced on 1 July 1926. Their avowed intention was to confine the levy strictly to professional graziers, and traders in cattle and milk. Yet unreconciled, the Reformed Council refused supplies under the head of commissions payable to collectors of the grazing dues.[95] The government decided, thereafter, to appoint a small committee to examine the working of the new grazing rules and to advise further action, if necessary, to limit the fee collection to the intended classes of people alone. N.C. Bardaloi refused to serve on it since a nominated committee headed by a Divisional Commissioner did not inspire his confidence. Finally, the committee was formed on 7 May 1927 with three members – Sadananda Dowerah, Keramat Ali and the Commissioner of the Assam Valley Division. It recommended a liberal application of the rules so as to bring down the total number of assessees listed in 1926–27.[96]

The grazing fees became a target of attack once more in the legislature in March 1934. Allegations that almost all cattle-owning Assamese peasants had been assessed remained unsubstantiated, and were not acceptable even to R.K. Chaudhuri. Nevertheless, the grazing fees continued to be unpopular. In disputed cases, the rules did not permit an assessee to move a civil court for relief. Besides, these rules were often differently interpreted in different districts – for example, more rigorously in Kamrup than in Nowgong. As a result, associations of professional graziers appeared on the scene to carry on the agitation. On 12 March, the Council's censure was recorded through a cut motion, carried by nineteen to seventeen votes.[97] The grazing rules were again revised, and these were implemented in September 1934. On 1 March 1935, M. Gohain moved a cut on the land revenue demand, to protest against the harassment of peasants at the time of assessing grazing fees. But this time the Council voted twenty-two to sixteen to reject the motion.[98] Grazing fees ceased to be a major economic grievance from then onwards.

---

[95] Government of Assam Resolution of 24 April 1925, cited by S. Barua, 12 March, *ALCP* (1934), Vol. 14, p. 345; Assam Government's resolution on 7 May 1927, cited in Revenue Department, Revenue A, June 1928, No. 6 (AS).

    Half the cut was restored by the Governor by way of certification, to meet the committed expenditure on account of the collections of 1926–27.

[96] 9–10 September, *ALCP* (1925), Vol. 5, pp. 1456–66 and 1491–1502 and 17 September, *ALCP* (1927), Vol. 7, pt. 2, p. 1689; Revenue Department, Revenue A, June 1928, Nos. 4, 6 and 15 (AS).

[97] 12 March, *ALCP* (1934), Vol. 14, pp. 345–51. In his speech, S. Barua demanded reduction in the rate of fees.

[98] *ALCP* (1935), Vol. 15, pp. 296–98 and 308.

Legislation on Land Revenue Settlement

Regulations under which the land revenue rates in Assam were revised and claimed from time to time had no legislative sanction. The Joint Parliamentary Committee noted this fact in 1919 and underlined the need for statutory land legislation. From then there was persistent agitation in Assam against arbitrary land revenue settlement operations. The first Reformed Council, though otherwise docile, refused the necessary grants when the executive government undertook resettlement operations in 1923 to replace the settlement of 1905–12. Funds for continued resettlement operations were restored, however, under the Governor's certificate. A resolution for recasting the Land and Revenue Regulations, 1886, within the frame of legislative sanction, and for postponing the resettlement operations until then, was carried in an amended form on 15 August 1925. But no such postponement followed.[99]

Then came the Assam Settlement Bill, 1925, to validate the resettlement operations. The select committee on it felt that the land revenue rate, calculated at 20 per cent of the gross produce, was too great a burden on the agriculturists and therefore should be fixed at 10 per cent. The official attempt to recommit the Bill having failed on 25 February 1926, the government allowed it to lapse, rather than remodel it in the recommended form. The resettlement operations went on as before under the executive authority. In the same year, thousands of peasants assembled at Golaghat to greet the visiting Governor with protests against the enhanced reassessment of land revenue rates in that sub-division.[100]

The legislature, too, reacted sharply to the enhancement of land revenue rates in 1927 and 1928. For example, it voted thirty-one to twelve to adjourn the house in order to discuss the arbitrary reassessment in Kamrup, soon after the relevant resolutions of the Governor-in-Council were published on 16 February 1927. It refused grants for the continued resettlement operations.[101] In September 1928, R.K. Chaudhuri's motion to stay further collection of land revenue at the newly reassessed rates until there was appropriate legislation on the subject, was adopted by the house. Another motion for realization of land revenue at the old rates was again adopted in September 1929.[102] But in no

[99] Kamakhyaram Baruah's speech, 28 March, *ALCP* (1924), Vol. 4, p. 228; Governor's address, 13 July, *ALCP* (1925), Vol. 5, p. 869; Kuladhar Chaliha's speech, 11 September, *ALCP* (1929), Vol. 9, p. 1112; Speech, 19 September, *ALCP* (1928), Vol. 8, p. 875. The 1925 resolution was moved by Nilmoni Phukan.

[100] *ALCP* (1928), Vol. 8, pp. 875–76; Faiznur Ali's minute of dissent in the Select Committee Report on the Assam Settlement Bill, 1925 and his speech of 26 February 1926, cited by Nilambar Datta, 12 September, *ALCP* (1930), Vol. 10, p. 872; M. Gohain's speech, 11 September, *ALCP* (1929), Vol. 9, p. 1100.

Some members even argued that the land revenue fixed at 10 per cent of the gross produce would fairly approximate one-third of the net produce, which had country-wide acceptance as a norm.

[101] *Assam Gazettee*, 16 February 1927, pp. 257–69; 2 March, *ALCP* (1927), Vol. 7, p. 291; R.K. Chaudhuri's speech, 11 September, *ALCP* (1928), Vol. 8, pp. 875–76.

[102] Sarveswar Barua's speech, 10 September, *ALCP* (1923), Vol. 9, pp. 1067–68; 11 September, ibid., p. 1116.

case did the government take any action to implement these resolutions.

The Assam Settlement Bill, 1925, was revived in the form of the Assam Land Revenue Reassessment Bill, 1930, and it was discussed in the Council on 11 September 1930. As a concession to popular demand, the Bill now fixed the land revenue ceiling for an assessment group at 12.5 per cent of the gross produce. This new formula was claimed to have resulted from an informal compromise reached between the government and all-party representatives on 16 March 1929. On 12 September, an amendment was moved to fix the ceiling of the total revenue demand on an assessment group at one-third of its net produce. Since the actual production cost was indeterminate because of non-monetized elements therein, the government argued that net produce was not a practicable concept. With twenty-two votes on each side, for and against, the amendment was rejected by the casting vote from the chair. However, the Council voted twenty-two to twenty-one to accept another amendment by which the revenue demand on an assessment group was limited to 10 per cent of the value of its gross produce. On 13 September, the amended Bill was passed without a division. But the Governor returned the Bill for reconsideration.[103]

On 17 March 1931, the house again refused to reconsider its earlier decision. The government, too, remained adamant. After years of a stalemate, when practically the same Bill was moved in 1935 by a private member, good sense at last prevailed. The government gave way and even cooperated with the house to circumvent certain procedural difficulties. The long-disputed Bill was thus passed into an Act in 1936.[104]

The hard-pressed peasants had been clamouring all these years for a reduction in land revenue rates, and their clamour had been repeatedly echoed in the Council since 1928. In March, and again in October 1931, R.K. Chaudhuri moved a resolution recommending the formation of district-wise standing committees to enquire into ryots' conditions and specify the quantum of relief (in the form of land revenue remissions) for slump years. On both occasions, his motion was rejected. Arrears in land revenue meanwhile piled up because of the ryots' inability to pay. The situation became so serious that, in the Governor's address to the house on 12 September 1932, a remission in the land revenue demand for the year 1932–33, to the extent of 3 annas in a rupee, was recommended. The remission of land revenue became an annual feature of the official policy during the 1930s and it continued till 1941–42. Resolutions recommending a 50 per cent or adequate land revenue reduction were passed almost every year in the fourth Reformed Council – for example, in September 1933, March 1934, and February

---

[103] *ALCP* (1930), Vol. 10, pp. 813, 872–87 and 985–86; Governor's message to the March session, *ALCP* (1931), Vol. 11, pp. 33–34. Both the amendments were moved by Nilambar Datta, a planter who was opposed to the Congress.

[104] 17 March, *ALCP* (1931), Vol. 11, pp. 385–97; *ALCP* (1936), Vol. 16, pp. 155–62 and 1048–50. The Council had already passed the Assam Land Revenue Regulations ˈˈˈ in 1933, thus for the first time providing a statutory basis for land legislation.

and October 1935.[105] Scores of Ryot Sabhas were voicing the same demand outside the Council. In the matter of advocating relief to the distressed people within the given constraints, the legislature was able to play a positive role even without the Congress–Swarajists.

Beginnings of Tenancy Legislation

How early official attempts to legislate in the field of landlord–tenant relations were thwarted by the landlord lobbies was discussed in Chapter Four. Councillors elected from the Brahmaputra Valley generally took a sympathetic view of the problem, not only in the first but also in the subsequent Reformed Councils, in contrast to Hindu members from the Surma Valley.

Landlord–tenant relations had been regulated in the permanently settled areas of Sylhet since 1869 and of Goalpara since 1892, under the adapted provisions of the Bengal Landlord and Tenant Procedure Act, 1869. In Bengal itself, this inadequate Act had long been replaced by the Bengal Tenancy Act of 1885. The latter Act required all contracts for rent enhancement to be registered, and all such enhancements not to exceed more than 2 annas in a rupee at one time. In the absence of similar provisions in the 1869 Act, zamindari tenants in Assam frequently suffered from exorbitant and arbitrary rent enhancements. An amendment of the existing law on the lines of the Bengal Tenancy Act, 1885, was therefore recommended by Abdul Mazid Ziaosshams in course of a motion on 11 September 1925. He proposed the formation of a nine-member committee to make necessary and detailed recommendations in this respect. To meet the lurking suspicion in the minds of gentlemen from the Surma Valley, Ziaosshams said:

> If we are clamouring for self-Government, if we are clamouring for more rights from our Government I suppose, Sir, that we have no right to deny the same rights to our under-ryots or to our tenants. If we want the equality of treatment from the British Government we should show the same equality of treatment to our tenants.

The Council voted seventeen to sixteen to pass the resolution, but that, too, after the mover agreed to drop Sylhet from its scope to enhance its general acceptability. The committee that was formed included *inter alia* two ICS officers and leading zamindars like Raja Prabhatchandra Barua.[106]

In 1926, A.J. Laine was once more appointed Special Officer on Duty to draft a Bill on the Goalpara tenancy, in pursuance of the committee's work. Introduced in 1927 in the face of dogged opposition from zamindars and *jotdars*, the Goalpara Tenancy Bill emerged through the select committee stage in a diluted form and was presented for the Council's consideration on 4 March 1929.

---

[105] 20 March, *ALCP* (1931), Vol. 11, pp. 547–70 and 3 October, ibid., pp. 1190–214; 20 March, *ALCP* (1934), Vol. 14, pp. 739–42 and 764; also 26 February and 14 September, *ALCP* (1935), Vol. 15, pp. 124–39 and 1453–63, respectively; Governor's address of 31 October, *ALCP* (1936), Vol. 16, p. 1657.

[106] 11 September, *ALCP* (1925), Vol. 5, pp. 1527–43; for quote, ibid., pp. 31–32.

The Bill granted occupancy rights to tenants over any land under their continuous cultivation for a period of twelve years or more. An infructuous attempt to get this provision dropped could muster only four votes. The Bill also provided that in no case should the rent be enhanced by more than 3 annas in a rupee at one time. The Swarajist attempt to limit such enhancement to 2 annas was defeated. On 12 March, the house voted twenty-six to five to pass the substantive Bill as amended. All the Goalpara zamindars voted with the officials for the Bill, while the Swarajists were divided among themselves.[107]

On 13 March 1931, Rai Sahib Pearimohan Das moved a resolution recommending that the Bengal Landlord and Tenant Procedure Act, 1869, still in force in Sylhet, be replaced by a suitable Bill drawn on the model of either the Goalpara Tenancy Act, 1929, or the Bengal Tenancy Act, 1885. He also proposed the formation of a committee for that purpose. In Sylhet, even occupancy tenants had no free right to sell their holdings. Nor were they protected against rent enhancements. Das implored that those who had entered the Council mainly on the strength of peasant votes should not play a traitor's role by opposing his harmless motion. Officially backed, it was passed by thirty to five votes. Of the dissenting votes, four were cast by British members.[108]

In pursuance of this resolution, the Sylhet Tenancy Act, 1936, was passed towards the close of the Reformed Council. Under its provisions, the collection of irregular cesses and the refusal to issue rent receipts by zamindars were punishable offences. The practice of distraint of crops was also abolished. All terms in a contract that sought to take away or restrict substantial rights conferred on the tenants by legislation, were declared inoperative. No tenant could be ejected, except in execution of a decree and on payment of a compensation for the improvements he made on the land. The landlord's right to enhance rent was regulated. Occupancy rights were clearly defined to include free rights of transfer. The Governor, however, considered that the Act required further liberalization in certain aspects. In the same year, the Goalpara Tenancy Act of 1929 was also further amended.[109]

The long-felt need for tenancy legislation in temporarily settled areas was voiced through R.K. Chaudhuri's motion, which the Council unanimously adopted on 21 March 1933. Accordingly, the government introduced the Assam (Temporarily Settled Districts) Tenancy Bill in 1934, provoking a storm of protest from landlords. The landlord-dominated select committee mischievously voted six to five to exclude all districts except Kamrup from the scope of the Bill, with a view to reduce it to nullity. The government refused to proceed with the truncated Bill. The Council then voted thirty-nine to one to adopt an official motion

---

[107] *ALCP* (1927), Vol. 7, pt. 2, pp. 977–79; *ALCP* (1929), Vol. 9, pp. 22, 128–73 and pp. 259–66. The five votes against the Bill included those of B.N. Chaudhury, R.K. Hatibarua and Sarveswar Barua. N.C. Bardaloi abstained from voting.

[108] *ALCP* (1931), Vol. 11, pp. 237–45. British planters had a large number of tenants on their own tea garden lands. This explains their objection to the reform.

[109] Governor's address, 31 October, *ALCP* (1931), Vol. 11, pp. 1657–59.

for its recommitment, and later passed it on 7 June 1935 with original jurisdiction restored. Coming into force in 1937, this Act provided for all such tenant rights in substance as were there in the Sylhet and Goalpara Acts.[110]

Legislation on Usury

Exorbitant interest rates and heavy peasant indebtedness constituted a normal feature of Assam's rural economy. According to K.L. Barua, the usual rate of interest charged by moneylenders was not less than 36 per cent per annum. The province's outstanding agricultural debt was conjectured by him in 1927 at Rs 90 to 100 million, in his memorandum before the Royal Commission on Agriculture. This debt burden was estimated at Rs 220 million by the Assam Provincial Banking Enquiry Committee in 1929–30 for the plains districts, which amounted to twenty-one times the annual land revenue. The average debt per family was Rs 242. With falling crop prices during the Depression years, the debt burden became increasingly heavier in the 1930s. According to the same Committee, 81.5 per cent of all agricultural families in Darrang and 78 per cent in Nowgong were indebted in 1929–30 to the extent of an average of Rs 229 and Rs 235, respectively, per indebted family. The provincial average price of unhusked winter rice per maund came down from Rs 3–14 as. during the years 1921–26 to Rs 2–14 as. during the years 1931–36; and that of mustard-seed, from Rs 7–2 as. to Rs 4 only.[111] This fall in agricultural prices was largely responsible for the increasing indebtedness. The debtors had virtually no legislative protection against usurious practices. Aggrieved parties could, of course, go to a court of law under the central Usurious Loans Act, 1918, but it was difficult to get any relief under that Act.

On 2 March 1923, Munawwar Ali infructuously moved in the Council that the province's moneylending practices be thoroughly enquired into for preparing a report. His motion was repeated on 10 April 1928 but was subsequently withdrawn on an assurance of official action in the near future. However, nothing came out of this assurance until interest in debt legislation was revived in the budget session of 1933. On 21 March, Khan Sahib Mahmud Ali moved a resolution recommending that the maximum rate of interest be fixed at 12.5 per cent per annum. Sanatkumar Das of Cachar, Rev. Tanuram Saikia and several Muslim members spoke about the debtors' plight in glaring terms. As the Council was told that a suitable official Bill would soon be sponsored, the resolution was withdrawn.[112] In due course, the Assam Moneylenders' Act, 1934 was passed.

[110] 21 March, *ALCP* (1933), Vol. 13, pp. 732–43; *ALCP* (1935), Vol. 14, pp. 717–39, 1023–43 and 1190–1204; Governor's address, 27 May, ibid., pp. 702–03. The lone voice against recommitment was Idris Ali Barlaskar – a big *mirasdar* of Cachar.

[111] *Assam Banking Enquiry Committee Report*, cited by Munawwar Ali, 5 August, *ALAP* (1937), p. 348; evidence of K.L. Barua, *Assam Banking Enquiry Committee Report, 1929–30*, Vol. 2, pp. 622–26; P.C. Goswami, *The Economic Development of Assam* (Bombay, 1963), pp. 61 and 250.

[112] *ALCP* (1923), Vol. 3, pp. 35–36; *ALCP* (1928), Vol. 8, pp. 539–41; *ALCP* (1933), Vol. 13, pp. 745–56.

Under its provisions, the charging of compound interest was forbidden, and the rate of simple interest was limited to 12.5 per cent on secured loans and 18.75 per cent on unsecured loans. In no case was the accumulated burden of interest charges to exceed the principal sum. In 1936, the Assam Debt Conciliation Act followed,[113] under which several debt conciliation boards were established to give relief to debtors. These measures satisfied the conscience of the legislators but not so much the real needs of the indebted people, because of the lack of a strong peasant movement.

The Line that Divided: 1921–36

Seeds of Conflict

Referring to the prevailing situation in the province, an Assamese member reminded the Council in 1936 that: 'the line of division in Assam politics is primarily not between Hindu and Muhammedan or on caste lines, but between the inhabitants of the Assam Valley and those of the Surma Valley' (*Report of the Delimitation Committee*, p. 89). Yet another member had said in July 1924 that the two Valleys were being forced to run a 'three-legged race in which no progress whatever is possible'.[114] Not that there was no political rivalry in terms of Hindu–Muslim communalism. But its open manifestation was much more subdued in Assam as compared to Bengal and other provinces. This was because each community was again sharply divided, linguistically and Valley-wise. Long before the birth of the Muslim League in Assam, men like Saadulla and local *anjumans* had persistently stood for the principle of separate Muslim electorates. But this did not create any deadlock or riots. In fact, the local authorities in Sibsagar had provided for communal representation as early as 1883, apparently without having provoked any local protest.[115]

The balance of power between the two Valleys was maintained on an even keel through a parity formula in the allocation of public expenditure and government jobs. What was of concern to the people, therefore, was the maldistribution of power and resources, not so much between the two Valleys as between the two major linguistic groups – the Assamese and the Bengalis. The Bengalis already had a much larger share in government jobs than their numerical strength in the province justified. On the census counts, those who returned Bengali as their mother tongue far outnumbered the Assamese-speaking population. The former's percentage in the population mix of the province tended to

---

[113] Governor's address, 31 October, *ALCP* (1936), Vol. 16, pp. 1658–59.

[114] Sarveswar Barua's speech, 16 March, *ALCP* (1936), Vol. 16, p. 329 and B.N. Chaudhury's speech, *ALCP* (1924), Vol. 4, p. 568.

[115] V. Venkata Rao, *A Hundred Years of Local Self-Government in Assam* (second edn, Gauhati, 1965), pp. 206–07.

Saadulla had demanded communal representation for Muslims also in local bodies in 1913 and 1914: 10 April, *ALCP* (1913), p. 80 and 2 April, *ALCP* (1914), p. 84. He reiterated the same view in the Council in 1917 when he said: 'Our voice too from the Assam valley would not have been heard in this Council but for the principle of communal representation.' 25 April, *ALCP* (1917), p. 128.

increase from census to census, due to the influx of immigrants. This also alarmed a major section of the Assamese. They insisted that the Assam government should allow only those immigrants who held domicile certificates to compete for local government jobs, scholarships and contracts. Such certificates, however, were a rare commodity. In 1935, for example, only 64 domicile certificates were issued by the District Magistrates of Assam. [116]

Under the circumstances, 'Valley jealousy', which was formerly limited to the job-seeking middle classes alone, was slowly percolating and being transformed into a cult of aggressive and defensive linguistic nationalism. Most of the Goalpara zamindars identified themselves with the Bengali culture, and launched a movement for the transfer of Goalpara to Bengal after World War I. Their agitation persisted throughout the 1920s and early 1930s.[117] It was then that the demand for containment of further influx of East Bengal Muslim immigrants into Goalpara and the rest of the Brahmaputra Valley began to be increasingly raised as a political issue. If the immigration continued unrestrained, would not the Assamese be turned into a linguistic minority in their own homeland – the Brahmaputra Valley? This was the question that plagued the minds of not only its urban middle classes, but also its peasant masses. It was in this context that public attention was focused on the 'Line system', which the officials had evolved in response to the situation since 1920.

Genesis of the Line System

It was in 1911 that the Census Commissioner first took note of the ongoing immigration as a peaceful invasion of Assam. However, immigration was no doubt a welcome phenomenon for labour-short, land-abundant Assam from the economic point of view. Landless immigrants from overpopulated East Bengal – of whom some 85 per cent were Muslims – found land in Assam's water-logged, jungle-infested, riverine belt. Used to an amphibious mode of living and industrious, they came by rail, steamers and boats up the Brahmaputra to reclaim these malarial areas. All they wanted was land. From their riverine base, they further pressed forward in all directions in search of more living space, to areas held by the autochthones. It was then that an open clash of interests began to take place.

---

[116] Speech by J.A. Dawson, 16 March, *ALCP* (1936), Vol. 16, pp. 349–50.

[117] The zamindars of Goalpara district petitioned to Lord Chelmsford and, later, in July 1921, addressed the Governor for its transfer to Bengal. Raja Prabhatchandra Barua of Gauripur brought out a pamphlet to publicize the demand. Bengali–Assamese feelings were tense in Goalpara sub-division at the time of the 1926 elections. The Swaraj Party candidate, though a *bonafide* Assamese, was rejected by his electorate there because a book written and published by him in Bengali had raised doubts about his linguistic affiliation. Mukundanarayan Barua, a Goalpara zamindar, suggested in 1929 to the Simon Commission that, 'the law, language and the social customs of the area concerned' justified the transfer of permanently settled parts of Goalpara to Bengal. Quote from Barua's note of dissent in the *Smiles Committee Report*, p. 11; N.C. Bardaloi's speech, 21 July, *ALCP* (1927), Vol. 7, p. 980; B. Ghosh's speech, 7 January, *ALCP* (1926), Vol. 6, pp. 104–05; *ALCP* (1924), Vol. 4, pp. 575–76.

Administrative measures had to be devised to contain the conflict. The Line system – first mooted in 1916 and adopted in 1920 – was such a device. The government encouraged immigration; at the same time, there was an increasing awareness since about 1913 that the indigenes needed some kind of protection. A consolidated set of rules for waste land settlement was published in September 1915. Only annual *pattas* were to be initially issued.[118] Under this system, a line was drawn in the districts under pressure in order to settle immigrants in segre-gated areas, specified for their exclusive settlement. The number of settlers, includ-ing children born after their arrival, increased from an estimated three lakhs in 1921 to over half a million in 1931.[119] Colonists were settling on government waste lands by families and not singly. They were better cultivators and, hence, could also offer higher and lucrative land prices to induce Assamese peasants to sell out portions of their holdings. Local Marwari and even Assamese money-lenders financed the immigrants so that the latter could reclaim land, and ex-pand the cultivation of jute, *ahu* rice, pulses and vegetables. Jagannath Bujar–Barua told the Assam Banking Enquiry Committee that immigration had led to all-round prosperity in the Barpeta area. Many Assamese farmers turned into land speculators. They sold off their lands to immigrants at a good price; they then cleared new plots (*pam*) on waste lands and sold them again. The immi-grants were financed by their own headmen (*matbar*), as well as by Marwari and Assamese (Barpetia) moneylenders. Even the *hati* (indigenous cooperative bank) funds of Barpeta were involved in this financing, to a small extent.[120]

Assamese public opinion began increasingly to clamour against the fail-ure of the Line system. Pressed by Bishnucharan Bora – a *mauzadar* member of the Council – the government admitted on 3 August 1923 that there was continu-ous immigration into Nowgong. But it also asserted that waste lands in Nowgong were plentifully available both for immigrant and local people. Bora had to concede that the policy of waste land settlement in racially segregated blocks in Nowgong during the years 1920–24 was not altogether unsatisfactory. Villages on waste land grants were classified into three categories: (i) those made avail-able exclusively to immigrants, (ii) those made available exclusively to local people and (iii) those available to both. No land settlement could be made with an immigrant family beyond a ceiling of 16 *bighas*. Sub-letting of land to immi-grants and their employment as agricultural labour by local people in Assamese lines were also prohibited. A large number of complaints nonetheless poured into the District Magistrate's office about encroachments on lands earmarked for the local Assamese people. The pencil-drawn alignments of the line on maps were often tampered by the corrupt revenue staff. Towards the end of 1924, the local

---

[118] AS File No. Rev. A, September 1926, No. 1–22, Governor's note.

[119] *Census of India, 1951*, Vol. 12, Part II-A, pp. 72–73; *Report of the Line System Committee*, Vol. 1 (Shillong, 1938), pp. 1–4.

[120] *Assam Banking Enquiry Committee Report, 1929–30*, Vol. 2, pp. 508–17.

administration was found to be increasingly indulgent of such encroachments and corrupt practices.[121]

The Assamese public demanded a rigid policy. Mahadev Sharma moved a resolution on 23 July 1927 with a view to prevent, or at least restrict, the settlement of waste lands with immigrants from other provinces and from foreign countries, including British planters. It recommended the appointment of a committee to examine, district by district, the actual position regarding (a) the availability of waste lands, (b) the desirability of reserving adequate area for future development, and (c) the implications of an immigration policy in terms of its impact on the requirements of grazing, fuel and forest reserves. B.K. Das of Sylhet spoke in favour of protecting the interests of the children of the soil. N.C. Bardaloi was one 'who would not restrict immigration, so far as can be helped'. He admitted that Sharma's motion was not happily worded. Nonetheless, he, too, emphasized the desirability of reserving adequate areas of waste land in each district for future development.[122]

Sharply divided on a Hindu and non-Hindu basis on Sharma's resolution, the house voted twenty-four to eighteen to reject it. The government was not prepared to commit itself to any kind of restrictive legislation, but nonetheless agreed to call an all-party conference to thrash out the issue.[123]

Colonization Schemes

A conference of district officers held at Shillong in 1928 decided that the number of 'lines' should be reduced, simplified and straightened as far as possible, with the objective of allocating considerable blocks of land communitywise. In September 1928, an all-party committee, with A.W. Botham as chairman, conferred on this issue. The official note that was circulated advocated a positive colonization policy, mainly on revenue considerations. It argued that administrative control over the process of natural migration, so necessary for a planned settlement, was in any case preferable to haphazard squatting. The committee consisted of four British and five Indian members, including Saadulla and N.C. Bardaloi.[124]

Bardaloi advocated for compact colonization areas outside which immigrants should not be allowed to settle afresh. He also suggested that enough land be left vacant to accommodate the future progeny of the Assamese people. All these points were acceptable to the government, although opinions varied as to the quantum of waste land actually available in the Brahmaputra Valley.[125] This was how the colonization schemes came into existence.

---

[121] Reply to Bishnucharan Bora, 13 August, *ALCP* (1923), Vol. 3, p. 521; Bishnucharan Bora's speech on 23 July, *ALCP* (1927), Vol. 7, pt. 2, pp. 1089–91.

[122] 23 July, *ALCP* (1927), Vol. 7, pt. 2, pp. 1084, 1091–93 and 1103.

[123] Ibid., pp. 1104–05.

[124] Rhode's speech, 16 March, *ALCP* (1931), Vol. 11, p. 307. *Report of the Line System Committee* (Shillong, 1938), Vol. 1, p. 4.

[125] Cited in R.K. Chaudhuri's speech, 24 February, *ALAP* (1938), pp. 410–12.

On 3 April 1928, the Council was told that the official policy of restricting and regulating land settlement with immigrants, by means of 'lines within villages' or 'exclusion from whole *mauzas* or villages', had been adopted mainly to protect the Assamese and aboriginal inhabitants – but partly also to avoid breaches of peace. The government was aware that a system of racial segregation was being practised thereby. Nevertheless, it found it desirable to settle waste lands – in the earlier stages at least – 'in blocks with persons of the same community and that land should remain for some time on annual basis in order to control transfers'.[126]

The colonization policy, though initiated by British officials, derived its legitimacy thus from the deliberations of an all-party conference, and initially had the approval of both Saadulla and N.C. Bardaloi. The first colonization scheme, started in Nowgong in 1928, was successively followed by one each in the Barpeta and Mangaldai sub-divisions. Under all these schemes, a small family was to be given about 20 *bighas* of land on payment of a premium. The areas allotted under the Nowgong scheme to 1,619 Muslim and 441 Hindu immigrant families amounted in all to 47,636 acres till March 1933.[127]

The total area of waste lands shown as cultivable was somewhat overestimated. For, in 1924, the proportion of settled to total area, exclusive of reserve forests, was officially stated to be 21.75 per cent in Nowgong, 41.12 per cent in Kamrup and 44.86 per cent in Darrang. In Goalpara, it was nearly 100 per cent.[128]

During the six years preceding 1936, as many as 59 grazing, forest and village reserves had been thrown open in Nowgong under the colonization scheme for settling immigrants. Out of the district's total occupied area of 5,41,160 acres

Agricultural Statistics: 1935–36

District	Net Area Sown (acres)	Percentage to Total Land Area	Cultivable Waste lands (acres)
Kamrup	9,83,260	(35)	4,19,050
Nowgong	4,99,689	(15)	14,38,790
Darrang	5,44,231	(25)	7,18,890
Sibsagar	7,54,856	(22)	14,82,573
Lakhimpur	5,03,442	(16)	14,86,599
Assam Proper	32,85,478		55,45,902

Source: Official data as cited by Munawwar Ali, 14 August, *Assam Legislative Assembly Proceedings (ALAP)* (1937), p. 711.

---

[126] *ALCP* (1928), Vol. 8, p. 247. In 1924, a colonization officer was functioning in Nowgong district to look after immigrants' settlement. *ALCP* (1924), Vol. 4, pp. 1189–90 and 1245–46.

[127] *ALCP* (1931), Vol. 11, p. 307; reply to B.C. Goswami, 24 March, *ALCP* (1933), Vol. 13, p. 888.

[128] Reply to Nilmoni Phukan, 25 September, *ALCP* (1924), Vol. 4, pp. 45–46.

– sown and fallow – in 1936, 2,04,078 acres or 37.7 per cent were under immigrant occupation, as against 62.3 per cent still in the hands of indigenous people.[129] The cultivable waste lands other than fallow in the district amounted to more than 1.4 million acres. The prevailing conditions of land abundance in Nowgong and other districts are indicated above in a tabular form.

The land-hungry Muslim immigrants, segregated and pitted against all odds, never appreciated the Assamese point of view. If all men were equal in the eyes of Allah, why should thousands of acres of land remain waste, particularly when men in search of a livelihood and *lebenstraum* were available to turn them into smiling fields? They resented being described in the press, the platform and even official reports as litigant, quarrelsome men with criminal propensities. They wanted the Line system to go. If it would only concede them the right to land and a new home, they would even follow the Congress flag. But this did not happen.

Politics of a Plural Society

The verbal support that the immigrants received from Assamese Muslim leaders was politically motivated. For example, on 16 March 1936, Khan Bahadur Nuruddin Ahmed of Nowgong told the Council that the Line system had been preventing the immigrants from being absorbed into the Assamese society.

> My Hindu friends of Assam Valley, in order to prevent them from falling into the hands of the organizers of the Domiciled and Settlers' Association, have been telling the immigrants that they regard them as Assamese people. But it is no use calling them Assamese without giving them the status of the Assamese.

He demanded abolition of the Line system.[130]

Despite such motivated support, many of the relatively better-off and educationally advanced Assamese Muslims were not too enthusiastic about social intercourse with the East Bengal settlers. Though they had a common religion, the two communities were wide apart from each other in culture, psychological make-up and socio-economic conditions. Unlike the immigrant Bengali Muslims, their Assamese counterparts neither practised strict *purdah* nor did they have any professed zeal for Urdu as a status symbol. Assamese Muslims in general welcomed the immigrants, nevertheless, with the hope that they would be Assamized in due course and thus numerically strengthen the base of Muslim communal politics in the province. 'They will become Assamese – not domiciled Assamese like many people – but Assamese in fact as much as the Ahoms and Kalitas became Assamese.' So, asked Sayidur Rahman in a speech on 23 July

---

[129] 29 September, *ALCP* (1936), Vol. 6, p. 1446; official data cited in R.K. Chaudhuri's speech in August, *ALAP* (1937), p. 714.

[130] Speech by Nuruddin Ahmed, 16 March, *ALCP* (1936), Vol. 16, p. 340. His resolution calling for the abolition of the Line system was defeated. He was a *mukhtear* practising criminal law for more than three decades. In 1930 he was chairman of the Nowgong Local Board.

1927 in the Council, 'why raise sentimental objections to their coming?'[131]

The Assam Valley Muslim Political Conference met under the presidency of Khan Sahib Mijanur Rahman on 8 September 1935 at Gauhati. It found the Government of India Act to be 'unsatisfactory' and 'inadequate'. Nevertheless, it recommended the capture of legislatures for promotion of the national cause. Appreciative of the Congress attitude towards solution of the communal question, it looked forward to further talks between Rajendra Prasad and M.A. Jinnah. It bitterly pointed out that the Communal Award had unduly favoured Assam's British community, at the cost of both Hindus and Muslims. The chairman of the reception committee also put forward a new formula for solution of the Sylhet question: to reconstitute the province as a homogeneous federating unit, Sylhet could be transferred to Bengal, provided the Jaintia Parganas and tea areas of the district were retained in Assam, and adequate minority safeguards for Muslims were built into the new arrangement. The Conference appointed a delegation, with Fakhruddin Ali Ahmed (1905–1977) as its secretary and Saadulla as its leader, to negotiate with the non-Muslim parties a common agreement on the separation of Sylhet with necessary safeguards. It even passed a resolution for reservation of jobs for Muslims of the Brahmaputra Valley, as distinguished from Surma Valley Muslims. But the interest it showed towards the immigrant question was rather perfunctory. The Conference suggested that an Assam Settlers' Welfare Committee be formed to work for the interests of the immigrants.[132]

Regional chauvinists – many of them Assamese Hindus – in turn, raised the slogan of the Assamese race being in danger. Ambikagiri Raychaudhury floated the Asamiya Samrakshini Sabha (Association for Conservation of the Assamese) in 1926 to propagate the Assamese cause. Nilmoni Phukan, who had thrice failed to get himself elected to the Council since 1923, soon joined his chorus. The Congress tried to steer a middle course because of its all-India character. But it was pressurized from below to take a chauvinistic line on such issues as land, jobs and the medium of instruction in schools. Publication of the 1931 *Census Report* aggravated the fear complex. In presenting the census results, C.S. Mullan, an irresponsible British civil servant, instigated a hate campaign against the immigrants. He wrote that during the years 1921–31, the immigrant army

> has almost completed the *conquest* of Nowgong. The Barpeta subdivision of Kamrup has also fallen to their *attack* and Darrang is being *invaded*. Sibsagar has so far escaped completely, but the few thousand Mymansinghias in North Lakhimpur are an *outpost* which may, during the next decade, prove to be a valuable basis of *major operations*. Wheresoever the carcass, there the *vultures* be gathered together. Where there is wasteland thither flock the Mymensinghias. (1931 *Census Report*, p. 51; emphasis ours)

---

131 Speech by Sayidur Rahman, *ALCP* (1927), Vol. 7, 1095.
132 *IAR* (July–December 1935), Vol. 2, pp. 315–16.

Mullan tried to peer into the future and mischievously forecast the future course of this 'invasion'. He prophesied that Sibsagar would ultimately remain the only district where an Assamese race would find a home of its own.[133] The motivation behind such irresponsible and unfounded utterings was clear. He wanted the Assamese and the immigrants to be set against each other.

So mischievous and blatantly fallacious were Mullan's observations that even the Governor, in his address to the Council on 6 March 1933, thought it expedient to quote the same 1931 *Census Report* to point out that:

> in spite of the large increase in the population of Assam at every Census since 1901, the percentage of speakers of Assamese to the total population has remained very steady. It is clear from the figures of increase in the speakers of Assamese at this Census that the language is at present in no danger of super-session.[134]

Time has proved that the Governor was right and Mullan wrong. However, it was the latter's false prophecy of 1931 that provided a rationale to the chauvinism which was to plague Assam for many years to come. An article on the gloomy future of the Assamese nationality was published in 1937 by Jnananath Bora, a leading intellectual of the province, in *Dainik Batori* (Jorhat), the mouthpiece of the Samrakshini movement. Bora argued that unless Sylhet was separated, unless Assamese was declared the only medium of instruction in schools and unless the influx of settlers was stopped, it would be difficult for the Assamese to survive as a nationality.[135] He was only echoing a cry raised on the floor of the Council the previous year: 'and now, sir, can this be reward from God that the Assamese people should confine themselves to Sibsagar alone. . . . We will not allow this to be!'[136]

A major section of the Assamese public was noticeably agitated over the outsider issue. In all the government schools of the Brahmaputra Valley, attended by both Bengali and Assamese pupils in sizeable numbers, there used to be a time-old arrangement for teaching not only their respective mother tongues, but also for imparting lessons through both the media up to Class VI and through the medium of English thereafter. Following Calcutta University's decision to adopt the mother tongues of pupils as media of instruction in place of English in Classes VII to X at the high school stage, the Assam government decided in favour of

---

[133] Citation in *Census of India, 1951*, Vol. 12, Part 1–A Report (Shillong, 1954), p. 73.
[134] Governor's address, *ALCP* (1933), Vol. 13, p. 5.
[135] In the bundle of *APCC Papers*, Packet No. 6, File 4, the present author came across a letter from Munin Barkataki, appealing to the Congress to remodel its stand in the light of Bora's article, 'Assam desh aru Congress', *Dainik Batori*, 24 October, Sunday, 1937. It is also interesting to note that the Asamiya Samrakshini Sabha, Gauhati, offered to issue non-official domicile certificates signed by its general secretary to boost the process of Assamization. Speech by J.A. Dawson, 16 March, *ALCP* (1936), Vol. 16, pp. 349–50. Dawson made fun of this attempt.
[136] J. Gohain's speech, 14 March, *ALCP* (1936), Vol. 16, p. 297.

unilingual schools. It encouraged, accordingly, the setting up of some four new aided schools exclusively for Bengali children from 1936. Bengali-medium sections were no longer provided in the government schools of the Brahmaputra Valley, except at Dhubri for another few years. A wedge was thus driven between the Assamese and Bengali communities through segregated schools.[137]

The Maulana of Bhasani

With the passage of the Moneylenders' Act of 1934, the prospect of further tenancy legislation and extended powers of the legislature under the forthcoming reforms, the influential Bengali Hindu urban middle class became increasingly panicky about their future status in the local power structure. While presiding over the first conference of the Assam Domiciled Peoples' and Settlers' Association held at Dhubri on 2 June 1935, Rai Bahadur Kalicharan Sen cited the Assam Tenancy Bill, the Assam Municipal (Amendment) Act and the Moneylenders' Act, 1934 as sources of great and grave danger to the land-owning settlers and factory owners of his community.[138] Also, concerned as they were about their cultural rights, they did not sit idle under the circumstances. In collaboration with some Marwaris, they founded the Assam Domiciled and Settlers' Association in 1935, for the protection of their own interests and to forge an alliance, if possible, with Bengali Muslim settlers on common issues. But the latter did not look to Assamese Muslim or Bengali Hindu politicians for leading them out of the wilderness. A new and autonomous leadership emerged slowly and silently within the community itself in Goalpara, after Maulana Abdul Hamid Khan Bhasani (1886–1976) immigrated there, not later than in the year 1928.[139]

The Maulana was born into a peasant family at a village near Sirajganj in the district of Pabna, East Bengal. After formal schooling at a madrassa, he taught for some time as a primary teacher in the village of Kagmari in neighbouring Tangail. After his first political experience as a Khilafatist and Non-Cooperator,

---

[137] For details on the medium of instruction prior to the change, see reply to Nichols–Roy, 15 September, *ALCP* (1933), Vol. 13, pp. 1190–94.

Following the establishment of a government-aided Bengali High School in 1936 at Gauhati, R.K. Chaudhuri said: 'the seed of the poisonous tree which will ever disunite the Bengalees and Assamese was sown with their blessings'. 14 March, *ALCP* (1936), Vol. 6, p. 262.

To forestall the segregationist move, local Congress leaders like Gopinath Bardoloi sought the cooperation of the so-called leaders of the Bengali community in running mixed schools under private managements. But the latter were too ready to play into the hands of the administration. Information from Brajamohan Lahiri, a former resident of Gauhati, in course of an interview at Calcutta on 7 March 1974.

[138] The second conference held at Tezpur in December 1935 unanimously passed a resolution expressing feelings of 'loyalty to the person and throne of His Majesty the King Emperor': *Assam Citizens' Association* (compiled by Dhubri Head Office, Gauhati, 1940), pp. 49 and 52. Needless to say, this reactionary platform failed to attract the Bengali masses or even the middle-class Bengali youth, even after changing its name later to Assam Citizens' Association.

[139] Mohammad Waliullah, *Yuga-Bichitra* (in Bengali, Dacca, 1967), p. 421.

he realized that Bengal's Muslim peasantry would have to continue their struggle against the zamindars and moneylenders, who were mostly Hindus. He did not hesitate to exploit religious sentiments to organize and unite oppressed Muslim peasants;[140] one of the issues he took up was restoration of a forgotten and dilapidated mosque within the premises of the zamindar of Santosh in Tangail.[141] In December 1932, Bhasani organized a conference of ryots (*praja sanmilan*) at Sirajgunj in Bengal, which passed resolutions calling for the abolition of zamindaris and for legislation to provide various types of relief to indebted peasants. It also passed a resolution extending support to the Communal Award of August 1932.[142]

The roving Maulana, with his simple and pious habits and great organizing abilities, was accepted by the rural folk not only as a political leader, but also as a *pir*, widely believed to have occult powers. Hounded out of Bengal by the zamindars and the police, he settled down on the waste lands of Ghagmari, a few miles from Dhubri, which extended to and included Bhasanir-char, an island in the Brahmaputra.[143] Both were in Goalpara district, where settlers already formed a fifth of the population. It was after the name of the latter place that he was nicknamed 'the Maulana of Bhasani' or simply 'Bhasani', in due course.

While still maintaining his contacts with Bengal during the years 1928–36, Bhasani used to move up and down the Brahmaputra to visit riverside immigrant Muslim villages in inaccessible areas of Assam, and he articulated their demand for land. The colonization of Ghagmari and Bhasanir-char was also partly due to his own personal efforts. Suffering from the oppression of zamindars and moneylenders in East Bengal, people were in any case flocking to the Brahmaputra Valley in large numbers in order to settle down on its beckoning waste lands. By 1936 Bhasani emerged as the accredited leader of the Muslim immigrants of Goalpara. He was an independent candidate in the 1937 election and was returned to the Assam Legislative Assembly. He remained an important figure to reckon with in Assam politics during the next ten years.

---

[140] Ibid., pp. 420–21.

[141] D.N. Banerjee, *East Pakistan: A Case Study in Muslim Politics* (Delhi, 1969), p. 62*n*; also information gathered at Tangail by the present author in 1948.

[142] Abul Mansur Ahmad, *Amar Dekha Rajnitiir Panchas Bachhar* (in Bengali, Dacca, 1970), pp. 80–82.

[143] Waliullah, *Yuga-Bichitra*, pp. 420–21.

CHAPTER SIX

Assembly Politics and Left Nationalism

Ministry-Making and Ministry-Breaking: 1937–38

Responsibility without Power

The Congress took part in the 1937 polls with the avowed objective of wrecking the new constitution from within. Twenty-six out of twenty-nine Congress candidates of the Brahmaputra Valley came out successful.[1] Altogether forty-one candidates fought the election battle in Assam on the Congress ticket; of them, thirty-three, including seven from the Surma Valley, were returned.[2] Whatever influence the Congress had in both the Valleys was conspicuously limited to non-Muslim general constituencies. The United People's Party led by T.R. Phookan stood for office acceptance and challenged the Congress in these constituencies. But, except for R.K. Chaudhuri, none of its leaders could get through. Gopinath Bardoloi, who was close to Phookan and shared his political views, was persuaded at the last moment to contest as a Congress candidate. He was elected. In the contest for the Jorhat Assembly seat, Heramba Prasad Barua (1893–1965), a planter and member of the Council of State during the years 1934–36, was defeated by Debeswar Sharma (b. 1896), a Congressman.

Under the Act of 1935, Governors were given veto powers even in the sphere of popular ministries. This was one reason why Left nationalist leaders like Jawaharlal Nehru and Subhas Chandra Bose had initially argued with great vehemence for a policy of outright rejection of office. But a majority of the All India Congress Committee (AICC) leaders regarded office acceptance as an inevitable corollary of poll participation.

Their view was supported by Gandhiji who was apparently moved by two considerations. First, the widely extended franchise now introduced the people

---

[1] 'APCC General Secretary's Report, 1937', *APCC Papers*, File No. 5, Packet 6 (Congress Bhavan, Gauhati).

[2] *Indian Annual Register* (hereafter IAR) (January–June 1937), Vol. 1, p. 168 (0).

    The minute book of the Assam branch of the Indian Tea Association (ITA) reveals that they had a political fund of Rs 1 lakh for use in the general constituencies. Obviously, the purpose was to ensure Congress defeat in the polls. Another Rs 1 lakh were at the disposal of the ITA's political secretariat at Shillong for other electoral purposes in 1937. For this information, I am grateful to Keith Ogborne of the University of Western Australia, Perth, who had access to the relevant ITA files.

to schooling in the art of self-government. Second, the Act of 1935 gave ample powers to the provincial ministers to propagate khadi and village industries, and to drive out drinking and drug habits. Nehru finally yielded to this pressure. Being the largest single party in the 108-member Assam Legislative Assembly, the Congress had fair prospects of forming a coalition government, but had no such inclination initially. 'The refusal to accept ministry and forming a solid bloc of opposition will, to my mind, be a more workable policy',[3] wrote Bardoloi to Rajendra Prasad, two days after being elected leader of the Congress Party in the Assembly, on 22 February 1937. In course of a resolution in March 1937, the Congress Working Committee (CWC) permitted the formation of Congress ministries in those provinces where the party commanded a clear majority, provided the concerned Governors assured that their special powers would in no case be exercised. In the absence of such assurance, no ministries could be formed even in the Congress-majority provinces. In an attempt to get out of this constitutional crisis, the Viceroy issued a message on 21 June to explain why a prior gubernatorial commitment on the issue was not possible; however, the message emphasized that the new constitution meant a real transfer of power so far as the ministerial sphere was concerned. This made the CWC feel that the substance of their demand had been conceded. On 7 July 1937, the Congress Party formed ministries in seven provinces.[4]

Meanwhile Assam remained free of any constitutional deadlock. Right from the beginning, Governor Sir Robert Reid's 'hopes had been centred on Sir Mohammad Saadulla' as Assam's first Chief Minister. Saadulla met the Governor on 15 March and took office as the head of a non-Congress coalition ministry on 1 April 1937 – the inaugural day of the constitution.[5]

Apparently the Act of 1935 meant some advance in the sphere of provincial government. The system of nomination to the lower house was done away with. The franchise was extended from about 3 per cent to some 8 per cent of the province's nine million population. This was done by widening the geographical coverage and also by lowering the property qualifications for voters. As a result, the size of the electorate expanded almost three times between 1929 and 1937 – from 2,88,832 to 8,15,341 electors.

There were discouraging aspects too. Assam's hills areas were kept, by and large, outside the scope of the provincial autonomy as before. These were classified under the 1935 Act into two categories: (a) excluded areas and (b) partially excluded areas. Both were outside the ordinary competence of the provincial legislature. The Balipara and Sadiya Frontier Tracts, the Naga Hills district, the Lushai Hills district, and the North Cachar Hills sub-division were

---

[3] Bardoloi to Rajendra Prasad, 24 February 1937, *APCC Papers*, Packet No. 35.

[4] Tarachand, *History of the Freedom Movement in India*, Vol. 4 (New Delhi, 1972), pp. 226–29 and 271; B.N. Chaudhury, 'Democracy in Action', *Assam Tribune*, 11 April 1941.

[5] Sir Robert Reid, *Years of Change in Bengal and Assam* (London, 1966), p. 87. Saadulla was knighted in 1928.

classified as 'excluded areas' and went unrepresented on the legislature. Their administration was vested in the Governor who acted 'in his discretion', without any reference being made to the cabinet. Of course, the necessary expenditures and staff came from the provincial pool of resources.

On the other hand, the Garo Hills district, the Khasi–Jaintia Hills district (excluding Shillong) and the Mikir Hills were classified as 'partially excluded areas'. These areas enjoyed franchise to elect members to the legislature. Their administration was primarily a ministerial responsibility under the 1935 Act. However, as per provisions under its Section 52 (e), the Governor had a special responsibility for their 'peace and good government'. In the exercise of his individual judgement, he could, therefore, over-ride his ministers' advice in this sphere, too.

More than a fifth of the province's total expenditure budget was non-votable – some of its items were not even open to discussion.[6] On certain specified subjects, a private Bill or resolution could be introduced in the legislature only after it had obtained the Governor's sanction. He had veto powers over all Acts of the legislature. He could even take the province's administration into his own hands, by invoking Section 93 of the Act, if he thought there was a break-down of the constitution. Lastly, there was the twenty-two-member upper house, called the Assam Legislative Council, with all but four of its members elected on a more restricted franchise. The four remaining seats were filled by nomination. This house acted as a brake on the popular will.

The existing provision for segregated electorates was expanded under the new constitution. Vested interests were thereby given heavy weightage in representation. For the province's less than 3,000 European population, there were as many as nine seats; whereas for the million-strong resident plantation population, there were only four seats in the 108-member Assembly. The detailed composition of the Assembly is shown below, in a tabular form.

The system of parliamentary politics that was built on such an electoral base could not but be divisive in its impact. The Congress Party's strength in the Assembly did not exceed thirty-three on 1 April 1937. It did not have a single Muslim member other than Fakhruddin Ali Ahmed. Even he was elected on an independent ticket. Nor did the Congress have any electoral foothold in the tribal and labour constituencies. Consequently, a large number of small, nebulous groups emerged – the largest of them being the Assam and Surma Valley Muslim Parties. The Muslim League was founded in the Surma Valley by Abdul Matin Chaudhury, who had resigned from the Central Legislative Assembly to enter the provincial Assembly.[7] The Muslim League had altogether four members in the Assembly in April 1937; it was yet to emerge as a viable Assembly party. Under

---

[6] Governor's address to a joint sitting of both the houses on 9 April, *Assam Legislative Assembly Proceedings* (hereafter *ALAP*) (1937), p. 40.

[7] Bureau of Public Information, Government of India, 'Provincial Autonomy: Ministries and Parties in Assam (1937–45)', File No. F 106/8/45-R, Morgue and Reference Series, No. 1, Reforms Department, National Archives of India (hereafter NAI).

Composition of the First Assam Legislative Assembly (under the Act of 1935)

	No. of Seats	No. of Electors	Poll Participation Rate in Contested Seats (%)
Territorial Constituencies			
1. Non-Muhammedan General (including seven reserved for Scheduled Castes*)	47	4,45,626	(76.0)
2. Muhammedan	34	2,77,677	(65.5)
3. Woman	1	2,199	(55.5)
4. European	1	2,357	–
5. Indian Christian	1	5,743	–
Special Constituencies			
1. (a) Backward Plains Tribes	4	27,588	(46.3)
(b) Backward Hills Areas	5	18,338	(64.6)
2. (a) European Planters	7	975	–
(b) Indian Planters	2	344	–
3. (a) Commerce and Industry (European)	1	18	–
(b) Commerce and Industry (Indian)	1	197	–
4. Tea Garden Labour	4	34,279	–
Total	108	8,15,241	(71.3)

Note: *Four depressed castes of the Brahmaputra Valley and ten of the Surma Valley were designated as Scheduled Castes.

Source: East India Constitutional Reforms: Elections, *Return Showing the Results of Elections in India 1937* (New Delhi, 1937), pp. 100–05.

the circumstances, the British planters and their allies were not only an important, but also the most organized group. They held the balance between the Congress and non-Congress camps. The legislature was thus destined to function as before, under the benign gaze of the British big brother. He could manipulate the strings of power slackly in ordinary times and firmly when necessary.

Sir Muhammad Saadulla had distinguished himself as the third Assamese ever to hold a master's degree and as a lawyer at the Calcutta High Court. He was an experienced parliamentarian with the longest record of membership in the province's Legislative Council. He also had to his credit an unbroken record of administrative experience of a whole decade, from 1924 to 1934, first as a minister and later as an executive Councillor. Moderate in his political views and a pragmatist, he was ready to cooperate with every move of the Raj for constitutional reforms, right from the beginning of his career. Claiming to promote the interests of the relatively advanced Assamese (Asamiya) Muslims of both his own Valley and the other Valley, he was determined to run the government with whatever support he could mobilize on his side – British planters not excluded. His five-member coalition ministry, which included R.K. Chaudhuri, Nichols–Roy and two Muslim ministers from the Surma Valley, was solidly backed by the British bloc in the Assembly.

B.K. Das of the Surma Valley was the seniormost and most experienced parliamentarian on the Congress side; most of the Congress legislators were from the other Valley. Under the circumstances, Das agreed to contest for Speakership, since the leader of the Congress Party had to be from the Brahmaputra Valley. Gopinath Bardoloi had suspended his law practice and undergone a jail term during the days of Non-Cooperation. Together with Tayyebulla, he was made a joint secretary of the Assam Pradesh Congress Committee (APCC) and was also elected as an AICC member in December 1926.[8] He was not with the Congress during the years 1930–36, nor did he have legislative experience. At a crucial hour in Assam politics, he came out of Phookan's influence and got himself elected to the Assembly on a Congress ticket.[9] The sudden demise of N.C. Bardaloi in 1936, the election of Kuladhar Chaliha to the central legislature in his place, the belated entry of B.R. Medhi into the provincial Assembly through a by-election in 1938 and Omeo Kumar Das's reluctance to assume the responsibility – all these helped Gopinath Bardoloi's almost overnight rise to the leadership. For the deputy leadership of the Congress Assembly Party, the unanimous choice fell on K. Deb, and, after his sudden death in June 1937, on Arun Kumar Chanda (1899–1947), both from the Surma Valley. Incidentally, B.N. Chaudhury was elected to the Central Legislative Assembly after B.K. Das had resigned therefrom to enter into Assam politics.

The Saadulla ministry, a government without a programme, was but a leaking boat. This was clear from the defeat of the official candidate for Speakership on 7 April. With the Muslim League opposed to him, Saadulla had to lean all the more on the European bloc. Bringing out the true character of the ministry, Dakshinaranjan Gupta-Chaudhury, a Congress legislator, pungently remarked: 'The white bureaucrats speak through their brown successors – the grip of imperialism – the chains of slavery tighten. It was well, sir, that the new constitution was inaugurated on All-Fools' Day – I mean the 1st of April, and the country had been befooled.'[10]

The Assembly proceedings came to a climax when, as per a strategy set out by the all-India Congress high command, all Congress legislators, except the Speaker, staged a walk-out and a boycott of the Governor's address on 8 April with a view to expose the futility of the constitution. The Governor missed their company at the official garden party the same evening, too.[11]

[8] The other four AICC members from Assam were N.C. Bardoloi, T.R. Phookan, Faiznur Ali and Kuladhar Chaliha. *The Bengalee*, 24 December 1926.

[9] After the Lahore Congress of 1929, Phookan and Bardoloi quit the Congress because of political differences. They did not participate in the Civil Disobedience movement of the 1930s. See Harendranath Barua *et al.*, eds, *Bharatar Mukti Yujat Asam* (in Assamese, Gauhati, 1972), pp. 24–25 and 169.

[10] Speech on 10 August, *ALAP* (1937), p. 512.

[11] *ALAP* (1937), pp. 1–11 and 35–36; Reid, *Years of Change*, p. 92.

Saadulla's Leaking Boat

As soon as serious business started in the first budget session (3 August–1 September 1937), the Saadulla ministry began to reel under heavy attacks. The budget Saadulla presented showed a small surplus after many years, despite the persisting economic depression. But this only indicated his failure to depart from the orthodox and bureaucratic principles of public finance. He suggested that Assam be assigned the whole or a portion of the central excise tax proceeds on petrol and kerosene produced within the province, as was done in the case of Bengal in respect of the jute export duty.[12] He also felt that the heavy expenditure on the Assam Rifles, a para-military force, should be borne entirely by the centre.[13] This latter demand was an old one raised in the legislature as early as 1926 by moderates like Nilmoni Phukan.[14] Both propositions gained unanimous support but with no immediate results. It took four years to devolve the maintenance cost of the Assam Rifles on the centre, through an amendment of the Assam Rifles Act, 1920.[15]

Fakhruddin Ali Ahmed moved an adjournment on 4 August to draw the attention of the house to the sufferings of the retrenched and locked-out Dhubri Match Factory workers, and to the hunger strike of their leader, Bipinchandra Chakravarty. The government managed to defeat the motion by 51 to forty-seven votes.[16]

Bardoloi, the leader of the opposition, launched an able attack on the budget. It was wretched, he said, in respect of its enunciated principles, as well as in its operational details. According to him, the maintenance of an army of occupation, an expensive public service and acute economic exploitation resulting in moral degradation of the Assamese people were among the causes of Assam's non-development. He charged that even the promised parliamentary form of government had been subverted in Assam through the European party's support to an otherwise minority government.[17]

From 12 August onwards, the Government began to sustain a series of heavy defeats – as many as eleven in twenty days till 31 August. It started with Abdul Matin Chaudhury's Local Rates Amendment Bill providing for reduced local rates, which was passed by 67 to thirty-seven votes. In an attempt to delay the measure, the Revenue Minister wanted the Governor to fix the time for its implementation. But his motion was rejected without even a division.[18]

More disastrous was the government's defeat on the question of retaining Divisional Commissioners – the administration's two white elephants – one in each Valley. As early as 1926, these offices were found somewhat superfluous

---

[12] *IAR* (July–December 1937), Vol. 2, p. 237.

[13] Speech on 3 August, *ALAP* (1937), p. 85.

[14] *The Mussalman*, 13 March 1926.

[15] File No. 159/40–R, 1940, Government of India Reforms Department (NAI).

[16] 3–4 August, *ALAP* (1937), pp. 75–76.

[17] Speech on 10 August, *ALAP* (1937), pp. 512–17.

[18] *IAR* (July–December 1937), Vol. 2, p. 239.

by the Webster Committee. The Retrenchment Committee of 1931, set up by the fourth Reformed Council, recommended abolition of one of them. But the proposal never found favour with the Secretary of State for India.

The Assembly voted 63 to eleven on 17 August 1937, to refuse the entire supply for the pay and establishment of Divisional Commissioners. A constitutional problem cropped up. Was a provincial legislature within its rights in refusing support to posts held by Indian Civil Service cadre? The matter was referred by the Speaker to the Advocate-General of Bengal and Assam for his legal opinion. The latter told the house that its decision was *intra vires* of the constitution. Accordingly, the Speaker's ruling of 27 August was that the refusal was perfectly in order and binding on the government.

Saadulla had earlier agreed to move the Secretary of State for the abolition of one Commissionership – that of the Surma Valley Division. Now he had to give the staff of both the Commissioners three months' notice of discharge. In the December session, the government presented a supplementary demand to meet the committed expenditure of four months, along with an assurance that the relevant staff would be discharged with effect from 1 January 1938. The demand was conceded by the Assembly. Acting contrary to his Chief Minister's advice, the Governor, however, sent a message on 21 December asking for a supplementary staff maintenance grant for another three months, till 31 March 1938. As the Assembly members were annoyed at this interference, the Speaker refused to admit the supplementary demand for discussion. The expenditure was validated later through the Governor's certification. On this occasion, Bardoloi felt that the Viceregal assurance of 21 June, on the basis of which the Congress had agreed to work the constitution, had been betrayed.[19]

On 23 August, the house refused the entire supply for the maintenance of the intelligence branch of the CID, which had been established eight years earlier to check terrorist activities. Unprecedented in any other province, it was yet another heavy blow for the government. In this case, the government accepted the verdict and abolished the establishment.[20]

Sarveswar Barua's cut motion, criticizing progressive enhancement of land revenue, was passed on 19 August. Another resolution recommending a 50 per cent reduction in the land revenue demand with effect from 1937–38 was moved by Siddhinath Sarma (Congress). Despite initial support from several members of the Muslim League, the long-drawn debate ended in a defeat for the Congress on 30 August. The resolution was interpreted by the government as a virtual no-confidence move against a Muslim-majority cabinet. It was this stance that helped mobilize Muslim support and tilt the balance of voting in its favour. Sayidur Rahman's amendment proposing a 33 per cent reduction in the land revenue demand came as a fig-leaf for the government, and it was adopted by the

---

[19] Ibid., pp. 240–42 and 245–47; Bardoloi to J. Nehru, n.d., File No. 11/37, Col. No. 4, Item No. 163, *Rajendra Prasad Collection* (hereafter *RPC*) (NAI).

[20] *Assam Administration Report*, 1937–38, p. I; *IAR* (July–December 1937), Vol. 2, p. 241.

house. The Revenue Minister subsequently formed a committee in an attempt to limit the proposed reduction to 25 per cent in the case of non-cultivating land-owners. Its report came under fire in the December session of the Assembly and was thrown out.[21]

Members from almost every group were keen on refusing a provision of Rs 35,260 towards the maintenance of the upper house. But it soon dawned upon them that the cut would bring the business of the upper house to a standstill and that, short of its confirmation, the Assembly's own legislative measures would also remain infructuous. Hence they decided not to push the matter to that length. The motion was withdrawn on an assurance that government support would be available for any forthcoming private resolution recommending abolition of the upper house.[22] A resolution moved by Munawwar Ali on 5 August 1937 demanding abolition of the Line system, if it had persisted, would have wrecked the ministry. But the mover was persuaded to withdraw it.[23] (This will be discussed in detail at the end of this chapter.)

From 12 August onwards, as defeat after defeat was inflicted on the Saadulla government, even its beneficiaries fought shy of supporting it. 'A Government which cannot control its own supporters and is continually humiliated by defeats', said the mouthpiece of British capital in eastern India, 'carries little authority and should either reassert its authority or resign.'[24] The annoyance of the Governor and the Government of India, as revealed in Sir Robert Reid's memoirs, was no less. Reid wrote: 'The Central Government was perturbed; but short of dismissing them, which could have caused a crisis we did not want to face, there was nothing that as a constitutional Governor I could do.'[25]

How Saadulla reasserted himself and avoided resigning, has already been discussed. The Congress lost its attempt to fix a minister's salary at Rs 500. A salary of Rs 2,800 per month for the Chief Minister and Rs 1,800 each for the other ministers was fixed by the house on 1 September. Despite Congress opposition, the Speaker's salary was fixed at Rs 1,000 per month. But he announced that he would draw only Rs 500 as salary.[26] The Assembly also voted emoluments for members of both the houses at the rates of Rs 100 per month and Rs 5 a day halting allowance. But the upper house returned the Bill with the amendment that a member's salary be reduced to Re. 1 a year. As the Assembly refused to revise the Bill, the upper house finally passed it in its original form on 19 February 1938.[27]

---

[21] *IAR* (July–December 1937), Vol. 2, pp. 240, 242–43 and 248; S.R. Dutta, Secretary of the Assembly Congress party to Rajendra Prasad, 29 October 1937, File No. 11/37, Item No. 162, *RPC*; 20 and 21 December, *ALAP* (1937), pp. 2359–609.

[22] 16–17 August, *ALAP* (1937), cited in *IAR* (July–December 1937), Vol. 2, pp. 239–40.

[23] Ibid., p. 236 and *ALAP* (1937), pp. 711–14.

[24] *The Statesman*, Sunday Dak edn, 22 August 1937.

[25] Reid, *Years of Change*, p. 92.

[26] *IAR* (July–December 1937), Vol. 2, p. 243.

[27] Ibid.; 19 February, *Assam Legislative Council Proceedings* (hereafter *ALCP*) (1938), pp. 97–104; *IAR* (July–December 1938), Vol. 2, p. 233.

Second Saadulla Ministry: 5 February–18 September 1938

By the end of August 1937, it became increasingly clear to Saadulla that he would have to bank heavily on his co-religionists from the Surma Valley for even bare survival, for, they formed the overwhelming majority of the Assembly's Muslim members. Led by Abdul Matin Chaudhury, the Muslim League in the Assembly had by then increased its strength to ten, and it sided with the Congress on most occasions. 'Grateful mention must be made of the invaluable support lent by the Surma Valley Independent Group, the Moslem League Party and the United Moslem Party', reported the secretary of the Assam Assembly Congress Party to Rajendra Prasad on 29 October 1937, 'but for whom the Congress Party might not have scored the victories it did in the last August session.'[28]

This trying situation forced Saadulla to woo the Muslim League. He attended its all-India annual conference held at Lucknow in October 1937. There he committed himself to advising his party's Muslim members to join the League.[29] For a cabinet reshuffle, he first tried to persuade two aged and inefficient Muslim colleagues to resign. As both of them refused to oblige, Saadulla himself resigned on 4 February 1938. He then formed a new ministry with Abdul Matin Chaudhury and Munawwar Ali, both of the Muslim League, and R.K. Chaudhuri, Nichols–Roy and Akshay Kumar Das (1900–1990), the last-mentioned a scheduled caste member from the Surma Valley, as his colleagues.[30] The reconstituted government faced the next budget session on 15 February with regained confidence. Rai Saheb Sonadhar Senapati (1868–1948) complimented Saadulla in the upper house for giving a start to scheduled caste politics in the province. It was Saadulla who had prompted their deputation to give evidence before the Simon Commission. 'The sight of a scheduled caste Minister in the Cabinet', said Senapati, 'has made me feel that I have begun to enter the fold of the Caste Hindus.'[31]

The second budget session was weathered by Saadulla somewhat better. The House voted 50 to forty-nine, to reject a no-confidence motion on 21 February.[32] All the budget demands were passed in full, except the provision for the Commissioners' staff. The instability of party alignments in the Assembly nevertheless soon loomed large with the changed Congress attitude to coalition for office acceptance.

Outside the Assembly, too, the situation was fast turning against Saadulla. There was widespread unrest amongst workmen in the oil fields, collieries and

---

[28] S.R. Dutt to Rajendra Prasad, 29 October 1937, *RPC*.

[29] Khalid B. Sayeed, *Pakistan: The Formative Phase 1857–1948* (second edition, New York/Karachi, 1968), pp. 87 and 213.

　In reply to a question on 5 September 1938, Saadulla claimed that he was a member of the Muslim League since before his election to the house. *ALAP* (1938), p. 11. Even if so, this connection was perfunctory.

[30] *IAR* (January–July 1938), Vol. 1, p. 229; Bureau of Public Information, Government of India, Morgue and Reference Series No. 11, New Delhi, 1 February 1946, File No. 106/8/45–R, Reforms Department (NAI).

[31] Speech on 16 February, *ALCP* (1938), pp. 33–34.

[32] *IAR* (January–July 1938), Vol. 1, pp. 229–30.

tea gardens, and amongst the tenants of certain zamindars. The 1938 local board elections were turned into a political battle, and the APCC claimed to have secured 65 per cent of the votes cast in the contested general seats.[33] Of the 324 elective seats in sixteen local boards, as many as 86, or an average 26 per cent, were to represent planter interests. Nevertheless, the prospect of these boards being captured by the Congress was not altogether bleak. But Saadulla abused his power and packed the local boards with such nominated members as would side with the planter group.[34] This raised a storm of protests all over Assam.

Because of the nomination system, the Congress was turned into a minority and was able to get chairmanship in only four local boards. On 5 September 1938, an adjournment was moved by Omeo Kumar Das to discuss the abuse of official nomination to various local boards. It was duly debated.[35] The mockery of local self-government was thus widely discussed and became a major issue in the anti-Saadulla agitation.

Bardoloi Throws His Net

Party policy did not permit formation of a Congress coalition government in Assam in July 1937 when Congress ministries were installed in several other provinces. However, there was no bar against attempts at overthrowing non-Congress ministries. B.R. Medhi, the APCC president, sent a telegram to Rajendra Prasad on 13 August, requesting him to send Abul Kalam Azad to help overthrow Saadulla. Although postponement of the requested visit was asked for the very next day, Calcutta newspapers reported that a shadow Congress coalition cabinet had already been chosen to take over the government. That some Assam Congressmen had started loose talk about ministry-making could not be denied. Rajendra Prasad angrily drew Bardoloi's attention to the then Congress policy and demanded an explanation. He wrote: 'even if a stage is reached when the Working Committee may be induced to permit alliances for forming ministries it is wholly undesirable and undignified to fix the personnel of the coalition ministry and to publish it in the Press'.[36]

---

[33] 'APCC's Report for the year 1938 to the President, National Congress, November 1938', *APCC Papers*, File No. 5, Packet 6.

[34] The twenty-three-member Jorhat Local Board, for example, had eleven general and nine other elective seats, besides three to be filled by nomination. The Congress won nine seats and failed, understandably, to establish control over the board. In Tezpur, all the eleven elective general seats of the local board had been captured by the Congress. But a *mauzadar*, defeated at the polls, was inducted into the board through the backdoor of nomination. Later, British, Muslim and nominated members combined to elect him as the board's chairman.

[35] 5–7 September, *ALAP* (1938), pp. 83–84 and 226; *Assam Administration Report*, 1938–39, p. ii; *Assam Tribune*, 25 April 1941.

Only in three of the nineteen local boards – Dhubri, Goalpara and Sunamganj – was there no separate representation for the planters.

[36] Telegrams dated 13 and 14 August from the APCC president to Rajendra Prasad, File No. 11/37, Col. No. 4, Item Nos. 128 and 129, *RPC*. Quote from Rajendra Prasad to Bardoloi, n.d., File No. 11/37, Col. No. 4, Item No. 133, ibid.

Bardoloi's reply of 25 August was typically that of a shrewd politician trying to wriggle out of an inconvenient situation. He blamed the *Amrita Bazar Patrika* for misreporting and asked Rajendra Prasad 'to send a warning to the A.P. against publishing such mischievous news'. He also informed him that their correspondent had already been asked to contradict the 'report appearing in the *Patrika* about Chaliha moving for a coalition. I believe his opinion is personal.' Thus he made his party colleague Kuladhar Chaliha the scapegoat. Bardoloi emphatically denied that the APCC or the parliamentary Congress Party had ever thought about a coalition, 'in spite of hundreds of suggestions coming from different places'. Nevertheless, he added:

> The stage has surely arisen when another coalition Government may take the place of the present one. My attitude has all along been that I would not go out to seek the alliance of any party, but if any party or group would come to us and give terms, I shall forward them to you and the Working Committee through you. Till then I remain where we were.[37]

There were people within his party, and many outside, who were egging Bardoloi on to the path of ministry-making. Compliments paid to the Muslim League for its oppositional role in the August session of Assembly, by him as well as by the party secretary, suggested that the feasibility of a Congress–League coalition to oust Saadulla was not outside the purview of their consideration. However, by the end of August, as noted earlier, the League was won over by Saadulla in the name of 'Muslim solidarity'.

An opportunity to overthrow Saadulla came again in September 1938. This time, the approval of the high command for a Congress coalition ministry was not lacking, provided there was an *ex ante* majority in its favour. In an attempt to gain allies among the tribal and labour members, Bardoloi raised the issue of tribal people in the plains losing their lands to immigrants. He demanded a protective system of tribal belts for them and pinpointed the utter lack of primary education facilities in tea gardens and tribal areas. This worked. The Congress and the Tribal League entered into an agreement to bring in a new coalition government. All sorts of temptations to induce floor-crossing were freely used by both the sides involved in this crucial struggle for power. While British planters helped Saadulla, most Indian planters supported Bardoloi with resources. Out of 1,103 tea gardens in Assam in 1936, 335 were Indian-owned. The Indian sector was relatively insignificant, in terms of acreage, investment and employment.[38]

On 12 September, four no-confidence motions were moved without any accompanying speeches. The next day, even before the debate could be resumed,

---

[37] Bardoloi to Rajendra Prasad, 25 August 1937, File No. 11/37, Col. No. 4, Item No. 136, ibid.

[38] *APCC Papers*, Packet No. 11; Reid, *Years of Change*, p. 125; Sadananda Chaliha, 'Barak Banam Brahmaputra', *Sapatahik Niilacal*, 27 (Ahrahayan, 1894 *shaka*); 7 September, *ALAP* (1938), p. 227.

Saadulla informed the house that his resignation had been submitted to the Governor. Bardoloi paid compliments to the outgoing Chief Minister for the spirit of democracy he displayed. As the Congress Party wanted some time for consultations at different levels, the Governor asked Saadulla to remain in office until it formed a new government.[39] For another week, the situation remained full of suspense, with hectic moves and counter-moves on both sides. The Congress was not yet very sure of a majority. Horse-trading in votes continued, even as Abul Kalam Azad appeared on the scene to supervise the take-over. Two more votes were still needed for a coalition majority. Azad therefore advised against ministry formation at that stage. Not satisfied with this decision, B.R. Medhi and Bardoloi invited the Congress president, Subhas Chandra Bose, to come down to Shillong and intervene. Bose himself started the wild goose chase for the two votes. 'Before the two birds were in hand, Subhas Bose counted them, and', says Tayyebulla in his memoirs, 'was inclined – nay decided to permit the coalition.'[40] Hurried telephonic consultations were held with Rajendra Prasad and Sardar Patel. While the former was in agreement with Azad, the latter approved of Bose's pragmatic strategy. Bose was finally able to have his way only because of the connivance of provincial leaders and Patel, chairman of the Congress Parliamentary Sub-committee. Later Bose reminded Gandhiji:

> But if Sardar Patel had not providentially come to my rescue, Maulana Sahib could never have given in at Shillong and perhaps you would not have supported my view-point against Maulana Sahib when the Working Committee met at Delhi. In that case there would not have been a Coalition Ministry in Assam.[41]

Bose also helped Bardoloi to iron out differences with Bengali Congressmen of the Surma Valley over the personnel of the ministry-in-the-making. Initially, only five non-Muslim ministers were named; the Governor was told that three more Muslim ministers would be appointed soon.

The formation of the Bardoloi ministry was announced in a gazette extraordinary published about noon on 19 September. On the same day, even before the new ministers had taken their oaths, Saadulla tabled a no-confidence motion signed by 56 members – a clear majority. The Speaker disallowed the motion since, technically, a no-confidence could not be moved against ministers who had not yet been sworn in. Bardoloi also prevailed upon him to adjourn the house *sine die* to avoid a critical situation. Under the chairmanship of F.W. Hockenhull, the leader of the European (planter) party, the 56 members of the

<hr>

[39] *IAR* (July–December 1938), Vol. 2, pp. 181–82.

[40] M. Tayyebulla, *Between the Symbol and the Idol at Last* (New Delhi, 1964), pp. 100–01.

[41] Bose to Gandhi, dated Bombay 21 December 1938, copy of letter in the possession of Nirad C. Chaudhuri, first published in L.A. Gordon, *Bengal: The Nationalist Movement 1876–1940* (Delhi, 1974), p. 284.

opposition met in the Assembly premises and unanimously resolved to remain together in all circumstances against the minority government. The oath-taking ceremony was suddenly postponed by the Acting Governor, and the few copies of the gazette extraordinary that had leaked out into circulation were recalled. However, at the peak of this confusion, it was realized by the Acting Governor that refusal to administer oath to ministers after the gazette notification would be scandalous. On 20 September, therefore, the oath-taking formality was completed posthumously, and the new ministry started functioning.[42] Thus, the nine-day drama that began on 12 September ended happily for Congressmen. The minority government was, of course, sure of becoming a majority one in no time.

First Bardoloi Ministry: 19 September 1938–16 November 1939

The five ministers who took their oath in September were Gopinath Bardoloi, Ramnath Das (Scheduled Caste), Akshay Kumar Das (Scheduled Caste), Kamini Kumar Sen and Rupnath Brahma (1902–1968), a Tribal League leader. Gradually, three Muslim ministers – Fakhruddin Ali Ahmed, Ali Hyder Khan and Mahmud Ali – were also taken in by 20 October, to complete the ministry. The new ministers faced the Assembly in December. It voted 54 to 50 to reject a no-confidence motion that was moved on 8 December. A huge crowd waiting outside the Assembly celebrated the victory with jubilations. Saadulla and Abdul Matin Chaudhury were no doubt behind the no-confidence move, but they did not take part in the debate. It was the leader of the European party who emerged as the *de facto* opposition leader.[43]

In the ministry thus formed, Bardoloi was the lone Congressman with a pre-election commitment. But his personal qualities and the abilities of his colleague, Fakhruddin Ali Ahmed, made up for his team's shortcomings, until it was put under the strain of a mass industrial unrest. In the eyes of the Governor, Chief Minister Bardoloi was 'a devout Gandhian, honest, obstinate, not very intelligent and with small gift of leadership'.[44] Wavell, the Viceroy, found in him in 1946 'a more forcible and quicker intelligence than the Khan Sahib but not a very pleasant personality'.[45] Opinions varied among others, including Tayyebulla – Bardoloi's rival for control over the party apparatus – as to how much of a Gandhian he was. In course of confidential notings on an official file when Bardoloi was a security prisoner, Saadulla assessed him rather uncharitably. He wrote on 1 October 1943: 'I know Mr Bardoloi personally. He was my student for a year . . . and then a colleague in the Gauhati Bar. He has been pitchforked into this

---

[42] Tayyebulla, *Between the Symbol and the Idol*, pp. 101–02; *IAR* (July–December 1938), Vol. 2, p. 183. For an official version of the episode, *Report of the Working of the Assam Legislative Assembly 1937–45* (Shillong, 1946), pp. 19–21.

[43] *IAR* (July–December 1938), Vol. 2, pp. 184–85; Reid, *Years of Change*, p. 125.

[44] Reid, *Years of Change*, p. 125.

[45] P. Moon, ed., *Wavell the Viceroy's Journal* (London, 1973), p. 233. Khan Sahib was the Chief Minister of North West Frontier Province.

position by adventitious circumstances. He was not a keen Congressman ever and did not go to jail in 1921 or 1931 movements.'[46]

However, a careful reader of Tayyebulla's memoirs and Bardoloi's correspondence with Gandhiji and other leaders cannot but conclude that Bardoloi knew the game of politics rather too well. Despite many shortcomings and contrary to Governor Reid's impression, he had enough gift of leadership to have his way at every critical stage, and with popular support. This was because he could always strike a balance between national and narrowly Assamese interests, as subsequent events indicated.

The Bardoloi government was committed to a programme and, therefore, was able to rouse popular expectations. The Congress accepted office, he said, with the definite object and purpose 'of easing the burden of taxation on the poor and of providing means for the uplift and betterment of the masses'.[47] Some features of the programme – such as abolition of the second chamber, reduction of the land revenue burden on the peasantry, progressive eradication of opium and abolition of Commissioners' establishments – were no longer controversial issues. Saadulla, too, had stood for them, though not vigorously in practice. After all, it was under Saadulla's orders that all political detenus (terrorist suspects), except one, had been released and six political convicts repatriated from the Andamans, after A.K. Chanda raised the issue in the Assembly on 27 August 1937. This process of political prisoners' release was completed by the new Bardoloi government, in response to a resolution moved again by Chanda and unanimously adopted by the Assembly on 5 December 1938. All the ten terrorist convicts serving various terms of imprisonment were released by 13 December.[48]

The opium eradication policy had also been in operation long before Bardoloi assumed power. Opium revenue progressively fell from Rs 3,826,000 in 1927–28 to Rs 1,007,000 by 1938–39; this was because the recorded consumption of opium had gradually decreased from 722 to 183 maunds. The opium prohibition scheme was inaugurated by the Congress coalition government in the two sub-divisions of Dibrugarh and Sibsagar on 15 April 1939. Omeo Kumar Das was appointed honorary prohibition commissioner. About 10,000 registered and 5,000 unregistered addicts were cured of the opium habit through hospitalization. By the end of March 1940, the opium revenue came down to Rs 5,20,000 and opium consumption to 94 maunds.[49] When he was installed Chief Minister

---

[46] Confidential B, 1945, File No. C 241/1945 (Assam Secretariat Files; hereafter AS). Saadulla was wrong to suggest that Bardoloi did not go to the jail in 1921.

[47] Budget speech on 9 March, *ALCP* (1939), p. 13.

[48] Ibid., p. 22; *Assam Administration Report*, 1937–38, p. I; *IAR* (July–December 1937), Vol. 2, p. 242; *IAR* (July–December 1938), Vol. 2, p. 184; *ALAP* (1939), pp. 13 and 258.

[49] *ALCP* (1929), Vol. 9, p. 4; Tayyebulla, *Between the Symbol and the Idol*, p. 56; Bardoloi's budget speech on 9 March, *ALCP* (1939), p. 22; *IAR* (January–June 1940) Vol. 1, p. 285; R.K. Chaudhuri's budget speech on 3 March, *ALCP* (1941), p. 167; Saadulla's budget speech on 22 February, *ALCP* (1940), pp. 13–14. Relevant reports of the Excise Department.

for the third time, Saadulla declared 26 February 1941 as Prohibition Day and brought all non-excluded areas of the province under the opium prohibition scheme with effect from 1 March 1941. Thus, by adopting a progressive opium prohibition programme, the new government only accelerated an established trend.

So was the case with the reduction of the land revenue burden. The 33 per cent remission of land revenue assessment for the year 1938–39, as effected by Saadulla, had amounted to Rs 28 lakh. This relief further increased to Rs 40 lakh a year in 1939–40 and 1940–41 because of a 50 per cent remission in the case of estates paying Rs 16 or less, and a 30 to 20 per cent remission in the case of other estates, under the Congress commitments.[50]

In its attitude to labour unrest, too, the Bardoloi government did not basically differ from its predecessor, as will be revealed later. What was new in the Congress programme was direct and bold confrontation with the British planters in fiscal matters, and a departure from the erstwhile orthodox policy of seeing virtue in surplus or balanced budgets. To compensate for the loss on account of the reduced excise and land revenue collections, the new Finance Minister, Fakhruddin Ali Ahmed, introduced five new tax efforts. These were:

  (i) The Assam Sales of Motor Spirit and Lubricant Taxation Act, 1939
  (ii) The Assam Sales Tax Act, 1939
  (iii) The Assam Amusements and Betting Tax Act, 1939
  (iv) The Assam Excise (Amendment) Act, 1939
  (v) The Assam Agricultural Income Tax, 1939.

The Assam Sales Tax Act, however, was not given effect to, in apprehension of an exodus of trade to neighbouring Bengal, where there was no such legislation.[51]

The introduction of agricultural income taxation, primarily to tax the plantations, proved to be literally an uphill task.[52] It was only after the 1921 movement that some of the Assamese planters had begun to lend support to the idea of taxing the tea industry for general benefit. Such taxation would have hit their own interests no doubt, but their British rivals much more. There was increasing realization on their part that such gestures alone would help sustain their hegemony over the local anti-imperialist movements. Planters – both British and Indian – let out a howl of protest. Even a section of Congressmen with plantation interests started feeling uneasy. Relatively better-off peasants were afraid that some of them who were on the wrong side of the exemption limit would have to pay tax. Maulana Bhasani opposed the Bill on the ground that surplus-yielding

---

[50] Saadulla's speech on 22 February, *ALCP* (1940), pp. 13–14; *Assam Tribune*, 10 November 1939; ibid., 26 September 1941.

[51] Atulchandra Sarma, 'A Study of Assam Finances – Structure and Trend 1948 to 1965–66' (unpublished Ph.D. thesis, University of Gauhati, March 1971), pp. 161–62.

[52] Himself a petty planter, Kuladhar Chaliha, for example, moved a resolution in the third Reformed Council recommending a levy of three pies on every pound of tea manufactured within Assam, so that the heavy government reliance on opium as a source of revenue could be decreased. The Council voted twenty-four to nineteen to throw out his motion. *The Mussalman*, 5 January 1926.

farmers would be unable to contribute to agricultural capital formation if they were to pay tax. Saadulla's motion for circulating the Bill to elicit public opinion was defeated. The select committee, which finished its job in two sittings in March, met the objections of the better-off peasants by raising the exemption limit from Rs 2,000 per annum to Rs 3,000. The house then voted, 57 to twenty-eight, to pass the modified Bill on 6 April 1939. Even thereafter, the Indian Tea Association doggedly continued its battle on the plea that the Bill was discriminatory to tea producers as compared to the producers of ordinary crops. It pulled strings in London to invoke the Governor's veto power, but the Secretary of State for India did not agree. Meanwhile, the upper house, where the vested interests were in a majority, rejected the Bill on 9 May 1939.

After much strain and tussle, on 4 August, a joint session of both the houses finally voted, 65 to 56, to pass the Bill. The rates of agricultural income taxation were fixed by the Assam Finance Act on 10 August. Having won the battle, the government declared its willingness to remove inequitable clauses, if any, through an amending Bill or appropriate provisions in the statutory rules. But before any such follow-up action could be taken, the Congress coalition ministry was out. With the come-back of Saadulla, statutory rules were framed in such a manner as to suit the planters.[53]

Of the remaining issues on the Congress programme, two – the immigrant problem arising out of the Line system and the growing labour unrest – defied any solution within the framework of provincial autonomy. The Congress coalition ministry betrayed hesitancy and indecision on these issues and exposed itself to severe criticism from even its own ranks. In the meantime, a new situation developed, relieving it of its committed responsibilities. Great Britain went to war with Germany on 3 September, and India was declared a belligerent the following day. As the declared war aims did not include India's independence, the Congress Working Committee meeting at Wardha on 22 October called upon all Congress ministries to resign.

Bardoloi did not want to resign immediately, for he had yet to spell out the official policy on immigration with reference to the report of the Line System Committee. He feared that once he was out, the old system of unrestrained immigration would be revived by the next government, much to the detriment of indigenous interests and his party's popularity. Press reports that the Congress coalition party was sending a deputation to the Congress Parliamentary Board for consideration of Assam's case as a special one were never contradicted. The APCC met in a plenary session at Sibsagar on 7 November 1939 to consider *inter alia* also the question of resignation. Several speakers at the meeting cast aspersions on Bardoloi for not having resigned so long. Both B.R. Medhi and B.C.

---

[53] *IAR* (January–June 1939), Vol. 1, pp. 251 and 254; Bhasani's speech on 3 August at a joint session of both the Houses, *ALCP* (1939), pp. 27–28; P. Griffiths, *The History of the Indian Tea Industry* (London, 1967), pp. 167–200.

Bhagavati reportedly charged the cabinet with lust for power. The meeting directed the Congress coalition ministry to resign not later than 15 November. It clung to power till that dead-line and was the last of the Congress ministries to resign. Because of this procrastination, Saadulla gained enough ground to caustically remark on 27 February 1940, that Bardoloi had resigned not to vindicate his moral stand against the war efforts but at the goading of the Congress high command.[54]

The Last Straw: Nichols–Roy

Resignation was not the end of the story. For some time past, Nichols–Roy had been with the Congress coalition party, and would have perhaps joined the ministry had there been no stiff opposition from the hills people he represented. Now, a plan was hatched to keep Saadulla out of power by bringing another coalition into power, with the necessary Congress support. The coalition party that emerged overnight, with Nichols–Roy as its leader and Ali Hyder Khan as president, pledged to execute the constructive programme of the Congress. It claimed the allegiance of twenty-three members and hoped to form a government with the backing of the thirty-five-member Congress Party. Brisk telephonic consultations were held on 15 November 1939 with Abul Kalam Azad and B.C. Roy of Calcutta. Baidyanath Mukherjee (b. 1900), a confidant of Bardoloi, rushed to Calcutta to plead the case before Azad. However, he was told that Congress support could not be pledged without its Working Committee's prior approval. In reply to Nichols–Roy's letter of 29 November 1939, Rajendra Prasad informed him that the Working Committee had met at Allahabad but did not approve of the plan. After a talk with Bardoloi in Calcutta, Azad finally issued a public statement on behalf of the Congress Parliamentary Sub-Committee on 14 December 1939, setting at rest all speculations about Congress support to Nichols–Roy.[55]

The third Saadulla ministry had to be double the size of the first one and larger than the Bardoloi ministry for ensuring the necessary support. Six ministers were sworn in on 17 November and four more within a few weeks. The new cabinet met on 16 December after Nichols–Roy's dreams were shattered, and then it dispersed for a 'merry Christmas'. Rupnath Brahma, who had been in Bardoloi's team, was the last and tenth minister to be sworn in on 9 January 1940.[56]

[54] *IAR* (January–June 1940), Vol. 1, p. 204; *Assam Tribune*, 10 November 1939.

[55] *Assam Tribune*, 17 November 1939 and 22 December 1939; Nichols–Roy to Rajendra Prasad, 29 November 1939, and Rajendra Prasad to Nichols–Roy, 2 December 1939, *AICC Files*, No. PL-32, 1939–40 (Nehru Memorial Museum and Library [hereafter NMML] New Delhi).

[56] Bureau of Public Information, Government of India, Morgue and Reference Series No. 11, New Delhi, 1 February 1946, File No. 106/8/45–R, Reforms Department (NAI); Reid, *Years of Change*, p. 134.

Industrial Unrest and the Emergence of Trade Unions
Strike and Lock-out at Dhubri

As early as in September 1937, A.K. Chanda – then a young barrister sympathetic to leftist thinking – sounded an ominous warning in the Assam Legislative Assembly. 'The spectre of class war', he said 'is worrying the world and I can see that this spectre is looming larger and larger on the horizons of this country everyday.'[57] Chanda's words were prophetic. The persistent economic depression of the 1930s had hit hard not only the agriculturists, but also the province's trade and industries. Planters and industrialists naturally tried to shift the burden on to the workers' shoulders. The latter, of course, resisted. On the peasant front, too, old-style Ryot Sabhas were giving way, here and there, to militant Kisan Sabhas (or Samitis) of a new type. The socialist and communist ideology began to play a significant role in organizing students, workers and peasants on a radical platform.

The lingering strike (and lock-out) of the organized workers of the Swedish-owned Assam Match Factory since 14 December 1936 came into prominence when, on 30 April 1937, the management fruitlessly tried to resume production with the help of new recruits. Besides arrests, a novel method adopted by the then Saadulla government to deal with the strike committee was to make twenty of their activists special constables for maintaining peace. The hunger strike by their leader Bipin Chakravarty and the animated Assembly debate that followed failed to pressurize the authorities concerned. The Board of Conciliation that was set up achieved nothing. Defecting workers drifted back to work by the end of December 1937.[58] After Dhubri, Dibrugarh came into the limelight when Kedarnath Goswami (1901–1965), then a Congressman, successfully led a strike of the steamer *ghat* workers there.

Saga of the Digboi Oil Strike

The Dhubri strike was of marginal concern to the government, since the employment at the match factory there had at no time exceeded 500. So was the strike at the Dibrugarh steamer *ghat*. But the smouldering unrest at the little oil town of Digboi in Lakhimpur district was a different matter as its 10,000 workers were concentrated in a sensitive industrial and plantation area. The *Administrative Report* for the year 1937–38 did not fail to note the signs of trouble brewing there. Jawaharlal Nehru addressed meetings at Moran, Khowang, Dibrugarh, Chabua, Tinsukia, Doomdooma and Digboi in the first week of December. He talked of capitalist exploitation with reference to the Assam Oil Company (AOC; a subsidiary of the Burma Oil Company) and the British plantation companies. Although Nehru's remarks at Doomdooma had little effect, 'the situ-

---

[57] 1 September, *ALAP* (1937), p. 1878.

[58] Fakhruddin Ali Ahmed's speech, 4 August, *ALAP* (1937), pp. 188–90; *Assam Administration Report*, 1937–38, p. I; A.K. Das to A.K. Chanda, 1 March 1938, *ALAP* (1938), pp. 583–86.

ation at Digboi', wrote the superintendent of police to his superior, 'gives cause for some concern'.[59]

The Assam Oil Company workers were agitated over the questions of low wages, retrenchment and non-recognition of bungalow servants as Company employees.[60] A general meeting of the workers was held on 13 February and again on 22 February 1938, as of consequence a which the AOC Labour Union was formed. In a letter of 29 April, the Company laid down certain preconditions for the Union's acceptance to facilitate its recognition. But these preconditions were not accepted. The Union applied to the government on 27 July for its registration under the Trade Unions Act, 1926. It also simultaneously submitted a twelve-point charter of demands and fourteen-day strike notice to the Company. The Company immediately moved the government for a conciliation. A Court of Enquiry, consisting of J.C. Higgins (chairman), O.K. Das and Sayidur Rahman, was formed by Saadulla on 16 August 1938.

The Court of Enquiry sat for two month from 29 August to 29 October 1938. The Union, having been registered under the Trade Union Act by 7 August, at first cooperated. But when a bungalow servant was dismissed for the 'offence' of giving evidence before this Court, it refused to cooperate any longer. Meanwhile, Bardoloi stepped into the shoes of Saadulla. All eyes now turned to the new government for a settlement within the framework of its declared policy. The Bardoloi government's resolution of 9 February endorsed only the unanimous part of the Court of Enquiry's recommendations, which were received on 7 January 1939. Neither the demand for a wage increase nor that for a 44-hour week was accepted. Even in clear cases of victimization and wrongful dismissals, the Court failed to pronounce judgment. The agitation therefore continued.

While the tripartite talks dragged on till the end of March 1939, the Company was busy preparing lists for further retrenchment. Between 14 November 1938 and 1 April 1939, at least 56 workers were either discharged or dismissed. In the face of these provocations, the Union became increasingly critical

<hr>

[59] *Assam Administration Report*, 1937–38, p. I; Supdt. of Police, Lakhimpur to Deputy I.G. of Police, Assam, 15 December 1937, D.O. No. 1-1/1-33 cited in Confidential B, December 1937, Nos 68–135, File No. 171–C/37 (AS).

[60] The account of the Digboi strike herefrom is culled from the following sources, except when stated otherwise.

   J.C. Higgins, *Report of the Court of Enquiry* (7 January 1939) and the relevant Government of Assam Resolution of 9 February, cited in *Assam Gazette Extraordinary*, No. 3, 10 February 1939; K.K. Hajra, *Report of the Board of Conciliation* (8 August 1939) and M.N. Mukerji, *Report of the Committee of Enquiry into the Affairs at Digboi* (25 November 1939); relevant Government of Assam Resolution of 18 December 1939, *Assam Gazette*, 20 December 1939 – Part II; 6 May, *ALCP* (1939), pp. 190–91 and 198; *Assam Administration Report*, 1938–39, p. ii; *IAR* (January–June 1939), Vol. 1, pp. 256 and 357–58; 'A note issued from Swaraj Bhavan, Allahabad 7 July 1939 with reference to Rajendra Prasad's statement', cited in *IAR* (July–December 1939), Vol. 2, pp. 206–08; Government's reply to S. Barua on 21 March, *ALAP* (1940), pp. 1095–98; *Assam Administration Report*, 1939–40, p. I; *ALCP* (1939), pp. 198, 157–58, and 323-3.

of the impotence of the Bardoloi ministry upon which it had placed so much trust. By a notification of 20 March 1939, the Company extended recognition to the Union, but at the same time saw to it that non-unionized workers could bypass the Union to represent their cases directly as before. The Union decided, therefore, to go on a week-long protest strike from 3 April. By 11 April the total number of victimized workers had increased to 74.

The strike was complete. More than 6,000 workers at Digboi and 4,000 workers at Tinsukia, where the Company had a tin container factory, struck work. Even sweepers and bungalow servants joined in. Only 138 men were allowed by the Union to remain on their jobs to maintain the minimum essential services. Following the Company's provocative threat of dismissal of all strikers, the strike persisted beyond the initially stipulated period. Pressurized by vested interests and to the discomfiture of Congressmen, the government had to provide armed escorts to the 'blacklegs' recruited by the Company. Chief Minister Bardoloi visited Digboi and Makum on 14 April, and publicly disapproved of the continuous strike. On 16 April, the day Bardoloi left the place, there was a large public meeting attended by several Assembly members and the APCC president, Hemchandra Baruah. In course of his speech, Baruah criticized the role of the police and demanded that they act upon the orders of the Congress coalition government alone.

The situation took a violent turn when three workers were shot dead by an Assam Rifles patrol on the night of 18 April. This incident roused anti-government feelings all over Assam. The findings of the judicial enquiry into the firing by a magistrate, which started on 23 April, did not satisfy the workers. The government therefore appointed M.N. Mukerji, a retired chief justice of the Calcutta High Court, on 10 July to enquire into the Digboi incident.

Because of the strikers' resistance, production at the AOC could be resumed only partially from 25 May. The AICC session held at Bombay on 24–27 June 1939 deplored the Company's refusal to accept a board of conciliation to go into such details of the dispute as the timing and manner of strikers' return to their jobs. It counselled the Assam government to make the decisions of such boards binding on the disputants through suitable legislation. It also threatened retaliation in the form of refusal by the Congress coalition ministry to renew the Company's oil field leases, which were soon to expire. In a series of meetings held in June, July and August all over Assam, the coalition government and its Chief Minister were charged, by local trade unionists and Left nationalists, of bad faith and weakness.

On 23 July 1939, K.K. Hajra, ICS, was appointed as the Board of Conciliation to try to settle the dispute. He found that out of 2,412 loyal workers working within the Company's precincts, 762 were old hands and 1,650 were new recruits. As against its pre-strike employment of 6,350 workers, the Company put its labour requirement now at some 5,560 hands. This meant that the declared vacancies could absorb only about 3,238 strikers, leaving the rest to their lot. The labour case was represented before the Board of Conciliation by

J.N. Upadhyay, Sadhu Singh, M.A. Chaudhury, Pritam Singh and Jadunath Bhuyan – president, vice-president and secretaries, respectively, of the AOC Labour Union. Sudhin Pramanik, a distinguished Bengal trade unionist, was also present at the conciliation proceedings. In the 1920s, he had played a prominent role in a steel workers' strike at Tatanagar and was now elected by the Digboi workers as the secretary of their strike committee. The Hajra Report, submitted on 8 August 1939, recommended that all strikers should be called back to their jobs and all new recruits discharged. Any surplus labour above the required strength could be later discharged after a discussion at the works council, to be set up soon. The Company, naturally, would not accept these recommendations. The Bardoloi government, too, postponed their further consideration and even publication, until the submission of the Mukerji Report.

On 4 September, the Digboi–Tinsukia area was declared protected under the Defence of India Rules. The District Magistrate explained the implications of such protected areas at a meeting of the strikers. Orders banning meetings and processions were issued under Section 144, CrPC. The six-month-old strike collapsed under these fierce attacks. Himself under a ban, Pramanik issued a frantic appeal reminding the AICC members of their commitment. 'The W.C. and the AICC ought to therefore direct the Assam Ministry by a clear resolution', he wrote on 7 October,

> to resist firmly any such interference in its administrative and labour policy and undue application of war emergency measures and to implement without further delay the AICC's last resolution 'to forthwith undertake legislation for making the acceptance of the decision of the Conciliation Board obligatory.[61]

Nothing of course came out of Pramanik's appeal. Nine principal Union and strike committee leaders were externed or forced to leave the area under threats of externment. After an ignoble and staggering existence for two-and-a-half months following the declaration of war, the Bardoloi government submitted its resignation on 15 November, and Saadulla formed his third ministry on 17 November. The Mukerji Report, submitted on 25 November and published on 3 December, validated the official policy of total surrender to the Company. It found the strike to be unjust. Registration of the Union was cancelled on 10 January 1940 on technical grounds. Thus ended the heroic struggle of oil workers that shook Assam for many months.

The Spirit of Digboi Spreads

Short-lived strikes in tea gardens and 'a good deal of trouble' among railwaymen and contractors' labour, working for the British-owned Assam Railways and Trading Company, took place in 1938–39.[62] This Company owned an industrial complex comprising the Dibru–Sadiya Railways, several collieries,

---

[61] A typed copy of the appeal in *APCC Papers*, File No. 4, Packet 6.
[62] *Assam Administration Report*, 1938–39, p. i.

saw mills, some shares in Digboi Oil, and four tea gardens in and around the towns of Margherita and Ledo. Benoybhusan Chakrabarty (1897–1967), a tea garden doctor who had resigned his job, Kedarnath Goswami and Nilmoni Barthakur (1912–2001) – Congressmen with sympathy for the socialist and communist ideology – helped the workers to organize.[63] The Assam Railways and Trading Company Workers' Union was registered on 29 March 1939. A few days after the oil strike was launched, it reportedly called for a general strike in all the Company's establishments. The strike spread even beyond and had spontaneously involved as many as twenty-one tea gardens by 23 May. Workers of the Ledo Tea Estate organized a march towards Tinsukia, protesting against alleged stoppage of water supply by the Company.[64]

The situation was so pressing that the Indian Tea Association had to set up, for the first time, a definite grievance-handling procedure and emergency committees to meet the challenge of the strike wave. The procedure adopted involved three successive measures: (a) enquiry into the labour grievances, (b) declaration of a lock-out if the strike was found unjustified, and (c) a publicity offensive against such strikes.[65] Several plantation labour unions – some of them perhaps paper unions – sprang up in the Brahmaputra Valley, while there was a lone one in the Surma Valley. These are listed in the table below.

Although far removed from the epicentre of labour revolts, the Surma Valley plantations did not lag behind. In the year preceding 30 September 1938, there were three tea garden strikes in Sylhet, each of one-day duration. In the same year, five tea gardens of Cachar were also on strike, involving some 2,000

Plantation Labour Unions: 1939–40

Name	Headquarters	Date of Registration
Upper Assam Tea Co. Labour	Dibrugarh	27 April 1939
Rajmai Tea Co. Labour Union	"	"
Greenwood Tea Co. Labour Union	"	6 May 1939
Makum (Assam) Tea Co. Labour Union	Margherita	30 May 1939
Sylhet–Cachar Cha-Bagan Mazdoor Union		27 April 1939

Source: Government's reply to A.K. Chanda, 14 November, *Assam Legislative Assembly Proceedings (ALAP)* (1940), p. 1313.

---

[63] In 1939, Bideshiram Tanti MLA, Benoybhusan Chakrabarty, Shyamchandra Choudhuri, Sardar Gurudat Singh, Lilaram Kakati, Bangshidhar Datta, Birochan Saikia and Shyam Goala – all were warned by the District Magistrate of Lakhimpur not to hold meetings in tea estates, in view of the formation of the Tea Garden Labour Unrest Enquiry Committee on 23 May the same year, which was also to look into the question of grievance procedure. Government of Assam, General and Judicial Department, immigration branch B, File no. I, 118, G.I.M. 49/47, 1939, p. 161.

[64] Sanat Kumar Bose, *Capital and Labour in the Indian Tea Industry* (AITUC, Bombay, 1954), pp. 114–15; *Assam Administration Report*, 1939–40, p. I; Bardoloi's reply to debate, 6 May, *ALCP* (1939), p. 198; 10 August, ibid., pp. 323–30; Government's reply to A.K. Chanda, 14 November, *ALAP* (1940), p. 1313.

[65] Griffiths, *History of the Indian Tea Industry*, p. 384.

workers and a loss of 6,326 man-days.[66] The Sylhet–Cachar Cha Mazdoor Sangathak Committee was formed in 1938 at the initiative of Barin Datta, Prabodhananda Kar and others. In the 1938 Cachar strikes, this Committee circulated a large number of leaflets among the workers. Renamed the Sylhet–Cachar Cha-Bagan Mazdoor Union, it was registered under the Trade Union Act on 27 April 1939.[67] With A.K. Chanda as its president and Sanatkumar Ahir as vice-president, the Union had a membership of about 900 in two circles of Cachar. They paid an annual membership fee of 2 annas per head. The Rege Committee (1946) noted that during the war years the Union had to carry on its activities in the plantations stealthily, because of lack of freedom of movement. Under the circumstances, it became practically defunct. A Bill entitled 'Assam Tea Garden Labourers' Freedom of Movement Bill' was tabled by O.K. Das as early as in 1937, and again in 1938, in the Assembly. But as the representatives of the tea industry assured the Congress ministry that they would see to it that the supposed grievances were removed, the Bill was withdrawn.[68]

A wave of strikes broke out in Cachar in the wake of the Digboi struggle. The most significant of them was the strike in the Arunabund Tea Estate that commenced in early April 1939 and continued for forty days. The main grievances of the workers were heavy workload, ill-treatment by the management and lack of freedom of movement in the plantations. This well-organized strike was able to mobilize popular support, like that of Digboi, from almost every walk of life.[69]

As the labour situation in the plantations of both the Valleys was getting out of hand, the Bardoloi government set up a Tea Garden Labour Unrest Enquiry Committee on 23 May 1939, for a probe. The Committee consisted of F.W. Hockenhull, Baidyanath Mukherjee, A.K. Chanda, Debeswar Sarma and a retired High Court Justice. The government warned that strikes, lock-outs and such other activities were unwelcome, and that it would not hesitate to enforce mutual forbearance, if necessary. Due to the Congress Party's persuasion and an official assurance, the strike was indiscreetly called off when the Committee visited the

---

[66] A.K. Das to A.K. Chanda on 12 September, *ALAP* (1938), pp. 420–23; *Annual Report on the Working of Tea Districts Emigrant Labour Act (XXII of 1932) for the Year Ending 30 September 1938*.

[67] Bose, *Capital and Labour in the Indian Tea Industry*, p. 114.

The house was told that leaflets were distributed by the Sylhet–Cachar Tea Garden Labour Association. Das to Chanda, 12 September, *ALAP* (1938), pp. 420–23. Thus there is some confusion over the name of the organization.

[68] Labour Investigation Committee (Chairman: D.V. Rege, Government of India), *Report on an Enquiry into Conditions of Labour in Plantations in India* (Delhi, 1946), p. 71. Also *Assam Administration Report*, 1938–39, p. ii. The grievances were indeed very real, and they persisted. It was only after independence that rules were framed under the Plantation Code of 1951 to guarantee freedom of movement in the plantations.

[69] Bose, *Capital and Labour in the Indian Tea Industry*, p. 115–17; *Amritabazar Patrika* (Calcutta), 23 April 1939 and 29 May 1939; *Naya Duniya* (in Bengali, Sylhet, 9 *Jaistha* 1346 [May 1939]).

Arunabund Tea Estate. The twelve militant workers who had been turned out of the tea garden along with their families were not taken back. The Indian Tea Association decided on 1 July 1939 not to cooperate with the Committee any longer. Accordingly, Hockenhull withdrew from it, and the Committee became totally defunct.[70]

Another notable strike took place in the Allenpur Tea Estate of Cachar. On 30 July 1940, about 200 working women there spontaneously went on a strike demanding higher wages and a decrease in workload. By 3 August, the entire labour force of the garden struck work at the instance of the union. A 200-strong procession of strikers proceeded to Silchar. Several organizers, including Gopendranath Ray, were arrested. All the strikers thereafter returned to work on 8 August. Digen Dasgupta, a communist organizer of the union, was prevented under Section 107, CrPC, when he tried to organize labour strikes in Shamsernagar and other tea estates in Maulvibazar sub-division. In 1940, the Surma Valley Dock Mazdoor Union was active in organizing the *khalasis* at Chhatak and Fenchuganj steamer stations in Sylhet. Some of the Sylhet communists were also active in the Bengal and Assam Railroad Workers' Union.[71] The Surma Valley (Shillong) Motor Workers' Union, with its headquarters at Sylhet, was registered on 6 May 1939. There was also the Sylhet Scavenger's Union, with Kaliprasanna Das as its secretary, in 1940.[72]

The phase of labour struggles during the years 1937–40 was a turning point in Assam's history in more than one respect. From the very beginning, these struggles, directed as they were against British capital, had a clear anti-imperialist character, as well as a broad Left–nationalist orientation. They inspired not only the anti-imperialist student masses of both the Valleys, but also the people on the cool heights of Shillong. In September 1937, a partial strike appears to have occurred in the Commercial Carrying Company's workshop in Shillong. At the initiative of Kirtibhusan Chaudhury, the Shillong Municipal Workers' Union was formed and registered on 10 August 1939. The municipal workers' strike, organized about this time, was widely supported by the local students. The Assam Government Press Industrial Association was registered on 7 August 1939. In 1940, it led a strike battle of the government press workers. Two other trade unions formed in Shillong were the Shillong Drivers' and Mechanics' Association, registered on 5 December 1938, and the Assam Provincial Shop Employees' Union, registered on 13 July 1940.[73]

---

[70] Same as footnote 69; also, *ALCP* (1939), pp. 323–30; Griffiths, *History of the Indian Tea Industry*, p. 384.

[71] 'Report of the political situation in Assam dated 26 August 1940 by J.C. Dutta, Deputy Central Intelligence Officer, Shillong', File No. A–8 (8A) 40, Police Department, Special Branch, Government of Assam; *IAR* (July–December 1940), Vol. 2, p. 241.

[72] *ALAP* (1940), p. 1313; *IAR* (July–December 1940), Vol. 2, pp. 179–82.

[73] Question from Karunasindhu Ray, 5 March, *ALAP* (1938), p. 887; Prafulla Misra, 'Communist Movement in Assam', *North Eastern Affairs* (Shillong, July–September 1972), p. 36; *ALAP* (1940), p. 241.

The number of strike-affected tea gardens all over the province increased from thirteen in 1937 to seventeen in 1938 and thirty-five in 1939. Police forces had to be rushed to nineteen out of these 65 strike-affected tea gardens. Lakhimpur and Cachar were the districts most affected. As a sequel to the labour upheaval, as many as 106 labourers in twelve tea gardens were victimized in the form of discharge, dismissal or forced repatriation during the period from November 1938 to October 1939, as per official admission. As a result of fifteen work stoppages of industrial nature, involving 20,000 workers in 1939, as many as 1,346,740 man-days were lost.[74] The growing power of militant trade unionism was demonstrated when Sanatkumar Ahir, a tea factory mechanic and communist sympathizer, won the by-election for the Silchar labour seat as a Congress candidate in 1940. He secured 3,165 votes as against 1,227 by his rival, set up by the British planters.[75] Students and youth were deeply impressed by the working-class awakening against the exploitation of British capital. No less, the peasants.

Unrest among the Peasantry

It was noted in Chapter Five that rural Assam, caught between a price slump and a fixed land revenue burden, was seething in discontent. The strife between the peasantry as a whole and the colonial regime persisted during the years 1937–40. In several places, there was confrontation even between landlords and the toiling peasants.

The demand for tenancy legislation in Sylhet was voiced by Karunasindhu Ray (d. 1949), a Congress candidate from Sunamganj, in his 1937 election battle. He and Bhasani separately introduced two tenancy Bills in the Assembly – for

[74] These figures are from a government statement in reply to A.K. Chanda, 21 March, *ALAP* (1940), pp. 1061–63 and the *Indian Labour Year Book* 1947–48 (Government of India), p. 118. According to another set of official figures, the number of strikes in Assam plantations was as follows:

Plantation Strikes in Assam: 1937–41

Year	No. of Strikes	No. of Workers Involved
1937	10	3,700
1938	7	3,700
1939	37	not given
1940	17	”
1941	7	”

Note: *The Indian Labour Year Book*, 1947–48, records only fifteen 'industrial work stoppages' for 1939, each involving ten or more workers. Obviously these relate to industrial workers alone.

Source: Labour Investigation Committee (Chairman: D.V. Rege, Government of India), *Report on an Enquiry into Conditions of Labour in Plantations in India*, p. 72.

[75] D.K. Borooah, assistant secretary of APCC to president, Indian National Congress, 14 July 1940, *APCC Papers*, File No. 5, Packet 6. Ahir's communist identity, though not mentioned by Borooah, was widely known.

Sylhet and Goalpara, respectively. They held the view that the abolition of permanent settlement was desirable and that, even short of this extreme step, substantial relief could be given to the oppressed tenants by introducing some of the salutary changes brought about in Bengal through tenancy legislation. The Sylhet Tenancy (Amendment) Bill became the rallying point of a massive peasant movement all over the district. The draft Bill was printed and circulated in thousands of copies. In many areas, the peasants themselves took the initiative in implementing some of the amendments, without waiting for their legitimization. Even before their consideration by the Assembly, these Bills had to be referred to the Governor-General-in-Council for clearance.[76] The initial constitutional hurdles having been overcome, the proposed Tenancy (Amendment) Bills for Sylhet and Goalpara were substantially modified at official initiative, and passed as official Bills in 1943. The two private Bills, as usual, lapsed.

Meanwhile, an organized *kisan* movement raised its head in the Sunamganj, Sadar and Karimganj sub-divisions of Sylhet. The number of Kisan Sabhas in Sylhet went on increasing during the years 1937–40. By 1938, tenants had succeeded in winning their immediate demand for suspension of zamindari rent collection in one case and remissions in another. In 1938–39 there was a considerable tension between landlords and tenants in the Karimganj sub-division. The first annual session of the Surma Valley Krishak Conference was held at Beheli in 1936 and the third at Maulvibazar in March 1939, with Bankim Mukherjee and Abul Hayat, respectively, in the chair. The Karimganj Sub-divisional Krishak Conference was held at Tegheria (Baraigram) on 28–29 May 1939, under the leadership of Sureshchandra Deb, then a Leftist Congressman. In the early months of 1939, the landlord–tenant conflict rose to such a height in Gauripur, Bhatipara and Selbores estates of Sunamganj that the government had to rush a party of armed police there to maintain the peace.[77]

Organized under the Congress flag, some 300 communist-led peasants from the Surma Valley marched to Shillong in the first week of September to present a memorandum of demands to the Saadulla government. This created a great stir.[78] A large number of participants had been arrested and convicted under the Defence of India Rules by November 1940, in connection with agrarian unrest in the district of Sylhet. Of fifteen Congressmen so arrested, at least nine appeared to be communists. Jagneswar Das (1914–1990) and Jitendrakumar

---

[76] File No. 4. 32/22/38–G 1938, Reforms Department, General (B) Branch (NAI). Ajay Bhattacharya, *Nankar Vidroha*, Vol. 1 (in Bengali, Dacca, 1973), pp. 104–29.

[77] *Assam Administration Report*, 1937–38, p. I; *Assam Administration Report*, 1938–39, p. I; *IAR* (January–June 1938), p. 354; the life-sketch of Karunasindhu Ray in *People's Age*, 30 December 1945; 'No. 1203: Notes on the political activities of Sureshchandra Deb', File No. C-319/1942, Confidential B, 1942 (AS). Also Bhattacharya, *Nankar Vidroha*, Vol. I, pp. 104–29 for details. Also *Naya Duniya*, 13 March 1939.

[78] *Asamiiya*, 7 September 1938; written testimony of Sibendranath Dam Roy, dated Shillong, 7 August 1972.

Bhattacharya were amongst them. Twenty-one Muslim peasants were also convicted.[79]

While the landlord–tenant conflict dominated peasant agitations in Sylhet, it was the conflict between the state and the peasantry as a whole that moved the peasant masses of the Brahmaputra Valley. There, the cry for a 50 per cent reduction in land revenue emerged as a universal demand, echoed and re-echoed at hundreds of meetings of the Congress and of Ryot Sabhas till the advent of World War II. Attempts by Congress Socialists (communists included) to form Kisan Sabhas on a class basis, on the other hand, were not many. A Halova Sangha (tillers' union) was formed at Golaghat by local rank-and-file Congressmen. Its name was changed in 1938 to the Golaghat Krishak Sabha, at the initiative of Jadunath Saikia (1909–1980), who had come under Congress–Socialist and communist influence while studying at Banaras. Under its auspices, the third session of the Golaghat District Krishak Sanmilan was held at Kamargaon on 14 October 1939. The conference called upon the peasants to assemble under the Congress banner and demanded a 50 per cent reduction in land revenue dues. Besides Saikia, Khageswar Tamuli and Dhirendrachandra Datta were the other early Congress Socialists who tried to radicalize this platform.[80] Devkanta Borooah (b. 1914) of Nowgong, who had his early initiation to Congress socialism at Banaras, wielded some influence as an assistant secretary of the APCC and secretary of the provincial Rastrabhasa Prachar Samiti, 1938–41.

Peasant conferences were not new in Goalpara sub-division. A Krishak Sanmilan was formed there as an allied body of the local Congress in 1935. On 29 November 1937, an organization styled 'Nikhil Goalpara Krishak Samiti' presented an address to Jawaharlal Nehru at Goalpara, to draw his attention to such local problems as the paucity of primary schools, bad drinking water and a deficient tenancy legislation. The Samiti claimed to have a membership of one lakh, spread over several local branches – an obviously exaggerated claim![81] The fourth annual session of the Nikhil Goalpara Krishak Samiti was held on 21–22 February 1939, with Hemchandra Baruah, APCC president, in the chair. Swami Sahajananda Saraswati presided over its fifth conference at Salkocha on 17–18 February 1940.[82] Indeed, that was the last annual session of the Nikhil Goalpara Krishak Samiti which was then still under the wings of the Congress.

---

[79] *IAR* (July–December 1940), Vol. 2, pp. 179–82; Saadulla's reply to Karunasindhu, 23 November, *ALAP* (1940), pp. 1717–19. In 1938–39, Muslim *nankars* (serfs) of several villages revolted against their Muslim zamindars, with the support of the Kisan Sabhas. They were led by Taqbir Ali, Md. Bedar Bakht, Abbas Ali Pattadar, Seikh Azahar Ali and others. See Bhattacharya, *Nankar Vidroha*, Vol. I, pp. 120 and 129.

[80] CPI, Assam State Council, *Silver Jubilee Souvenir* (in Assamese, Gauhati, May 1969), p. 3; *Assam Tribune*, 27 October 1939.

[81] An anonymous note on Goalpara in the Office of the Editor of the History of Freedom Movement (hereafter OEHFM), Government of Assam (Gauhati); *APCC Papers*, Packet 35.

[82] Swami Sahajananda Saraswati, *Mera Jiivan Sangharsha* (in Hindi, Patna, 1952), p. 539.

Thereafter, Kisan Sabhas with a new ideology struck roots there, under the leadership of Pabitra Ray (an externee from Bengal), Jalabindu Sarkar, Pranesh Biswas, Nandeswar Talukdar (1921–2003) and others.

At Bhasani's initiative, the Goalpara District Praja Conference was held in December 1940 at Ghagmari, with Nazi Ahmed Chaudhury in the chair. It condemned the action of legislators who were opposed to the Goalpara Tenancy (Amendment) Bill in the Assembly. Resolutions were passed by the conference demanding: (i) reduction of rent in the Bijni and Mechpara estates; (ii) suitable rules for effective debt conciliation boards; (iii) extension of primary education in Goalpara; and (iv) use of Bengali as the medium of instruction for Bengali children of the Brahmaputra Valley in all primary and secondary schools.[83]

Peasant agitations were organized in some places of the Brahmaputra Valley by the underground Communist League. The Assam Peasant and Labour Party (Krishak–Banuwa Panchayat) was formed as its open platform at a meeting of delegates from several districts, held at Gauhati on 2 May 1940. Kedarnath Goswami, a journalist and disillusioned Congressman, presided over this meeting. Earlier he had been elected president of the Dibrugarh District Peasant and Labour Party.[84]

Birth of a New Ideology and Left Nationalism
Growth of Left Parties

By the time the war broke out, the workers and peasants of Assam were thus building up their class organizations. In contrast to the sweep of the working-class struggles, militant peasant struggles and organized Kisan Sabhas were not many. Their combined impact was nevertheless significant. The socialist and communist thoughts that gripped the youth and the student intelligentsia in both the Valleys bore relevance to the experiences of toilers all around them. There was also increasing awareness even among nationalists that the demand for national freedom had to be concretely linked to workers' and peasants' aspirations. Since 1938, Subhas Chandra Bose had been advocating an uncompromising struggle against imperialism with methods more effective than the ones Gandhiji had prescribed. In course of his visits to Assam in 1938 and October 1939, he gained popularity in the local Congress circles. It was in the context of these developments that several Left parties – the Congress–Socialist Party, Communist Party, Communist League and Forward Bloc – gained a foothold on the soil of Assam. Their early formations are briefly described below.

Banned during the years 1934 – July 1942, the Communist Party of India (CPI) carried on its underground activities under the cover of mass organizations.

---

[83] *Assam Tribune*, 17 January 1941.

[84] Ibid., 10 May 1940. Goswami was the president of the Dibrugarh DCC in 1938 and the editor of the *Times of Assam* (Dibrugarh weekly) during 1930–39. The Communist League – a splinter group of the CPI – was later renamed after its parent body and remained so until it was finally designated as the Revolutionary Communist Party of India in 1943.

It viewed the Congress as a national front of anti-imperialist forces and was keen on using its platform. It stood for socialist unity within the Congress and constituted the mainstay of the Congress–Socialist Party, formed in 1934. The Communist League, also formed in the same year by Saumyendranath Tagore of Bengal, was a recalcitrant offshoot of the CPI. It viewed the Congress as a bourgeois party, and believed in organizing the toiling masses for socialism and national freedom on an independent political platform.[85] All these Left parties made their belated but simultaneous appearance in the Brahmaputra Valley after 1937. The communist and socialist ideology appeared in the Surma Valley a little earlier, but the Communist League was totally absent there. Founded in 1939, the Forward Bloc struck its roots in a few districts of Assam during the early war years.

By 1938, Congress–Socialist Party (CSP) groups were functioning not only in the district of Sylhet, but also in Golaghat, Dibrugarh and Goalpara. Jadunath Saikia and Dhirendrachandra Datta of Golaghat, Benoybhusan Chakrabarty and Nilmoni Barthakur of Dibrugarh, Pabitra Ray of Bengal, then residing in Goalpara, and Sriman Prafulla Goswami (b. 1911), a student and youth leader of Gauhati – they all conferred and decided to take steps towards forming the Assam Congress–Socialist Party.[86] 'At present four districts are organized and there are four Congress–Socialist Parties,' wrote Goswami to Jayaprakash Narayan on 18 January 1939, 'but we must make a provincial party in Assam.'[87]

The anniversary of the October Socialist Revolution of Russia was observed in the form of a public meeting at Golaghat on 7 November 1939 – an unprecedented event for the Brahmaputra Valley. A provincial (Brahmaputra Valley) conference of Congress–Socialists was held at Missamara near Golaghat on 29–31 January 1940, under the presidency of Somnath Lahiri of Calcutta. Two prominent communist student leaders – Biswanath Mukherjee and Amiya Dasgupta – also attended it. There, the Assam Congress–Socialist Party was formed with Prafulla Goswami as general secretary and a twenty-one-member executive committee. The same night, a more exclusive inner group was formed with Benoybhusan Chakrabarty, Dhirendrachandra Datta, Pabitra Ray, Nilmoni Barthakur, Bishnu Bora (1918–1981) and Jadunath Saikia, to carry on secret communist

[85] Tagore had first-hand experience of the international communist movement during his few years' stay in the Soviet Union and Europe as an insider. He was a critic of Stalin's leadership and the role of the Third International. He was also critical of Trotsky's views.

[86] Misra, 'Communist Movement in Assam', p. 26. Biswanath Mukherjee, while on an Assam tour on behalf of the AISF in 1938, had established contacts with them and suggested such a move.

[87] Goswami to Jayaprakash, Jorhat, 18 January 1939, copy of intercepted letter in Secret Memo No. 876 S.N., File No. B–2 (17) 39, Police Department, Government of Assam, Shillong. Also a file of private papers of Sriman Prafulla Goswami, containing extant proceedings of the Assam CSP, 1939.

In an interview at New Delhi, Goswami made it clear that the Assam CSP units followed the national front policy of the communists from the very outset and, hence, did not accept Jayaprakash's leadership. Nor were they affiliated to his party's all-India centre.

activities. Later, Jagannath Bhattacharyya was also taken into the group. On 20 April 1940, the executive committee of the Assam CSP held its first meeting at the house of Siblal Pandit at Lumding.[88] By a resolution, it disapproved of individual *satyagraha* as a form of struggle but nevertheless decided to adopt it for the sake of discipline within the Congress. Its impact was soon felt on Assam politics, mainly through the radicalization of the student masses.[89]

The Assam Chhatra Sanmilan, the platform of a united student movement since 1916, decided in its annual conference at Jorhat in April 1939 to affiliate itself to the All India Students' Federation (AISF), founded in 1936. Gaurishankar Bhattacharyya (1915–2002) was elected its general secretary and Dadhi Mahanta (1915–1987), the editor of its organ – *Milan*. Amiya Dasgupta, AISF leader, remained in Assam for purposes of organization until he was externed from the province in June 1940. He was deputed by the Bengal Committee of the CPI to organize a communist group in the Brahmaputra Valley under the cover of the CSP. He helped radicalization of the Students' Federation and formation of Marxist study circles in several towns of the Brahmaputra Valley.[90] A Marxist youth study club styled 'Progressive Union' was established at Gauhati about 1939. In August 1940, a police intelligence report noted that communist literature was being circulated amongst students and youth by 'a branch of Communist Party' formed at Dibrugarh. Steps were being considered to restrain the activities of Nilmoni Barthakur and other suspected communists there.[91]

In Sylhet, a regular group of the Communist Party, constituted of Chittaranjan Das, Digen Dasgupta and others, had been functioning since 1936. Praneshchandra Biswas and Jyotirmoy Nandy, who had become communists in Calcutta, came back to Sylhet in 1938. The latter edited *Naya Duniya* – the local organ of the communists. The seventh session of the Surma Valley Students' Conference, which was held at Habiganj in December 1939, bore the imprint of the growing influence of communist ideology and organization. The Surma Valley District Committee of the CPI was reportedly formed in an underground conference held at Dhaka-Dakshin in December 1940. It was in that year that Biresh Misra (1905–1991), district Congress secretary of several years' standing, secretly joined the CPI.[92] Achintyakumar Bhattacharya of Cachar also joined it

---

[88] Misra, 'Communist Movement in Assam', p. 26. Interview with Dadhi Mahanta on 7 October 1975 at Calcutta. Mahanta was a participant in the conference.

[89] 'Notes on the Political Activities of Bistoo Bora', Police Department, Special Branch, Government of Assam Shillong. Private papers of Prafulla Goswami.

[90] Misra, 'Communist Movement in Assam', p. 26 and the interview with Amiya Dasgupta.

[91] 'Report of the political situation in Assam dated 26 August 1940 . . .'.

[92] Written testimony of Praneschandra Biswas, dated Shillong, 12 June 1973 (also interviewed on 2 August 1973 at Shillong); 'No. 1179: Notes on the political activities of Praneschandra Biswas', File No. C-319/1942 Confidential B, 1942 (AS). Also, the life-sketch of Biresh Misra in *People's Age*, 30 December 1945. In June 1940, the government demanded a security of Rs 1,000 from *Naya Duniya*, for publishing an objectionable article – 'Council, Assembly and the Kisan Movement'. IAR (July–December 1940), Vol. 2, pp. 191–92.

in 1939. He was elected secretary to the Cachar District Congress Committee in 1940.[93]

Throughout the year 1939, organized students all over Assam had expressed their solidarity with the Digboi workers. A joint conference of the Students' Federation bodies of both the Valleys, as well as of Manipur and Shillong, was held at Shillong on 29–30 July 1940, with Humayun Kabir in the chair. The conference elected Gaurishankar Bhattacharyya as president and Praneshchandra Biswas as secretary of the emergent confederation. The conference passed resolutions condemning the Defence of India Rules and directing students not to render any assistance to the war efforts. Biswas and Anjali Das, and later Bishnu Bora, went on an organizational tour of Assam districts, carrying on anti-war propaganda.[94] About the Students' Federation activities in Jorhat, Bora reported to Amiya Dasgupta in November 1940:

> In Jorhat there are 4 study circles, 16 night schools, 27 primary committees and 13 libraries. After J.B. College students' strike we are able to get many active student workers not only in colleges but in high schools also. After your departure I attended no less than 150 meetings and tried my best to clear out (*sic*) about war, national struggle and students' duty. Now there are many who support our party. This year we enrolled 500 members (S.F.) in Jorhat.[95]

Another batch of young men, committed to the Communist League, were also indoctrinating and organizing students since 1939 with the same anti-war message, but on a different platform. In November 1938 Saumyendranath Tagore, founder of the Communist League, visited Gauhati[96] and met a group of students associated with the Gauhati Vyayam Sangha (established about 1935). Already disillusioned with the Congress leadership, they were much impressed by Tagore's independent Left platform and international experience, and the Marxism he talked of in the context of the Digboi strike and the general unrest. The group started working for consolidation of all the Left forces and invited Bose, founder of the Forward Bloc, to pay a visit to Assam.

In a representative provincial youth conference presided over by Bose at Gauhati, the All Assam Progressive Youth Association was formed on 6 October 1939. Its fifteen-member working committee, drawn from both the Valleys and diverse Left groups, included *inter alia* Debendranath Sarma (president), Upendranath Sarma (general secretary), Khagen Barbarua, Haridas Deka, Nalinikumar Gupta and Kirtibhusan Chaudhury. A Left Consolidation (Organizing) Commit-

---

[93] Interview with Achintyakumar Bhattacharyya on 1 July 1973 at Gauhati.

[94] 'No. 1179: Notes on the political activities of Praneschandra Biswas' and his written testimony; Misra, 'Communist Movement in Assam', p. 29; File No. A–8 (8A)–40: 'Notes on the political activities of Bistoo Bora'.

[95] Extract from intercepted letter, Bora to Dasgupta, quoted in 'Notes on the political activities of Bistoo Bora'. Refers to Students' Federation.

[96] On 4 November 1938, Tagore was invited to Cotton College to speak on 'India and Socialism'. *Asamiia*, 5 November 1938.

tee was also formed at the same conference.[97] However, both the Youth Association and the Left Organizing Committee became defunct soon after Bose's departure.

The Gauhati Vyayam Sangha group, which had organized the conference, could not be drawn by Bose towards the Forward Bloc. Led by Haren Kalita, they joined the Communist League instead. An underground organizing committee of the League and an open Marxist youth study club, styled 'Radical Institute', meanwhile, came into existence at Gauhati.[98] The Progressive Union and the Radical Institute, between them, played a significant role in drawing the cream of Assamese students towards Marxism and the broad front of 'Left' nationalism.

Leftist Impact on Congress

From 1937, the Congress went on expanding and improving its organization. In the years following the Civil Disobedience movement, its organization had fallen into disarray. Its membership in the Brahmaputra Valley came down to only 2,620 in 1935–36. However, by September 1937 it increased to 15,646.[99] The organizational weakness of the Congress shocked Nehru when he visited Assam in November 1937. He found that one District Congress Committee was itself a primary body and consisted of only 60 members. 'The basis of your organization will inevitably be the peasantry and therefore,' he advised the APCC, 'you should keep the agrarian reforms ever before you and discuss this with the peasantry.' He advised the Congress legislators to organize Primary Congress Committees in their constituencies and ventilate the grievances of plantation workers.[100] In November 1938, the APCC reported that nearly 300 Primary Committees had been formed, and that Congress activities had been extended to Shillong. Congress membership in the Brahmaputra Valley shot up thereafter to 37,321 in 1938–39, partly as a result of the party coming to power in the province. The membership remained between 56,000 and 57,000 during the next two years. A large number of the members were allegedly enlisted without realization of membership fees – a measure of organizational weakness. Of all the Congress districts in the Valley, the most organized was Sibsagar. In 1939 it had 12,619 primary members and 99 Primary Committees.[101]

---

[97] Confidential D.O.No. 1424–C, Supdt. of Police, Kamrup to the I.G.P., dated Gauhati, 3 November 1939; File No. B–2 (17) 39, Police Department, Government of Assam; *Assam Tribune,* 13 October 1939.

[98] Interview with Haridas Deka, 27 February 1974, Gauhati.

[99] 'APCC General Secretary's Report, 1937', *APCC Papers*, File No. 5, Packet 6.

[100] Nehru to B.R. Medhi, APCC president, camp Jorhat, 1 December 1937, *AICC Files*, File No. p. 4: 1937: 39 (NMML, New Delhi); a copy of the six-page typed letter was also found in *APCC Papers*, File No. nil, Packet 6.

[101] *Assam Tribune*, 8 December 1939; Secret No. 37/Cong./ 40 Intelligence Bureau, Home, dated Simla, 24 May 1941 in Home: Pol. (I) File No. 4/6/41 (NAI). According to the latter source, primary membership claimed by the APCC was 37,321 in 1938–39, 56,633 in 1939–40 and 56,000 in 1940–41. The comparable figures claimed by the PCC of Bengal were 4,83,158, 4,40,729 and 2,18,878, respectively.

In 1936, Sylhet had 2,831 Congress members and 15 Primary Committees; Cachar had 516 members and three Primary Committees. During the preceding thirteen years, according to the Sylhet District Congress Committee's (DCC) own admission, the constructive programme on khadi and untouchability had failed to create any enthusiasm in the district.[102] Factionalism persisted there, dividing the Congress into two rival groups. Later, these groups identified themselves with the Right and Left trends. Organizationally under the Bengal Provincial Congress Committee (BPCC), the Sylhet DCC was dominated by radical nationalists from 1937. The rightist group included, among others, B.N. Chaudhury, B.K. Das and Shibendrachandra Biswas (1871–1946). A 1937 by-election made the rift wider still. R.N. Aditya, a rightist election candidate, applied to the AICC Parliamentary Board for the Congress ticket through the BPCC, and Biresh Chandra Misra through the Assam Provincial Congress Committee (APCC). Misra was nominated. But just eight days before the poll, the Board reversed its decision under pressure from the rightists. Misra was persuaded by his patron, Jawaharlal Nehru, to step down and, since it was too late for a formal withdrawal, also to issue an appeal to the electorate to vote for Aditya. The Left forces refused to reconcile themselves to this position and continued their campaign for Misra. The result was that Aditya was elected with only a narrow margin of 240 votes. When Nehru came to Sylhet in the first week of December 1937, two rival reception committees were there to welcome him. The rightist leadership of the BPCC failed to discipline the Sylhet DCC, even by removing its leftist secretary, Abalakanta Gupta Chaudhury (b. 1897). For, Biresh Misra who replaced him was no less a leftist.[103] The next secretary, Probodhananda Kar, was also a communist.

The Cachar DCC, too, was dominated by leftists patronized by A.K. Chanda, deputy leader of the Assam Congress Legislature Party. While the APCC itself had no Right–Left rivalry within its organization, Chanda's strong advocacy of the labour cause kept the Congress Legislature Party under pressure. Bardoloi and his cabinet colleagues became unpopular because of their failure to intervene in the workers' favour in the Digboi and Arunabund disputes. Later, in

---

[102] DCC's replies to items 1/1 and 1/5 of the questionnaire, 'Report of Congress and Mass Contact Sub-Committee, BPCC', enclosed in 'BPCC to Congress Mass Contact Committee', *RPC*, IX/36/31, cited by John Galagher, *Locality, Province and Nation: Essays on Indian Politics 1870 to 1940* (Cambridge, 1973), pp. 315–17.

[103] Letter from Sylhet DCC to Nehru, 29 November 1937, in File No. p. 4 (i)–37 (Assam Tour Files), *AICC Files* (NMML, New Delhi); 'Notes on the left movement'; R.N. Aditya, *From the Corridors of Memory* (Calcutta, 1970), pp. 42–44.

Aditya further writes that Rammanohar Lohia, secretary of the Foreign Department, AICC, criticized Sardar Patel in an article in the *Congress Socialist* for the reversal of the nomination under factional pressure from the BPCC. Patel, chairman of the Congress Parliamentary Board, took exception to this and subsequently raised this matter in the Working Committee. This episode finally resulted in the Socialist group resigning in a body from the AICC. Besides, 'a very energetic group of Congress workers was lost to the Sylhet district (committee), who slowly went over to the communist ideology'. Ibid., p. 44.

1940, when the Saadulla government was considering action against persons aggravating labour disputes, it was emphasized in an official communication that Chanda should be the 'first person in this province to be dealt with'.[104] Significantly, the Cachar DCC had a communist secretary from 1940 onwards till about the end of the war.

The Tangled National Question
'Save the Assamese Race!'

The Saadulla ministry had an uneasy existence. It incurred the displeasure of not only Congress but also the Muslim League, because of its indecision on the question of abolition of the Line system. Almost all the Muslim members of the Assembly were united on this demand. But Saadulla was powerless to move in that direction on account of R.K. Chaudhuri's opposition inside the cabinet. Like the Congress leaders, Chaudhuri also believed that segregation was necessary to avoid conflicts between autochthones and immigrants. Munawwar Ali exposed the inconsistency of this stand in a speech in the Assembly on 14 August 1937. 'But if the line prevents friction, then,' he asked, 'why do my friends of the Congress Bloc press for joint electorate?' He even drew a parallel with the segregationist practice in South Africa. He finally withdrew his resolution calling for abolition of the Line system only after the government agreed to accept a committee to enquire into the question.[105] The Congress Party allowed its members to serve on this committee.

Meanwhile, the Congress high command was kept informed of the gravity of the Assam situation. 'If Karachi resolutions are literally interpreted, the immigrants have every right to acquire land, property etc., and there cannot be a Line system', Bardoloi wrote to Rajendra Prasad in November 1937. 'On the other hand, our people whether Congressmen or otherwise, all feel that adequate reservations must be there.' He apprehended that, short of a rigid Line system, the linguistic problem would become, in the coming years, 'a source of constant friction resulting in violence, incendiarism and crimes of all kinds'.[106]

Segregationists tried to thrash out the issue with Nehru when he came to Assam in November 1937. Nilmoni Phukan and Ambikagiri Raychaudhury represented to him on behalf of the Asamiya Samrakshini Sabha that a 'purely local and racial question' had recently been given a communal colour by the Muslim League. According to them, Bengali Muslim immigrants were willing to identify themselves with the Assamese people in matters of language and culture, but were now being persuaded and 'forced' to read Bengali. The effect of each national movement and the constitutional advance that followed in the province

---

104 File No. C 314/1942, Confidential B, 1942 (AS).
105 Speeches on 5 and 14 August, *ALAP* (1937), pp. 233–34 and 712–33; R.K. Chaudhuri's speech, ibid., p. 714.
106 Bardoloi to Rajendra Prasad, 13 November 1937, File No. 11/37, Col. No. 5, Item No. 165, *RPC* (NAI).

had been, according to them, disastrous to Assamese interests. They pointed out that

> as a means of saving the Assamese race from extinction, a considerable section of the Assamese intelligentsia had even expressed their minds in favour of *the secession of Assam from India*. This is how the present situation appears to the average Assamese, and they look to you, the National Congress, to help the Assamese to get out of these dangers. (Emphasis ours.)

If Sylhet and the Cachar plains were separated from the province and the mass immigration into the Brahmaputra Valley stopped, the Assamese people would be – they said – the staunchest Congress supporters.[107]

Aware of his limitations in understanding the local problems, Nehru was confused. The desire of the Assamese to preserve their own culture and language, and not to be overwhelmed by non-Assamese people, appeared to him perfectly legitimate. He agreed on the desirability of separating Sylhet from Assam. But, at the same time, he argued that sparsely populated and land-rich Assam could no longer continue to remain so with an overcrowded province flanking it. Immigration was, therefore, bound to take place as an economic necessity. No amount of sentiment, not even laws, would stop it. 'Indeed, even from the point of view of developing Assam and making it a wealthier province,' he wrote to the APCC president, 'immigration is desirable. The real problem is how to control and organize this immigration.'[108] Thus, though not in favour of its total abolition, he nevertheless wanted relaxation of the Line system.

Nehru's was an idealist point of view that was neither palatable to the Assam Congress leaders nor acceptable to all his colleagues in the all-India leadership. The proportion of Muslims in the population of the Brahmaputra Valley increased from 9 per cent in 1881 to 19 per cent in 1931, 23 per cent in 1941 and 24 per cent in 1951. In 1911, Muslims had constituted 0.1 per cent of the population of Barpeta sub-division; by 1941, they constituted nearly 49 per cent. The area of land settled with immigrants from other Indian provinces was about 1.1 million acres in 1940–41, that is, one-fifth of the total temporarily settled area, inclusive of waste land grants, in the Brahmaputra Valley. As against this, East Bengal immigrants alone accounted for nearly half a million acres.[109]

---

[107] Memorandum presented to Nehru at Rangiya on 28 November 1937, File No. p. 4 (i)–1937, *AICC Files* (NMML, New Delhi).

Yet another memorandum was submitted on behalf of the 'Asamiya Deka Dal'. It suggested a six-point programme to save the Assamese: (i) transfer of Sylhet to Bengal, (ii) total ban on Bengali immigration to the Brahmaputra Valley for a period of twenty years, (iii) strict naturalization laws for resident Bengali immigrants, (iv) outlawing all anti-Assamese organizations in the Brahmaputra Valley, (v) a ten-year moratorium on agricultural indebtedness and (vi) exclusion of the planters' bloc from the legislature.

[108] Nehru to Medhi, 1 December 1937, *AICC Files*.

[109] Percentages are worked out from the relevant census figures. The analysis of the Barpeta population is from Saadulla's speech in the Assam Muslim League Conference at Barpeta in April 1944. *Assam Tribune*, 5 May 1944.

These facts were sufficient not only to unnerve many local Hindus, but also some Congress leaders of national stature. What was initially an economic issue was turned into a communal one, not only by the Muslim League, but also by some Congress leaders. Rajendra Prasad, for example, had first-hand knowledge of the problem as far back as the 1920s. At that time he had toyed with the idea of populating Assam with Bihari Hindu immigrants so that the Muslim influx from East Bengal could be held back. He wrote in his autobiography:

> I sounded the Assamese on the subject and they welcomed it. . . . Some thought it better to have the Hindus of Bihar than the Muslims of Mymensingh. . . . They welcomed the idea also because by themselves the Assamese were unable to bring the land under the plough. But the influx of Muslims from Mymensingh was upsetting the population ratio, and the Assamese wanted to retain a majority in the Brahmaputra Valley. The influx from Mymensingh could be countered only by Bihar Hindus to settle down on the land.

In partnership with his brother and Anugraha Narain Sinha, Rajendra Prasad even joined a Bengali Hindu gentleman to acquire 1,000 acres of land and a tractor in a jungle-infested malarial tract. This joint venture in farming, of course, ended in failure. Even after this costly experience, Rajendra Prasad continued to view the successful immigration of Bengali Muslims into Assam as an unwelcome phenomenon.[110]

The Bengali–Assamese Question

Another dimension of the immigration problem was the burning language issue. The expatriate Bengali Hindus, who were dominant in the towns, and many of the Muslim immigrants demanded equal rights for the Bengali language. Matiur Rahman Mia (west Goalpara) told the Assembly on 16 February 1938: 'We are Bengalees. Our mother tongue is Bengalee. . . . Under the circumstances if this Assamese language be imposed as a new burden on our shoulders, on our children's shoulders and if we are deprived of our mother tongue, then that will amount to depriving our children from opportunities of education.'[111] The same demand re-echoed from the Goalpara Praja Sanmilan at Ghagmari in December 1940. By and large, however, the Muslim immigrants were more concerned with acquiring land rights than preserving their language. This was particularly so in Assam proper.

The land settlement figures are worked out from *Assam Valley Division Land Revenue Report, 1940–41*. Inclusive of all settled lands – permanent, temporary as well as waste land grants – the total settled area in 1940–41 amounted to 6,788,000 acres in the Assam Valley Division, that is, the Brahmaputra Valley. No figures are available for the amount of land settled by zamindars with immigrants in the permanently settled portion.

[110] Rajendra Prasad, *Autobiography* (Bombay, 1957), pp. 259–60; also see his *India Divided* (Bombay, 1946), pp. 246–48.

[111] Speech in Bengali, *ALAP* (1938), pp. 66–71. Translation ours.

The attitude of a major section of the Bengali Hindu settlers, particularly its influential urban section, was quite different. Their leaders viewed the Brahmaputra Valley as a bilingual area. They built their case on the available census figures on Assam. S.M. Lahiri moved a resolution in the upper house on 31 August 1938, for the removal of racial discrimination in recruitment to government jobs. Despite official opposition, his resolution recommending revision of the existing domicile rules – in accordance with accepted legal principles – was passed, but it was not taken up by the lower house. Therefore, on behalf of the Bengali community, a memorandum was submitted to Chief Minister Bardoloi in March 1939, drawing his attention to this resolution and the Congress Working Committee's commendable award of January 1939 on the Bengali–Bihari question. The memorandum demanded equal rights and privileges, civil and political, for all persons having domicile in Assam, whether of origin or choice.[112]

The Congress Working Committee's award of 1939 had recommended abolition of the practice of issuing domicile certificates, and suggested that birth in the province or ten years' continuous residence should be regarded as sufficient proof of domicile. It had also recommended educational facilities through the medium of any language, wherever there was a local demand for it. Instead of implementing these model recommendations, the Bardoloi government opted for deliberate procrastination in this matter. While replying to S.M. Lahiri on 9 May 1939, Bardoloi promised to consider action on the memorandum, but his assurance remained unfulfilled. The third session of the Assam Domiciled and Settlers' Association (renamed Assam Citizens' Association), held at Nowgong on 24 March 1940, reiterated the demand for equal citizenship rights and education through the medium of one's mother tongue, irrespective of race and language.[113] The conference was permeated with a spirit of challenge to the unilingual concept of the Brahmaputra Valley, as upheld by Congress since 1920.

Unpalatable as this attitude was to the Assamese people in general, it provided a grand opportunity to the Governor to pose himself as a champion of Assamese nationalism. In reply to an address presented by the Bengali Association at Nowgong, he said:

> Though I fully sympathize with you in your desire to preserve your mother tongue, I cannot – as a purely personal view – but ask two questions. First would not the possession of a common tongue tend towards the creation within Assam of a united nation? And secondly, if we accept a united nation as a desirable aim, could its tongue be other than Assamese? I do not think that it could.[114]

---

112 *ALCP* (1938), pp. 72–83; for the text of the memorandum, see *Assam Citizens Association* (Head Office – Dhubri, 1940), appendix A, pp. 56–66.

113 Ibid., appendices B and C, pp. 66–74; *ALCP* (1939), pp. 235 and 277–78; *Assam Tribune*, 29 March 1940.

114 Cited by Nilmoni Phukan in a speech at the annual session of the Assam Students' Union, held at Shillong, as reported in *Assam Tribune*, 23 August 1940.

The Governor was enthusiastically quoted in a speech by Nilmoni Phukan when he addressed the Assamese students of Shillong in August 1940. Phukan, who had consistently opposed the Congress till 1938, joined it towards the latter part of that year and was elected president of the Jorhat Town Mauza Congress Committee.[115] His decision to join the Congress was obviously influenced by its acceptance of office. In the economic crisis of the 1930s, the tea garden he built with borrowed funds had to be sold to a Marwari trader. This frustration perhaps made him aware of the imperialist stranglehold on Assam's economy, and salvaged him from his heretofore impeccable, collaborationist politics. Nevertheless, it could not cure him of the fear of his own countrymen.[116] Together with Ambikagiri Raychaudhury, he continued his tirade against Bengali settlers, which was quite out of tune with the popular anti-imperialist struggles of the period.

Aftermath of the Hockenhull Report

In an atmosphere of growing distrust between Hindus and Muslims, as well as between the Assamese and the Bengalis, F.W. Hockenhull, leader of the European party, had the honour of presiding over the deliberations of the Line System Committee. Its report, submitted in February 1938, emphasized that indigenous people alone would be unable, without the aid of immigrant settlers, to develop the province's enormous waste land resources within a reasonable period. Nevertheless, it viewed the Line system favourably and even advised its tightening to protect the tribal lands.[117] The situation was too delicate for Saadulla to take a decision on the matter.

Even the Bardoloi government, which followed Saadulla's, procrastinated. Only a few days before its resignation was it able to adopt a resolution on the subject, which was gazetted on 4 November 1939. Its main features were:
  (i) denial of land settlement to anybody in village and professional grazing reserves;
  (ii) regulated settlement of landless people, including immigrants on available waste lands, subject to a holding of 30 *bighas* per family; and
  (iii) eviction of all immigrant squatters from areas declared 'protected tribal blocks', in the submontane region.[118]
The policy, on the whole, reflected a reasonable approach. But since much would depend on how and by whom it was going to be implemented, it hardly satisfied anybody. The first provincial conference of the Assam Muslim League, held at Ghagmari in November 1939, rejected the Line and demanded its total abolition.[119] On the other hand, many thought that the policy adopted was not sufficiently protective, so far as tribal peoples' interests were concerned.

---

[115] Ibid.; also see *Assam Tribune*, 6 October 1939.
[116] Dilip Chaudhuri, *Nilmoni Phukanr Cintadhara* (in Assamese, Gauhati, 1972), pp. 24–27 and 91.
[117] *Report of the Line System Committee* (Shillong, 1938).
[118] *Assam Tribune*, 1 December 1939.
[119] *ALCP* (1940), p. 103.

While speaking on the budget on 26 February 1940, Bhimbar Deuri refused to make any distinction between the policies of Saadulla and Bardoloi in this matter. He complimented 'the farsighted British officers' for innovating the Line system 'with a view to do even justice to all concerned', and demanded strict implementation.[120] In an editorial on 29 March 1940, the *Assam Tribune* commented that the Saadulla government was following 'a completely anti-Assamese policy' in the matter of immigration. With Bardoloi out and Saadulla in, the policy could not in practice be what it was originally intended to be.

To work out the operational details of the policy in consultation with the opposition, Chief Minister Saadulla held an all-party conference on the Line system on 31 May and 1 June 1940. A Development Scheme, as envisaged in the majority report of the Hockenhull Committee, was officially advocated, with some modifications to accommodate the minority view as well. The government resolution that followed on 21 June put a ban on the settlement of waste lands with any immigrant entering Assam on or after 1 January 1938. It also decided to go ahead with the Development Scheme for providing land to indigenous landless persons and eligible immigrants, in an order of priorities in favour of the former.[121]

The salient features of the Development Scheme were published in the *Assam Gazette* of 4 December 1940. Under the scheme, a special officer was to be appointed by the government to examine whether the proposed areas could be opened for settlement without any detriment to the districts' normal requirements of grazing and forest reserves. The settlement was to be confined to only indigenous landless people and pre-1938 immigrants. Besides, the flood-and-erosion-affected people, then illegally squatting in some 'Lined' villages and reserves, were also to be accommodated. Eligible applicants were to receive waste lands in specified development areas, on payment of stipulated premia, in blocks segregated for different communities as before. The government promised to put the scheme into operation as early as possible, after the land scrutiny was completed. To appease the Muslim public, an assurance was given that the Line in respect of the non-tribal and non-backward people would soon be done away with.[122]

Line or no Line, the law of competition was in full operation. Whatever feeble attempts were made to set up Lines in Goalpara, for example, were found to be self-defeating. Local people there could not be stopped from selling their lands even in 'Lined' villages to immigrants at high prices. The district being contiguous to Bengal and the bulk of the people speaking a language akin to Bengali, they could easily accommodate themselves – as was reported by the District Magistrate – to the immigrants' ways of life, and live in peace and amity

---

[120] *Assam Tribune*, 28 June 1940. The minority view in the Report was presented by Sarveswar Barua, Kameswar Das and Rabichandra Kachari.

[121] Harendranath Barua, 'The Development Scheme, Position of Indigenous People', *Assam Tribune*, 29 August 1941.

[122] Goalpara District Magistrate to Government of Assam, 1 January 1938, cited in R.K. Chaudhuri's reply, 25 February, *ALAP* (1938), pp. 464–66.

with them.[123] But any such breakdown of the Line system in Assam proper was certain to have more serious implications.

Assamese public opinion – the opinion among articulate Hindus, to be more precise – was therefore almost hysterical in denouncing the Development Scheme. The Muslim League was gaining ground. It was in this atmosphere that the Congress launched its anti-war, individual civil disobedience in Assam, in December 1940. The people could not be split on the linguistic issue. The Assam Citizens' Association failed to strike roots among the local Bengali youth. The latter allowed it to go into liquidation after one more annual conference at Gauhati. They had meanwhile turned to militant nationalism and a leftist ideology, and taken their place in the mainstream of struggle side by side with others. The Congress was evidently successful in containing the Bengali–Assamese conflict for larger political interests.

CHAPTER SEVEN

War, National Struggle and Assembly Politics

Third Saadulla Ministry

Satyagraha against War Efforts

The third Saadulla ministry (17 November 1939 – 24 December 1941) was born with a commitment to war efforts and to the Defence of India Rules. As such, it was not free to act in a manner prejudicial to either. On 11 November 1940, the Assembly voted 50 to forty to reject an adjournment moved by the Congress opposition, to discuss an order under the Defence of India Rules banning processions and meetings in Sylhet.[1]

But Saadulla was in a fix when Delhi pressed for the revival of the long-abolished police intelligence branch. The Viceroy wrote to the Assam Governor on 21 May 1940: 'the war has created special obligations. . . . I have come to the conclusion that this matter should be delayed no further.' Ministers could hardly deny the necessity for such an intelligence staff. They were also aware that the Governor's special powers were not to be ordinarily and lightly invoked to relieve them of responsibilities that were precisely theirs. Nevertheless, being afraid of public reaction, they were unwilling to initiate the necessary action in the legislature on their own. For a way out, they rather willingly looked forward to the Governor's interference from above under Section 126 (5).[2] Such interference was of course not lacking. The Assembly was told on 3 March 1941 that the intelligence branch had been revived by the Governor, as per the requirements of his special responsibilities.[3]

The ministry's cooperation with the war efforts was not just passive and perfunctory. At a cabinet meeting on 1 June 1940, the question of enabling Assamese of all classes to join the armed forces was discussed. The proposal that an Assam Regiment be raised took concrete shape in due course. In July the government contributed Rs 1 lakh to the War Fund. The relevant supplementary demand, declared out of order by the Speaker on technical grounds on 19 November, was

---

[1] *Indian Annual Register* (hereafter *IAR*) (July–December 1940), Vol. 2, p. 169.

[2] Reforms Branch File No. 20/126/40-R 1940, Government of India: Reforms Dept. (National Archives of India; hereafter NAI).

[3] Robert Reid, *Years of Change in Bengal and Assam* (London, 1967), p. 137; *IAR* (July–December 1940), Vol. 2, p. 170; *IAR* (January–June 1941), Vol. 1, p. 247.

revived in the next budget session and passed on 20 March 1941. For the war efforts, even local board funds were not spared. Eleven Congress members of the Tezpur Local Board, led by Jyotiprasad Agarwala, had to resign in a body in April to record their protest against the contribution of Rs 3,000 to the War Fund.[4] Both Saadulla and his seniormost colleague, R.K. Chaudhuri, were associated with the National War Front, as its chairman and vice-chairman, respectively. In July 1941, Saadulla even joined the National Defence Council as a representative Muslim leader.[5]

While Saadulla was thus busy helping the war efforts, the Congress launched its programme of anti-war agitation. Congress legislators stopped attending the Assembly sessions. By June 1940 the APCC Working Committee had converted itself into the provincial Satyagraha Committee. District Congress Committees (DCCs) were asked to hold meetings in villages to explain the Congress programme of individual *satyagraha*, as envisaged by Gandhiji. 'It is wrong to help the British war effort with men and money' – was the simple slogan to be raised by carefully selected *satyagrahis* courting arrest.[6] According to an APCC report, *satyagrahis* enrolled up to 15 June 1940 in the Brahmaputra Valley numbered 1,576 – mostly villagers. They included eleven Muslims and fifteen women. Several training camps were opened for their orientation.[7] All these preparations being over, the first individual *satyagraha* in Assam was offered by Gopinath Bardoloi on 11 December 1940 at Gauhati.[8]

A repressive policy was already in operation since early 1940 to deal with communists and other leftists, many of whom were served with orders of internment and externment. The deliberate violation of the Defence of India Rules by Congress *satyagrahis* now added a new dimension to the law and order problem. In many cases, the authorities took no cognizance of the solo performances of the garlanded *satyagrahis* and it ended in just great fun for the onlookers. The APCC president himself had to offer *satyagraha* twice to qualify for a jail term. Bardoloi failed to offer *satyagraha* for the second time, after his premature release from jail in August 1941, much to the displeasure of the APCC president. He had, of course, obtained Gandhiji's prior approval for exemption on health grounds. But many others avoided the ritual for other reasons. A group

---

[4] *IAR* (July–December 1940), Vol. 2, p. 170; Reid, *Years of Change*, p. 137; *Assam Tribune*, 25 April 1941.

[5] To fall in line with the then Muslim League policy, later he had to resign from the National Defence Council, under directives from Jinnah. Khalid B. Sayeed, *Pakistan: The Formative Phase 1857–1948* (second edition, New York/Karachi, 1963), pp. 183–84.

[6] *IAR* (January–June 1940), Vol. 1, p. 247; M. Tayyebulla, *Between the Symbol and the Idol at Last* (New Delhi, 1964), pp. 105–07.

[7] *APCC Papers*, File No. 5, Packet 6 (Congress Bhavan, Gauhati); 'Report of the political situation in Assam dated 26 August 1940 by J.C. Dutta, Deputy Central Intelligence Officer, Shillong', File No. A-8 (8A) – 40, Police Dept., Special Branch, Government of Assam.

[8] *Asamiiya*, 14 December 1940.

of Congress Assembly members even petitioned the APCC president to absolve them from offering *satyagraha* again. Their plea was that the political conditions then prevailing in Assam, particularly the immigration problem, required their intervention.[9] On the other hand, Left nationalists of all brands and the communists were highly critical of the individual *satyagraha* programme. They urged for mass action instead. Nevertheless, as Congressmen, many of them offered *satyagraha* and went to jail.

The movement did achieve its limited objective – that of making people aware of the imperialist character of the war and of their moral right to denounce it. Up to 31 May 1941, altogether 334 *satyagrahis* were arrested, of whom 231 were convicted to terms of imprisonment ranging from one day to a year. Many more went to jail even thereafter. The *satyagraha* campaign – 'both grim and light' in the words of Tayyebulla – petered out by the end of December.[10] There was increasing reluctance on the part of registered *satyagrahis* to repeat their feats. For example, Sarveswar Barua wanted to withdraw his name from the *satyagrahi* list for domestic reasons. Rajanikanta Barua and Jadav Prasad Chaliha, both Assembly members and planters, expressed their inability to sign the *satyagraha* pledge.[11]

Congress Returns to Legislature

Growing concern over Saadulla's migrant-friendly land settlement policy was largely responsible for Congressmen's hesitancy in pursuing the individual *satyagraha* programme. Many of them grudged Saadulla an easy walk-over in the Assembly for his Land Development Scheme. The scheme was announced in the Government Resolution of 28 July 1941 for the district of Nowgong, to begin with. Similar schemes for other districts were soon to follow. The special officer appointed to draw up a scheme for the whole Brahmaputra Valley submitted his report, but it was withheld from publication.[12] There was persistent public agitation in Nowgong from September to pressurize the Congress to renew parliamentary activities. A public committee was formed to urge the Congress high command to allow Congress legislators to participate in the ensuing Assembly session. Even the local press recommended this course for the Congress.[13]

---

[9] Tayyebulla, *Between the Symbol and the Idol*, pp. 107–11 and 156; Gandhiji to Bardoloi, Sevagram, 3 July 1941, photostat copy in Gopinath Bardoloi, *Gandhiji* (in Assamese, Gauhati, 1969); Bardoloi's statement on 22 December 1941, cited in *IAR* (July–December 1941), Vol. 2, p. 165.

[10] For arrest and conviction figures, reply to K.P. Agarwala, 18 June, *Assam Legislative Council Proceedings* (hereafter *ALCP*) (1941), pp. 355–56; Tayyebulla, *Between the Symbol and the Idol*, pp. 113–14.

[11] 'APCC Gen. Secretary's report, 12 March 1942', *APCC Papers*, File No. 5, Packet 6. The latter had purchased rolling mills in Calcutta and was obviously busy developing this new unit of his business enterprise.

[12] 8 December, *Assam Legislative Assembly Proceedings* (hereafter *ALAP*) (1941), pp. 1440 and 1444.

[13] *Assam Tribune*, 17 October 1941; ibid., 31 October 1941; ibid., editorial, 24 October 1941.

After his release from jail, Bardoloi visited Wardha to consult the high command on this issue. His own opinion, as he claimed, was that *satyagraha* could be made a real success only through complete withdrawal from the legislatures. However, twenty-seven out of the thirty-three Congress members of the Assam Legislative Assembly were reportedly in favour of resuming parliamentary activities, at least on vital matters. He found that representatives from all quarters, particularly from the Congress-minority provinces, who had come to Wardha for consultations, were of the same opinion. Most of the Congress Working Committee (CWC) members also favoured resumption of parliamentary activities, whenever needed. On his return from Wardha in late November 1941, Bardoloi announced that the Congress legislators of Assam were free to attend the ensuing winter session of the Assembly and work for a no-confidence motion. 'That is what the public has all along wanted them to do; the regret is that', it was editorially commented in a local weekly, 'Wardha has not seen its way to allow them to continue their parliamentary activities beyond this session.' However, a new orientation in the Congress policy was hoped for even before the year was over.[14]

Students Lathi-Charged: Saadulla Out

In the Assembly session that commenced on 1 December, Lakheswar Barua moved a resolution on land settlement, incorporating an amendment by Bardoloi, to disapprove Saadulla's policy.[15] This caused a flutter in the ministerial party, since R.K. Chaudhuri's conscience was not clear on this issue. Meanwhile, a new development outside the Assembly precipitated a ministerial crisis. Two Cotton College students were manhandled by a prominent National War Front organizer, when students were boycotting and picketing at the gate of a week-long War Fund-raising scientific exhibition in the science laboratory of their college. In protest, they instantly organized a big procession which paraded the streets shouting – 'Not a man, not a pie to the imperialist war!' The procession was broken up by brutal bayonet and lathi charges, resulting in severe injuries to a large number of students. This occasioned a province-wise, continuous student strike and a wave of protest *hartals*. At the initiative of the All India Students' Federation (AISF), a 'Gauhati Day' was observed for anti-war demonstrations all over the country.[16]

---

[14] *Assam Tribune*, 28 November 1941. Bardoloi's statement of 22 December 1941, cited in *IAR* (July–December 1941), Vol. 2, p. 165. The offer of *satyagraha* being purely one of personal conviction, the APCC president and his colleagues came to the conclusion that those who had not offered *satyagraha* for one reason or other should be allowed to attend the Assembly and participate in its discussion. The Parliamentary Sub-Committee was accordingly moved and the permission obtained.

[15] 6 December, *ALAP* (1941), pp. 1401–24; *Assam Tribune*, 12 December 1941.

[16] Same as footnote 15 and *Assam Tribune*, 19 December 1941; also information gathered from the then student leaders – Umakanta Sharma, Nandeswar Talukdar and Tarunsen Deka; *The Golden Jubilee Volume, Cotton College* (Guwahati, 1951–52), p. 73.

Under the circumstances, secret talks were held between some Congress leaders and R.K. Chaudhuri. If a coalition ministry headed by Allah Baksh could be supported by the Congress in Sind, why not one led by Chaudhuri in Assam's special circumstances? Chaudhuri submitted his resignation from the ministry on 9 December, in the wake of which several no-confidence motions were tabled. The Congress Assembly party held a meeting the same evening to consider the issue of support to Chaudhuri in his attempt to form a new ministry. Out of thirty-one Congress legislators present at the meeting, twenty-eight voted for support to Chaudhuri. O.K. Das, Krishnanath Sharma and Siddhinath Sharma were the three dissidents. B.R. Medhi and Fakhruddin Ali Ahmed were still in jail. Tayyebulla, APCC president, attended the meeting upon invitation. He recorded his strong opposition in view of Chaudhuri's association with the National War Front.[17]

A crisis thus developed in the relationship between the parliamentary and organizational wings of the Congress Party, over the issue of ministry formation. A majority of the APCC Working Committee members supported Tayyebulla's stand. In the next few days, both Bardoloi and Tayyebulla were busy keeping the high command informed of their appraisal of the situation. Abul Kalam Azad, the national Congress president, summoned them by turn to Calcutta for discussions and advised them to clinch the issue at a meeting of the APCC.[18]

Meanwhile, on 12 December, Saadulla submitted his resignation and, pending its acceptance by the Governor, made a statement to that effect in the house the very next day. Bardoloi, too, made a statement on the Gauhati lathicharge. A vote of no-confidence was moved after Saadulla and his supporters had walked out. Both the Land Development Scheme and the Gauhati lathicharge came under fire. The Assembly passed a vote of no-confidence, 56 to nil. Chaudhuri and two parliamentary secretaries voted for the motion.[19]

The constitutional deadlock that lingered thereafter stemmed from the Congress indecision. As per Azad's advice, the APCC Working Committee met for two days, on 14–15 December, at Gauhati, and was apprised by both Bardoloi and Tayyebulla of their talks with Azad. The outcome of the meeting was kept a guarded secret.[20] Subsequently, further instructions were received from the Congress Parliamentary Sub-Committee, but these were ambiguous and vague. Bardoloi reiterated on 22 December:

[17] M. Tayyebulla, *Karagarar Cithi* (Gauhati, 1962), pp. 285–94; Tayyebulla, *Between the Symbol and the Idol*, pp. 114–16.

[18] Same as footnote 17; also Bardoloi's statement of 22 December 1941, cited in *IAR*. Since Bardoloi and Tayyebulla did not see eye to eye, their accounts have to be compared and collated to get at the facts.

[19] *IAR* (July–December 1941), Vol. 2, pp. 163–64; *Assam Tribune*, 19 December 1941.

[20] *Assam Tribune*, 19 December 1941; Bardoloi's statement of 22 December 1941, cited in *IAR*. For a slightly different version of the development, see Tayyebulla, *Karagarar Cithi*, pp. 285–94.

> If a new Ministry is formed, the Congress Party would not oppose it so long as
> the Government would be carried on the basis of the Congress policy and
> programme excepting war measures. It is also open to such members of our
> Party to offer Satyagraha as would like to do so.[21]

In any case, the proposed Chaudhuri ministry never saw the light of day.

Section 93 and Fourth Saadulla Ministry

Asked on 18 December to form an alternative ministry, Bardoloi refused
to oblige, except on terms prejudicial to the war efforts. If Chaudhuri formed a
new coalition cabinet instead, Congress support would in general be given, he
said, but not for supporting the war. Chaudhuri claimed to head a twenty-six-
member party in the Assembly and looked forward to Congress support. However, in the given circumstances, the Governor's interview with him was understandably an empty formality. Even the possibility of an all-party war cabinet
minus the Congress was explored, but without success. Finally, Section 93 of the
Government of India Act, 1935 was proclaimed on 25 December 1941. This
meant suspension of the legislature and take-over of the reins of administration
personally by the Governor.[22]

Governor's Regime and Congress Challenge

One of the first acts of the Governor's regime was the Resolution of 6
March 1942 scrapping the Land Development Scheme. It was stated that the
policy of waste lands settlement, if continued further, would seriously prejudice
'the interests not only of the indigenous population, but also of those who have
already come from Bengal and settled in the last twenty or thirty years'. The
pressing need to extend forests and preserve grazing grounds was particularly
emphasized.[23] This was no doubt a calculated move to appease Hindu and Assamese public opinion at a critical juncture, when the war was rapidly approaching
India's eastern frontier, and when the Congress was being pressed by the people
all over the country to throw the gauntlet to the Raj.

By mid-1942, the war situation was serious. The invading German army
had penetrated deep into Russian territory. With the fall of Singapore on 15 February, Rangoon on 7 March and the Andamans on 12 March 1942, the Japanese
were almost at the doors of mainland India. The mission of Sir Stafford Cripps
for a political settlement failed in April. The rulers were nervous, but so were the

---

[21] Bardoloi's statement of 22 December 1941, cited in *IAR*.

> Whatever instructions were received from the high command regarding support to
> Chaudhuri were interpreted differently by Bardoloi and Tayyebulla. According to the
> latter, the advice of the high command, as early as in 12 December, was clearly
> against lending support to any ministry. See *Karagarar Cithi*, pp. 285–94 and
> Tayyebulla, *Between the Symbol and the Idol*, p. 115.

[22] *IAR* (July–December 1941), Vol. 2, p. 164; Reid, *Years of Change*, p. 147; letter to the
editor, dated 21 December 1941, *Assam Tribune*, 26 December 1941.

[23] Communique cited in *Assam Tribune*, 1 September 1944.

ruled, though for different reasons. Many national leaders with genuine sympathies for the USSR and equally genuine hatred for fascism were in a mental conflict. They would have liked to support the Allied forces against fascism. But could they do so effectively while remaining in bondage? C. Rajagopalachari even advocated a conciliatory attitude to the Muslim League demands – a stand that culminated in his virtual support to the demand for Pakistan in July 1944 – to ensure a quick political settlement in order to meet the emergency. But the AICC remained firm on its stand and reiterated the principle of non-violent non-cooperation as the right means for resisting invasion from any quarters.

By its resolution of 14 July 1942, the AICC Working Committee served the Raj with an ultimatum. In a tense atmosphere, the AICC met at Bombay on 7–8 August and asked the British to quit. Its historic resolution of 8 August sanctioned the starting of a non-violent mass struggle 'on the widest possible scale', under Gandhiji's leadership. Once started, the struggle was to be carried forward indefinitely. In the absence of leaders, under compelling circumstances, every participant was to act for himself or herself within the limits of the general instructions issued. 'Do or die' was Gandhiji's message to the people. His draft statement containing detailed instructions for the movement was scheduled for discussion on 9 August, but the AICC failed to take it up. No formally sanctioned programme for controlled civil disobedience could therefore be issued.[24] For, on that day the government struck. In anticipation of the AICC resolution, lists of persons to be detained had been kept ready in advance in every province. The list for Assam, finalized by 7 August, included the names of eleven important Congress functionaries of the Brahmaputra Valley and five of the Surma Valley.[25] Gandhiji and other leaders were thrown into jail. Between 9 and 15 August, all the important leaders of the Assam Congress, including Tayyebulla, were arrested. While returning to Assam from the AICC meeting, Bardoloi and Siddhinath Sharma were arrested at Dhubri on 15 August. In blind fury, the people hit back. The months of August and September saw spontaneous mass protests and violence all over India. The Government of Assam declared the AICC and the APCC

---

[24] Tarachand, *History of the Freedom Movement in India*, Vol. 4 (New Delhi, 1972), pp. 375–77; Tayyebulla, *Between the Symbol and the Idol*, pp. 130–40.

[25] These sixteen leaders were – M. Tayyebulla, Siddhinath Sarma, Liladhar Barua, B.R. Medhi, Fakhruddin Ali Ahmed, O.K. Das, Padmadhar Chaliha (1895–1969), Lakheswar Barua, Harekrishna Das, Gopinath Bardoloi, Debeswar Sarma, A.K. Chanda, Kedarnath Bhattacharya, Purnendukishor Sengupta, Chanchalkumar Sarma, and Achintyakumar Bhattacharyya. The latter two, who were also members of the CPI, were detained despite their viewing the war as a people's war, because they were also office-bearers of the Congress Party.

The arrest of O.K. Das was delayed, in consideration of his ill health and his firm faith in non-violence. The District Magistrate of Darrang reported on 20 August: 'When some Congressmen had broken down telephone wires, Omeo Kumar Das issued a notice announcing that such acts were against the Congress policy.' Confidential B, File No. C 351/1942, 'Subject: Congress movement 1942 – progress of the movement in Assam' (Assam Secretariat Files; hereafter AS).

as unlawful bodies on 10 August by its notification no. 15-H. Later, the lower committees were also banned.

The detention of Congress legislators created conditions for Saadulla's return to power on 25 August 1942. The Raj was pleased to revoke Section 93 so that the popular resistance could be confronted by a 'popular' ministry. A secret report to the Eastern Army Headquarters, Barackpore, anticipated that Saadulla 'will maintain a policy compatible with the maintenance of loyalty, law and order'. The expectations were not belied.[26]

1942 Struggle and Fourth Saadulla Ministry

Processions and protest *hartals* were spontaneously organized by the people in many parts of the province. In an appraisal of the situation, the Chief Secretary to the Government of Assam noted on 21 August that Nowgong and 'perhaps' Darrang were more troublesome than the other districts. Two platoons of the Assam Rifles were sent to Nowgong to maintain the peace. By the end of August, according to a report received by the Chief Secretary, there was obviously 'an atmosphere of rebellion around Nowgong and from all accounts also in the area around Kamrup and Jamunamukh' (Secret No. 3983 C., 29 August 1942). People were shot dead by the police and military at several places in Nowgong district in August.[27]

Some serious acts of sabotage took place in Nowgong district in the second half of August 1942. Railway tracks were displaced at least at three places, and two paramilitary officers were assaulted at Puranigudam. Several excise shops, the Kathiatoli inspection bungalow and the Raha Circle Office were burnt. People turned violent also in other districts. A mail van was sacked at Goalpara and a military depot was burnt at Palasbari in Kamrup. On 28–29 August, a crowd burnt the Garrison Engineering Office, the Post and Telegraph Office, and an inspection bungalow at Sarbhog in Barpeta sub-division. In Sylhet, an angry crowd destroyed the records and furniture of three government offices. In September, similar disturbances spread to Sibsagar and other districts. A collaborating pleader's house, a forest bungalow and several liquor shops were burnt at Barpeta.[28] There were cases of sabotage on the railways near Shahajibazar

---

[26] Secret Government of Assam No. 76/PS, Office of Military Liaison Officer, Confidential B, 1942, File No. C 251/1942, 'Subject: Congress Movement' (AS).

[27] Ibid.

Five freedom fighters died from gunshots in the district of Nowgong – Hemaram Patar, Gunabhi Bardoloi and Hemaram Bora on 26 August 1942; Tilak Deka on 28 August; and Bhogeswari Phukanni on 18 September.

[28] Home (Pol.) File No. 18/8/42 and Fortnightly reports, Assam, August and September 1942, cited by A.C. Bhuyan, 'The Second World War and Indian Nationalism: A Study of the Quit India Movement' (unpublished Ph.D thesis, School of International Studies, Jawaharlal Nehru University, New Delhi, 1972), pp. 109–10; also see Confidential B, 1943 File No. C 243/1943 (AS) and No. 214 S Confidential B, 1942 File No. C 351/1942 (AS).

in Habiganj, at Barpathar in Golaghat, near Saffrai in Sibsagar and Rangiya in Kamrup.[29]

There were brutal police firings at Gohpur and Dhekiajuli, in the district of Darrang, when hundreds of unarmed people led by *satyagrahis* attempted to enter the police station compounds on 20 September, to hoist the Congress flag. Thirteen persons were killed at Dhekiajuli; and at Gohpur, Mukunda Kakati and a teenaged girl, Kanaklata Barua. Lathi-armed volunteers of the village defence committees, which were organized by the Saadulla government for its support at the grass roots, helped the police in many places in suppressing the 1942 movement.[30] There were also cases of police firing at Patacharkuchi in Barpeta sub-division on 25 September, and at Fakiragram in Goalpara sub-division in October.[31] Nidhanu Rajbansi, a poor peasant of Fakiragram, was brutally bayoneted to death for resisting the imposition of a collective fine. During the Quit India movement of 1942, 'all attempts at sabotage caused only six derailments', whereas there were thirty-three derailments and six collisions since the Americans took over the Assam Railways in early 1944. It was so observed by Wavell on 22 August 1944.

The consolidated statistical picture of the movement that was officially compiled at the end of 1943, and reproduced below, throws some light on its extent and nature, and on the government's punitive measures. A more telling report was later compiled by Gopinath Bardoloi. Never before were so many people killed or arrested in the province – neither during the 1921–22 movement nor in the Civil Disobedience movement of 1930 and 1932. The toll of police and military atrocities in 1942 was no less than twenty-seven deaths from gunshots – all in the Brahmaputra Valley. About 3,000 people were arrested. Of four death

[29] K.N. Dutt, *Landmarks of the Freedom Struggle in Assam* (reprint, Gauhati, 1969), p. 102. See P. Moon, ed., *Wavell the Viceroy's Journal* (London, 1973), p. 88.

[30] Confidential B, File No. C 351/1942, 'Subject: Congress movement 1942 – progress of the movement in Assam'.

 The police officer who was then in charge of the police station of Dhekiajuli published his own version of the firing incident exactly thirty-two years after it had taken place. See Mahidhar Bora, 'Biyallish biplavar eta aitihasik din', *Niiacal* (Assamese weekly), 14 August 1974.

 For a list of martyrs, an account of people's heroism, and the details of police and military atrocities, see Tayyebulla, *Between the Symbol and the Idol*, pp. 149–54 and Dutt, *Landmarks of the Freedom Struggle in Assam*, pp. 101–06 and 139–40.

[31] The mood of the people is indicated by the report of the officer in-charge of the Pathacharkuchi police station to the Supdt. of Police, Gauhati:

 'Mob about 1,000 Congressmen armed with lathis attacked me with two armed constables at Jalah to rescue three Congress leaders . . . Fired three rounds . . . at Rehabari again surrounded, about 500 Congressmen armed with big lathis. Fired three rounds, probably killed two men. On the road to EKAYA, similarly two big mobs attacked, fired one round to sky. At NITYANANDA surrounded, about 500 Congressmen armed with lathis, blocked road. Fired one round, probably killed one . . . no police party injured.'

 Cited by R.C.R. Cumming, IGP, to Chief Secretary, 26 September 1942, Confidential B, File No. C 248/1943 'Subject: Congress Movement 1942 – progress of the movement in Assam' (AS).

sentences passed for alleged sabotage activities, that on Kushal Konwar was confirmed by the Governor-General. He was executed on 15 June 1943 for alleged implication in the Sarupathar train derailment case. The other three co-accused were each given ten-year terms of imprisonment.[32]

An Assessment of the 1942 Struggle

Although the movement was carried on in the name of the Congress and mainly by Congressmen, many Congress leaders like O.K. Das condemned the violence and sabotage activities.[33] The all-India leadership was arrested even before it could formally launch the movement and issue the necessary instructions. Hence, it was not a Congress movement as such. The people – the non-Muslim masses in general – started it spontaneously.

The Communist League, renamed the Revolutionary Communist Party since 1943, the Forward Bloc and the Congress–Socialist followers of Jayaprakash Narayan – all plunged into the struggle. They had never accepted non-violence as a creed. Leaderless Congress masses in many places of Assam came under their influence and direction. Clandestine literature exhorting violence and sabo-

---

[32] Dutt, *Landmarks of the Freedom Struggle in Assam*, pp. 101–06; Tayyebulla, *Between the Symbol and the Idol*, pp. 149–50; also the table that follows.

Official Statistics of Congress Disturbances: Assam
(9 August 1942–31 December 1943)

Nature of Case	No.
Police Firing Occasions	4*
Fatal Casualties	15*
Non-Fatal Casualties (Inflicted)	19
Non-Fatal Casualties (Suffered)	17
Police Stations Destroyed/Damaged	4
Government Buildings Destroyed/Damaged	64
Other Public Buildings Destroyed/Damaged	66
Private Buildings Destroyed/Damaged	61
Bomb Explosions	10
Explosives Discovered without Damage	9
Cases of Sabotage to Roads	43
Arrests Made	2,707
Case of Imposition of Collective Fine	1
Defection from Government Service	nil
	Amount
Estimated Loss to Government	Rs 2,84,582
Estimated Loss to Other Parties	Rs 1,94,847
Collective Fine Imposed	Rs 3,39,487

Notes: *Fatal casualties were no less than twenty-seven; the actual number of police and military firings was more than what has been indicated above. See Dutt, *Landmarks of the Freedom Struggle in Assam*, appendix IV, p. 139.

Source: Home Pol. File No. 3/52/43 (NAI) cited in Bhuyan, 'Second World War and Indian Nationalism', appendix table 1 (abridged and adapted by us). This source fails to give a complete picture, because of under-reporting.

[33] Confidential B, File No. C/351/1942; also, Dutt, *Landmarks of the Freedom Struggle in Assam*, p. 102.

tage activities was in circulation. Attempts were made by the underground workers to collect firearms: six licensed guns were stolen in Nalbari and nineteen in Nowgong.[34]

Jail-going was no more a soft business. Thousands were jailed or home-interned; some were externed from the province. Many Congressmen, like Jyotiprasad Agarwala, Lakshmiprasad Goswami (1918–?), Sankarchandra Barua (1895–1966), Mahendra Hazarika, Brajanath Sharma (1894–1960) and Gahanchandra Goswami, went underground to sustain the movement. Attempts were made in a few rural areas to establish a sort of parallel government, through village panchayats and *shanti-senas* (soldiers of peace).[35] But these did not attain much success. The underground resistance movement made limited headway in Assam in terms of actual operations. But it did help sustain hope and occasional symbolic defiance. News about the Indian National Army, formed abroad, kept up their morale. Hemchandra Baruah, the ailing Congress leader, maintained contact from his sick bed with all the groups of underground freedom fighters.

There was an unprecedented concentration and movement of troops in Assam. Students and teachers of Cotton College were pushed out from its extensive campus to make room for the armed forces during the years 1942–45. The Cotton College Students' Union Society had, since its democratization in 1937, played a vanguard role in politicizing the students. Its activities, however, remained virtually suspended in the post-1942 war years, because of repression and communal dissensions.[36] The government contained the August movement through repressive measures like the preventive detention of political leaders and suspects. There were 227 security prisoners in the Assam jails on 15 March 1943, 349 on 1 November 1943 and 162 on 31 October 1944. During the whole period from 9 August 1942 to 31 October 1944, altogether 463 persons were held as security prisoners.[37]

The August uprisings were confronted ideologically by the Communist Part of India (CPI). It argued that the USSR, the vanguard of the international

---

[34] *IAR* (January–June 1943), Vol. 1, pp. 242–43.

[35] Dutt, *Landmarks of the Freedom Struggle in Assam*, pp. 99–102.

'1087 Kamrup, 29-4-44 – It is reported that the Head Office of the Assam Congress Socialist Party has been started at Nowgong with the following workers: (1) Deba Kanta Barooah, (2) Lakshmi Goswami, (3) Ghanakanta Hazarika and (4) Tilak Hazarika. This Party is being supported by Dr Bhubaneswar Barua and Hemchandra Baruah. Lakhyadhar Barua (Chaudhuri? A.G.) is the treasurer of this party and he used to get money from Achyut Patwardhan of United Provinces. Absconder Sankarchandra Barua is the leader of this party throughout Assam Valley.' Extract from the Assam Police Abstract of Intelligence No. 19 dated 6 May 1944, Police Dept., Special Branch, File No. B. 2 (12) (a) 44/111, Shillong.

Shriman Prafulla Goswami, a socialist Congressman close to the communists, had no links or rapport with this group.

[36] *Golden Jubilee Volume, Cotton College*, pp. 56–58 and 65.

[37] *IAR* (January–June, 1943), Vol. 1, p. 243; *Assam Tribune*, 24 November 1944; Saadulla to Bardoloi, Shillong, 2 August 1945, *APCC Papers*, File on leaders' correspondence, Packet 43.

working-class movement, being under attack since 22 June 1941, the imperialist war had turned into a people's war. The immediate task before the Indian people, therefore, was not to impede the war efforts through an open revolt against an ally of the USSR. The party had taken six months from 22 June to rectify its erstwhile anti-war stand and accept the new line in December 1941. In recognition of the change in its attitude, the ban on the party was lifted in July 1942. Biresh Misra, a leader of the Sylhet District Congress Committee (and also a communist), who had been in jail since 1940, was released in time for participation in the first legal meeting of the CPI at Sylhet on 27 July 1942.[38] Communists of both the Valleys openly came out of their Congress–Socialist Party (CSP) shell. Late in 1942, the Assam Valley District Committee of the CPI was formed.

The new CPI line was first pushed among the students through the platform of the Assam Chhatra Sanmilan (Students' Federation). With some difficulty and despite an organizational split in May 1942, it continued to retain substantial influence over the student community.[39] Communists held key offices in the District Congress Committees of Sylhet and Cachar, and were thus able to keep these committees somewhat in restraint in course of the August turmoil. Hitler's invasion of the USSR, and the threat of a Japanese invasion of India within a few months thereafter, brought about a significant, if not radical change in the war situation and its character by December 1942. India's confused reaction to this change was hesitant, half-hearted and self-defeating, as was evident in Assam.

The INA's Shadow over Assam

Turned into a war base even before the August struggle had commenced, Assam was burdened with a field army of six divisions under British command. Besides, there were American armed forces, too, committed to help China from their Assam base. The Assam Railways, placed under the latter's control in 1944, catered primarily to war needs. Aerial bombings on Imphal on 10 and 16 May 1942 and again on 20 April 1943, on the Chittagong dock on 8 May 1942, on Calcutta for two consecutive days in December 1943, and on several places in Assam in 1943 and 1944, created a general panic. Subhas Chandra Bose, who had secretly left India in 1941 to carry on the liberation struggle from abroad, reorganized the Indian National Army (INA) into a formidable force of some 20,000 fighting men, stationed in Southeast Asia.[40] The establishment of the Provisional Government of Free India at Singapore by Bose on 23 October 1943 was, for India, the year's greatest event.

Bose's radio broadcasts were listened to in Assam eagerly and exten-

---

[38] *People's War*, 6 September 1942.

[39] In fact, the All–India Students' Federation was already split into two rival bodies in 1940. In Assam, one was represented by the CPI-led Assam Chhatra Sanmilan and the other by the RCPI-led Assam Provincial Students' Federation. A third body emerged in Assam in due course, after the aforesaid split of 1942, to accommodate Congress-minded students.

[40] Moon, ed., *Wavell the Viceroy's Journal*, pp. 53–54 and 161–62.

sively throughout the remaining war years.[41] The Japanese advance across the Indian frontier into Manipur and the Naga Hills began on 8 March 1944. Three regular divisions of the Japanese army were employed in the campaign that lasted from March to July. The INA, too, employed three organized divisions – each of 2,000 men. The rest of the INA men moved as auxiliaries. Fighting was heavy all along the Imphal–Kohima–Dimapur sector. The advancing Japanese army, assisted by the INA, was finally overcome in the siege of Imphal and Kohima, and the campaign ended in a disaster. Lack of adequate air support and the Japanese contempt for the politically-inspired INA men, who had broken a soldier's pledge, contributed towards the disaster. Ordered to retreat on 8 July, the remnants of the defeated army fell back on Burma. In December 1944, a British campaign was opened to push them out of Burma. It was all quiet again on the eastern front with the surrender of Japan on 14 August 1945.

Congressmen and Local Issues

It was during these uneasy war years that the fourth Saadulla ministry (25 August 1942–23 March 1945) had an unenviable existence. There was inflation and scarcity of essential consumption goods. The high foodgrain prices perhaps helped better-off peasants to liquidate old debts, but the bulk of the peasantry and wage-earners were in distress, despite increasing war-induced employment. The years 1942 and 1943 witnessed a general exodus of non-Assamese wholesale and retail traders from the province. Markets were so affected thereby that angry Bodo–Kachari peasants in Goalpara looted several *haats* in November 1942, allegedly with such slogans as 'land is ours', 'we are the *raij*' and 'turn out the foreigners'. The police intervened and one Deobar Boro was shot dead at Ramfalbilhat. Enquiries revealed that village meetings had preceded these disturbances, which were caused partly by the economic distress and partly by the dislike of non-indigenous traders.[42]

Uncertain trade conditions forced the Assam government to undertake large-scale commercial operations on its own account. It appointed Shaw Wallace and Co. Ltd., a British-owned managing agency firm, as its agent for wholesale purchase of salt, sugar, wheat, flour and standard cloth from outside Assam. Similarly Steel Bros. Ltd., also a foreign-owned firm, was appointed the agent for purchase of products like rice, paddy and mustard oil from the local markets, with a view to stabilizing their prices and ensuring supplies. The latter firm had

---

[41] Inside the prison, some top Congress leaders started discussing what was to be done after Bose had ejected the British from Assam with Japanese help. Tayyebulla, O.K. Das and Krisnanath Sharma did not like this 'Un-Gandhian' attitude of their comrades. Tayyebulla, *Between the Symbol and the Idol*, p. 124; *Karagarar Cithi*, pp. 346–47. Tayyebulla's insinuations against Bardoloi in his memoirs, however, need not be taken at their face value in this respect.

[42] Goalpara District Magistrate's report on the incident dated 6 November 1942 in Confidential B, 1943, File No. C 249/1943 (AS); also speech by Abdul Matin Chaudhuri, 12 November, *ALAP* (1942), p. 15.

extensive experience of similar business in Burma and Malay, which of late, were lost to the Japanese.[43]

The supply system was so mismanaged in 1943 that salt was selling in the black market at Rs 8 per *seer* in some places. The evils of hoarding, black-marketing and profiteering were rampant all over Assam. In neighbouring Bengal, three million people died of famine in 1943. A class of contractors, traders and corrupt government servants minted money. Communists, charged with collaboration with imperialism, used the opportunity to prove their *bonafides* by organizing relief work and protest movements directed against hoarders, profiteers and black-marketeers.[44]

In the absence of Congress leaders in the field, the CPI was able to build up a band of dedicated cadres in both the Valleys, despite its unpopular stand on the war. Its two Valley district committees came under a provincial organizing committee, formed at the first Party Congress held at Bombay on 23 May–1 June 1943. Under its guidance, a campaign was carried on for the release of national leaders and for Congress–League unity to achieve a national government. On 26 January 1944, Bardoloi was prematurely released on health grounds, but his movements were put under restriction. In a discussion with CPI leaders, Bardoloi agreed that the release of national leaders, the formation of a provisional government on the basis of Congress–League unity and an organized defence against the Japanese aggression were the key tasks before the people. He even issued a well-publicized statement to that effect on 10 April 1944.[45]

In a similar statement in April 1944, B.K. Das, Speaker and a Surma Valley Congress leader, said: 'Our country today is face to face with a threat from the Japanese aggressors. This is the moment when we should forget our narrow

[43] Speech by Chaudhuri, ibid.

Shaw Wallace and Co. Ltd. controlled half-a-dozen tea companies owning some twenty-five tea gardens and about 16,000 planted acres in Assam. Besides, the Company was also the managing agent of Nazira Coal Co., with an annual output of about 20,000 tons of coal.

[44] Prafulla Misra, 'Communist Movement in Assam', *Northeastern Affairs*, 1 (July–September 1972), p. 30. *People's War*, 14 March 1943.

To maintain its patriotic image, the CPI refused to cooperate with the National War Front and tried to forge unity with Congressmen and Leaguers for peaceful agitation on matters of public concern. Although its condemnation of Bose's supporters. as fascists and fifth columnists was rejected by the people in general, it nevertheless was able to recruit quite a large number of young participants of the Quit India movement of 1942 to swell its ranks.

[45] For the statement, *Janayuddha* (Bengali weekly), 19 April 1944; and for the date of Bardoloi's release, *Assam Tribune*, 4 February 1944. Also *People's War*, 28 May 1944 and Bhowani Sen's article in *People's War*, 2 July 1944.

It was suggested in the 'APCC Report for 1945' (typed copy, pp. 1–15, in the Office of the Editor of the History of Freedom Movement [hereafter OEHFM], Government of Assam, Gauhati) that communists often publicized the views of Congress leaders in a distorted manner so as to suit their own point of view. Bardoloi's indulgent stand was that Congressmen, being non-violent, need not be shy of the communists.

squabbles and petty interests and devote ourselves to the supreme task of defending our homes.'[46]

Congress legislators who were then outside prison bars were eager to resume their normal parliamentary activities. One local consideration, in particular, weighed heavily on their minds. They wanted to halt the implementation of Saadulla's controversial land settlement and immigrant policy, which had been revived in August 1943.

Fourth Saadulla Ministry under Pressure
Resuscitated Land Development Scheme

The Bengal Legislative Council carried a motion on 16 July 1943, calling upon the Government of India to take immediate steps to remove all existing restrictions imposed by the Assam government on land-hungry, emigrant cultivators from Bengal. Exactly a year after its formation, the fourth Saadulla ministry, therefore, adopted a new resolution on land settlement under the slogan of 'grow more food'. What it really meant, according to the Viceroy, was 'grow more Moslems'. The salient features of this resolution of 24 August 1943 were as follows:

   (i) resumed distribution of waste lands in proportion to the needs of different communities in Nowgong and de-reservation of select grazing reserves for that purpose, as per the resolution of 21 June 1940;

   (ii) de-reservation of professional grazing reserves in Kamrup and Darrang if found surplus to actual requirements; and

   (iii) opening up of surplus reserves in all the submontane areas, and in Sibsagar and Lakhimpur, for settlement of landless indigenous people.[47]

S.P. Desai, a senior ICS man, was appointed special officer in September 1943 to ascertain what portion of professional grazing reserves could be declared as surplus available for settlement. Desai reported that forcible occupation of grazing lands by immigrants had already taken place to a large scale, even in the predominantly Assamese or tribal areas. His conclusion was that there was no surplus land available for new settlement.[48] Ignoring the report, Saadulla's Muslim League coalition government threw select professional grazing reserves open for settling immigrants. The Revenue Secretary to the Government of Assam bluntly wrote to the Bengal government in May 1944 that gradual abolition of

---

[46] *Assam Tribune*, 21 April 1944.

[47] *Assam Tribune*, 3 September 1943; also, *IAR* (July–December 1943), Vol. 2, pp. 279–80, citing *Assam Gazette*, 25 August 1943; Moon, ed., *Wavell the Viceroy's Journal*, p. 41.

[48] *Assam Tribune*, editorial, 27 October 1944; Rajendra Prasad, *India Divided* (Bombay, 1946), p. 247; S.P. Desai, 'My thirty five years in Assam' in K.L. Punjabi, ed., *The Civil Servant in India* (Bombay, 1965), p. 66.

   Also see S.P. Desai, *Report of the Special Officer Appointed for the Examination of the Professional Grazing Reserves in the Assam Valley* (Assam Government Press, Shillong, 1944.)

the Line system was a process that had already been under way 'in areas where Caste Hindus are in a majority'. It was a committed policy, he stated, 'as far as is consistent with the necessity for reservation for indigenous people and protection of the tribal classes'. The policy, thus elaborated, was claimed to have undergone considerable liberalization in the recent past, to meet Bengal's objections.[49]

This anti-Line policy gave an opportunity to the Asam Jatiya Mahasabha, as well as the All-India Hindu Mahasabha, to raise respective cries of the Assamese and Hindus being in danger. They pointed out that the new resolution was nothing but a resuscitation of the discarded Land Development Scheme under a new garb.[50] On the other hand, nothing short of the abolition of the Line would satisfy the land-hungry Bengali Muslim immigrants and their leader, Bhasani, president of the provincial Muslim League.

The provincial Muslim League conference was held in April 1944 at Barpeta, Bhasani's stronghold, with Chowdhry Khaliquzzaman in the chair. 'Ministers give us land or resign' was literally the writing on the walls of the *pandal* to greet Saadulla. Replying to Bhasani's long harangue, Saadulla charged that the greedy headmen of immigrant villages, *dewanis* and *matbars*, had unceremoniously managed to get for themselves *pattas* for 70 to 100 acres of land each, with a view to induct sub-tenants thereupon. It was their greed that was at the root of the evil of the Line system. He cited instances of them driving out even Assamese Muslims from newly reclaimed lands. To drive home the point, he drew a parallel with unrestricted Jewish migration to the Arab homeland. He pleaded for protection of Assam's tribals in the plains from the onslaught of more enterprising settlers. Finally, he appealed for support for his policy, since the Line system had already been relaxed a great deal with a view to its gradual abolition.[51]

The debate was carried on before an assembly of some 25,000 people. Bhasani, of course, won the day. The ministry was thus confronted with a deep political crisis. Despite an enquiry ordered by the all-India Muslim League's working committee, the quarrel between Bhasani and Saadulla remained unresolved.[52]

[49] A.G. Patton to Revenue Secretary to Government of Bengal, Shillong, 5 May 1944, Revenue Dept. Development Branch, File No. RD 25/44 (AS).

[50] *IAR* (July–December 1943), Vol. 2, pp. 258 and 279–80; *Assam Tribune*, 31 March 1944; ibid., 1 September 1944.

[51] *Assam Tribune*, 5 May 1944.

[52] Mohammad Walliullah, *Yugabicitra* (in Bengali, Dacca, 1967), pp. 420–24. According to a police report, altogether about one lakh people were believed to have attended the conference. Town D.I.B. to Supdt. of Police, 13 February 1945, Confidential B 1945, File C 27/45 (AS).

Congress Assembly Party and Land Settlement Question

The Congress Assembly party had officially absented itself from the Assam Legislative Assembly for about three years, though three or four of its members attended some sessions in their individual capacity.[53]

On the publication of Rajagopalachari's partition formula of 10 July 1944, Bardoloi became apprehensive of further Congress concessions to the Muslim League that might result in Assam's inclusion in the so-called East Pakistan. He wrote to Rajagopalachari that, if the province or any of its parts excepting Sylhet were grouped with Bengal to form a single unit under the formula, 'the whole Province will join to a man opposing it'. Forwarding a copy of this letter to Tej Bahadur Sapru on 14 August, Bardoloi requested him 'to take a special interest in the matter and kindly to see that no injustice is done to Assam'.[54] Bardoloi apprised Gandhiji also of Saadulla's anti-national policy and asked for his advice. If the people really felt that the government's policy was oppressive and anti-national, let them fight it non-violently or even violently, if necessary, was what Gandhiji advised in course of a message.[55]

In September 1944, the Assam government was considering further relaxation of restrictions on the movement of the released Congress legislators, so that they could attend the Assembly sessions. The Chief Secretary was in favour of relaxing the internment order on Bardoloi, in particular, but both the Governor and the Chief Minister were against it. Finally, after some consultation, it was decided that all the interned legislators, Bardoloi not excepted, should apply for the government's permission to attend the Assembly, and each case would be judged according to the concerned District Magistrate's report. Those who were outside the jails asked for permission and, except Purnachandra Sharma and A.K. Chanda, all of them were given it. Out of thirty-one members of the Congress Assembly party, only sixteen could attend the November session.[56]

Back in the Assembly as opposition leader, Bardoloi declared on 14

---

[53] On 11 March 1943, four Congress Party members were present in the house. *IAR* (January–June 1943), Vol. 1, p. 243.

[54] Bardoloi's letter to Sapru, 14 August 1944 and a copy of his letter to Rajagopalachari, intercepted by CID, Special Branch, Lucknow, in 'Government notes regarding Bardoloi's intention to attend Assembly session at Shillong in November 1944', Confidential B 1945, File No. C 241.1945 (AS).

[55] This was what Bardoloi told the United Press of India in December 1944. Congress decision to attend the Assembly session to protest against the anti-national policy was claimed to have stemmed from Gandhiji's advice. Later, in clarification, Bardoloi issued a statement that what Gandhiji had said four months ago was in consonance with his general attitude to cowardice. *Assam Tribune*, 22 December 1944 and also 5 January 1945. See *Hindustan Standard* (Calcutta), 15, December 1944.

[56] 'Government notes regarding Bardoloi's intention to attend Assembly session at Shillong in November 1944'. Saadulla noted on 12 September 1944: 'When I find that this class of people who publicly speak of unity but secretly write to Gandhiji and Sir Tej Bahadur Sapru against the same move as in Mr Bardoloi's case, no reliance can be placed on their word'. Ibid.

Also 'APCC Report for 1945' (typed copy, pp. 1–15, in the OEHFM, Gauhati).

November 1944 that his party's outlook on parliamentary activities remained unchanged. It would continue to take advantage of its position in the house to prevent the harm that was being done to the people. He demanded a shift in the land settlement policy in favour of the landless indigenous people, as well as pre-1938 immigrants.[57]

The opposition suggested that the land settlement question be considered once more by an all-party conference. The Governor, too, threw a similar hint in his address to the Assembly. Saadulla accepted the offer, without any prior consultation with the Muslim League Party. An all-party conference was duly held under his chairmanship on 16–19 December 1944, to recommend a suitable land settlement policy. He chose not to stand by the rigid Muslim League policy on this issue and agreed, in essence, to whatever was suggested by the Congress Party. Reservation of 30 per cent of the available waste lands as provision for future expansion of the indigenous people, planned settlement of the residual waste lands with landless sons of the soil and pre-1938 immigrants, and a system of protection for tribal people in belts specially reserved for them – these were the measures recommended by the conference. It was also agreed that the integrity of grazing reserves should be strictly maintained and all trespassers evicted. The decisions were not unanimous, however. Two Muslim League participants, both of them immigrants, dissented.[58] During the negotiations, Saadulla always had the advantage of pointing out that, under the existing law of the land, the Government of Assam had no right to discriminate between communities in the matter of restricting freedom of movement and property rights. Strictly speaking, the Line had no legal basis. Nevertheless, the outcome of the conference was a victory for the Congress. But soon it came out that there was many a slip, indeed, between the cup and the lip.

Government Resolution: 16 January 1945

In response to the conference decisions, the government adopted a fresh resolution on waste lands settlement on 16 January 1945.

This resolution envisaged a plan for waste lands settlement in Goalpara, Kamrup, Darrang and Nowgong with landless people of all categories, including pre-1938 immigrants. Subject to availability, land was to be allotted to members of various communities in separate community-wise blocks, in accordance with their requirements. The ceiling of such allotment was fixed at 30 *bighas* (10 acres) per family. If enough land was not available in the aforementioned four districts for settling the landless, north Lakhimpur sub-division was also to be

---

[57] *Assam Tribune*, 24 November 1944.

The Congress Assembly party took part only in the land settlement and procurement policy debates. 'APCC Report for 1945' notes that, according to many, the retention of Assembly seats by Congress did harm to the province, and that this should be brought to the notice of Gandhiji.

[58] *Assam Tribune*, 22 and 29 December 1944; ibid., 29 June 1945; Rajendra Prasad, *India Divided*, p. 248; *People's War*, 24 December 1944.

opened up. A landless person was defined as one who owned less than 5 *bighas* of agricultural land. Tribal belts were to be constituted, and the total area required for the tribal people was to be calculated at double the area already in their possession plus a reservation for their future progeny on a basis similar to that for non-tribals. Altogether, 30 per cent of all cultivable waste lands in each district, as of 1940, was to be reserved to provide for future population growth. Lands in professional grazing reserves, even if surplus, were henceforth to remain untouched, except where these had already been settled. If any community failed to fully occupy its quota of the allocated waste lands within two years, the unoccupied plots were to be allotted afresh to members from other communities.[59]

The Ministerial Crisis Matures

As expected, the resolution was not acceptable to the immigrant Muslims. A meeting of the Assam Provincial Muslim League Council held at Gauhati under Bhasani's chairmanship on 28 January 1945, and attended by 525 representatives, demanded total abolition of the Line system.[60] Even Assamese public opinion was adverse to the resolution, because of a number of built-in loopholes. Most of the indigenous cultivators owned uneconomic holdings of more than 5 *bighas* of land. They could not claim to be landless under the prescribed conditions; the 5-*bigha* clause operated as a handicap for them. Secondly, since tribal belts had yet to be delimited, much room was still left for administrative manipulation and bungling. Contrary to the conference decisions, the resolution allowed wide discretionary powers to the local officers 'to keep in possession encroachers who had been in occupation of and cultivating land in the grazing reserves over three years'. This meant that even the post-1937 immigrants could get land if they were already in illegal occupation of plots in the grazing reserves. The Congress therefore refused to back the resolution.[61]

Because of this rejection of the land policy both by the Congress and the League, the Saadulla ministry became shaky. By the end of January 1945 the press began to talk about a forthcoming Saadulla–Chaudhuri coalition ministry, as an emerging alternative to Section 93.[62] On 6 February, armed police intervened in a clash between local graziers and Bengali Muslim encroachers in the Kawaimari grazing reserve of Barpeta sub-division. Two of the latter group were injured from gunshots. This was followed by communal tension in the district. Due to administrative interference from above, the local police failed to take any

[59] *Assam Tribune*, 26 January 1945.

[60] Ibid., 9 February 1945. Incidentally, on 14 November 1942, Bhasani had charged Abdul Matin Chaudhuri, a Muslim League minister, of betraying the immigrants. 'Whoever goes to Lanka, becomes a Ravan' was what he said bitterly on the Assembly floor. *ALAP* (1942), p. 79.

[61] Rajendra Prasad, *India Divided*, p. 248; Bardoloi's letter to Gandhiji, 14 March 1945, reproduced in Bardoloi, *Gandhiji*, pp. 139–41.

[62] *Assam Tribune*, 2 February 1945.

effective action against the illegal encroachments, much to the resentment of the Assamese population.[63]

That Chaudhuri would try to fish in troubled waters was understandable. Though a trusted colleague for years until he crossed the floor in December 1941, he was thereafter kept out of Saadulla's cabinet. Now he was once more available for Bardoloi to play a decisive role at this critical stage.[64] With special government permission, he, together with eighteen Congress legislators, attended the Assembly session that commenced on 1 March 1945. Afraid of a defeat and eventual resignation, Saadulla was by this time in search of fresh allies. A hairbreadth's escape on a cut motion on 17 March forced him to enter into secret negotiations with Chaudhuri and Bardoloi.[65]

Bardoloi had come to the conclusion that, in the given situation, the Congress Assembly party had only two courses open before it. One was to launch a mass struggle against the unpopular Muslim League coalition government. But that involved the risk of raking up communal feelings and violence. The other course, that is, to participate in the legislature and try to pull down the government, was therefore the only workable line of action left. However, since tribal and scheduled caste politicians would not welcome Section 93, a no-confidence moved by the Congress would fall flat unless the formation of an alternative coalition government was also kept in view. Three possibilities, therefore, emerged:

   (i) a Congress-supported coalition ministry without Saadulla, in which Congressmen would not accept any office;
   (ii) a coalition ministry headed by Saadulla that would include Congressmen and would be committed to a minimum programme;
   (iii) a full-fledged Congress coalition ministry.[66]

The Congress Assembly party met to decide upon the strategy. Bardoloi told his colleagues that personally he was opposed to Congressmen serving on any cabinet, in the given situation. But as a democratic leader, he was prepared to act according to the party's mandate. Excepting two, all his colleagues were ready to go to any length to bring down the Muslim League coalition government. So the path for him was clear. He felt he only needed Gandhiji's moral sanction for his forthcoming action. In a long letter to him dated 14 March 1945, Bardoloi graphically described Assam's burning land settlement and immigrant

---

[63] Confidential B 1945, File No. C 27/45 (AS). A hue and cry was raised by the Muslim League press over the Kawaimari shooting incident. Two League ministers held spot enquiries on 12 February 1945. Saadulla noted on the file on 20 February 1945: 'The entire Police officers in the Barpeta circle are Hindus, and the immigrants have reported to me various things against Hindu officers of Police.' Saadulla concluded that he had 'never come across so blatant and outrageous Police report'. Saadulla ordered transfer of the police inspector pending further enquiry.

[64] 15 March, *ALAP* (1945), p. 519.

[65] Tayyebulla, *Karagarar Cithi*, p. 349; *People's War*, 8 April 1945.

[66] The strategy as elaborated in Bardoloi's letter to Gandhiji, 14 March 1945, in Bardoloi, *Gandhiji*, pp. 139–41.

question. He explained the rationale of his strategy to oust, or at least curb, the Muslim League's power, and concluded:

> If I am continuing as a parliamentarian, it is only because there is no alternative for me just at present, and that I would do all that is possible for me to do not to become a minister consistent of course only with the safety of my province. . . . I have made up my mind for the action on the understanding that I have your approval.[67]

Gandhiji's reply to this letter on 17 March was non-committal. 'Do what is best. Kill corruption. Adopt that alternative which is the best under the circumstances', he wrote.[68] Apparently, even without waiting for the reply, Bardoloi had set to work. On 18 March, he and Chaudhuri jointly sent a concrete five-point proposal to Saadulla inviting him to head a Congress-supported reconstituted ministry. The very next day Saadulla's coalition party agreed by more than a two-thirds majority to accept the proposal to form a stable ministry. They authorized their leader to negotiate the details, particularly about the land settlement policy and the allocation of cabinet seats.[69]

The Tripartite Agreement

On 20 March, the three leaders – Bardoloi, Saadulla and Chaudhuri – met to thrash out issues. The five points they agreed upon after three days' discussion were the following:

(i) restoration of civil liberties and gradual release of political prisoners;

(ii) a suitable policy for procurement and distribution of essential goods, with a view to remove corruption;

(iii) revision of the land settlement policy with a view to accommodate the claims of sons of the soil;

(iv) an agreed distribution of local board seats among the main contending groups; and

(v) reconstitution of the Saadulla ministry on an all-party basis.

Fifth Saadulla Ministry: 'A New Era'?

According to the agreement, Saadulla resigned on 23 March and reconstituted his cabinet to include all the five Muslim ministers from his last cabinet, one tribal minister chosen by the tribal group and four non-Muslim ministers, including one representative of the scheduled castes selected by the opposition, that is, the Congress.[70]

---

67 Ibid.

68 Cited in *IAR* (January–June 1945), Vol. 1, p. 214.

69 Chaudhuri and Bardoloi to Saadulla, Shillong, 19 March 1945 and Saadulla's reply to Chaudhuri and Bardoloi, Shillong, 19 March 1945. See *APCC Papers*, Packet No. 43, 'Leaders correspondence'.

70 *IAR* (January–June 1945), Vol. 1, p. 213; Tayyebulla, *Karagarar Cithi*, pp. 351–55; Tayyebulla, *Between the Symbol and the Idol*, p. 158. Also see in this connection

Bardoloi and Tayyebulla at Loggerheads

Although all the five Muslim League ministers were retained in the cabinet, the two important portfolios of land revenue and finance were taken out of their hands. All the non-Muslim ministers were practically Congress nominees, although Congressmen themselves did not accept any office. The Congress achieved what it wanted. Relieved and relaxed after the Assembly show was over, Bardoloi wrote to Gandhiji on 25 March: 'In whatever has happened, I felt the hand of God and your good wishes and blessings working through them.'[71] In course of a press statement, Bardoloi, like Saadulla, even said that 'a new era in Assam' had been ushered in. It was noted by the *Assam Tribune* that 'the Congress and the Moslem League have joined hands in Assam'.[72] The Provincial Congress Constructive Workers' meeting held at Goalpara on 27 March, with the participation of Bardoloi, Hemchandra Baruah and other leaders, was a clear sign of renewed Congress initiative in public activities.[73]

But all were not happy. Not Tayyebulla, certainly, who claimed to be no less a Gandhian than Bardoloi. Released on 27 March, he issued a press statement in his capacity as the APCC president, expressing strong opposition to the Tripartite Agreement. Bardoloi had no right to use the name of the Congress, he said, in signing an agreement with war collaborators like Saadulla and Chaudhuri. In June he sent a memorandum to the Congress high command and asked it to discuss the matter at the next meeting of the Working Committee. But the Congress–League *entente* in the Assam Legislative Assembly was already showing signs of a breakdown. Under the changed circumstances, the Congress high command was not in a mood to discipline Bardoloi for his non-conformist role in ministry-making. The controversy within the APCC on this issue became pointless by early August 1945 with the end of World War II and with new developments in the province.[74]

Burial of the Tripartite Agreement

Ministry-making with personnel acceptable to everybody was an easy task, as compared to fulfilment of the remaining part of the Saadulla–Chaudhuri–Bardoloi agreement. Particularly, the revision of the resolution of 16 January 1945 needed careful handling. The working committee of the CPI-controlled Assam Provincial Kisan Sabha met on 30 May at Gauhati, and appealed to all the concerned political parties for a compromise on this controversial issue. On the one hand, it recognized the prior right of the Assamese people to the local soil; on the other hand, it also supported the demand of the landless Bengali

---

Bardoloi's letter to Gandhiji, 14 March 1945, in Bardoloi, *Gandhiji*, and speeches by Saadulla and Bardoloi, 22 March, *ALAP* (1945), pp. 780–82.

[71] *APCC Papers*, Packet No. 43, 'Leaders correspondence'; *IAR* (January–June 1945), Vol. 1, p. 213.

[72] *Assam Tribune*, 30 March 1945.

[73] *People's War*, 8 April 1945.

[74] Tayyebulla, *Between the Symbol and the Idol*, pp. 158–60.

peasants for settlement on Assam's surplus waste lands after a proper survey.[75]

Due to the intricacies of the situation and various obstacles put forward by the League, the cabinet dared not adopt a new resolution on the subject until 18 June; even this was not published until 13 July 1945. Thus, it was only about four months after the signing of the agreement that the new land settlement policy was officially announced. A landless family was now re-defined as one possessing less than 20 *bighas* of land. All grazing reserves were to be maintained intact and all encroachers were to be indiscriminately evicted therefrom, as a matter of policy. In short, the principles agreed upon in the December conference were, in all respects, fully restored.[76]

The new government's halting and half-hearted action in fully implementing the agreement provided Bardoloi with a plea to wriggle out of the marriage of convenience – an arrangement already under heavy fire from his critics in the APCC as unwise and unprincipled. On 10 July 1945, he wrote to Abul Kalam Azad, the national Congress president, giving him a detailed report of the Assam situation. He also privately wrote to Saadulla on 13 July, charging him with deliberate procrastination in implementing the agreement *in toto*. The contents of the last-mentioned letter leaked out to the press. Since he was out of station, Saadulla presumably received it only after his return from Simla on 19 July. Rajendra Prasad wrote on 21 July to the APCC president, Tayyebulla, that his complaint about the unprincipled tripartite deal was receiving Azad's attention and that it might be taken up at the next Working Committee meeting. Azad advised Bardoloi to carry on the negotiations with Saadulla, and to allow the latter a few weeks' time so that 'our attitude may remain straightforward and unambiguous' until the Congress Working Committee decided on the next step.[77]

If Bardoloi was working under constraints from above, so was Saadulla. The Central Parliamentary Board of the Muslim League frowned upon the resolution of 18 June and advised its modification. Accordingly, on 28 July, Saadulla apprised R.K. Chaudhuri, the Land Revenue Minister, of the suggested modification. The crux of the proposed amendment was that immigrants who had already sown at least one crop should also be entitled to land settlement, irrespective of their arrival date in the Brahmaputra Valley or the legality of their squatting on grazing reserves. Chaudhuri handed this letter of 28 July to the APCC leaders.[78]

Caught on the horns of a dilemma, Saadulla could do very little to

---

[75] Biresh Misra's despatch in *People's War*, 15 July 1945 and *Assam Tribune*, 8 June 1945.

[76] *Assam Tribune*, 27 July 1945.

[77] For reference to Rajendra Prasad, see Tayyebulla, *Karagarar Cithi*, p. 366. Azad to Bardoloi, 22 July 1945 and Bardoloi to Saadulla, 21 August 1945, in *APCC Papers*, Packet No. 43, 'Leaders' correspondence'.

[78] Saadulla to Chaudhuri, 28 July 1945, ibid.

The rift between Saadulla and Bhasani over the land settlement issue had divided the provincial League into two warring factions in 1945. Two all-India League leaders – Chowdhry Khaliquzzaman and Liaquat Ali – came to Shillong in mid-May 1945 to patch up the quarrel. But it was never patched up. Bhasani worked up sentiments over the eviction question and cornered Saadulla. *People's War*, 15 July 1945.

improve the worsening relations. In vain did he stress that Assam was the first province to lift the ban on the Congress and that the new ministry had already released 70 security prisoners, retaining only thirteen. Denying the charge of non-implementation of the terms of the agreement, he bitterly wrote to Bardoloi on 2 August: 'You are welcome to take whatever course your conscience dictates. I know you are not a free agent.'[79] The Congress coalition party and the Independent Muslim Party thereafter held a joint meeting on 14–15 August, which was attended by twenty-four members besides Bardoloi himself. The suggestions from the Muslim League quarters regarding further modification of the land policy were discussed and rejected. Finally, the joint meeting authorized Bardoloi to protest, on their behalf, against the non-implementation of the agreement. Bardoloi accordingly wrote to Saadulla on 21 August.[80]

Thus 'the new era in Assam' came to an end. The superannuated Assam legislature was dissolved on 1 October 1945, while the fifth and last Saadulla ministry was to continue until the general election in the second week of February 1946.

War and the Working Class
The Burden of the War
Inflation and mounting corruption in the administration made the people all the more indignant towards the Raj for dragging them into England's war with its enemies. All civil liberties vanished under the severe war-time emergency measures. While the Congress leaders were either behind prison bars or under internment orders, the communal parties used every opportunity to strengthen their bases. The CPI also tried its best to win over the nationalist masses, but its success was limited. This was because of its post-1941 reluctance to take such popular actions as were likely to hamper the war efforts. The war definitely brought a setback to the workers' and peasants' class struggles that were at their peak in 1939 and early 1940.

The entire plantation economy, controlled as it was by the Indian Tea Association, was tied to the wheels of the chariot of war. With the fall of Java and Sumatra in March 1942, India and Ceylon remained the sole sources of tea supply to the markets in the UK and Allied countries. The UK government emerged as the sole foreign purchaser and distributor of Indian tea. Under its bulk purchase scheme, the entire tea production was brought under a strict monopolistic control to ensure that producers did not gain at the cost of British consumers.

---

[79] Saadulla to Bardoloi, 2 August 1945, File containing 'Leaders' correspondence', *APCC Papers*, Packet No. 43.

[80] Proceedings of the meeting and Bardoloi's letter to Saadulla, 21 August 1945, ibid. The APCC met at Nowgong after forty-two momentous months, but did not discuss the tripartite deal, although its Working Committee had, the day before, approved of Tayyebulla's stand on the issue. His memoirs indicate some confusion over the dates of these meetings. See Tayyebulla, *Between the Symbol and the Idol*, pp. 159–60 and *Karagarar Cithi*, p. 367.

Even under this system, the tea companies of Assam – of whom British companies owned 84 per cent of the acreage – made 'satisfactory' profits. At the same time, they yielded a high tax revenue to the government. The Indian Tea Association also provided thousands of labourers from its own work force, and under its own supervisors, to build strategic roads and airstrips all over Assam.[81] British planters even served as members of the auxiliary volunteer corps. With their local knowledge of the country and their command over a big labour force, they were very useful to the army.

Trade Union Activities

Only one of the several plantation workers' trade unions established in the 1930s, the Sylhet–Cachar Cha-Bagan Mazdoor Union, continued to function through the war years. Its activities, however, had to be carried on stealthily. There is evidence that the Chhotanagpur Association, a labour organization founded by Professor P.M. Surwan, a Munda Christian, was functioning in April 1938. But the bishop of Assam ordered missionaries to disassociate from it. At one of its meetings, the Association advised labourers not to be misled into strikes.[82] It was also not heard of during the war years. To forestall the advance of communists in the plantations, five individual plantation labour unions, and an Assam Tea Labourers' Federation affiliating them, were formed in Sibsagar in May 1945 through the efforts of P.M. Surwan.[83] An enlightened member of the depressed community of plantation coolies and ex-coolies, Surwan strived for the welfare of his community in alliance with the British planters. At the end of the war, the Indian Tea Association laid down the conditions under which trade unions could be recognized: the office staff and the labour were not to belong to one and the same union, and one-third of the relevant labour force had to be paying members. Besides, in no case was it to be directly or indirectly affiliated to the CPI.[84]

While touring Assam in 1945, the Rege Committee noticed that 'there was virtually no improvement in such important matters as cash wages, real freedom of movement and association, education and organization of work' during the war years. In the area of hard-earned repatriation rights, the planta-

---

[81] H.A. Antrobus, *A History of the Assam Company 1839–1953* (Edinburgh, 1957), pp. 225–32. For the British share of the tea acreage, see P.C. Goswami, *The Economic Development of Assam* (Bombay, 1963), table on p. 149.

[82] Home (Pol.) File No. 18/4/38 Pol., D.O. No. 260-C.B., Fortnightly report for Assam, first half, April 1938.

[83] Labour Investigation Committee (Chairman: D.V. Rege), Government of India, *Report on an Enquiry into Conditions of Labour in Plantations in India* (Delhi, 1946), pp. 71–72.

[84] Percival Griffiths, *The History of the Indian Tea Industry* (London, 1967), p. 391.

The ITA Circular Letter No. 6868 dated 23 June 1948, cited in the ITA *Labour Manual* for tea garden managers in Assam, reiterated: 'It is the accepted policy of the Indian Tea Association to refuse to have any dealings with Unions organized by the CPI or bodies connected therewith.'

tion workers had suffered a setback.[85] Practically no plantation strike took place in 1942. During the three years from 1943 to 1945, altogether no more than five spontaneous such strikes appear to have taken place.[86] In the industrial field as a whole, there were only five work stoppages in 1945, involving 1,988 workers and a loss of only 2,208 man-days.[87] Thereafter, the situation began to change.

The third annual conference of the Assam Railways and Trading Company Labour Union was held in March 1942 at Dibrugarh, with Jadunath Saikia in the chair. Nilamoni Barthakur was arrested on the spot for his violation of the internment order served on him a few months earlier. Later the same year he was released and externed from Upper Assam. A conference of the trade unions of Assam was held also at Dibrugarh on 28 November 1943. On the one hand, it called on workers to boost war efforts through increased production; on the other, it urged the government to release national leaders. The progress of trade unionism was bound to be slow with a pro-war policy, although such a policy did help the early communists to circumvent the lack of civil liberties. The transfer of a bunch of class-conscious workers – mostly Bengalis – from Chittagong to Assam's railway workshops around 1942, helped the Bengal and Assam Railroad Workers' Union to expand in the province in a big way. By the end of the war, it had bases all along Assam's 1,300 miles of railway tracks. It held its fourth annual conference at Lumding on 6–8 December 1946. The provincial branch of the All India Trade Union Congress (AITUC), the only centrally organized labour body till then, held its annual conference at Gauhati on 26–27 May 1945.[88]

The CPI wanted to contest all the four tea labour seats in Assam with the necessary Congress support, or at least connivance, which was not forthcoming. Finally, it contested three labour seats on its own strength and was miserably defeated. It also contested and lost three general seats.[89]

While exposing the weakness of the CPI vis-à-vis the nationalist upsurge under the Congress flag, the 1946 polls also facilitated its limited entry into the otherwise forbidden plantation settlements. In several tea gardens of Upper Assam, like Mikirpur, Hatipati and Barbari, trade unions were formed. Railwaymen,

---

[85] *Report on an Enquiry into Conditions of Labour in Plantations in India*, p. 70.

[86] Griffiths, *History of the Indian Tea Industry*, p. 385.

[87] *The Indian Labour Year Book 1947–48* (Government of India), p. 118. The figures covered disputes involving ten or more workers for any duration in mines and factory establishments. It is not clear whether the coverage of these figures also included the non-factory workers of tea gardens.

[88] *Assam Tribune*, 3 December 1943 and ibid., 1 June 1945. *People's War*, 9 January 1944. The next conference of the APTUC was held at Dibrugarh on 14–15 December 1946.

[89] The party received not more than 21,000 votes in all. It did fairly well in the contest for a rural seat in Cachar, where its candidate, Irawat Singh (1896–1951), received 13,357 votes as against 17,340 cast for the Congress candidate. *People's Age*, 12 May 1946 and also its election supplement, 17 February 1946. Singh was the founder of the State People's Congress movement in Manipur. He turned a communist while in Sylhet jail for three years till 1943. After his release, he worked for some time in Cachar among the local Manipur peasantry.

who had served a strike notice in June 1946, fraternized with the tea garden workers and helped them organize. Labour meetings were also held in other tea gardens like Myzan and Duklingia. The CPI popularized such demands as old age pension, rations for children, supply of cheap cloth, minimum daily wage of Rs 1.25 and dearness allowance of Rs 25 per month, etc., in some of the tea gardens. These developments led to the formation of the Assam Cha-Bagan Mazdur Union with Gaurishankar Bhattacharya (1915–2002) as president and Mani Bhoumik as general secretary in mid-1946; the union was registered in due course, with its headquarters at Tinsukia. About 900 workers of the Suntak Tea Estate, belonging to the Assam Company, went on a lightning strike on 16 September 1946 for such wage-related demands as already mentioned.[90] Under a strike threat, the management of the Barbari Tea Estate yielded to some of the workers' demands. Later it turned for cooperation to the Indian National Trade Union Congress (INTUC) to confront the red flag.[91]

INTUC Leaps into Prominence

Congress victory in the labour constituencies in the 1946 polls brought home to the APCC the need for regular political and welfare work among the workers, particularly those of the plantations. A Congress labour cell was formed, with R. Kakati and B.C. Bhagavati as its leading members, to pursue the matter. According to a police intelligence report for the week ending 8 January 1947, continual efforts were being made by Congressmen in the district of Lakhimpur to gain a foothold among the workers of some tea gardens and the steamer *ghats*. The Congress labour cell made considerable progress in its work. It decided to form a trade union of the office employees of the plantations first, so that their influence could later be utilized to unionize the remaining categories of plantation labour. The Assam Chah Karmachari Sangha was accordingly formed on 9 February 1947 at a meeting held at Tinsukia, and was registered under the Trade Union Act on 21 April 1947. Its headquarters were set up at Dibrugarh. The formation of this powerful trade union, with B.C. Bhagawati as president, marked the beginning of a new phase of the labour movement in Assam.

The second Bardoloi ministry was keen on developing an understanding among labour, capital and the government, with a view to maintaining industrial peace in the province. R. Kakati of the INTUC and Bardoloi, Assam's Chief Minister, negotiated an agreement with the Indian Tea Association on 9 July 1947. The ITA agreed to allow free access in the tea gardens to only such INTUC

---

[90] In a confrontation that followed on 18 September, one of the strikers, Bankuru Saora, was fatally stabbed by the British manger and his Indian assistant fired to disperse the mob, injuring many. The police immediately arrested thirty-eight strikers but none from the management. The strike fizzled out thereafter.

[91] Griffiths, *History of the Indian Tea Industry*, p. 391; District Magistrate, Sibsagar to Chief Secretary, No. SJC. 27 34, Jorhat, 8 July 1947 on 'Congress Labour Union', Confidential B, Confidential Dept., File No. C. 233/47 (AS); Sanat Kumar Bose, *Capital and Labour in the Indian Tea Industry* (AITUC, Bombay, 1954), pp. 118–19.

organizers as were accredited by Kakati. INTUC, on its part, gave an assurance that its organizers would make speeches only for the purpose of legitimate trade union activities and not to upset existing labour–management relations. The Indian National Trade Union Congress was formed on 3 May 1947 and its Assam branch came into existence with K.P. Tripathi (b. 1910) as president on 3 September 1947.[92] Thus, by the time national independence dawned, INTUC had entered the plantations in a big way with the blessings of both the ITA and the government. What united them was their common interest in keeping the communists out. By November 1947, trade unions had been formed by INTUC organizers in about 200 tea gardens, and the spadework was extended to many more. Delegates from the tea garden primary units met in a provincial labour conference at Jorhat in the last week of December 1947,[93] where the Assam Chah Mazdoor Sangha was formed with M.N. Sarma and J.N. Bhuyan as joint secretaries.[94] It emerged, in due course, as the biggest trade union to be formed in the province.

With the restoration of civil liberties under the Bardoloi government, some old bases of the labour movement became active again after years of wartime suppression. The heretofore defunct Assam Oil Company Labour Union got itself registered once more under the Trade Union Act on 9 May 1947. It preferred not to seek affiliation to any central labour organization like AITUC or INTUC. The coal, timber and plantation workers of the Assam Railways and Trading Company were also once more unionized – at the initiative of RCPI activists. According to a police intelligence report of August 1947, they popularized the demand for a wage of Rs 85 per month in some tea gardens of Lakhimpur.[95] However, all the leftist efforts in the plantation labour field, even when taken together, paled into insignificance before the predominant position of the INTUC.

The number of registered trade unions in Assam increased from nine in 1944–45 to 19 in 1945–46 and 36 in 1946–47; and the corresponding membership from 2,486 to 3,680 and then to 13,518. These figures do not cover trade unions registered outside Assam as inter-provincial organizations. According to an unofficial source, there were no less than 16,000 unionized workers in Assam's

---

[92] G.C. Sarma, general secretary of the Assam Chah Karmachari Sangha, 'Trade union movement – a study of Assam Chah Karmachari Sangha', *The North Eastern Research Bulletin* (Dibrugarh), Vol. 5, Summer 1974, pp. 79–82; and 'Assam Police weekly intelligence report for the week ending 8th January 1947', typescript in the OEHFM, Gauhati.

[93] 'ITA Circular to Garden Managers, No. LD–600, dated Dibrugarh 21 July 1947', reproduced as Appendix 12. A version of the same circular and two letters – one from Ravindra Kakati, general secretary of Assam INTUC, dated Jorhat, 18 November 1947, to Labour Officer, Assam Branch, ITA, and another in reply from the latter – leaked out and were reproduced in two consecutive issues of *People's Age*, 13 June and 18 June 1948. About the government's role, G.C. Sarma writes: 'The Labour Department agreed to make a vehicle available on payment of Rs 44 a day.' Sarma, 'Trade union movement – a study of Assam Chah Karmachari Sangha', p. 81.

[94] Ibid.

[95] 'The fortnightly report for Assam for the first half of August 1947', typescript in the OEHFM, Gauhati.

forty-one registered and unregistered trade unions in December 1946. The number of work stoppages, as per official returns, increased from twenty-six in 1946 to 64 in 1947; the number of workers involved in these correspondingly increased from 9,137 to 24,021, and the loss of man-days from 35,673 to 78,541.[96] Thus, the year that saw the transfer of power also saw a mounting wave of industrial unrest in Assam.

The National Question and Peasants

A Divided Peasantry

The bulk of the peasants, who had no surplus to sell, suffered from the war-time increase in the cost of living. But, like the workers, they failed to organize themselves effectively for agitation from a class platform. What loomed large in their minds in the Brahmaputra Valley was the big question mark posed by the Line system. Was it to stay or go? The local peasants refused to accept an open society lest their separate cultural heritage was eroded through loss of their lands to the more enterprising immigrants. Already in their second and third generations, the immigrants, on the other hand, always welcomed further immigration. Line or no Line, they wanted an open and competitive but nevertheless electorally divided society. The national question in Assam obviously involved – and integrally so – the peasant question, which evolved around the land problem.[97]

Assamese nationalism (or sub-nationalism) was essentially the ideology of the small, unconsolidated Assamese middle class. It projected its cause as a national cause, and was successful in rallying peasants and various petty bourgeois elements under its banner. Almost entirely non-indigenous in origin, the working class of the Brahmaputra Valley was not, however, involved in this ideology. Competition with the immigrants for land and jobs supplied fuel to the fire of regional chauvinism. This was because the Bengali bourgeoisie was believed to be getting the better of its Assamese counterpart. This 'Assamese nationalism' was both agrarian and linguistic in character, and it specifically raised the demand for Assam's administration by its own (Assamese) officials.[98]

---

[96] *The Indian Labour Year Book 1947–48*, pp. 108 and 118; ibid., *1946*, p. 116 and *People's Age*, 29 December 1946.

    Some of the trade unions which got themselves registered about this time are: Assam Chah Co.; Karkhana Mazdoor Sangha; Nazira (regd. on 5-8-47); Cachar Motor Drivers' Union, Silchar (regd. on 27-8-46); R.S.N. – I.G.N. Workers' Union (regd. on 12-9-46); Kamrup Mill Mazdoor Union, Gauhati (regd. on 14-8-47); and Gauhati Electric Supply Workers' Union (regd. on 14-8-46).

[97] 'The very question of self-existence of the Assamese people as a distinct and growing nationality now hinges on this problem and, naturally enough, the people of Assam are seriously perturbed with an intense desire for checking further immigration which has been the primary cause for complicating the question of land settlement.' 'Resolution on land settlement and eviction in Assam', *Assam Fights for Freedom and Democracy: Draft Resolutions of Assam Communists* (Assam Provincial Organizing Committee, CPI, Gauhati, n. d.), pp. 41–50.

[98] The 'Jatiya' movement, under Ambikagiri Raychaudhury's leadership, degenerated into a series of petty collisions, squabbles and fights over signboards. The Congress

Since the legislature had the power to retain or abolish the Line, parliamentary activities assumed increasing importance in the eyes of the middle class and the peasantry. The Congress leaders who mattered soon found that if they bypassed the legislature and the opportunities of ministry-making for the sake of mere principles, they would lose their mass following. In the same way, Saadulla, too, could not afford to lose the support of the Muslim peasants by denying land to newcomers, even if he had a mind to do so.

Through its communal electorates, the constitution of 1935 helped maintain the segregation of the two communities. The peasants, so divided, failed to thrash out the issue on a common political platform. During the war years, the League in the Brahmaputra Valley managed to reach the Muslim peasant masses – mainly the immigrants – and its base expanded. In alliance with Assamese Muslim student leaders of lower middle-class and peasant origin, Bhasani was able to establish his grip over this organization. It was then that the leaders, with a more 'respectable' and sons-of-the-soil background, faced a growing challenge. Saadulla, Sayidur Rahman, Keramat Ali – they were all also government title-holders at some time or other.[99]

In this confused state of affairs, no agreed solution acceptable to the masses could or did emerge from any quarter – not even from the CPI, a majority of whose members then spoke Bengali, or from its associated mass organizations. The CPI failed to support in unequivocal terms the demand for a policy of waste lands settlement with the landless irrespective of their race, creed and language. It had to concede that the Assamese people should have the first right to such lands in their own homeland, and that the problem required a political solution. It did not, of course, fail to condemn the government violence in dealing with the immigrant encroachers and their forcible eviction. But such pragmatic gestures were hardly meaningful. The CPI tried its best to remain above petty and communal considerations, and sug-gested the following principles for acceptance by the Congress and the League: (i) stop immigration; (ii) postpone evictions pending working out of planned settlement; (iii) withdraw voluntarily from 'reserves' illegally encroached upon; (iv) recognize the right of self-determination for the people of Assam, and democratic and cultural rights to the minorities.[100]

Despite an organizational tour of the Brahmaputra Valley by Mansur Habibullah, joint secretary of the All-India Kisan Sabha, in mid-1942, the growth of Kisan Sabhas remained sluggish through the war years.[101] The first conference

---

and the CPI decried it and tried to raise it to a mass anti-imperialist struggle for regional autonomy in an independent federal India. For a general discussion of the problem in multinational states see J.V. Stalin, *Works*, Vol. 2: *1907–13* (Moscow, 1953), pp. 314–23.

[99] Interview with Md. Akram of Jorhat on 12 August 1974 at Assam House, Calcutta.

[100] See 'Resolution on land settlement and eviction in Assam'.

[101] *People's War*, 19 July 1942. The membership of the AIKS increased from 1,500 in 1944 to 7,900 in the Brahmaputra Valley in 1945, and from 8,000 to 16,000 in the Surma Valley. Ibid., 25 March 1945.

of the CPI-controlled Assam Provincial Kisan Sabha was held at Thekeragaon in Nowgong district in 1946. It talked of peasant unity and wanted Gandhi and Jinnah to come to terms, but could suggest no agreeable political solution other than mere patchwork. The growing demand for Pakistan and the grim prospect of a divided India heightened the Assamese people's nervous concern over their future political and cultural status. Unrestrained immigration from Bengal was increasingly viewed as a calculated move to turn Assam into a Muslim-majority province, so that it could qualify for inclusion into East Pakistan.

Revolt of the Nankars

In the Surma Valley, the prospects of an effective class organization on the basis of Hindu–Muslim unity was somewhat brighter, despite minor engineered communal clashes here and there. By 1945, a militant struggle for occupancy rights and for the abolition of certain feudal obligations developed among a class of serfs known as *nankars*, attached to the households of zamindars.[102]

Nankars were peasants settled on rent-free lands in lieu of obligatory personal service to their zamindars. The menfolk were obliged to take up lathis in defence of their respective masters' interests against rebellious tenants and rival zamindars, whenever so asked. The womenfolk had to perform miscellaneous domestic services in their masters' households and were often also used as concubines. Under the law, *nankars* had no right to the land they lived on and could be ejected at any time by their zamindars. The storm-centre of the movement was Lauta-Bahadurpur, where a prolonged class war was carried on between the zamindars and the *nankars*, involving clashes and casualties on both sides. This abominable system of serfdom was more deep-rooted among the Muslim zamindars than their Hindu counterparts. Also, a majority of the several thousand *nankars* were Muslims. Led by the Kisan Sabhas, they refused to serve their masters any longer and defended their lands against the landlords' private armies. Thus, in Sylhet, the CPI was able to build up a united platform of Hindu and Muslim peasants in certain pockets of their influence, against all provocations. Red flags in hand, Muslim *nankars* were even seen campaigning against Pakistan at the time of the Sylhet referendum in July 1947.

Post-War Electoral Politics

Freedom in Sight

After the Labour Party came to power in post-war Great Britain, its new Prime Minister, C.R. Attlee, announced on 19 September 1945 that a Cabinet Mission would go to India by end-March, to help Indians frame their own constitution. By that time, both the rulers and the ruled had the growing feeling that

---

[102] The following account is based on an interview with Jyotirmay Nandy in Calcutta on 3 August 1974, and Ajay Bhattacharya, *Nankar Vidroha*, Vol. 1 (in Bengali, Dacca, 1973). The *nankar* system was abolished by legislation in Sylhet by the Government of East Pakistan in 1950.

India could no longer be directly governed as a colony, and that its independence would come in a form determined primarily by the nature of the confrontation.

The provincial elections, therefore, were of crucial importance to the Congress and the Muslim League, since they both wanted to achieve their respective goals through constitutional means, if possible. In November 1945, R.K. Chaudhuri and A.K. Chanda were elected unopposed to the Central Legislative Assembly on Congress tickets.[103] The Muslim seat went to the League, as before.

The Congress high command took a keen interest in the Assam elections. Azad helped the Congress leaders of both the Valleys to bury their differences and agree to a joint parliamentary board for the province, although the nomination of Congress candidates for the Surma Valley was entrusted to the Bengal board.[104] Prabhudayal Himmatsingka, a prominent Marwari Congressman of Calcutta having business interests in Assam, apprised Sardar Patel in November of the hopeful election prospects there, despite poor collection of local election funds. Asking for an advance of Rs 3 lakh from the central fund, he wrote: 'I have advanced money for the present, and I shall arrange it with Shri B.M. Birla.'[105] Jawaharlal Nehru concluded his election tour of the Brahmaputra Valley on 18 December 1945.

APCC's Election Pledge on the National Question

In its widely publicized six-point election appeal, the APCC claimed that it was only after incessant Congress agitation that the British had agreed to allow an indirectly elected constituent assembly to frame India's constitution in accordance with its people's wishes. The appeal reminded the electorate of the Congress endeavours for redrawing provincial boundaries on the basis of language and culture, and it solicited votes particularly on that count.[106] It further implored:

> Unless the province of Assam be organized on the basis of the Assamese language and Assamese culture, the survival of the Assamese nationality and culture will become impossible. The inclusion of Bengali-speaking Sylhet and Cachar (plains portion) and the immigration or importation of lacs of Bengali settlers on wastelands has been threatening to destroy the distinctness of Assam and

---

[103] *Assam Tribune*, 9 November 1945.

[104] Azad to Patel, 19 October 1945, in Durga Das, ed., *Sardar Patel's Correspondence 1945–50*, Vol. 2 (Ahmedabad, 1972), p. 30.

[105] Copy of Himmatsingka's letter to Patel, 23 November 1945, found along with Bardoloi papers in the possession of Mrs Lily-Majindar-Barua, Gauhati. Also see Patel to Azad, 26 October 1945, in Das, ed., *Sardar Patel's Correspondence*, Vol. 2, p. 34. According to the Supdt. of Police, Tezpur, in the early 1940s 'the local businessmen (Marwaris) appear to be all Congress-minded' and 'all Marwaris are involved in the matter of financial help to the Congress'. Office of the Supdt. of Police, Tezpur, Confidential branch, Memo No. 1812–C/1/43, dated Tezpur, 1 June 1943, in Police Dept., Special Branch, File No. B-2 (1), 43, Shillong.

[106] Congress election leaflet (in Assamese) printed at the Jayanti Art Press by Jadunath Das and published by Hemkanta Barua and Harendranath Barua, joint secretaries, Publicity Dept., APCC, found in *APCC Papers*, Packet 43.

has, in practice, caused many disorders in its administration. For an appropriate solution and redress of this big problem, the Congress party should be installed as the majority party in the Assembly.[107]

Arithmetic of Votes

Needless to say, from such an election platform, the Congress could hardly look forward to winning the Muslim seats. Of the thirty-four Muslim seats, as many as thirty-one were bagged by the Muslim League, three by the Jamiat-ul-Ulema and none by the Congress. The Jamiat's success is explained by the influence of the Deoband school of Islamic theology and of Hussain Ahmad Madani (1879–1957) – the national leader of that school. Of the 2,72,871 Muslim votes polled in Assam, almost 69 per cent were in favour of the League. However, the Congress swept the general constituencies, securing 78 per cent of the votes therein. By taking up the national question in its provincial context as its main election platform, it was able to keep the Asam Jatiya Mahasabha completely out of electoral politics. Altogether the Congress got 3,56,797 votes in Assam. The second Assembly constituted under the Act of 1935 consisted of 58 Congress, nine British and seven independent members, besides others.[108] Both Baidyanath Mukherjee and Nichols–Roy came to the new house as Congress members and clients of Bardoloi. Thus there was a comfortable Congress majority for ministry formation.

Second Bardoloi Ministry

After the election victory, Bardoloi, the master tactician, had yet another battle to win before choosing his cabinet – this time within his own party. The canker of Valleyism had gone so deep in Assam that even ministry-making was not free from it. Azad came to Shillong to ensure that Valley and group feelings did not surge up any further. The function of a joint parliamentary board for advising the ministry was discussed with him. Azad first thought that the APCC itself was competent to advise the ministry on policy matters, leaving the latter free to carry on the day-to-day administration. But the Surma Valley was not constitutionally represented on the APCC. Since it, too, needed participation in policy-making, a joint standing committee for the purpose was agreed upon. It was to consist of ten members – three from the two Surma Valley District Congress Committees, four from the APCC, the secretary of the BPCC, the secretary of the APCC, and the leader of the Congress Assembly party of Assam. This was a unique arrangement indeed, the workability of which appeared doubtful even to optimists like Bardoloi and Patel.[109]

---

107 Ibid. We have translated 'Asamiya *jati*' as Assamese nationality (it could be 'race' as well) and '*pamua*' as settlers on wastelands. The latter term generally stands for Muslim settlers on the waste lands in the Brahmaputra Valley.

108 The Muslim League secured 1,88,011 votes and non-League Muslims 85,387 votes.

109 Bardoloi to Patel, 18 February 1946 and Patel to Bardoloi, 1 March 1946, in Das, ed., *Sardar Patel's Correspondence 1945–50*, Vol. 3 (Ahmedabad, 1972), pp. 194–97.

Azad was particularly keen on adopting a 'generous attitude' towards the Muslim League in the matter of ministry-making. In several of the Congress-majority provinces, he approached the League legislators and asked for their cooperation in this respect.[110] Patel did not like this coalition business; nevertheless, he was willing to be guided by Azad, the Congress president, in this delicate matter.[111] According to Azad, the Muslim League legislators in Bihar, Punjab and Assam would have been glad to come in but for Jinnah's disapproval.[112]

Having recently burnt his fingers over a proposed Congress-supported coalition ministry in Assam, Bardoloi was cautious. Though, in his heart of hearts, he wanted a coalition once more, he stood publicly committed to forming a government on strict party lines. Azad came to his rescue. He told the Assam Congress Assembly party that the League's active cooperation should be solicited in order to undermine the latter's 'morale' while boosting that of the Congress. This advice emboldened Bardoloi. While forming his ministry on 11 February 1946, he included in it only one Muslim minister from the Jamiat-ul-Ulema and kept two cabinet posts – also meant for Muslims – vacant as a bait for Saadulla, who was requested to recommend his party men for the same.[113] The League, of course, turned a deaf ear to the proposal, although the posts remained long vacant.

The second Bardoloi cabinet (1946–50) had altogether seven members to begin with – three from each Valley and Rev. Nichols–Roy from Shillong. B.R. Medhi was made the Finance and Revenue Minister, while B.K. Das, the former Speaker, was given the Home portfolio. Debeswar Sharma was elected the Speaker. Having put the cabinet on an even keel, Azad wrote to Patel on 15 February: 'I have found that the whole province was satisfied and happy over it.'[114] By July the president and secretary of the Assam Plains Tribal League accepted the principle of joint electorates with reservation of seats, and joined the Congress Assembly party. So did Abdur Rashid by early September. Bhimbar Deuri, the Tribal League leader, and Abdur Rashid were both taken into the ministry.[115] But the events that followed soon proved that there was no basis for Azad's complacency. Valleyism assumed its ugliest form in the context of the partition of the country.

[110] Abul Kalam Azad, *India Wins Freedom: An Autobiographical Narrative* (Calcutta, 1959), pp. 127–28.

[111] Patel to Bardoloi, 1 March 1946, in Das, ed., *Sardar Patel's Correspondence*, Vol. 3, pp. 194–97.

[112] Azad, *India Wins Freedom*, pp. 127–28.

[113] Bardoloi to Patel, 18 February 1946 and Azad to Patel, 15 February 1946, in Das, ed., *Sardar Patel's Correspondence*, Vol. 3, pp. 193–96. Also see S. Chaliha, 'Barak banam Brahmaputra', *Saptahik Niilacal*, 20 December 1972 (serialized).

[114] Azad to Patel, 15 February 1946, in Das, ed., *Sardar Patel's Correspondence*, Vol. 3, pp. 193–94.

[115] Telegram from Fakhruddin Ali Ahmed to Patel and Patel's telegram in reply, both dated 8 September 1946, in Das, ed., *Sardar Patel's Correspondence*, Vol. 3, pp. 198–99.

CHAPTER EIGHT
Final Bid for Power

Anti-Imperialist Upsurge: 1945–46

The war years, particularly those following the movement of 1942, slackened Gandhiji's grip on a politically awakened India. Large sections of Indian nationalists became increasingly aware that, for the final bid for power, the Gandhian method would not do. The road to freedom trodden by other nations, as illustrated in history, appeared to be relevant even in the Indian context.[1] The new mood, deriving inspiration also from Bose's exploits abroad, found expression in the post-war national upsurge, in comparison with which all previous movements appeared insignificant. Assam, too, shared this new mood in a modest way, although the local Congress leaders were still very much under the spell of Gandhiji's influence.

'Release the INA' Campaign

The public trial of some Indian National Army (INA) officers as war prisoners in Delhi in November–December 1945 rocked the country from one end to the other. Everywhere – Assam included – demonstrations were held to demand their unconditional release and rehabilitation as national heroes. On 21–22 November 1945, and again on 12–14 February 1946, even after the British cabinet's decision on 22 January to send its mission soon to India to negotiate the transfer of power, troops had to be called out. Scores of people were shot to suppress an anti-British upheaval and barricade resistance in curfew-bound

---

[1] Tarachand, *History of the Freedom Movement in India*, Vol. 4 (New Delhi, 1972), p. 398.

Tayyebulla reflected on the attitude of some of the Congress leaders who were with him in the same jail, as follows: 'The story of Subhas Bose's unfurling the "Flag of Independence" somewhere near Imphal, and of his appointing a "governor" of Assam under his "Liberation Government" . . . made that confusion worst confounded! "To fight for liberty at any cost!" One esteemed comrade and co-prisoner, during the talks, even ironically asserted: "This time we have not registered any document in favour of the old man, Gandhi"! Another exclaimed: "Non-violence when possible, violence when necessary!"' M. Tayyebulla, *Between the Symbol and the Idol at Last* (Bombay, 1964), p. 124.

Calcutta. *Hartals* and demonstrations to protest against the massacre were held in Assam, Bengal and other provinces. A distinguishing feature of this anti-imperialist upsurge was the growth of a popular initiative. Students, office employees, workers and slum-dwellers – Hindus and Muslims – unitedly moved into action with Congress, League and communist flags in their hands.[2]

Discontent Spreads to Armed Forces

The year 1946 witnessed quite a few mutinies and acts of defiance in the armed forces. Reduction in ration scales, low pay, fraternal concern over the fate of the INA prisoners, uncertainty about their own release conditions and, above all, racial discrimination in favour of Britons – all these were factors that contributed to the growing discontent. Peaceful hunger strikes and work stoppages by defence personnel found their way as news to the press, and had a cumulative effect in the context of the wide sympathy for the INA prisoners. The Royal Indian Navy (RIN) revolt at Bombay and Karachi in February 1946 took a distinctly political turn.[3] The flags of the Congress Party, the Muslim League and the Communist Party – all together – were unfurled on some ships' masts, and there was large-scale fraternization between the sailors and citizens.[4]

When battle-ready British troops took up their positions and threatened the use of overwhelming force 'even if it meant the destruction of the navy', the Bombay working class declared a total strike and *hartal* on 22 February, and barricaded the streets to resist the army patrols and the police. All ships of the RIN excepting ten and all except two of its shore establishments were involved, one after another, in a hunger strike and work stoppage movement that affected some 20,000 naval ratings. The affected stations were Bombay, Karachi, Jamnagar, Madras, Vizagapatam, Cochin and the Andamans. The duration of the mutiny in these places ranged from one day to a week, between 18 and 24 February 1946. A majority of the ratings, concentrated at Bombay and Karachi, were also involved in an open armed revolt, coordinated by the Central Naval Strike Committee.[5] The uprising was drowned in blood, with an officially estimated toll of more than 250 citizens and ten navy men killed, and hundreds wounded, in three fateful days. Congress and League leaders, with whom the ratings had established contact, refused to ride the crest of the upsurge in support of the rebels. On the contrary, they advised the ratings to surrender. This followed on 23 February.

---

[2] Gautam Chattopadhyay, 'The Almost Revolution: India in February 1946', *Indian Left Review*, 3 (April 1974), pp. 33–46. *Amrita Bazar Patrika* (Calcutta), 12–19 February 1946, and official documents cited by Chattopadhyay, ibid.

[3] V. Longer, *Red Coats to Olive Green: A History of the Indian Army 1600–1974* (Bombay, 1974), pp. 247–49; *Summary of the Report of the Commission of Enquiry into the RIN Mutiny*, February 1946 (Government of India Press, New Delhi, 1946), Chapters III and IV.

[4] R. Palme Dutt, *India Today* (second Indian edition, Calcutta, 1970), pp. 579–85.

[5] The quote is from Admiral Godfrey's ultimatum, broadcast on 21 February, cited ibid., pp. 580–81.

The communists and various Left parties came forward to support the struggle, but they were yet too weak to inspire confidence.[6]

The historic uprising, as R.P. Dutt has pointed out, 'laid bare in a flash all the maturing forces of the Indian revolution' – their points of strength as well as weakness.[7] Even after their surrender, open outbursts of discontent persisted. There were fresh acts of defiance in the air force and the army – in Calcutta and Jubbalpore, on 27 and 28 February, respectively.[8] Factory workers, office employees, students and even policemen, in their thousands, were caught in a wave of strikes, *hartals* and demonstrations. In Assam, preparations for the all-India railway strike, which was to start with effect from 27 June 1946, became a rallying point of all anti-imperialist political forces. The Railway Board had to concede almost all the demands to avoid the strike. Anti-feudal peasant struggles that broke out in Telengana, Kerala, Bengal and many other regions inspired the share-croppers' struggles in Kamrup and Cachar. On 29 July 1946, there was an inter-provincial general strike in support of the striking post and telegraph workers.

This post-war upsurge from November 1945 to July 1946 assumed an all-India dimension. Solidarity actions in the wake of all these events of national importance were organized by various student organizations and workers' trade unions in Shillong, Gauhati, Tezpur and other towns.[9] It was in course of such political activities that the Communist Party of India (CPI) in Assam was able to restore its patriotic image that had been damaged after 1942, following its pro-war stand. In course of a month-long tour of the Brahmaputra Valley in 1945, the Surma Valley Cultural Squad, sponsored by the Sylhet and Shillong branches of the Indian People's Theatre Association (IPTA), laid the foundations of a patriotic and revolutionary cultural movement that kept pace with the post-war upsurge. Jyotiprasad Agarwala, by then a disillusioned Congressman, was elected president and Hemanga Biswas general secretary of the provincial branch of the IPTA, at its first conference at Silchar on 3–4 May 1947.

Enter Cabinet Mission

If the national scene had its credit side during the stormy months from February to July, it had its debit side, too. The British Cabinet Mission's negotiations with national leaders in March–June 1946, and the Congress and League leaders' squabbles over its offer of transfer of power to Indian hands, vitiated the atmosphere. Failing to arrive at a scheme approved by all parties, the Mission declared itself in favour of a three-tier federal government with only three

---

6 Ibid., pp. 578–85; *Summary of the Report of the Commission of Enquiry into the RIN Mutiny*, Chapter IV; Chattopadhyay, 'The Almost Revolution', pp. 41–46.

7 Dutt, *India Today*, p. 579.

8 Longer, *Red Coats to Olive Green*, p. 250 and Chattopadhyay, 'The Almost Revolution', p. 43.

9 Prafulla Misra, 'Communist Movement in Assam', *North-Eastern Affairs*, 1 (July–September 1972), p. 32. Interviews.

subjects – defence, foreign affairs and communications – vested in the centre, and all residuary powers in the existing provinces, to be grouped into three zones. It also recommended an interim national government to start with, pending the final arrangements. What was a novel feature in the plan was that the groups might have, if they so wished, legislatures and executives forming an intermediate layer of government between those in the provinces and the Union. This provision was there to secure the advantage of a Pakistan for Muslims without the troubles of a partitioned India.[10]

The offer satisfied nobody. The British were now in the role of a mediator in the power struggle between Indians and Indians. The League refused to participate in the proposed interim government. Its Direct Action Day, observed in protest on 16 August, brought in its wake the Calcutta killing, in which hundreds of lives were lost and properties reduced to ruins. The month of August saw a sudden and swift turn of the national situation for the worse. Soon the Noakhali, Bihar and, later, Punjab riots followed. The communal harmony that had been developing during the months November to July at the grass-roots level was now reversed, and the people were led to a communal frenzy. In Assam, although communal riots could be kept at a safe distance, a big question mark loomed large in the minds of the people. What would happen to Assam's autonomy if the Cabinet Mission Plan was accepted?

Assam in the Cabinet Mission Plan
CPI Memorandum

In a memorandum to the Cabinet Mission, the CPI emphasized its stand for an undivided, federal India. At the same time, it suggested that the proposed interim government be entrusted with the task of setting up a boundary commission to re-draw the boundaries on the basis of the natural ancient homelands of every people. This would enable the re-demarcated provinces to develop into linguistically and culturally homogeneous national units such as Sind, western Punjab, Baluchistan etc.[11] 'The people of each such unit should have the unfettered right of self-determination, that is, the right to decide freely whether they join the Indian Union or form a separate sovereign state or another Indian Union.'[12]

The CPI's stand was perfectly in tune with popular aspirations, and it vindicated J.V. Stalin's ideological formulation in 1912 that India was still a melting pot of several growing nationalities.[13] It also appeared to be the most pragmatic solution of the divisive question, in the given context. In Assam this line had a popular appeal, and it soon emerged there as an acceptable proposition to a major section of the people who were opposed to the grouping plan.

---

[10] Broadcast by Pethick-Lawrence, Secretary of State for India, New Delhi, 16 May 1946, quoted by Tayyebulla, *Between the Symbol and the Idol*, p. 171.

[11] CPI memorandum of 15 April, quoted in *Indian Annual Register* (hereafter *IAR*) (January–June 1946), Vol. 1, pp. 220–21.

[12] Ibid.

[13] J.V. Stalin, as cited by Dutt, *India Today*, p. 473.

Anti-Grouping Agitation

Under the Cabinet Mission Plan, the representatives of the provinces were to divide themselves into three sections – A, B and C, after a preliminary session of the proposed Constituent Assembly was over. Section C was to consist of Bengal and Assam. Each section was to decide its own provincial and group matters. A province was free to opt out of its allotted section only after the first elections under the new constitution were over. The Constituent Assembly members supposed to sit in Section C were going to be almost evenly balanced, as shown below:

Composition of Sections under Cabinet Mission Plan

	General	Muslim	Total
Bengal	27	33	60
Assam	7	3	10
Total	34	36	70

The Congress had earlier expressed itself against compelling a province to join a particular section against its will. But, under the Plan, the provinces were to come into their respective sections automatically. As this involved infringement of the basic principle of provincial autonomy, Assam was quick to react, and sharply.

As soon as the Cabinet Mission's White Paper of 16 May 1946 was announced, the Assam Provincial Congress Committee (APCC) president consulted his Working Committee and telegraphically apprised the Congress high command of Assam's resentment against the grouping clauses. Chief Minister Bardoloi, who was then in New Delhi, placed before the Working Committee of the All India Congress Committee (AICC) a memorandum to the same effect on 19 May. In June, a nine-member Congress delegation from Assam met the Working Committee, then in session at New Delhi, and presented yet another memorandum. The Congress leaders found a saving clause in paragraph 15 of the Cabinet Mission's statement, which could be construed as suggesting inherent freedom on the part of a province to join or not join a section. They therefore advised that, even if the Plan was accepted by the Congress, the Assam legislature could, by a mandatory resolution, direct its representatives to the Constituent Assembly to shun the section it was supposed to join.[14] Throughout May, June and July, hundreds of meetings were held all over Assam to record vehement protest against the grouping clauses. Resolutions to that effect were forwarded to national and government leaders, as well as to the press.[15]

At the instance of the Congress Party, the Assam Legislative Assembly passed the historic, mandatory resolution of 16 July 1946, by which it was

---

[14] Tayyebulla, *Between the Symbol and the Idol*, pp. 175–82.

[15] Assam Governor's Secretariat, Military Secretary's Office, Home Department, Misc. Branch, File No. HMI 67/46 (Assam Secretariat Files; hereafter AS).

resolved that the provincial constitution could be framed only by Assam's own representatives to the Constituent Assembly, and that it would be detrimental to the province's interests if they joined others in a section for that purpose. The original suggestion to do so had come from Nehru and Patel, when an APCC delegation met them at Delhi on 8 and 9 June, respectively.[16]

In its operative part, the resolution directed all the ten representatives of the province to sit in the Constituent Assembly only for purposes of framing the Union Constitution, and to sit in an exclusive meeting or meetings attended by themselves alone to frame the provincial constitution. When the resolution was moved, the League members refused, after recording their protest, to take part in further deliberations and voting. They nevertheless participated in the election to the Constituent Assembly. Under the system of proportional representation with single transferable votes for the purpose, seven Congressmen and three Leaguers were elected.[17]

On 10 August, the Working Committee of the AICC accepted the Cabinet Mission Plan and proposed to proceed with the Constituent Assembly.[18] The League was also initially committed to the Plan. But meanwhile, because of the Assam legislature's mandate, the situation changed. 'This clearly repudiated one of the fundamental terms of the statement of 16th May', said Jinnah in course of an angry statement on 12 August, 'and this is an instance how the majority acted although it is highly doubtful whether the Assam Assembly was competent to give such a mandate to the representatives of the Constituent Assembly.'[19]

In Jinnah's view, the 'groups' were an essential part of the Cabinet Mission Plan. The provision that it could later opt out was sufficient protection for any province that did not wish to belong to the group. The Assam Congress leaders, on the other hand, held that a province could stay out from the very beginning and frame its own constitution independently. The Cabinet Mission confirmed Jinnah's interpretation.[20]

At this stage, Wavell, the Viceroy, decided to go ahead with the formation of the interim government, even before the League could be committed to it. When the interim government, led by Nehru, was formed on 2 September, some berths were kept vacant for the League. The League joined the government on 25 October, but boycotted the Constituent Assembly that was summoned on 9 December.[21]

The stalemate in the situation led to an increasing outburst of communal

---

[16] A.C. Bhuyan and S. De, eds, *Political History of Assam,* Vol. III: 1940–47 (Government of Assam, Gauhati, 1980) pp. 360–61 and 366.

[17] *Assam Legislative Assembly Proceedings* (hereafter *ALAP*) (1946), pp. 785–801.

[18] Tayyebulla, *Between the Symbol and the Idol,* p. 187.

[19] Jinnah's statement on Congress Resolution, Bombay, 12 August 1946, reproduced in J.S. Sharma, *India's Struggle for Freedom: Select Documents and Sources,* Vol. 3, (Delhi, 1965), p. 1059.

[20] A.K. Azad, *India Wins Freedom: An Autobiographical Narrative* (Calcutta, 1959), pp. 173–74.

[21] Tarachand, *History of the Freedom Movement,* pp. 484–90.

feelings that threatened the very fabric of day-to-day administration in many parts of the country. At this critical stage, the British government came out with its statement of 6 December upholding the interpretation that sectional decisions, in the absence of any agreement to the contrary, should be taken by a simple majority vote of representatives in the respective sections. But, should the Constituent Assembly desire that this fundamental point be referred for a decision to the Federal Court, such reference might be made at a very early date. This position appeared to be acceptable to Jinnah.[22] Among the Congress leaders, Nehru and Azad were also conciliatory. According to Azad, Assam's fears were unjustified and 'there was much force in Mr Jinnah's contention'.[23] The Congress was officially committed to the position that differences between the Congress and the League could be resolved, if necessary, through the mediation of the Federal Court.

Congress Discomposure

Meanwhile Assam was rocked by another spell of protests. In no circumstances was the APCC agreeable to accept the grouping as a given fact or the Federal Court as a mediator in the matter. It rushed a delegation to New Delhi to pressurize its high command in rejecting the British government's statement of 6 December. Nehru and Azad tried hard to soften the attitude of the Assam delegation but they listened to neither, since Gandhiji had already thrown his weight on their side.[24] When Bardoloi's emissaries consulted Gandhiji at Srirampur on 15 December, he reiterated: I told Bardoloi that if there is no clear guidance from the Congress Working Committee, Assam should not go into the Sections. It should lodge its protest and retire from the Constituent Assembly. It will be a kind of Satyagraha against the Congress for the good of the Congress.[25] Accordingly, Bardoloi took a bold stand and informed Nehru, the Congress president, that Assam would stand by Gandhiji's advice of 'framing our own constitution, and grouping accordingly'.[26] A Congress delegation from Assam again met the Congress Working Committee and Gandhiji at Delhi on 4 January 1947.

The AICC met in a plenary session in the first week of January 1947 to review the situation. It was eager to proceed with the Constituent Assembly and was in no mood to retrace its steps. However, in the face of the apprehensions of the Sikhs and Assamese non-Muslims, its acceptance of the British statement of 6 December was qualified with many reservations. It resolved to advise action 'in accordance with the interpretation of the British Government in regard to the procedure to be followed in the Sections'. Acceptance of the Federal Court as a

<hr>

[22] P. Moon, ed., *Wavell the Viceroy's Journal* (London, 1973), pp. 393–94.

[23] Azad, *India Wins Freedom*, pp. 172–74.

[24] Ibid., p. 172.

[25] Verbatim report, signed and circulated by Nirmal Kumar Basu, 15 December 1946, *AICC Files*, File No. 71, 1946–47 (confidential Government of India) (Nehru Memorial Museum and Library; hereafter NMML).

[26] Ibid.

mediator was also reiterated, but with a new rider that there should be prior agreement among the parties concerned to abide by its decision. The resolution also made it clear that, in the event of any attempt at compelling a province to go against its wishes or at jeopardizing the rights of the Sikhs in Punjab,

> a province or part of a province has the right to take such action as may be deemed necessary in order to give effect to the wishes of the people concerned . . . the A.I.C.C. therefore directs the Working Committee to advise upon it (the future course of action) whenever circumstances so require, keeping in view the basic principle of provincial autonomy.[27]

The original draft had underwent substantial revision at the instance of the Assam members; yet, when the resolution was moved by Nehru, it failed to remove their fears. Of Assam's eight members present at the crucial AICC meeting, Tayyebulla alone voted for the resolution. As the news reached the Assam public, they angrily disapproved the resolution and his stand on it.[28]

The Congress–Socialists and Communists also played a significant role in spearheading the open anti-grouping agitation that seized the people. The Assam Provincial Organizing Committee of the CPI called the AICC resolution a death-blow to Assam's birthright to decide her own constitution, and her relations with Bengal and other provinces. It called upon the Assamese people and 'their mighty Congress Organization' to break away from the compromising policy of the leadership. It expected that 'the Assam Ministry and the Legislatures shall be fully utilized in a revolutionary manner to aid and support the patriotic resistance of Assam'.[29] In a press statement, Tayebulla however argued that acceptance of the resolution was in no way going to affect Assam's stand. Finding Congressmen still clinging to Gandhiji's advice from Srirampur, Tayyebulla sought clarification from him on 15 January 'as to whether the AICC resolution on 5 January 1947 had provided "clear guidance" to Assam and whether Assam should sit in the section initially or opt out from the very beginning'. After the Working Committee of the Assam Congress reiterated on 17 January that the province's constitution should be framed by its own representatives alone, Gandhiji wrote back to Tayyebulla, the APCC president. He deplored 'the panic on the part of the Assamese and said that the AICC resolution 'gives enough guidance, if not clear guidance, for it will not compel Assam to act against the declared wish of the people through the Legislative Assembly'. Hence, he claimed that Gandhiji's full support was with him.[30]

---

[27] Text of the AICC Resolution of 5 January 1947, as reproduced by Tayyebulla, *Between the Symbol and the Idol*, pp. 201–02 and Moon, ed., *Wavell the Viceroy's Journal*, 6 January, p. 406.

[28] Tayyebulla, *Between the Symbol and the Idol*, pp. 202–04.

[29] *Assam fights for Freedom and Democracy: Draft Resolutions of Assam Communists* (Assam Provincial Organizing Committee, CPI, Gauhati, n. d.), p. 1.

[30] Tayyebulla, *Between the Symbol and the Idol*, pp. 200–07 and Bhuyan and De, eds, *Political History of Assam*, Vol. III, pp. 385–87.

Both the Congress and the League had at one stage accepted the Cabinet Mission Plan and, for a while, a solution of the communal question without partition of the country was in sight. But Assam's determined opposition to its grouping with Bengal provided an opportunity to the League to repudiate its earlier acceptance. The Cabinet Mission Plan fizzled out and, in its wake, Wavell had to quit his office in March 1947.

March of Communalism

Never was the communal situation in Assam so tense as in the last year of the British rule. In the 1940s, the demand for abolition of the Line system had converged on the demand for a six-province Pakistan that would include Assam. In January 1946, the province's Muslim electorate stood massively behind these demands and their champion, the Muslim League. If Assam could now be yoked with Bengal in one and the same section, that is Group C, which had a 51 per cent Muslim majority under the Cabinet Mission Plan, these demands would be substantially achieved.

Dangers of Eviction Policy

Under the circumstances, the Bardoloi government's routine measures to evict thousands of immigrant squatters from grazing and forest reserves, which had the sanction of the tripartite agreement of 22 March 1945, looked like a counter-measure to curb the League. Jinnah's statement issued from Gauhati on 6 March and the provincial Muslim League Working Committee's resolution of 8 March 1946 expressed grave concern over the future of many immigrants facing eviction. A sub-committee of the League's Working Committee was formed, with Saadulla as its treasurer, to collect funds from all over India in their aid.[31] The government armed itself, in due course, with special powers by promulgating the Assam Maintenance of Public Order Ordinance on 18 November 1946, to deal with the League movement.[32]

Communal feelings were running high, particularly since the observance of the Muslim League's Direct Action Day on 16 August. There was a minor communal clash in Sylhet resulting in injury to some thirty people and loss of property worth a few thousands of rupees. Bardoloi alerted all district and sub-divisional officers to control the situation through the formation of local peace committees and, if necessary, through the sternest police measures.[33] The District Magistrate of Darrang felt in November that in many areas 'the eviction operations would require strong military aid not only to give protection to officers

---

[31] Bhasani's appeal (in Bengali), 15 March 1946, cited in Revenue Department, Development Branch, File No. RD/46 (AS).

[32] *Assam Gazette*, Part VI, 1947, cited by M. Kar, 'Muslim Politics in Assam', *North-Eastern Affairs*, 2 (July–December 1973), p. 19.

[33] Bardoloi to Chief Secretary, 7 September 1946, Confidential B, 1946, File No. C 241/46 (AS).

. . . but also to protect Assamese villages against . . . retaliation'.[34] Apprehending retaliation in Sylhet in the wake of the proposed evictions in the Brahmaputra Valley, the Governor of Assam apprised Delhi of the impending perils of the situation.[35] Eviction of immigrant encroachers was nevertheless in progress in the Mangaldai sub-division in the beginning of January.[36] Ultimately, however, Bardoloi wisely decided to go slow with his policy and was able to keep the province free from communal riots.[37]

Ambikagiri and Bhasani

The divisive League politics of carving out of India a new state of Pakistan that was to include Assam provided an opportunity for the chauvinistic influence of Ambikagiri Raychaudhury to thrive, particularly when the Congress leaders were in jail from 1942. No doubt, his patriotism was genuine; but there was also an aspect of his life and works that gave rise to controversies and encouraged anti-Bengali chauvinism. In his concept of a future Indian federation of linguistic nationalities, he laid emphasis on the principle of dual citizenship and opposed multiculturalism at the provincial level. He even presented some constitutional ideas for an ideal Indian confederation on these lines. This was printed as a pamphlet in September 1942 and reprinted in 1946. While explaining his life's mission in his presidential address to the Assam Sahitya Sabha Conference at Margherita in 1950, he blamed the Bengali community of Assam for so long endangering the Assamese culture and language. 'That is why', he concluded, 'that the Bengalis residing in Assam had been more hostile than the British to them – this belief of the Assamese is getting stronger day by day, keen as they are on self-defence' (translation ours).[38]

Neither his concept of dual citizenship nor that of secession, as was earlier suggested by Jnananath Bora, had any general acceptance among the Assamese people. Their commitment obviously was to the Congress ideal of single Indian citizenship alongside regional autonomy within a federal structure. Raychaudhury's call for the organization of a two-lakh-strong Assamese volunteer corps styled '*Asam Atmarakshini Vahini*', to resist further immigration and

---

[34] S.N. Maitra, District Magistrate to the Divisional Commissioner, 11 November 1946, ibid.

[35] G.E. Abell to Patel and Bardoloi to Patel, both dated 15 November 1946, in Durga Das, ed., *Sardar Patel's Correspondence 1945–50*, Vol. 2 (Ahmedabad, 1972), pp. 294–99.

[36] 'Assam Police Weekly Intelligence Report for the week ending 8th January 1947' (typescript in the Office of the Editor of the History of Freedom Movement of Assam [hereafrer OEHFM], Government of Assam, Gauhati).

[37] S. Chaliha, 'Barak banam Brahmaputra', *Saptahik Niilacal*, 20 December 1972 (serialized).

[38] Ambikagiri Raychaudhury, *Swadhiin Panchayat Rashtragathanar Anchani* (in Assamese, second edition, Gauhati, August 1946) and his *Rachanavalii* (Guwahati, 1986), pp. 836–41.

the alleged Muslim League invasion of Assam, went unheeded,[39] although he was acclaimed as a true son of the people. His party, the Asamiya Samrakshini Sabha – renamed Asam Jatiya Mahasabha in 1935 – flourished as a platform for articulation of the widely shared 'sons-of-the-soil' sentiment, and also as a pressure group within the Assam Congress.[40] Although without much formal education, poor of means and somewhat unconventional in his ways, Raychaudhury was nonetheless a first-rate poet with wide contacts and a record of jail-going as a freedom fighter. Congress leaders found a man of his background handy at times, and useful as a mouthpiece of Assamese reaction to the divisive League politics.

The provincial League observed 3 January 1947 as 'black flag day' to protest against the evictions and to offer prayers to save Muslims from Congress 'oppression'. Assamese-speaking Muslims, however, responded poorly to this call.[41] The Working Committee of the All-India Muslim League, meeting at Karachi on 31 January and 1 February 1947, urged upon the Assam government to halt its allegedly inhuman eviction policy.[42]

Bhasani, the provincial League president, contemplated a civil disobedience movement and gave out a threat of leading a march of one lakh volunteers upon Assam from the borders of Bengal, in course of a speech delivered at Bahadurabad. He sounded out Bengal's League leaders as to how much and what kind of help he could bank upon from them. But the response was poor. Yet he selected Dhubri, on the Assam–Bengal border, as the venue for a series of simultaneous conferences of such bodies as the Bengal–Assam Mujahadins, the Bengal–Assam National Guards, the Bengal–Assam Literary Conference and the Committee for Action against the Line system – all to be held on and around 3–4 March 1947. He established a centre at Mankarchar to train volunteers for a civil disobedience movement that was soon to be declared against the Line system. With Gandhiji's historic salt march in mind as a model, he hoped to lead a similar peaceful march from Mankarchar against the Line system.[43]

The march was supposed to formally start on 30 March, but neither the agitated League followers nor the government had the patience to wait for action till then. Civil disobedience broke out sporadically and large-scale arrests followed. Under the circumstances, Bhasani changed his plan. Having secretly arrived at Tezpur, he held a public meeting there on 10 March, in defiance of the promulgation of Section 144 of the Indian Penal Code (IPC). He was immediately

---

[39] Ambikagiri Raychaudhuri, 'Atmarakshmii Vahinii Gathan', reproduced in *Dekadekeriir Ved* (in Assamese, second edition, Gauhati, 1958) by the same author, pp. 72–94.

[40] See Tilakchandra Das, *Ambikagiri Aru Teonr Jiivan Darshan*, Vol. 1 (in Assamese, Gauhati, 1952), pp. 1–172. The party never took the shape of a well-knit organization; it remained just a forum for a particular viewpoint on the national question.

[41] 'Assam Police Weekly Intelligence Report for the week ending 8th January 1947'.

[42] *IAR* (January–June 1947), Vol. 1, p. 112 (b).

[43] Mohammad Waliullah, *Yugabichitra* (in Bengali, Dacca, 1967), pp. 523–24 and the *Shillong Times*, 14 February 1947.

arrested and detained.[44] The Muslim members of the upper house staged a walk-out in protest on 11 March.[45] Bhasani had nominated a number of persons to court arrest one after another by defying certain government orders. Such *satya-grahas* and encroachments on grazing and forest reserves continued despite large-scale arrests during the next three months. Though the civil disobedience movement was by and large peaceful, the police had to resort to firing on the evicted encroachers who resisted at the Kawaimari Reserve in Barpeta sub-division on 21 March, killing twelve persons, and in the Kumolia Reserve on 14 May 1947, killing three. Both before and during the movement, police firing was resorted to in several places to disperse mobs, causing deaths and injuries.[46] But, in view of the receding prospect of Assam's inclusion in the eastern wing of Pakistan in the changed situation, the League had to retrace its steps. The movement was officially withdrawn on 11 June 1947,[47] and Bhasani was released on 21 June from the Gauhati Jail.

Towards Partition

The decision that India should be granted independence by a fixed date-line was taken largely because of Wavell's insistence. Even the country's partition with the consent of the two major parties was conceived before his unceremonious departure.[48] However, as Attlee and Wavell had differences – both of temperament and of judgment over the announcement of a final date for the British withdrawal – the latter was asked to quit. On 20 February, it was announced that the transfer of power to responsible Indian hands would be completed not later than 30 June 1948 and that Louis Mountbatten was to be the new Viceroy.[49]

Sworn in on 24 March, Mountbatten picked up the threads where they had been left by his predecessor. He quickly discovered, in the wake of the Punjab riots, that the Cabinet Mission Plan had already gone to pieces. He worked out a plan for the country's division on a communal basis, got it accepted by the two major parties and announced it on 3 June. Under this plan, a referendum was to be held, *inter alia*, in Sylhet to decide whether that district should remain a part

---

44 Syed Abul Maksud, *Maolana Abdul Hamid Khan Bhasani* (in Bengali, Bangla Academy, Dhaka, 1994), pp. 57–58.

45 *Assam Legislative Council Proceedings* (hereafter *ALCP*), 11 March 1947, cited by M. Kar, 'Muslim Politics in Assam', p. 18.

46 Waliullah, *Yugabichitra*, pp. 523–24, and Bhuyan and De, eds, *Political History of Assam*, Vol. III, pp. 281–89. Bhasani had apparently launched his movement without prior approval of the Muslim League high command. See Chowdhry Khaliquzzaman, *Pathway to Pakistan* (Lahore, 1961), p. 373.

47 Bhuyan and De, eds, *Political History of Assam*, Vol. III, pp. 278–89 (we have corrected a printing mistake, while accepting the dates given for the police firings' at Kawaimari and Kumolia); *Amrita Bazar Patrika* (Calcutta), 22 and 25 March 1947; Syed Abul Maksud, *Maolana Abdul Hamid Khan Bhasani*, pp. 57–58.

48 Moon, ed., *Wavell the Viceroy's Journal*, pp. xi–xii.

49 Ibid., pp. 421–23.

of the province of Assam in India or go to Eastern Bengal in a truncated and moth-eaten Pakistan. In the case of opting for Eastern Bengal, a Boundary Commission with terms of reference similar to those for Punjab and Bengal was to be set up to demarcate the contiguous Muslim-majority areas of Sylhet for their transfer to Pakistan. The date of transfer of power was advanced to 15 August 1947. The Indian Independence Bill, 1947, was rushed through the British Parliament, and it received the royal assent on 18 July.

Sylhet Referendum

The Sylhet referendum was held on 6 and 7 July 1947. It was a vote virtually on the twin issues of the reorganization of India on a communal basis, and of the province of Assam on a linguistic basis. Sylhet Hindus who had for decades agitated for reunion with Bengal now clung to Assam. On the other hand, Sylhet Muslims who, on political considerations, had been consistently opposed to the move since 1928, now reversed their position. Some local scheduled caste leaders, too, sided with them. The local Jamiat-ul-Ulema, led by Husain Ahmad Madani, remained consistently opposed to the idea of Pakistan and advised all Muslims of the district to vote for an undivided Assam.[50] Though otherwise influential, they failed to make any impact on the Muslim voters.

On the Sylhet question, Assamese public opinion, too, remained understandably cold, but consistent with its earlier stand. The APCC election manifesto had pledged to the electorate in 1945–46 that the Congress Party would work for separating Sylhet from Assam. 'Maulana Sahib (that is, Azad) seemed to come to the conclusion that the only alternative to this state of things', wrote Bardoloi to Patel in February 1946, 'is to separate the Bengali district of Sylhet and a portion of Cachar from Assam and join these with Bengal – a consummation to which the Assamese people are looking forward for the last 70 years.'[51] Bardoloi had let the Cabinet Mission understand in April that Assam would be quite prepared to hand over Sylhet to Eastern Bengal.[52]

A year later, under the changed circumstances, it was no longer possible for the APCC to say this so openly. However, Congress control of the Assam administration was so 'correctly' exercised that it hardly provided any advantage to the local Congress during its campaign in Sylhet to win the referendum. It was indeed a lifetime's opportunity for the Assamese leadership 'to get rid of Sylhet' and carve out a linguistically more homogeneous province. When the

---

[50] Rabindra Nath Aditya, *From the Corridors of Memory* (Karimganj, 1970), pp. 29 and 33–34.

    Madani believed in the peaceful spread of Islam in a united India and the latter's evolution into an Islamic state in due course. Meanwhile, the Jamiat stood for provincial autonomy, a minimal federation and communal electorates. See P. Hardy, *The Muslims of British India* (Cambridge, 1972), pp. 243–45 and 194.

[51] Bardoloi to Patel, 18 February 1946, in Das, ed., *Sardar Patel's Correspondence*, 1945–50, Vol. 3 (Ahmedabad, 1972), pp. 194–96.

[52] Moon, ed., *Wavell the Viceroy's Journal*, 1 April 1946, p. 234.

results of the referendum were declared, there was a feeling of relief in the Brahmaputra Valley.[53] It was widely suggested, for example, by the *Assam Tribune* and Raychaudhury, that the Bengali-speaking plains portion of Cachar district, at the least its Hailakandi sub-division, and also the four Bengali-speaking *thanas* of the Dhubri sub-division, the stronghold of Bhasani, should have been transferred to Pakistan. The Sylhet leaders were discouraged when they tried to salvage a portion of the district through an effective representation to the Boundary Commission.[54] The representation of truncated Assam in the Constituent Assembly was fixed by the Governor-General at eight seats – six general and two Muslim seats. Accordingly, Assam's representatives were elected afresh. Among several others, Saadulla, too, retained his seat.

Saadulla could have migrated to Pakistan and politically thrived there, to begin with, as a provincial governor. But he refused. As an efficient and moderate time-server, he was ready to serve the Congress regime in his own province, in the same way as he had served the earlier one. Wavell wrote about him on 22 December 1943: 'I saw all the Assam ministers and chief officials, not a very impressive lot, except the chief minister, who is a shrewd and competent politician, though how he would do in better company – I am not sure.' K.N. Dutt assessed Saadulla as 'an astute politician and a capable administrator not without touches of nobility and generosity in his personality and character'.[55]

Sylhet was 60 per cent Muslim. Of the valid votes cast in the referendum, 2,39,619 (56.6 per cent) were in favour of Sylhet's inclusion in Pakistan and only 1,84,041 (43.4 per cent) were for an undivided Assam in India. This verdict was not unexpected, and it almost reflected the communal composition of the district population. The Boundary Commission, presided over by Cyril Radcliffe, published its award three days after independence. Only the three *thanas* of Patharkandi, Ratabari and Badarpur, and about one half of the *thana* of Karimganj were to remain in Assam, as per terms of the award; the rest of the district went to Pakistan.[56] Sylhet, 'the golden calf' that was sacrificed in 1874 to usher in a new province, was now once more sacrificed at the altar of a new state.

[53] Aditya, *From the Corridors of Memory*, p. 31; also Kar, 'Muslim Politics in Assam', p. 18. See also Moon, ed., *Wavell the Viceroy's Journal*, p. 41. Saadulla has to be judged indeed by the company he kept.

[54] Editorial of *Assam Tribune* (Gauhati), 17 July 1947 and Ambikagiri Raychaudhury's statement, ibid., 23 July 1947.

[55] S. Chaube, *Constituent Assembly of India: Springboard of Revolution* (New Delhi, 1973), pp. 77 and 112; and K.N. Dutt, *Landmarks of the Freedom Struggle in Assam* (Gauhati, 1958, reprinted, 1969), p. 107.

[56] Aditya, *From the Corridors of Memory*, pp. 31 and 35–36. *Amrita Bazar Patrika*, 14 July 1947.

Emergence of Hills Politics

The Background: A Resumé

Under-administered and kept in seclusion as museum specimens of 'backward tracts', the hills areas remained excluded from all constitutional reforms until 1937. The two districts of Garo Hills and Khasi–Jaintia Hills, as well as the Mikir Hills area, all of which were 'partially excluded areas' under the Act of 1935, gained some legislative experience in the pre-independence decade. The 'partially excluded areas' sent representatives to the legislature and were placed under ministers, subject, however, to the Governor's discretionary control. The 'excluded areas' – that is, the present Nagaland, Mizoram and North Cachar Hills – on the other hand, were not represented at all in the legislature, and their administration was vested in the Governor, under the same Act. In any case, both the categories were outside the ordinary competence of any legislature – provincial or central.[57] This meant that no Act of any legislature could apply to these areas unless the Governor so directed or wished.

Under this policy of seclusion, there was practically no political development in the hills, except for the Khasi–Jaintia Hills district, until the end of World War II. Christianity and literacy, however, made rapid progress in the twentieth century, due to the exertions of Christian missionaries. There were only twenty-six Christians in Mizoram, 579 in Nagaland, 3,629 in the Garo Hills and 17,125 in the Khasi–Jaintia Hills in 1901; but by the time of independence, they were dominant in some of these districts.[58] In the matter of literacy, the level achieved in the hills compared favourably with, and in some cases even excelled, the all-India average.[59] The hills' tribal languages were developed into written ones by the Christian missionaries, in the Roman script. Thus scripts became a unifying and modernizing factor at the district level.

The early emergence of political consciousness in the Khasi–Jaintia Hills is explained by two factors. The location of the provincial capital there dates from 1874. Besides, unlike in the other hills, tribal state formations appeared

---

[57] Verrier Elwin, *Nagaland* (Shillong, 1961), pp. 36–39.

[58] According to the 1951 Census, the proportion of Christian to total district population was 90 per cent in Mizoram, 30 per cent in Khasi–Jaintia Hills, 16 per cent in Garo Hills and 8 per cent in the combined North Cachar and Mikir Hills. Between 1941 and 1951, the percentage of Christian to total population of the Assam hills area, as a whole, increased from 21.7 to 35.4 per cent. The comparable percentage figures for the 1971 Census are as follows:

Mizoram Hills	*Khasi–Jaintia Hills*	*Garo Hills*	*Naga Hills*	*N. Cachar Hills*	*Mikir Hills*
86	51	41	67	22	8

[59] The number of literates per hundred (aged five and over) in the Assam hills in 1951 was 15.5 against 15.8 in India, as a whole, and 18.5 in the Assam plains. However, Mizoram ranked first in the province both in male and female literacy, these being 46.2 and 16.7 per cent, respectively. Census of India 1951, Vol. 12, Part I-A *Report* (Shillong, 1954), pp. 343–44. Male literacy in Mizoram increased to 59 per cent and female literacy to 43 per cent by 1971. The overall literacy rate stood at 88 per cent in Mizoram in 2001 as against Assam's 64 per cent.

there centuries before the advent of the British rule. The chiefs of some twenty-five petty polities, partly elected and partly hereditary Siems, played a significant role in the evolution of modern political consciousness. The formation of the Jaintia Durbar in 1900, the Khasi National Durbar in 1923 and the Khasi States' Federation in 1934 were early landmarks of the growing politicization. This process was marked by a conflict between the Siems and those who grabbed communal land with their connivance, on the one side, and the commoners, on the other. The Government of Assam told the Simon Commission that the Khasis had a keen desire to come under the reforms, though the chiefs and their subjects might not favour it.[60]

In Nagaland, some marginal activity of a political nature may be traced back to 1918 when the Naga Club was formed with government officials and leading village headmen, to discuss social and administrative problems. In January 1929, it submitted to the Simon Commission that the Nagas should be excluded from the proposed reforms.[61] No club or association comparable to the Naga Club ever existed in the Garo Hills at least till 1940.[62] Conditions were no better in the remaining hills. In Mizoram, some 60 hereditary chiefs, deemed as owners of the soil, ruled over the people, and the District Magistrate ruled over them. Before 1937 some people in the district town of Aizawl reportedly put forward a demand for representation in the legislature; this resulted in their imprisonment.[63]

It may, however, be noted that in Mizoram, as well as the other hills, communal ownership of land was progressively giving way to the rise of private property during the twentieth century and even earlier. The formation of an educated Christian elite helped the process. During the war years, when panic-stricken immigrant shopkeepers and petty traders left the hills, circumstances compelled some of the local hillsmen to take up these lucrative professions as well as petty war contracts. Thus there emerged a small stratum of middle-class people of local origin, which was not in existence earlier, except in the Khasi–Jaintia Hills. Besides, the war-time contacts with soldiers from many provinces and many nations exposed the hillsmen to the world outside and allowed them to be politicized. Lastly, the partition of the country largely disrupted the hills' economy, since some parts of the Garo, Mizo, Khasi and Jaintia Hills had long been economically more integrated with Eastern Bengal than with the plains of Assam. People in these areas had to undergo untold hardships because of the disruption of their normal trade channels. This experience further strengthened their urge for local autonomy.

[60] S. Chaube, *Hill Politics in North-East India* (Calcutta, 1973), pp. 62–65.

[61] Elwin, *Nagaland*, pp. 49–50.

[62] Parimalchandra Kar, 'A point of view on the Garos in transition', in Pannalal Dasgupta, ed., *A Common Perspective for North-East India* (Calcutta, 1967), pp. 99–100.

[63] R.N. Prasad, 'Evolution of Party Politics in Mizoram', *North-Eastern Affairs*, 2 (Annual 1973), p. 47.

Two War-time Influences

All-India political parties and organizations had been making some attempts, since 1938, to draw the hills people into their fold, but with little success. They had no access to the 'excluded areas' or even to the interior of the 'partially excluded areas'. As a result, their contacts were limited to Shillong and to the hills students studying in other district towns. Neither the Shillong local unit of the National Congress, formed in 1938, nor that of the CPI, formed a little later – both at the initiative of local Bengalis – was able to recruit tribal cadres, excepting one or two, during the war years.

However, the Students' Federation was able to establish rapport with the hills students in the various colleges of Assam and Calcutta. For example, G.G. Swell, a Khasi student then studying in Calcutta, was a member of the Working Committee of the Bengal Provincial Students' Federation in 1943–44 and took a leading part in forming the Calcutta-based Assam Hills Students' Association in 1945.[64] At the same time, the Assam Hills Students' Federation was formed in Assam, with T. Aliba Imti Ao, a Naga student, as its secretary. This body, jointly with the Assam affiliate of the All India Students' Federation, organized the All-Assam Students' Educational Conference in 1946 at Shillong, which adopted a charter of demands for the spread of education in the province in general and in the hills in particular. Several tribal students who actively participated in this conference later emerged as local leaders in their respective regions.[65]

Because of their deep religiosity and the fierce opposition they faced from the church, the communist influence on the Christian hills students was neither stable nor deep. What appealed to them most was the communist approach to the national question. They collected from bookshops at Shillong, Gauhati and Jorhat dozens of copies of such Marxist publications as were relevant to the subject, particularly copies of the USSR constitution, for the consumption of their reading public at home.[66] The Soviet concept of a multi-national state (each nationality therein with a formal right to secede) and of autonomous regions was to their liking, afraid as they were of domination by the plains people. The impact of the USSR constitution was soon to be seen on the growth of their group consciousness.

Another extraneous factor that made the hills people concerned about their future political status was British official thinking on the subject. Towards the end of the war, when talk of transfer of power was in the air, some British civil servants and other interested quarters began to toy with the idea of a 'Crown

---

[64] Swell was also a joint secretary of the United Teachers' and Students' Famine Relief Committee, Calcutta University.

[65] Chaube, *Hill Politics in North-East India*, pp. 73 and 141; Misra, 'Communist Movement in Assam', p. 32.

[66] Misra, 'Communist Movement in Assam', p. 37. Also information obtained from the relevant bookshops.

Colony' consisting of all the contiguous hill areas of Burma and Assam.[67] To prepare the ground for this, British officials in charge of the hills districts took the initiative in forming district-level political bodies in which the tribal elite could participate. Such attempts were made in the North Cachar Hills, Nagaland and Mizoram, but with varying and indifferent results. In the atmosphere of an anti-colonial upsurge all over India, it was but natural that the idea of a 'Crown Colony' or guided participation in politics did not appeal to the tribal mind.[68] However, the official efforts were successful to the extent of kindling an urge for autonomy and political participation, and, above all, in nurturing the seeds of suspicion in tribal minds against their more developed neighbours in the plains.

Formation of Local Political Parties

The year 1946 saw the formation of several district-level tribal political organizations in the hills. The Garo National Council was formed in March 1946.[69] On behalf of it, a draft constitution for an autonomous Garo region was submitted in mid-1947 to the Bardoloi Sub-Committee of the Advisory Committee of the Constituent Assembly on tribal affairs. It envisaged maintenance of links with the provincial as well as the central government.[70]

From towards the end of 1945, politics took a new orientation as a reaction to the alleged Congress interference through Nichols–Roy in Khasi political life. Failing to get a Congress ticket in the 1946 election, MacDonald Khar-Kongor, Nichols–Roy's rival, initiated a Hills Union with members drawn from different hills. It raised the demand for a separate hills state within India. The tribal response to his move was, however, cold. In early 1946, a Khasi–Jaintia Political Association was set up, mainly with the backing of the Siems.[71] In its memorial to the Cabinet Mission, it emphasized that the Khasis were a historically evolved distinct community of people 'living in democratic communes'. The Association, therefore, raised the demand for a federation of the Khasi areas – both the British portion and the native states – with adequate 'cultural and political autonomy' within a 'sovereign Assam'. At their own initiative, the Siems organized their states into a federation in 1946 and signed the Instrument of Accession to India on 15 December 1947. All formalities of accession were completed on 17 October 1948.[72] Later, the states were merged in the administrative set-up of the district, with the acceptance of the Indian Constitution of 1950.

In the Mikir Hills, the first political organization of the Mikir (Karbi)

---

[67] R. Coupland, *The Constitutional Problem of India*, Part III (Oxford University Press, 1944), p. 164 and R. Reid, *Years of Change in Bengal and Assam* (London, 1966), p. 110. Also Major A.G. McCall, *Lushai Chrysaiis* (London, 1949), pp. 241.

[68] Elwin, *Nagaland*, pp. 51–52.

[69] D.N. Majumdar, 'A Glimpse of Garo Politics', *North-Eastern Affairs*, 2 (Annual 1973), p. 10.

[70] Chaube, *Hill Politics in North-East India*, p. 72.

[71] Ibid., pp. 67–68 and 73.

[72] Ibid., pp. 67–68 and 79.

people – the Karbia Durbar – was formed in early 1947 with a modest programme of protection of local customs, consolidation of the Mikir areas into a single administrative unit and extension of the franchise.[73] Thus, all over 'the partially excluded areas', the post-war trend was one of growing desire for local autonomy within Assam and India.

The Naga Hills District Tribal Council was officially sponsored in April 1945 with the objective of uniting the multilingual Nagas and repairing some of the damages of the war through self-help. Within a year of its formation, this semi-official body had to be reorganized as the Naga National Council (NNC), a federation of several tribal councils, under the leadership of T. Aliba Imti Ao. For a few years, it published a small newspaper, the *Naga Nation*.[74] In June 1946, it adopted a resolution demanding autonomy within Assam and opposing both the 'Crown Colony' and the grouping plan, as envisaged in the Cabinet Mission Plan of 16 May. However, by the turn of the year, the NNC substantially changed its position. In February 1947 it formally demanded an interim government for Nagaland with financial provisions initially for a period of ten years, at the expiry of which the Nagas would be free to reconsider their political status. This demand was voiced before the Governor in June. Angami Zapu Phizo (1904–1990), who had lived for seventeen years in Burma and collaborated with the Japanese Occupation Army there, returned home and slowly built up the case for Naga independence.[75]

Still in office as secretary of the NNC, Ao had to face an increasing challenge from the extremists. In July 1947, Phizo led a deputation to Delhi with the suggestion that Nagaland would automatically become sovereign after the British withdrawal on 15 August. Akbar Hydari, Governor of Assam, rushed thereafter to Kohima. After prolonged talks with the Naga leaders, he entered into a nine-point agreement with the NNC, which was to remain valid for ten years. Under the terms of this agreement, the NNC was made responsible for the imposition, collection and expenditure of land revenue, house tax and such other taxes as might be imposed by it. According to the NNC interpretation of the agreement, the Nagas were to decide afresh after ten years whether they were to continue with the arrangement or opt out to assert independence. This interpretation was not accepted by the other side, that is, the Government of India. Naga politics became increasingly too hot for Ao, but were congenial to Phizo's ascendancy within the NNC power structure. The movement for autonomy was thus transformed into one for independence from India after Phizo was elected

---

[73] Ibid., pp. 71–72.

[74] Elwin, *Nagaland*, pp. 51–53. According to a news item published in *Shillong Times*, 1 November 1946, the two-day session of the Tribal Council of Kohima demanded, *inter alia*, recognition of the Ao and Angami languages up to the Matriculation standard of Calcutta University.

[75] Chaube, *Hill Politics in North-East India*, pp. 69–70, 107–08 and 140–45. Also see *The Naga Problem* (External Publicity Division, Ministry of External Affairs, Government of India, New Delhi, n.d.), pp. 1–20.

president of the NNC in November 1949. The NNC virtually transformed itself into a sort of parallel government for the district. On 20 February 1950, it decided to organize a plebiscite on the question of independence. The results encouraged the Nagas to stand aloof from the 1952 general elections. No elections could be held in Nagaland that year for lack of candidates.

In Mizoram, the District Magistrate tried to set up a tribal political body by convening a district conference in January 1946 with representatives of chiefs and commoners in equal numbers. Because of its undemocratic character, the response was poor and it practically ended in failure. The conference was revived after a few months, in 1947. But the Mizo Union, formed meanwhile at popular initiative in April 1946, boycotted it.[76] By February 1947, the Mizo Union claimed a membership of 20,000 and an associate membership of 1,00,000, the latter figure obviously a conjectural estimate. A weekly in the Mizo language was brought out in 1948 by the Mizo Publishing House, which owned a small press.[77]

The Mizo Union adopted a memorandum on 22 April 1947 for submission to the Constituent Assembly. The document urged consolidation of all Mizo areas into a single administrative unit and its self-determination within Assam.[78] It was opposed to the chiefs' domination, and it desired integration with the rest of India. On 20 July 1947, dissidents floated a second political party – the United Mizo Freedom Organization – to propagate secession of all contiguous Mizo areas from India and their union with the Mizo areas of Burma. But on 14 August, the eve of India's independence, this party, too, fell in line with the Mizo Union in accepting the *fait accompli*, that is, the inclusion of Mizoram in India. However, both parties demanded a review after ten years.[79]

The Mizo Union served an ultimatum on the Chiefs' Council in November 1947, demanding:

    (a) abolition of *begar* (corvee) towards house-building for chiefs;

    (b) abolition of the paddy rent, payable to chiefs;

    (c) abolition of the flesh tax, also payable to chiefs;

    (d) abolition of trials by chiefs; and

    (e) suspension of the practice of *jhum* land distribution by the 'running system'.[80]

---

[76] Prasad, 'Evolution of Party Politics in Mizoram, pp. 47–48 and Chaube, *Hill Politics in North-East India*, pp. 161–64. Also, *Shillong Times*, 15 October 1948.

[77] Mizo Union's note to the President, Constituent Assembly, cited in *Shillong Times*, 14 February 1947 and ibid., 7 September 1947.

[78] *Shillong Times*, 16 May 1947.

    Later, in 1949, a Mizo Union delegation consisting of R. Thanliara, Saprange and H.K. Bawi-Chhuaka again represented to the Governor-General, C. Rajagopalachari, demanding amalgamation of the contiguous Mizo areas of Tripura, Manipur, Mizoram and Cachar to form an autonomous greater Mizoram. See *Shillong Times*, 6 December 1949.

[79] Chaube, *Hill Politics in North-East India*, pp. 162–64.

[80] As per custom, each year the chief declared certain portions of the village land open for *jhuming*. The chief and the elders, numbering a fifth of the village households,

As the grievances were not redressed, a civil disobedience movement was started in late 1948 for early achievement of local self-government in the form of a district council, and for abolition of the privileges of the chiefs. The movement often involved riotous assaults on the chiefs. Funds amounting to Rs 14,000, collected by the Mizo Union for purposes of the movement, were frozen by the government. The movement was withdrawn following a definite official assurance in January 1949 that the grievances would be redressed.[81] It was the Mizo Union's urgent desire to get rid of the chiefs that guided the Mizos to throw in their lot with the rest of the Indians. They realized that the task would be more difficult in a 'Crown Colony', or even in an independent Mizoram headed by feudal elements. Separatism once more raised its head, in the form of the Mizo liberation struggle, long after the abolition of chiefships there.

Thus, all the hill areas, excepting Nagaland, were on the whole politically reconciled to the changes brought in by the Constitution of India, on 26 January 1950.

Independence and After

With the sun having set over Britain's empire, one epoch of India's anti-imperialist struggle came to an end. But many of its tasks were yet to be fulfilled. The period from 15 August 1947 to 26 January 1950 was period one of hopes and fears, facilities and strains, bold promises and cautious administrative measures. Nevertheless, the foundations of a parliamentary democracy, based on universal adult suffrage, were laid. How strong these foundations were, was a matter to be judged by posterity.

Everything did not and could not, of course, change overnight. The stranglehold of foreign capital on the economy remained very much there. The ministers and legislators were the same who had been on probation in the erstwhile British regime, and their outlook was largely conditioned by that experience. The same old bureaucracy, now manned by Indians, held the reins of administration. The British had gone but the habitual dependence, in many respects, persisted.

Some long-standing popular demands were fulfilled within a few years of independence. Assam, for the first time, had a university, a medical college, an engineering college, several technical institutions and a high court, which opened up new avenues of influence for the province's upper classes. But the progress towards the goal of universal primary education remained slovenly as

---

made the first choice. After that an announcement was made by the village crier on an appointed day or night, so that the villagers could rush to the jungles to make their choice, sometimes spending the whole night in the jungle. With increasing population pressure on the land, this 'running system' had already become impracticable and unpopular. Modernists therefore preferred allotment of *jhum* land by lottery.

[81] *Shillong Times*, 7 September 1948. Also Chaube, *Hill Politics in North-East India*, pp. 163–64.

before. Assam still remained 82 per cent illiterate and 96 per cent rural in 1951.[82] By and large based on subsistence agriculture, its economy remained poor in techniques and resources. There were no engineering industries or even light consumption industries worth their name. The annual per capita consumption of electricity in Assam was only 0.58 kwh in 1950–51, as compared with 13.3 kwh for all-India – a measure of its industrial backwardness.[83] Some foreign-owned extractive industries like tea, coal, a mini-oil refinery and a few saw mills, with the supporting infrastructure of railways and inland navigation, were the hall-marks of more than a century of colonial development until the 1950s.

Direct colonial domination of Assam's economy remained intact until independence. Less than fifteen managing agency houses, through their control over some 200 joint-stock sterling and rupee companies, and all of them with head offices outside the province, dominated the economy. With control over one-and-a-half million acres of land – only a third of which was under tea plants – and a half-a-million work force, the planters wielded financial power before which the provincial government's own budgetary resources paled into insigni-ficance.[84] That is why, in course of his pre-independence budget speeches, B.R. Medhi, Finance Minister, announced in a flush of enthusiasm that important British-owned industries of the province would be nationalized at the earliest convenience. But for many years no such nationalization followed.[85] Such nationalization, if with heavy compensation, would not have benefited the economy either. Immediately after independence, however, the Assam Assessment of Rev-enue-free Wastelands Grants Act was passed, to deny the privileges so long en-joyed by the tea industry in land taxation.

Under the provisions of a new opium prohibition Act enforced on 1 April 1948, an honorary prohibition committee and about 500 honorary prohibition officers were appointed to bring the long-drawn opium eradication programme to its completion. The province was also freed of the vestiges of the illicit trade in opium within a few years. But liquidation of the vestiges of feudal and semi-feudal exploitation, which could have made democracy meaningful to the peas-ants, remained an unfinished task. Permanently settled zamindaries were abol-ished with compensation in due course, and some tenancy reforms – for example, the Assam Adhiars Protection and Regulation Act, 1948 – were introduced, but

---

[82] These percentage figures came down to 72 and 92, respectively, by 1971, and to 36 and 87 by 2001.

[83] National Council of Applied Economic Research, *Techno-Economic Survey of Assam* (New Delhi, 1962), pp. 82–83. By 1970–71, these figures increased to 21.5 kwh and 99.2 kwh, respectively.

[84] Data published in the annual issues of *Assam Directory and Tea Areas Handbook* (issued annually, Calcutta) around 1947 corroborate this point. Increasingly, during the post-independence years, British tea gardens and substantial shares in the manag-ing agency houses were sold out to Indians – mainly Marwaris.

[85] The foreign-owned joint steamer companies as well as other foreign-owned compa-nies like private railways and coal were nationalized by the central government under totally different circumstances, long after this policy statement was made.

in a manner that hardly benefited the poor peasants. The poor tenants remained where they were or were reduced to the status of wage labour. These half-hearted reforms were further watered down in course of their actual implementation. Those at the helm of the provincial government were themselves mostly landlords, planters and rich peasants. Even otherwise, the government could not but heavily depend for electoral support on these classes.

A new chapter was added in 1948 to the Assam Land Revenue Regulations, 1886. It provided for reserved tribal belts in different regions with the ostensible purpose of protecting the tribal people from the competition of non-tribals, mainly immigrants, for land. To discourage Muslim immigration from Eastern Pakistan, the Indian Parliament also passed the Immigrants' (Expulsion from Assam) Act on 13 February 1950, following an earlier January ordinance on similar lines. The Act provided for the removal of immigrant persons (excepting *bonafide* refugees) whose stay in Assam was politically undesirable. Empowered by the new law, the Government of Assam ordered a sizeable number of Muslim immigrants to quit the province. This created a general panic among them.

Immigration of Bengali Muslim peasants from East Bengal stopped, thereafter, with the introduction of the passport system and customs checks. But a huge influx of Bengali Hindus, Buddhists and Christians refugees from the same area created new problems that defied any immediate solution. The new immigrants – peasants, artisans, petty traders and *bhadralok* numbering 2,73,000 at the time of the 1951 Census – settled down in the towns as well as villages. With their coming, a new dimension was added to the existing tensions between the major religious and linguistic communities. In the early part of 1950, communal feelings in Assam were worked up to an unprecedented height in the wake of anti-Hindu riots in Eastern Pakistan. Thousands of Muslim immigrants, nearly a lakh according to Indian official estimates, had to quit riot-affected Lower Assam for Eastern Pakistan in search of security.[86] It was indeed the province's first big riot against a religious minority community. Henceforward, it was the language question that was to increasingly become the rallying point of anti-social, divisive forces and vested interests, to organize riots.

The post-independence period was therefore a period of economic and social tensions, especially after the Indo–Pak Standstill Agreement came to an end on 29 February 1948, disrupting Assam's normal channels of communications. Industrial strikes and peasant struggles, unleashed after the war, persisted. The great earthquake of 1950 severely damaged the economy. More than one Left party characterized the newfound freedom either as a sham or as transfer of power to a dependent bourgeois class reconciled to the domination of foreign

---

[86] Census of India, 1961, Vol. 3, Part II-C, Table D. 3, p. 218; also Census of India, 1951, Vol. 12, Part I-A *Report*, pp. 32–33 and 78. The total number of displaced persons (non-Muslim) who had immigrated to Assam increased from 2,73,000 in 1951 to 6,28,000 by 1961. Another big influx of refugees took place in 1964.

capital and integrally linked with feudal vestiges. These parties, organizationally much weaker than the ruling party in Assam, lent their weight to transform
the economic struggles into a maturing political crisis for the new regime.

There were peasant struggles all over the Assam plains during the years
1948–51, in which a large number of poor and landless peasants, most of them
tribals, participated under the guidance of the red flag. But the prestige of the
government leaders as front-rank freedom fighters, the repressive police measures and the legitimized preventive detention – a combination of all these proved
to be more than a match for the challenge. The communist call for a railway
strike on 9 March 1949 did not click. The newly organized plantation workers
all along remained with the INTUC and the ruling party. The Plantation Labour
Act passed by the Indian legislature on 2 November 1951 raised the promise of
certain welfare measures to be implemented by the provincial government in the
near future. The clouds passed off as quickly as they had gathered, though the
basic problems were hardly solved. With the completion of the Assam Rail Link
project through a difficult terrain, Assam's railway and road communications
with the rest of India were once more established from 1950. Civil liberties were
restored through the mediation of the Supreme Court and High Courts. Even the
CPI was attracted to the parliamentary path, when the first general election
under the new Constitution was held in 1952.[87] British planters no longer had
any representation either in the legislature or in the local bodies.

Not only in the matter of expectations, but also in the matter of political
participation, there was a revolution indeed. The system of joint electorates was
promulgated in Assam under Governor's notification with effect from 15 August
1947.[88] Involvement of common men in electoral politics, based on adult suffrage, increased their chances of entry into realms so long held as the preserve of
a privileged few. The caste factor in local and provincial power politics now
assumed greater importance. It allowed the underprivileged but numerically
viable castes to pose an effective challenge to the traditional balance of social
power. The same was true in the case of linguistic groups. The process of Assamization (*Asamiyaization*) of most positions of power and influence in the province was hastened. For the first time, Assamese (*Asamiya*) emerged as the
acclaimed language of more than half the people of Assam in the Census of 1951,

[87] It is interesting to note that the communist response to parliamentary activities since
1952 bears a close resemblance to the model set by Congressmen during the period
1924–47. To begin with, the purpose is to wreck the Constitution; then, to take part
in the process of legislation as a responsible opposition; and, finally, to assume ministerial power even under constraints, if possible, to give relief to the people and widen
the base of influence. In between, walk-outs and boycotts add colour to the drudgery
of parliamentarism. The process is one of collaboration and conflict, not outright
rejection of the system under attack.

[88] Tayyebulla, *Between the Symbol and the Idol*, p. 209. The change facilitated
Tayyebulla's election to the Assam legislature in November 1947 and his induction
into the Bardoloi ministry in March 1948.

thus preparing the ground for declaring it as the state language in 1960. The separation of Sylhet alone would not have sufficed to bring in this change. It was the census figures for the district of Goalpara that tilted the balance. In all the census operations up to 1931, Bengali was returned as the mother tongue of more than half of the district population. This figure came down to less than 18 per cent in 1951 and 12 per cent in 1961. This was mainly because, meanwhile, on political considerations, Bengali Muslims and a section of the sons of the soil who had earlier recorded Bengali as their mother tongue, declared themselves to be Assamese-speaking. The composition of local bodies, legislatures, the bureaucracy, medical and legal professional bodies, even political parties began to change with a continuous erosion of linguistic and caste power groups within them. The social change and political development that took place in the province's post-independence generation indicate that linguistic nationalities and their institutionalized inter-relations are still in the process of further development through conflicts, understanding and adjustments.

CHAPTER NINE

Epilogue

The above survey of more than a century of nationalism in Assam and its interaction with electoral politics centering around doled-out, half-hearted reforms tentatively suggests that the evolution of nationalism in our country was simultaneously along two intertwined tracks – one pan-Indian and the other regional. Great nationalism was grounded in a feeling of all-India unity; and little nationalism was based on regional–linguistic unity. The former essentially suited the interests of India's big bourgeoisie; and the latter was largely related to the small bourgeoisie – the regional middle classes. (see footnote no. 85, p. 56)

This two-track nationalism is nowhere so prominently traceable as in the case of Assam. In the long run, language there proved to be a stronger binding element than caste, religion or isolated local ties. The incipient regional middle class did clash with its counterparts from other regions, but only up to a point. Beyond that, they generally coalesced to put forward a common front against imperialism. Despite the strains and stresses in their relationship, they moved in unison towards a fusion, the model for which need not be searched in western nationalism with no tradition as such of a federal process of its own.[1] Much of our misunderstanding of Indian nationalism so far has stemmed from a false framework of reference.

The involvement of Maniram Dewan in the national revolt of 1857, and of the new Assamese middle class in the modernist and tactically collaborationist politics of the last quarter of the nineteenth century indicate Assam's early identification with the then mainstream of Indian nationalism. This was despite the fact that early all-India Congress sessions refused to take up matters of mere provincial importance on their agenda. At another level, the repeated outbreaks of peasant struggles against the colonial tax policy – the *raij mels* of 1861, 1868 and 1893–94, as well as the Jaintia people's war of resistance in 1861–63 – were in line with broadly similar peasant and tribal revolts in many parts of India. Unorganized plantation workers in Assam, too, went on frequent strikes at the individual tea garden level, and had national support for their cause.

---

[1] One could, however, profitably look into the experience of Eastern Europe and the area that was the Czarist Empire.

At the beginning of the twentieth century, Assam, like Bengal, had enough grounds to react strongly to the Curzon Plan of welding East Bengal and Assam into a single province, but it did not. The yet incipient and unconsolidated Assamese middle class was neutralized by Fuller through the promise of favoured treatment henceforth in the matter of public services and promotion of its language interests. The Swadeshi movement and Bengal terrorism could not strike roots in the Assamese homeland. Nevertheless, their impact was not altogether absent. A number of political memoirs bear this out.

In fact, in the first two decades of the twentieth century, Assam passed through a period of introspection. The Assam Association (1903–20), the Asam Chhatra Sanmilan (estd. 1916) and the Asam Sahitya Sabha (estd. 1917) – all attempted to articulate their Valley's unsettled quest for a linguistic–regional identity, their concern over the government-blessed opium evil, and their desire to be administered, at least at the lower levels, not by recruits from Bengal but by sons of the soil. All these were no doubt important and legitimate issues, but they side-tracked attention from the root cause – colonial rule. Until 1873, this rule had resisted all local pressures to allow the Assamese language a recognized status in the Brahmaputra Valley, which was then administered as a division of Bengal. Later, this recognition was conceded, but Assam proper and the populous Bengal district of Sylhet were forced into an involuntary partnership in the newly constituted Assam province. Imperialism encouraged ethnicity to play a divisive role and thus hinder the growth of nationalism.[2]

The separation of Sylhet, the eradication of the opium evil and the restrictions on land-hungry peasants' immigration from Bengal into the Assamese homeland – these were believed to be issues on the solution of which depended the very existence of the Assamese 'race'. But it was also increasingly realized that the planter Raj that tyrannized the entire people was at the root of all these problems.

The first rumblings of the storm that was Gandhi did not, therefore, fail Assam's ears. By 1921, the Assam Association voluntarily liquidated itself to usher in the formation of the Pradesh Congress. After 1939, the Asam Chhatra Sanmilan also became a Branch of the AISF. Little nationalism yielded its hegemony to great nationalism, even in the arena of local issues. Great nationalism, though challenged from time to time and put to the test by intricate issues of local and communal interests, very much held its ground through the remaining three pre-independence decades. Gandhiji's stand on linguistic provinces helped the process.

The biggest events in the 1920s and early 1930s were not the dyarchy and the elections, but Non-Cooperation and Civil Disobedience. The role of the legislature in politicizing Assam was minimal up to the introduction of the 1935 reforms. During the sixteen years of dyarchy, the Congress (Swarajists) chose to be present in the legislature only for six consecutive years, 1924–29, and had no

---

[2] See Appendix 13.

occasion to regret its decision. The only other organized party in the house until 1937 was the European party. It was only after a substantial widening of the franchise in that year under the Act of 1935 that the Congress decided in favour of a policy of responsive cooperation, alternating with struggles. Yet, in the subsequent decade, the debates in the legislature were overwhelmed by stirring events outside.

The Assam experience thus does not suggest that 'the constitutional reforms of 1935 granted almost full self-government in the provinces', and that 'Indian politicians had prizes worth fighting for'.[3] For one thing, the permitted autonomy was self-defeating. The politicians had to swallow an upper house and a strong British lobby built into the legislature, as well as a 'white' Governor with special responsibilities and wide discretionary powers, which were indeed exercised on several crucial occasions. For another, Gopinath Bardoloi, the Congress politician and statesman, would not have chosen to give a walk-over to Saadulla to form five of the six ministries during the period from 1937 to 1946, had the prize been worth fighting for or if the nationalist struggle had only been a fight for prizes.

Bardoloi cared neither for prizes nor for the dictates of his party's high command when Assam's interests were concerned. With Gandhiji's blessings, he led a successful resistance to the proposed inclusion of Assam in Group C of the Cabinet Mission Plan, acceded to by the All India Congress Committee (AICC). People widely believe that it was mainly because of him that Assam was saved from being a part of Pakistan. It was he, again, who flagged off the Sylhet referendum to comply with the public opinion of his constituency, the Brahmaputra Valley, thus inviting a rebuke from his mentor, Gandhiji.[4] His mission in life was to serve Assam to the best of his abilities and with vision. However, his government's failure to do justice to the workers on strike at Digboi and the Arunabund Tea Estate, as well as its failure to establish the right to free movement within and across plantations, made him unpopular even within the Congress. In fact, his labour policy in general and his pragmatism in decision-making, as opposed to the rigid and principled stand of Tayyebulla, the Assam Provincial Congress Committee (APCC) president, became highly controversial. Nevertheless, during Bardoloi's second stint in office as Chief Minister, his experience, priorities and policy initiatives matured him into a seasoned statesman.

The establishment of the University of Gauhati, which he had campaigned for almost for a decade, was indeed a gift of his to the people. A notch ahead of his peers in understanding Assam's tribal question, he reinforced the existing Line system and added a new chapter, as mentioned earlier, to the Assam Land Revenue Regulations, providing for reserved belts and blocks of land for the

---

[3] Quote from Anil Seal, *The Emergence of Indian Nationalism: Competition and Collaboration in the Later Nineteenth Century* (Cambridge, 1968), p. 350.

[4] Lily Mazindar Baruah, 'Lokapriya Gopinath Bardoloi, a devotee of Mahatma Gandhi', *Assam Tribune*, 5 August 1979.

plains tribes in select regions. The Adhiars' Protection and Regulation Act of 1948, a response to the post-war, communist-led peasant movement, was an important reform that also benefited the people. Besides, in the Constituent Assembly, Bardoloi was instrumental in providing a degree of autonomy for the hill tribes under the Sixth Schedule of the Constitution. All said, while appreciating Bardoloi's statesmanship, we should also keep in mind the constraints of his middle-class background and Gandhian ideology.

The opium monopoly, a source of provincial revenue second only to land tax, was imperialism's weakest link in Assam. And it was there that the Congress struck hard. Congressmen – despite many of them being petty planters themselves – attempted, during their short ministerial tenures, to tax the tea industry, to relieve the government of its heavy dependence on the 'tainted' excise revenue. They gave substantial relief to the depression-hit peasantry. These measures helped strengthen the Congress mass base. However, the Congress policy of refusing settlement of waste lands with post-1937 immigrants alienated the immigrant peasants. The immigrant question quickly matured into a political crisis in the last pre-independence decade. During the controversy over 'grouping' under the Cabinet Mission Plan, a demand for the self-determination of Assam was brought into the limelight to forestall its threatened inclusion in East Pakistan. That danger having passed, the mainstream of little nationalism, overcoming stresses and strains, once more, anchored itself on the firm base of pan-Indian nationalism. But for how long a period, only time will tell us. The political and economic issues such as the centre-periphery conflicts syndrome, xenophobia due to influx of migrants, under-development and secessionism – all these discussed in this book – still haunt and challenge the 21st century Assam of today, exhibiting striking similarities.

Appendices

APPENDIX 1

Urban Population of Assam: 1881–1931

(in eighteen towns, each with more than 5,000 population in 1931)

	Towns having above 10,000 population in 1931	Towns having 10,000 population or less in 1931	Total
	(1)	*(2)*	*(3)*
1881	62,612	24,057	86,669
1891	63,803	30,312	94,115
1901	71,711	35,284	1,06,995
1911	82,941	42,654	1,25,595
1921	1,01,028	49,350	1,50,378
1931	1,30,793	65,435	1,96,228

Note: Of the eighteen towns, only three – Sylhet, Gauhati and Barpeta – had more than 10,000 population each in 1881, and they together accounted for a population of 37,434, Sylhet being the largest town (14,407). Only three other towns – Silchar (6,567), Goalpara (6,697) and Dibrugarh (7,153) – were in the 5,000–10,000 bracket in that year. The population of the remaining twelve towns in that year ranged from 1,020, in the case of Sunamganj, to 4,583, in the case of Sibsagar.

All the towns, except Shillong, were in the plains districts. Gauhati emerged as the largest town (21,797) in 1931. Throughout the period 1881–1931, the urban population as a percentage of the province's total population remained below 2 per cent.

In 1931, eleven places with less than 5,000 population each were also listed as towns. These together accounted for a population of 33,885 in 1931 and less than 8,000 in 1881. These, obviously, are not included in the above list.

Source: Census of India, 1931, Vol. 3, Assam Part II, p. 8.

APPENDIX 2
Population of the Province of Assam (in thousands)
(excluding Manipur but including the Khasi states)

	Brahmaputra Valley (6 districts including the Mikir Hills)	Surma Valley (2 districts including the North Cachar Hills)	Hills Districts (excluding North Cachar and Mikir Hills)	Province Total
1872	1,917	1,955	291*	4,162
1881	2,251	2,285	372*	4,908
1891	2,476	2,543	459*	5,478
1901	2,618	2,700	525*	5,842
1911	3,107	2,973	634*	6,714
1921	3,856	3,071	680*	7,606
1931	4,723	3,295	784*	8,802
1941	5,762	3,758	898	10,418
1951	6,815	–	1,073	–

Note: Figures for 1872 are from *Statistical Abstract Relating to British India from 1868/9 to 1877/8*, No. 13 (London, 1879), Table No. 5, p. 9. For the rest, see Census of India, 1931, Assam Part II – *Tables*, and Census of India, 1941, Vol. 9, Assam (rearranged). The 1951 Census figures have been adjusted to make them comparable.

The Brahmaputra Valley also includes the Frontier Tracts (plains portion); the latter's population increased from 8,692 in 1881 to 58,493 in 1931.

* These figures suffer from under-coverage, in respect of the Lushai Hills (Mizoram) and a part of the Naga Hills. The gaps were progressively eliminated over the years. Between 1901 and 1911, new areas with a population of 39,586, and in 1931, an area of 908 sq. miles with a population of 15,711, were added to the Lushai Hills district.

According to the 1921 Census (uncorrected for distortions), 35,24,318 persons were Bengali-speaking and 17,18,712 persons Assamese-speaking in the province of Assam. The latter population was almost wholly found in the Brahmaputra Valley.

APPENDIX 3
Density of Population per sq. mile (Brahmaputra Valley)

District	1872	1881	1891	1901	1911	1921	1941	1951	1961
Kamrup	146	167	164	153	173	198	328	387	542
Darrang*	69	80	90	99	110	170	263	326	383
Nowgong	68	82	90	68	79	108	299	409	559
Sibsagar*	64	79	96	120	138	162	301	351	437
Lakhimpur*	27	40	56	82	104	143	219	265	317
Goalpara	98	113	115	117	152	193	254	278	385

Note: Immigration into the tea gardens during the years 1872–1931, and into rural settlements during the years 1901–61, contributed heavily to the density increase. The increase in the density of Nowgong and Sibsagar in 1951 is partly explained by the boundary re-adjustments to exclude the thinly populated Mikir Hills.

All the hills districts together had a low average density of 44 per sq. mile even as late as 1951, and Garo Hills, the densest hill district, 77.

* Important tea districts.

Source: Census of India, *Assam Census Reports* and *District Census Handbooks*.

APPENDIX 4
Opium Statistics of Assam: Select Years, 1875–76 to 1939–40

Year	Assam Proper			Assam Province (including Manipur)		
	Consumption (maunds)	No. of Shops	Wholesale Price (Rs per seer)	Consumption (maunds)	Opium Revenue (Rs 1000)	No. of Shops
1875–76	1,689	2,740	–	1,874	1,225	3,151
1878–79	1,520	1,116	24	1,655	1,561	1,342
1879–80	1,481	1,152	26	1,619	1,584	1,367
1880–81	1,557	1,179	"	1,686	1,638	1,397
1881–82	1,464	1,179	"	1,583	1,554	1,404
1890–91	1,208	829	37	1,308	1,812	946
1891–92	1,272	843	"	1,370	1,916	953
1897–98	1,128	662	"	1,228	1,723	758
1900–01	1,201	674	"	1,291	1,804	761
1901–02	1,126	685	"	1,228	1,723	775
1905–06	1,321	657	"	1,415	1,982	728
1908–09	1,499	427	"	1,640	2,353	495
1909–10	1,398	381	40	1,540	2,367	443
1910–11	1,391	355	"	1,512	2,462	416
1911–12	1,394	347	"	1,507	2,522	409
1919–20	1,640	279	50	1,748	3,837	324
1920–21	1,519	272	57	1,615	4,412	315
1921–22	967	264	65	1,048	3,917	306
1922–23	920	261	68	998	3,586	303
1923–24	817	254	75	884	3,810	307
1925–26	761	248	"	838	4,494	300
1926–27	681	245	"	750	3,992	296
1927–28	673	245	"	722	3,826	297
1930–31	472	243	"	512	2,664	293
1931–32	387	243	"	423	2,775	294
1932–33			95	356	2,121	297
1933–34			"	317	1,870	296
1934–35			"	294	1,614	293
1935–36	230		"	269	1,557	292
1938–39			"	183	1,007	282
1939–40	68	179	"	94	520	217

Source: Collated from *Annual Reports* of the Excise Department, Government of Assam; *Excise Statistical Tables for the Province of Assam* (Shillong, 1927), pp. 96–97; official data cited in *Assam Congress Opium Enquiry Report* (*ACOER*) (Jorhat, 1925), pp. 23–24, 45 and 91. In the case of some figures, the sources do not tally; but the relevant discrepancies, not being significant, are overlooked.

The supply of opium to the state of Manipur, which had only one shop, was marginal, e.g., hardly 5 maunds in 1920–21, and later, much less. It appears that opium was introduced there only in the twentieth century through the British political agency.

APPENDIX 5
Assamese Middle Class (last quarter of the nineteenth century): A Cross-Section

AGARWALA, HARIBILAS (1842–1916): Keont from mother's side; son of a Marwari trader-settler; educated at Sibsagar Government School and Hindu School, Calcutta; owned saw mills, printing press, tea garden and agricultural lands in course of a successful trading and publishing career; father of Chandrakumar Agarwala, poet and founder of the pro-Congress Assamese biweekly, *Asamiiya*; grandson, Jyotiprasad, was a committed Congressman until independence.

BARDOLOI, MADHAVCHANDRA (1847–1907): Daivajna; Gauhati High School; college education at Calcutta; by turn teacher, lawyer and government servant; Rai Bahadur. His son, Nabin Chandra – lawyer and petty planter – was a committed Congressman.

BAROOAH, JAGANNATH (1851–1907): Brahmin, son of a government servant who had started a tea estate; matriculated, 1868; graduated from Presidency College, 1872; owned several tea gardens in due course; Rai Bahadur; vice-president and later president, Jorhat Sarvajanik Sabha; employed in 1893 about 500 labourers – 300 Bengali, 100 local Assamese and 100 Kachari recruits from Kamrup and Goalpara. After his death, his brother, Rai Bahadur Krishnakumar Barooah, and son-in-law, Chandradhar Barua, rose to be members of the Assam Legislative Council; and the latter also of the Indian Council of Sate.

BAROOAH, MANIKCHANDRA (1851–1915): Kayastha; son of a government servant; educated at Gauhati High School and Presidency College; matriculated, 1868; started business in European partnership; in course of the ups and downs of his business career, owned tea gardens, a small steamer, an ice factory and saw mills; related to Bholanath Barooah who was, for some time, manager of his timber business; a business partner of Annadaram Dhekian–Phukan until the latter's death; member of the East Bengal and Assam, later Assam, Legislative Council, 1909– 15; honorary magistrate and municipal chairman; had interests in the short-lived periodical *Assam News* and in the Assam Printing Corporation.

BARUA, ANUNDORAM (1850–1889): Kayastha; educated at Gauhati High School and Presidency College, Calcutta; Gilchrist Scholar; B.A., 1869; ICS, 1872; reputed Sanskrit scholar; planned to purchase a tea garden after retirement; left a legacy of about Rs 45,000. Unmarried.

BARUA, BISTURAM: Kayastha; had no English education worth the name; government servant; Rai Bahadur; started Thengalbaree Tea Estate and acquired two more tea estates – all before 1900. His son, Shivaprasad Barua, was a member of the Reformed Assam Legislative Council and founded the Assamese daily *Batori*, in the 1930s, with Nilmoni Phukan as editor. Shivaprasad added several tea gardens to his family property; was chairman, Jorhat Local Board, 1928–31; and was considered the biggest Indian tea planter of his time.

BARUA, DEVICHARAN (1864–1926): Kayastha; educated at Dibrugarh Government School; college education in Calcutta: matriculated in 1882; graduated in 1886; B.L., 1888; married to daughter of Bisturam Barua, planter; secretary, Jorhat Sarvajanik Sabha and lawyer; owned three tea gardens by 1917 and four by 1924; employed, around 1906, 170 permanent and twenty to twenty-five seasonal labourers on his Kakodonga Tea Estate; Rai Bahadur; member of the Indian Legislative Assembly, 1921–23, and Council of State, 1923–26. His son, Herambaprasad Barua, also planter, rose to be a member of the Council of State (1934–36) and president, Assam Legislative Council (upper house). Herambaprasad married the daughter of another tea planter, Rai Bahadur Nilambar Datta.

BARUA, GHANASHYAM (1867–1923): Kalita; son of a *mauzadar*; matriculated in 1882; higher education in Calcutta; B.L., 1888; chairman, Golaghat Local Board and Golaghat Municipal Board for some time until 1913; member, Imperial Legislative Council, 1913–16; member, Assam Legislative Council, 1916–23; minister, 1921–23; Rai Bahadur; started Dolowjan Tea Estate in the 1890s. One of his sons was educated in the UK.

BARUA, GUNABHIRAM (1837–1894): Brahmin; educated, Kolutola School, Calcutta and Presidency College; initiated Brahmo, 1869; social reformer, government servant, author; Rai Bahadur; settled in Calcutta after retirement; left a legacy of Rs 50,000. Got his son educated in the UK. Married a widow.

BARUA, HEMCHANDRA (1835–1896): Brahmin; atheist; self-educated; social reformer, government servant, author; edited an English weekly, *Assam News* (Gauhati), 1882–85; had a share in the Assam Printing Corporation; left a modest legacy.

BARUA, MALBHOG: Daivajna; son of a government servant; traditionally educated; started Rajabheta Tea Estate and owned a couple of tea gardens; honorary magistrate. His son, Prasannakumar Barua, and son-in-law, N.C. Bardaloi, were both planters and Congressmen.

BEZBARUA, DINANATH (1813–1895): Brahmin; traditionally educated; a promoter of English education; government servant; owned two small tea gardens. His son, Lakshmi Nath – a timber merchant and initiated Brahmo – was the doyen of modern Assamese literature. Had another son educated in the UK. Both were married to Bengalis, and they lived outside Assam.

BHATTACHARYA, KAMALAKANTA (1853–1936): Brahmin; initiated Brahmo; unsuccessful trader in natural rubber and other products; nationalist poet; editor, *Asam Hitaishii*; upheld the Congress cause to the last.

BORA, BOLINARAYAN (1852–1927): Kalita; son of a government servant; Gauhati High School and Presidency College; Gilchrist Scholar; graduated in civil engineering at Cooper's Hill, UK, 1877; government servant; proprietor and *de facto* editor of the Assamese periodical *Mau*; had his son educated in the UK; married a Bengali and settled in Bengal. His maternal uncle, Bholanath Barooah, was a millionaire timber merchant.

BORA, Col. SIBRAM (1847–1907): Caste Hindu; educated at Gauhati High School and Calcutta Medical College; later Glasgow University; matriculated, 1865; joined Indian Medical Service, 1874; after retirement, acquired Rowriah Tea Estate, in partnership with Jagannath Barooah; married a Bengali and settled in Calcutta.

CHALIHA, KALIPRASAD (1862–1914): Kayastha; son of a tea garden employee of the Assam Company; matriculated from Sibsagar High School in 1878; employee of Assam Company; later, lawyer; Rai Bahadur; started four tea gardens, with encouragement from European patrons. His sons, Jadavprasad and Bimalaprasad, both planters, were distinguished Congressmen.

CHALIHA, PHANIDHAR (1855–1923): Kayastha; educated at Dibrugarh Government School and Presidency College; matriculated in 1871; retired from government service in 1903; a cooperator and member of Assam Legislative Council, 1915–19; Rai Bahadur. He started a tea garden which could not be developed and, long after his death, was sold to a Marwari. His sons, Kuladhar Chaliha and Padmadhar Chaliha, were both lawyers and Congressmen. Kuladhar developed two small tea gardens.

CHANGKAKATI, RADHANATH (1853–1923): Daivajna; owned a printing press and a self-edited English weekly, *Times of Assam* (estd. 1895), which was backed by European planters.

DHEKIAL–PHUKAN, ANNADARAM (d. 1884): Brahmin; son of Anandaram Dhekial–Phukan; business partner of Manik Chandra Barooah in the firm Barooah–Phukan Bros. His England-educated elder brother settled in Europe.

HANDIQUI, RADHAKANTA (1857–1952): Ahom; matriculated in 1881; educated at Sibsagar Government School and City College, Calcutta; government servant till 1916; Rai Bahadur; started a 10-acre tea garden, Tirual Tea Estate, and expanded its acreage to 150; also owned Bar Timan Tea Estate; had his two sons educated in the UK; nominated member, Assam

Legislative Council; married to P. Gohain-Barua's sister. His son, Krishnakanta, reputed Sanskrit scholar, was also a planter.

HATIBARUA, KRISHNAKANTA GOGOI: Ahom; designed a new machine for spinning *muga* silk thread; participated in the Calcutta Exhibition, 1883; started a tea garden in Sibsagar district.

PHUKAN, GANGAGOVINDA (1841–1926): Brahmin; educated at Sibsagar Government School; government servant; started several tea gardens; share-holder and director of Amola Tea Co.; first chairman, Sibsagar Municipality.

MUNSHI, RAHAMAT ALI: Hailed from Puranigudam; did not know English; pleader; honorary magistrate; owned a plantation since 1870s. In 1893, he employed 200 permanent and 100 casual labourers in the two tea gardens covering 300 acres. His son, Kutubuddin Ahmed, rose to be an executive Councillor during the days of the dyarchy.

Col. ZALNUR ALI AHMED (1848–1931): Son of a poor villager; educated at Gauhati High School, and at Calcutta and Glasgow Universities in medicine and surgery; joined the Indian Medical Service, 1872; married into an Urdu-speaking family of Delhi and settled there. His son, Fakhruddin Ali Ahmed, was educated in the UK and became the President of the Indian Union.

Source: Collated from published memoirs and biographies; year books; evidences before the Assam Labour Enquiry Committee, 1906 and the Royal Commission on Opium, 1893.

APPENDIX 6
Brahmaputra Valley Delegates to National Congress Sessions: 1886–1921

Session/Year/Place	Names of Delegates	Remarks
1886/Calcutta	Kalikanta Barkakati	Shillong Association
	Devicharan Barua, B.A.	Upper Assam Association
	Gopinath Bardoloi, B.A.	” ” ”
	Satyanath Borah, B.A.	Nowgong Rayat Association
1887/Madras	Radhanath Changkakati	Secretary, Upper Assam Association and also Assam Conference
	Lakshmikanta Barkakati	Tezpur Rayat Sabha and also Assam Conference
1888/Allahabad	Ghanashyam Barua	Cultivator, Nowgong; Nowgong Rayat Association
	Harendranarayan Singha-Chaudhuri	Zamindar, Bagribari
	Ram Chandra	Merchant, Shillong
1889/Bombay	Haridas Ray	Cultivator, Dibrugarh
1890/Calcutta	Baradachandra Haldar	
	Manikchandra Barua*	
1891/Nagpur	Meghanath Banerji	Medical practitioner, Joypur, Dibrugarh
	Durgakanta Ray	Dhubri
1892/Allahabad	Bholanath Barooah	Merchant, Gauhati
	Lakshmi Nath Bezbarua, B.A.	Editor of *Jonaki*
	Radhanath Changkakati	Secretary, Upper Assam Association
1893, 1894, 1897, 1899 and 1902	None	
1895, 1896 and 1898	Not checked	
1901/Calcutta	Hariprasad Nath	Mukhtear, Goalpara
	Basantakumar Chaudhuri, M.A.	Headmaster, Goalpara School
1903/Madras	Lakshmi Nath Bezbarua	Merchant, representing Jorhat Sarvajanik Sabha
1904/Bombay	Lakshmi Nath Bezbarua	Jorhat Sarvajanik Sabha
	Chandrakamal Bezbarua	Jorhat
	Bhabanikanta Das	Pleader, Dhubri
1905	n.a	n.a
	Lakshmi Nath Bezbarua	Calcutta, merchant
1906/Calcutta	T.R. Phookan	Barrister, Calcutta
	C. Barooah	Assam Association
	Hariprasad Nath	Mukhtear, Goalpara
	Mukundalal Dasgupta	Pleader, Goalpara
	S.N. Haldar, Bar-at-law	Barrister, Goalpara
	Ashwinikumar Sen	Headmaster, Goalpara
	Durga Das	Pleader, Dhubri
	Abdul Aziz	Religious preacher, Goalpara
1907	Nagpur Session was not held	
1908–16	None on record	

APPENDIX 6 (contd)

Session/Year/Place	Names of Delegates	Remarks
1917/Calcutta	S.C. Bagchi, Bar-at-law	Planter, Tengakhat
	Debendranath Bezbarua, B.L.	Pleader, Jorhat
	Gopalchandra Dutta	Manager, Borashali Tea Estate, Sapekhatii
	Bhabaniprasad Barua	Tea Estate, manager, Sibsagar
	Nabin Chandra Bardaloi, B.L.	
	Ratneswar Dasgupta	Lawyer, Mangaldai
	Bistuprasad Chaliha	Tea Estate, Manager
	Sadananda Dowerah, B.L.	
	Kanakchandra Sarma	
	Chandrakamal Bezbarua	Tea planter
	Umeshchandra Das	Merchant, Barpeta
	Bachalal Barah	Zamindar, Dibrugarh
	Brahmananda Dutta	Pleader, Golaghat (all representing Assam Association)
1918/Delhi	Nabin Chandra Bardaloi	Assam Association
1919/Amritsar	Nabin Chandra Bardaloi	Kamrup Association
	Ambikanath Borah	
1920/Nagpur	Nabin Chandra Bardaloi	
	Kanakchandra Sarma and others	
1921/Ahmedabad	Chandranath Sharma	
	G.N. Bardoloi	
	Paramananda Agarwala	
	Jyotiprasad Agarwala and fifteen others.	

Note: * See Prafulladatta Goswami, *Manikchandra Baruva Aru Teour Yug* (in Assamese, Gauhati, 1970), p. 47. We did not find the name in the official list of delegates.

Source: Reports of the annual sessions of Indian National Congress, 1886–1921; also *Assam Congress Opium Enquiry Report* (September 1925), pp. 55–57 for the year 1920; A.M. Zaidi and S. Zaidi, eds, *The Encyclopaedia of National Congress*, Vol. I–III (New Delhi, 1976, 1977).

Bholanath Barooah was elected a delegate from Tezpur, in *absentia*, to the Ahmedabad Congress (1902). See, *Bezbaruar Dinalekha*, edited by Maheswar Neog (Jorhat, 1969), p. 169. Apparently, he did not attend.

APPENDIX 7
Surma Valley Delegates to National Congress Sessions: 1886–1920

Session	Names of Delegates	Remarks
1886	Dinanath Dutt	Manager, C.N. Joint Stock Co., Cachar
	Bipin Chandra Pal	Land-holder, Sylhet
	Joy Govinda Shome, M.A.	Vakil of Calcutta, Sylhet
	Kamini Kumar Chanda, M.A.	Land-holder, Habiganj People's Association
1887	Bipin Chandra Pal	Journalist, Lahore (elected by public meeting at Sylhet, 23 December)
1888	-do-	Journalist, Lahore (elected by public meetings at Sylhet and Shillong)
1889	-do-	(elected by public meeting at Sylhet/ Shillong on 28 December 1889)
	Joy Govinda Shome, M.A.	Vakil of Calcutta (elected by Bengal Christian Conference and Sylhet public meeting)
1890	Bipin Chandra Pal	Sylhet
1891–94	None	
1897	Bipin Chandra Pal	Sylhet
1898, 1899	Ramani Mohan Das	Zamindar–merchant–banker, Cachar
1900	-do-	Karimganj Peoples' Association to represent Sylhet
1901	-do-	-do-
	Sundari Mohan Das, B.A.	Maulvibazar/Sylhet
	Kamini Kumar Chanda	Silchar/Karimganj
	Bipin Chandra Pal and five others	
1904	Ramani Mohan Das	Karimganj
	Harendrachandra Sinha	Pleader, Sylhet
1906	Ramani Mohan Das	
	Promod Chandra Datta	
	Brojendralal Chaudhuri	
	Bipin Chandra Pal	
	Mahendranath De, M.A. and thirty-four others	
1908–10, 1912, 1913 and 1915	None	
1911	Ramani Mohan Das	Zamindar–merchant–planter–banker
1914	Ramani Mohan Das	
1916	Kamini Kumar Chanda	Member, Imperial Legislative Council
1917	-do-	
	Ramani Mohan Das	Karimganj
	Radha Binod Das	Sylhet
	Bipin Chandra Pal and thirty-four others	
1918	Kamini Kumar Chanda	Silchar
	Kaliprasanna Das	Sylhet
	Khitischandra Das	Pleader/Mirasdar, Sylhet
	Ramani Mohan De, B.L.	Zamindar, Karimganj
	Pandit Ambikaprasad Tripathi.	Sylhet
1919	Kamini Kumar Chanda	Bengal PCC
1920	-do-	

Note: Only those years have been shown for which we could check recorded information.
Source: Reports of the annual sessions of Indian National Congress, 1886 to 1920.

APPENDIX 8
Legislative Councillors of Assam (Indians only) 1912–20

	Term*	Mode of Representation	Period of Service
Officials:			
A.Majid	(I–II)		(For most of the period)
Col. H.E. Banatvala	(I–II)		(For most of the period)
Non-Officials:			
Brahmaputra Valley			
Rai Sahib Padmanath Gohain-Barua	(I)	Nominated	
Raja Prabhatchandra Barua (zamindar of Goalpara)	(I)	"	
Rajendranarayan Chaudhuri (zamindar of Goalpara)	(II)	"	
Saiyid Muhammad Saadulla, M.A., B.L. (knighted in 1928)	(I–II)	Muslim	
Tarun Ram Phookan, Bar-at-Law	(I–II)	Land-holder	(Resigned in 1919)
Rai Bahadur Ghanashyam Barua (planter)	(I–II)	Local Board	(Could attend only the first meeting of the first term which elected him to Imperial Legislative Council in 1913)
Manik Chandra Barooah (planter)	(I)	Municipality	(Died in July 1915)
Rai Bahadur Phanidhar Chaliha (retired government servant)	(I–II)	"	(From October 1915 until resignation in 1919)
Rai Bahadur Krishnakumar Barua (planter)	(II)	Land-holder	(From September 1919)
Chandradhar Barua (planter)	(II)	Municipality	(From September 1919)
Surma Valley			
Rai Bahadur Dulalchandra Deb	(I)	Nominated	(For a short period till early 1913)
Rai Bahadur Sitamohan Das	(I)	"	(After Deb)
Radha Binod Das (lawyer)	(II)	"	(Resigned in 1919)
Khan Bahadur Muhammad Bakht Mazumdar (zamindar)	(II)	Nominated	
Khan Bahadur Saiyid Abdul Majid (planter)	(I–II)		
Munshi Riaz Baksh	(II)	Muslim	
Rai Bahadur Nalinikanta Ray Dastidar	(I–II)	Land-holder	
Ramani Mohan Das (zamindar–planter–merchant–banker; Rai Saheb)	(I–II)	Local Board	(I – nominated)
Kamini Kumar Chanda, M.A., B.L. (lawyer)	(I–II)	Municipality	(Could attend only the first meeting of the second term which elected him to the Imperial Legislative Council in 1916)
Nagendranath Chaudhuri (zamindar–planter)	(II)	Nominated	(From September 1919)

Note: * (I) First three-year term, 1913–16. (II) Second term, 1916–19, extended till 1920. Those who were neither officials nor nominated were elected from their several constituencies, as mentioned.

Source: *Assam Legislative Council Proceedings*, as published in *Assam Gazette* from time to time (1913–19).

APPENDIX 9 *Sorbojanik Sobha's Memorandum to Royal Commission on Opium, 1893*
Royal Commission on Opium, *Minutes of Evidence*, Vol. II (London:, 1894)

APPENDIX XXXVI   (Page 462)
(Received through the Secretary to the Government of India in the Department of Finance and Commerce)

From
The President and Secretary, Jorhat Sorbojanik Sobha.

To
William Erskine Ward, Esq., M.A., I.C.S., C.S.I., Chief Commissioner of Assam.

The Humble Memorial of the Jorhat Sorbojanik Sobha

1. That your memorialists beg, on behalf of themselves and of the general public, desire to approach you with this memorial and to give expression to the feeling of regret and alarm which they believe is shared in by the people of this province at the proposed enquiry into the cultivation and consumption of opium with a view to its prohibition and suppression.

2. That the people of Assam, in common with those of other provinces of India, have been in the habit of using opium and other narcotics from the remotest times. Opium is an invaluable medicine in many disorders of the stomach; it alleviates pain and possesses a sedative power of restoring health. It is useful after 40 years of age in prolonging life and is an undoubted preventive against malaria. The hard-working classes in the malarious plains of Assam require some stimulant to keep up their powers. On the whole, opium taken in a moderate quantity is beneficial, and positively necessary for a large number of people earning their livelihood by manual labour in the swampy rice fields and in the tea gardens of Assam and of boatmen and others.

3. That amongst the inhabitants of the province of Assam the aboriginal tribes, such as the Kacharis, Mikirs, Noras, Tooroongs, Sawdangs, Muttucks, Miris, etc., consume more opium than other races, and yet these aboriginal tribes are the strongest and the hardiest amongst the population, and no degeneration has been observed amongst them. The thousands of Kachari coolies from Kamroop and Goalpara Districts, who come every year to Upper Assam tea gardens for work, use opium for the most part, and they are those who work hardest and the least liable to illness. They build wretched houses, and the sanitation of their lines is never necessary to be looked into. As a rule they don't take English medicines and don't suffer from diseases.

4. That some of the hardiest races in India, such as the Sikhs and Rajputs, indulge in opium, and there appears to be no deterioration in the physique or the vitality of those races.

5. That the prohibition of the cultivation of opium will deprive a large number of Her Majesty's subjects of the means of livelihood, and set free a large quantity of land which would be unfit for other purposes, the misery and distress thereby caused to the people concerned being very serious indeed.

6. That the prohibition of the sale of opium to China will not do the least benefit to that country, there being already large areas under opium cultivation which again admits of unlimited expansion. The only result of the stoppage of opium from India will be that China will have to be content with her own opium of an inferior quality, while Persia and other Non-British countries will be afforded an opportunity of pushing their opium into the Chinese market, and while the Indian exchequer will suffer a loss of about seven crores of rupees per annum.

7. That the taxation of the people of India has reached the highest possible limit, and that no further addition can be made to it without generating serious distress and discontent, and how far this would be wise and politically sound, your memorialists would leave to the Government to decide.

8. That so far as the people of Assam are concerned, the case is still stronger. A large proportion of the people have been in the habit of using the drug for centuries. In the time of the Native Government the higher classes of the people also indulged in opium, but

when the cultivation of opium in Assam was abolished about 1859, the use of opium has almost gone out of fashion from the higher classes, but the working classes largely make use of the drug as a necessity of life. It is positively advantageous in advanced age and also to those who worked hard and are constantly exposed to the inclemencies of the weather. There is very little abuse of opium.

9. That if the sale of opium be stopped in Assam, those who now indulge in opium are certain to take to some other stimulant, and they would in natural course take to spirits. The consumption of spirits, it is hardly necessary to remark, would be hundred-fold more injurious than opium. Drinking is liable to excess, and the misery and distress that would be caused by excessive drinking in a hot climate would be simply appalling.

10. That the stoppage of the sale of opium will drive the inveterate users of opium of advanced age to certain death and the others to the use of spirits. The energy said to be wasted in opium will be again despoiled by the use of spirits. The amount of money spent by the Assam people in buying opium will not be saved and invested in reproductive industry, but will be squandered away in purchasing a positive poison. It may be alleged that religious scruples will come in the way of any large use of spirits. To this the simple answer would suffice that the bulk of those who use opium in Assam have no objection to, and often indulge in spirits, and have no religious scruples on that score.

11. That your memorialists would, however, welcome any measures that Government may adopt for the suppression of madak-khanas where chandoos are sold and for the discouragement of the consumption of opium by persons of tender age as a luxury, and your memorialists should not omit to mention that the number of young persons indulging in opium is very limited.

12. That your memorialists would respectfully submit that, even if the Government of this country adopt any measures for the limitation and restriction of the sale of this drug to any extent in this province, under instructions from the Home Government, the people of this province are not able, and would not be willing, to make up by the contribution of other taxes, any deficit in the revenues of the province caused by such measures holding as they do the views above set forth. The Government of this country will no doubt see the injustice of levying a tax upon the whole population for the supposed benefit of a minority who now use opium of their own accord for their own benefit and satisfaction, and on whom the Government has not forced the consumption of opium.

13. That the policy hitherto pursued by the British Government in respect of opium is the soundest imaginable. The restrictions imposed on the sale of opium and the gradually increasing price fixed on it have the effect of gradually diminishing the quantity consumed in each year. In the opinion of the people of this province there is no reason whatever to make any departure from the policy above described.

14. That your memorialists would in conclusion respectfully request that you may be pleased to submit this memorial for the consideration of the Government of India and of the Royal Commission apointed by Her Majesty's Government.

JAGANNATH BARUA
President
Debicharan Barua, B.A., B.L.,
Secretary.

Extract from the Proceedings of the Jorhat Sorbojanik Sobha, held on the 11th November 1893.

The chair was taken by the President Mr. Jagannath Baruah, B.A. About 300 members were present on the occasion, all classes of the people were represented including tea-planters, pleaders, landholders, Marwari merchants, Mahomedans and ryots, etc.. The chairman fully explained to the audience the object of the meeting.

Proposed by Mr. Debi Charan Baruah, B.A., B.L. Seconded by Srijut Benund Ram Baruah and carried unanimously. That the memorial read in this meeting be adopted for submission to the Chief Commissioner of Assam.

Jorhat Sorbojanik Sobha,
21st December 1893.

DEVI CHARAN BARUA
Secretary.

APPENDIX 10

Annual Immigration of Labour including Children into Assam Plantations

Year	No.	Year	No.
1902–03	26,684	1919–20	1,02,089
1903–04	22,162	1920–21	25,472
1904–05	24,209	1924–25	33,727
1905–06	31,830	1925–26	33,009
1906–07	25,617	1926–27	45,694
1907–08	84,824	1927–28	42,845
1908–09	60,773	1928–29	68,900
1909–10	39,332	1929–30	59,796
1910–11	43,657	1930–31	53,519
1911–12	58,646	1931-32	50,997
1912–13	59,873	1932–33	39,901
1913–14	58,646	1933–34	47,960
1914–15	63,638	1934–35	19,968
1915–16	1,10,376	1935–36	23,876
1916–17	48,130	1936–37	27,842
1917–18	19,407	1937–38	32,335
1918–19	2,22,171		

Note: Indentured labourers had to be continually brought from outside the province to compensate for inadequacy of local recruitment, deaths, discharge, desertions and loss by way of repatriation under the relevant Emigrant Labour Acts. After 1937–38, all leakages, taken together, exceeded what was added to the plantation labour force by way of immigration. But until then, a positive trend of increase in labour population through immigration was continuously there. The land settlement figures also indicate the pressure of this trend. Owned land-holdings of ex-coolies of plantations in the Brahmaputra Valley increased from 1,36,216 acres in 1908–09 to 2,27,362 acres in 1920–21 and 3,79,325 acres in 1940–41.

Source: *Assam Labour Enquiry Committee Reports* of 1906 and 1921–22; *Reports on Immigrant Labour in the Surma Valley and Hills Division as well as the Assam Valley Division* for the year ending 30 June 1929; *Annual Reports on the Working of the Tea Districts Emigration Labour Act* (XXII of 1932). Also, relevant *Reports of the Land Revenue Administration*, Government of Assam.

APPENDIX 11

Deployment of Armed Police Units to Suppress the 1921–22 Movement

Proclamation of Disturbed Areas (date of order)	Thana	Staf	Punitive Levy Rs. P.
23 Dec. 1921	Boko	One Platoon, Assam Rifles	2,779
1 Feb. 1922	Dharampasha (Sylhet)	Police	5,843
6 Feb. 1922	Simoluguri Teok Chowkat and Haligarh (Sibsagar)	1 Platoon, Assam Rifles	5,200
17 Feb. 1922	Barkhola (Cachar)	Police	6,332
20 Feb. 1922	Kanairghat (Sylhet)	"	25,529
21 Feb. 1922	Lakhipur (Sylhet)	"	2,481
23 Feb. 1922	Raha and Jamunamukh	"	2,542 2,529
1 March1922	Mangaldai and Kobigaon	1 Platoon, Assam Rifles	4,981
3 March1922	Ghiladhari, Moronge and Dergaon Mauzas	1 Platoon, Assam Rifles	4,790
10 March1922	Wards I-II, Karimganj Town	Police	9,982
20 March1922 25 April 1922 8 May 1922	Habiganj and Bahubal	"	16,658
8 May 1922	Ratabari	"	6,448
	Golapgunj, Karimganj and Jaldhup	"	22,210
20 March 1922 25 April 1922 8 May 1922	Muchikandi and Nabiganj	"	12,412
8 May 1922	Kulaura and Jaldhup	"	8,882
-do-	Maulvibazar, Kamalganj and Rajnagar	1 Platoon, Assam Rifles	17,951
-do-	Sylhet Sadar	Police	5,237
24 March 1922	North Salmara	Police	1,221
4 April 1922	Sonai	"	4,913
22 April 1922	Hailakandi and Katlichera	"	5,477
27 April 1922	Patharkandi	½ Platoon, Assam Rifles and Police	18,626

Source: Government statement, *Assam Legislative Council Proceedings* (1922), Vol. 2, pp. 791–78.

APPENDIX 12
ITA Circular to Garden Managers, 21 July 1947
Assam Branch Indian Tea Association, Labour Department

Private and Confidential and not for publication   Dibrugarh P.O.
No. L.D.—600   The 21st July, 1947

To
All Managers of Tea Gardens,
Assam Branch Indian Tea Association.

Dear Sir,

Labour
1. Babu Rabindra Kakoti of Sibsagar has been made responsible by the Indian National Trade Union Congress and the Hon'ble Prime Minister for the organization of tea garden labour in the Assam Valley.

2. To enable Babu Rabindra Kakoti to proceed with the Organization of labour, it was agreed at a meeting on 9th July, 1947 attended by your Branch Chairman and Labour Adviser, that a list of accredited labour workers would be forwarded to this office for circulation to all Managers. It was further agreed that all such labour workers would be in possession of an authority signed by Babu Rabindra Kakoti. (It follows therefore that Managers would be at liberty to refuse facilities to persons not in possession of this authority; in the event of such persons applying for permission to hold meetings on garden land they should be referred to Babu Rabindra Kakoti).

3. At this meeting an assurance was given by Babu Rabindra Kakoti that the speeches made by his labour workers would be directed solely to the purpose of organizing labour for the eventual introduction of Trade Unions, and would contain no material of any subversive nature that might upset the present relations between management and labour.'

Sd/- Labour Office.

Source: Copy forwarded by D.C., Sibsagar to Govt. of Assam on 'Congress Labour Union', No. SJC 27/34, dated Jorhat, 8 July 1947, Home, Confidential B, Confidential Branch File No. C253/47 (Assam Secretariat Files). The Hon'ble Prime Minister of Assam, as mentioned in the circular, was Gopinath Bardoloi.

APPENDIX 13
Community-wise Share of Government Jobs: Select Data

A: *Police Inspectors and Assistant Sub-Inspectors: Community-wise Breakdown, March 1936*

Belonging to Category	Surma Valley Division		Assam Valley Division		Provincial Total	
	No. of posts held	% share of all posts held by the communities mentioned	No. of posts held	% share of all posts held by the communities mentioned	No. of posts held	% share of all posts held by the communities mentioned
Hindu (other than Scheduled Castes)	130	(24.6)	151	(28.6)	281	(53.2)
Muslim	97	(18.4)	51	(9.7)	148	(28.0)
Scheduled Castes	5	(0.9)	11	(2.1)	16	(3.0)
Domiciled	9	(1.7)	12	(2.3)	21	(4.0)
Total	241	(45.6)	225	(42.7)	466	(88.2)
Non-Domiciled Bengali (including four Muslims)					52	(9.8)
Other outsiders to the province					10	(2.0)
Total					528	(100)

Source: Tabulated from P.C. Datta's reply, 11 March, *Assam Legislative Council Proceedings* (1936), Vol. 16, p. 39–40. Tribals, constituting 16 per cent of the population, presumably held a few posts, outside those listed above or none.

B: *Posts of Sub-Asst. Surgeons: Medical and Public Health: March 1935*

Incumbents belonging to	Surma Valley Division	Assam Valley Division	Of Outside Origin		Hill Tribes	Provincial Total
			Domiciled	Others		
	122	91	9	55	23	300
	(40.7)	(30.3)	(3.0)	(18.3)	(7.7)	(100)

Source: Tabulated from K.L. Barua's reply, 4 March, *Assam Legislative Council Proceedings* (1935), pp. 390–93.

(contd)

APPENDIX **13** *(contd)*

C: Posts of Sub-Asst. Surgeons; Medical and Public Health: September 1935

Category	No.	% share of posts
Assamese	57	(19.2)
Non-Muslim Sylhet–Cachar Natives*	103	(34.9)
People of Hills Districts	23	(7.8)
Muslims	51	(17.2)
Outsiders (including Domiciled)	62	(20.9)
Total	296	(100)

Note: * Including Scheduled Castes and plains tribals.

According to the 1931 Census, (i) Surma Valley non-Scheduled Caste Hindus consti-tuted 9 per cent, (ii) Assam Valley non-Scheduled Caste Hindus 26 per cent, (iii) Muslims of the province 31 per cent, (iv) Scheduled Castes 6 per cent, (v) tribals 16 per cent, and (vi) others 12 per cent of the provincial population.

The first group had a disproportionately large share of the jobs. For example, about 25 per cent of the police inspectorial and about 33 per cent of the medical jobs were held by this group. As a matter of policy, vacancies had been closed to outsiders to the province, as long as qualified persons were available locally. To compete for jobs, domiciled Bengalis had generally to produce domicile certificates.

In the wake of the 1935 Reforms, altogether eight communities were recognized by the government as distinct groups, with a view to securing for them population-wise, proportionate shares in the public services. These groups were: (1) Europeans and Anglo-Indians, (2) Hindus of the Surma Valley (excluding those falling in categories 5 and 6), (3) Hindus of the Brahmaputra Valley (excluding those falling in categories 5 and 6), (4) Muslims, (5) Scheduled Castes, (6) domiciled Hindus (other than ex-tea garden coolies), (7) hills and plains tribals, and (8) other communities.

Still earlier, for most of the period after 1917, there prevailed a slightly different practice of categorization into nine groups. Under this, the Ahoms were recognized as a separate group, but not the Scheduled Castes. In place of the Surma Valley Hindus, the term used then was 'Bengalis other than the people of Sylhet–Cachar'. In place of tribals in general, only the 'Khasi–Syenteng' community was mentioned. There was yet another group – 'Bengalis who were not domiciled'.

For a reference, see September, *Assam Legislative Council Proceedings* (1922), Vol. 2, p. 704. Speeches by S.M. Lahiri and S.M. Saadulla, 31 August, *Assam Legislative Council Proceedings* (1938), pp. 63–90 and *Assam Citizens Association* (Head Office, Dhubri, 140), pp. 74–133.

Source: K.L. Barua's reply, 18 September, *Assam Legislative Council Proceedings* (1935), Vol. 15, p. 1669.

Appendix 14

Elections to the Assam Legislative Assembly, 1946

Summary of Elections to the Assam Legislative Assembly

Class of constituency	No. of seats	No. of seats filled without contest	No. of candidates for contested seats	Total electo-rate	No. of scheduled caste voters	No. of woman voters	Total No. of voters in contested constituencies	No. of electors who voted	Col. 9 as % of col. 8 (poll participation rate)
(1)	(2)	(3)	(4)	(5)	(6)	(7)	(8)	(9)	(10)
1. General	47	12	101	8,10,700	59,195	1,09,232	6,11,799	3,02,023	49.3*
2. Muhammadan	34	1	108	5,19,627	–	35,275	5,14,752	2,73,398	53.1
3. Women's	1	–	4	5,087	–	5,087	5,087	2,878	56.5
4. European	1	–	2	2,837	–	977	2,837	1,130	39.8
5. Indian Christian	1	–	3	13,977	–	929	13,977	5,81˙	41.5
6. Backward Tribal (Plains)	4	1	9	46,220	–	2,890	37,567	11,440	30.4
7. Backward Areas (Hills)	5	–	19	26,142	–	9,766	26,142	16,436	62.8
8. Planting	9	7	5	2,006	–	3	758	701	92.5
9. Commerce and Industry	2	1	6	646	–	11	624	549	87.9
10. Labour (Tea Gardens)	4	–	9	38,444	–	10,632	38,444	14,755	38.3
Total:	108	22	266	14,65,686	59,195	1,74,802	12,51,987	6,29,121	50.3

Note: * This figure is worked out, to avoid an obvious typing or copying mistake (52.3).

       * Only four selected tea gardens.

Elections to the Assam Legislative Assembly, 1946

Number of Votes Polled by Various Political Parties in Elections to the Assam Legislative Assembly

Class of Constituency	Total no. of votes polled	Congress		Hindu Mahasabha		Muslim League		Nationalist Muslims		Communists		Others	
		No. of votes polled	% of votes polled	No. of votes polled	% of votes polled	No. of votes polled	% of votes polled	No. of votes polled	% of votes polled	No. of votes polled	% of votes polled	No. of votes polled	% of votes polled
1. General	4,16,848	3,26,304	78.3	5,337	1.3	–	–	–	–	17,851	4.3	67,356	16.1
2. Muhammadan	2,72,871	844	0.3	–	–	1,88,071	68.9	46,159	16.9	–	–	37,797	13.9
3. Women's	2,872	1,454	50.6	–	–	–	–	–	–	–	–	1,418	49.4
4. European	1,058	–	–	–	–	–	–	–	–	–	–	1,058	100.0
5. Indian Christian	5,772	950	16.5	–	–	–	–	–	–	–	–	4,822	83.5
6. Backward Tribal (Plains)	11,440	5,631	49.2	–	–	–	–	–	–	–	–	5,809	50.8
7. Backward Areas (Hills)	16,419	7,389	45.0	–	–	–	–	–	–	–	–	9,030	55.0
8. Planting	699	499	71.4	–	–	–	–	–	–	–	–	200	28.6
9. Commerce & Industry	541	536	99.1	–	–	–	–	–	–	–	–	5	0.9
10. Labour (Tea Gardens)	14,755	13,190	89.4	–	–	–	–	–	–	558	3.8	1,007	6.8
Total	7,43,275	3,56,797	48.0	5,337	1.3	1,88,071	68.9	46,159	16.9	18,409	2.5	1,28,502	17.3

Source: *Returns showing the Results of Elections to the Central Legislative Assembly and the Provincial Legislatures, 1946* (Govt. of India, Delhi, 1948), pp. 65 and 76.

APPENDIX 15

Number and Membership of Registered Trade Unions in Assam,
1938–39 to 1949–50

Year ending 31ˢᵗ March	No.	No. of Trade Unions Submitting Return	Membership
1938–39	3	–	–
1939–40	11	3	982
1940-41	6	6	1,476
1941–42	5	5	1,502
1942–43	5	5	1,948
1943–44	7	7	1,580
1944–45	9	9	2,486
1945–46	19	12	3,680
1946–47	36	25	13,518
1947–48	80	43	46,706
1948–49	71	43	1,07,725
1949–50	67	39	1,18,188

Source: A.S. Mathur and J.S. Mathur, *Trade Union Movement in India*, pp. 36 and 283–84.

APPENDIX 16
List of Ministers in Assam: 1 April 1937 to 15 August 1947

Name	No. of Terms	Particular Ministries Served*					
Saiyid Muhammad Saadulla[†]	5	I	II		IV	V	VI	
Abu Nasr Mahmud Waheed	1	I						
J.J.M. Nichols-Roy	3	I	II					VII
Rohini Kumar Chaudhuri[†]	4	I	II		IV		VI	
Muhamad Ali Haidar Khan	2	I		III				
Munawwar Ali	4		II		IV	V	VI	
Abdul Matin Chaudhuri	4		II		IV	V	VI	
Akshay Kumar Das[†]	3		II	III			VI	
Gopinath Bardoloi	2			III				VII
Ram Nath Das[†]	2			III				VII
Kamini Kumar Sen	1			III				
Rupnath Brahma[†]	4			III	IV	V	VI	
Fakhruddin Ali Ahmed[†]	1			III				
Muhamad Ali	1			III				
Hirendrachandra Chakravarty	2				IV	V		
Mudabbir Hussain Chaudhuri	3				IV	V	VI	
Mahendranath Saikia[†]	2				IV	V		
Sayidur Rahman[†]	3				IV	V	VI	
(Miss) Mavis Dunn	2				IV	V		
Nabakumar Datta[†]	1					V		
Baidyanath Mukherjee	2						VI	VII
Surendranath Buragohain[†]	1						VI	
Basanta Kumar Das	1							VII
Bishnu Ram Medhi[†]	1							VII
Abdul Matlib Mazumdar	1							VII
Bhimbar Deuri[†]	1							VII
Abdur Rashid	1							VII

Note: [†] Belonging to the Brahmaputra Valley.

* Of the seven ministries functioning during 1 April 1937–15 August 1947, as detailed below, II and VII were headed by G.N. Bardoloi as Chief Minister and the rest by Saadulla.

Ministries
I: 1 April 1937–5 February 1938
II: 5 February 1938–20 September 1938
III: 20 September 1938–17 November 1939
IV: 17 November 1939–25 December 1941
Governor's Regime under Section 93, Act of 1985 (26 Dec. 1941–24 August 1942)
V: 25 August 1942–23 March 1945
VI: 23 March 1945–(caretaker till general elections) 11 February 1946
VII: 11 February 1946–14 August 1947

Source: File No. F. 106/8/45-R, Bureau of Public Information, Government of India, Morgue and Reference Series, No. 11, New Delhi 1 February 1946, Reforms Dept., Government of India (NAI); also, *Indian Annual Register*, January–June 1947, Vol. 1 and relevant year-books.

Glossary

abkari	the excise on drugs and liquors
abwab	illegal cesses claimed by and paid to revenue collectors
ahu (aush)	a variety of short-maturing rice suitable for dry farming
ali	a road
Angami	a particular tribe of Nagaland
Ao	a particular tribe of Nagaland
Anjuman	an association of Muslims
arkatti	agents employed to recruit labourers for a concern or concerns
bari	land suitable for homestead site, so classified for taxation purposes
bigha	land measurement unit equivalent to one-third of an acre
bhadralok	a person claiming or believed to have a superior social and cultural status because of his caste and/or literacy; a status group consisting of such persons
Bodo (Bodo–Kachari)	a plains tribe of the Brahmaputra Valley and North Cachar Hills
brahmottar	revenue-free land grants to Brahmins
char	a river island or banks seasonally submerged in water
Charing Raja	a high-ranking Ahom prince, so named after the estate in his charge
chaukidari tax	a local tax collected in permanently settled areas to maintain a village watchman
Daivajna	a high caste in Assam, claiming equal status with Brahmins
Dangariya	an Ahom noble; a *bhadralok* in modern usage
devottar	revenue-free land grants to temples

Dewani	the headman of a Bengali Muslim immigrant village in the Brahmaputra Valley
dharmottar	revenue-free land grants for religious purposes
dhewa/dhawa	a battle; a hot chase
Fauzdari Mohrur	a petty employee of the Criminal Court
fatwa	an opinion on a point of Islamic law given by a competent religious person or a body of such persons
feringhee/feringhi	a white man; Europeans
ganja	the top leaves and tender part of Indian hemp dried for smoking as an intoxicant; hashish
gaon-burha	a near-hereditary, government-appointed village headman in Assam
Garo	a tribe mostly living in the Garo Hills district
gherao	to surround a person in authority and pressurize non-violently
Goswami	a Vaishnava preceptor
haat	a weekly or bi-weekly market serving a group of villages
Hitaishini Sabha	a welfare association
Jaintia	a section of Khasis living in the Jaintia sub-division of the Khasi and Jaintia Hills district
jhum/jhuming	slash and burn cultivation
Kachari	see Bodo
kala azar	black fever
Kalita	a peasant caste ranked high in the Brahmaputra Valley
Kamakhya	a mother goddess
kaniya	an opium-eater ('*kani*' is opium).
Kayastha	a high caste in the Brahmaputra Valley, often inter-marrying with Kalitas
kear	a land measurement unit in Sylhet, equivalent to one-third of an acre
Khasi	a tribe mainly living in the Khasi and Jaintia Hills district
khiraj	full revenue-paying land
la-khiraj	land freed from payment of revenue
Lalung	a plains tribe of the Brahmaputra Valley
Lhota	a tribe of Nagaland
Lushai	a tribe of Mizoram
Mahanta	a non-Brahmin head of a Vaishnava monastery; also used as a surname
Mandal	a village surveyor in government employ

mauza	an areal unit of a group of villages, for purposes of land revenue collection
mauzadar	a revenue collector, on a commission basis, in charge of a *mauza*
maund	a measure of weight equivalent to a little more than 82.1 lbs.
Matbar	same as '*Dewani*'
mel	an assembly of people
mirasdar	a person owning a superior tenure of land in Cachar
Moamaria (Mayamaria)	a religious sect of the Vaishnava faith in the Brahmaputra Valley
muga	a kind of silk with a golden hue
Mujahadin	those who are engaged in a *jihad*, a struggle enjoined upon the faithful by Islam
Mymensingia	people hailing from the district of Mymensingh; in the Assam context, Bengali Muslim immigrants, most of whom were from that district
nisfkhiraj	land paying revenue at half the going rate
paan	betel-leaves
panchayat	a traditional court of arbitration
panda	a temple priest in a pilgrimage centre
pargana	a traditional grouping of villages for revenue purposes, in those parts of Assam that were once under Mughal rule
praja	ryots; tenants
raij	public; a local public
rupit	transplanted rice land
Sabha	an association
sadhana	practice with single-minded devotion
sali	a long-maturing variety of rice requiring transplantation
Samiti	an association
Sammilan	a conference; an associate body
Samrakshini Sabha	a society for conservation (of)
Sarbajanik	for all; universal
sardari	a system of recruitment through a *sardar* or head coolie
satra	a Vaishnava monastery, typical of the Brahmaputra Valley
satradhikar	the head of a *satra*
seer	one-fortieth of a maund
Siem	the chief of a Khasi tribal state
Singpho	a Kachin tribe of Assam–Burma border tracts

Synteng	see Jaintia
tola	a measure of weight equivalent to 180 grains troy
tahsil	an areal unit for land revenue collection
ulema	Arabic plural of *alim*, a scholar; loosely used to describe the Muslim ecclesiastical class as a whole
Shakta	those following a mother goddess cult
Vaishnava	worshippers of Vishnu

Selective Bibliography

Primary Sources
Manuscript Collections
Official Records and Reports – unpublished and published
Newspapers and Periodicals
Other Works and Reports

Secondary Sources
Books and Unpublished Theses
Articles and Papers

Fuller details of sources, listed below, will be found in the relevant footnotes running page-wise for the text. Here it is simply intended to indicate their nature.

PRIMARY SOURCES

Manuscript Collections

All-India Congress Committee Files, 1927–47, and Nehru Papers (Nehru Memorial Museum and Library, New Delhi).

Rajendra Prasad Collection (RPC) (National Archives of India, New Delhi).

Assam Pradesh Congress Committee Papers, 1930–47 (Congress Bhavan, Gauhati).

Gopinath Bardoloi Papers, by courtesy of his daughter, Mrs Lily Majindar-Barua of B. Barooah College, Gauhati. [This is a thin collection of a few extant letters and transcripts of other letters not in her possession.]

A file of private papers of Sriman Prafulla Goswami, relating to the Congress Socialist Party for 1939 and 1940.

K.K. Chanda's notebook and the transcript of a letter received by him from Surendranath Banerjee, by courtesy of Mrs Anuradha Chanda of the Department of History, Jadavpur University, Calcutta.

A file containing 'Notes on the left movement and growth of the CPI in the Surma Valley and comments thereon by Jyotirmay Nandy, 12 November 1972', by courtesy of Chinmohan Sehanavis, Calcutta. [The notes were compiled by Prafulla Misra of Shillong for the years beginning the 1930s.]

Materials collected up to 15 November 1955 by Regional Committee for Assam, compilation of the History of the Freedom Movement in Assam, by courtesy of A.C. Bhuyan, Editor of the 'History of Freedom Movement', Government of Assam, Gauhati. [This collection includes *inter alia* a number of notes submitted by freedom-fighters. Some of these notes are no doubt exaggerated, even faulty accounts of their own individual roles. But some are informative and useful.]

Jenkins, Capt. Francis, *Journal of a Tour in Upper Assam, 1838* and some other documents in the collection of the Department of Historical and Antiquarian Studies (Government of Assam, Gauhati).

Official Records and Reports – unpublished and published

Government of Assam

Assam Secretariat Files in the State Archives of Assam, Shillong. [The Archives were in the process of being shifted to Gauhati, when I was working there. It was interesting to find that the files available for the years 1937–47 were extremely scant, compared to the preceding years. The authorities were obviously reluctant to expose their files to researchers' scrutiny.]

Police Records at the Office of the Deputy Inspector-General of Police, Shillong. [Only a few documents related to the 1940s were released for consultation, after due scrutiny of each by a responsible officer. However, by courtesy of the Editor, 'History of Freedom Movement', Government of Assam, Gauhati, select extracts from *Assam Police Intelligence Abstracts* were available to us. Police intelligence reports, though often unreliable otherwise, help restore the chronology, if missing in other kinds of evidences.]

Dutt, K.N., comp., *History of Freedom Movement in India: Compilation of Materials in the State of Assam – A Synopsis and a Catalogue of Materials Collected up to 15th November 1955*, Bulletin No. I (Shillong, 1956). [This useful printed catalogue was withdrawn by the Government of Assam from circulation, as some of the materials collected were apparently of doubtful historical value. We found it useful, as the collection is well-preserved in the Office of the Editor, 'History of Freedom Movement', Government of Assam, Gauhati.]

An Account of the Province of Assam and Its Administration (Shillong, 1903) and other *Annual Administration Reports* of Assam.

Allen, B. C., ed., *Assam District Gazetteers* (1905 onwards).

Proceedings of the Assam Legislative Council, 1912–1947. [The Council was the sole provincial legislature till 1936, and its second chamber thereafter.]

Report of the Working of the Assam Legislative Assembly 1937–45 (Shillong, 1946).

Report of the Working of the Assam Legislative Assembly, 1937–47.

Excise Department, Government of Assam, *Excise Statistical Tables for the Province of Assam* (Shillong, 1927) and annual reports.

Report of the Committee Appointed to Enquire into Certain Aspects of Opium and Ganja Consumption (Botham Committee, Shillong, December 1913).

Report of the Committee Appointed to Enquire into Certain Aspects of Opium and Ganja Consumption (Nichols–Roy Committee, Shillong, 1933).

Report from the Committee of the Assam Legislative Council Appointed to Co-operate with the Indian Statutory Commission (W.D. Smiles Committee, Shillong, 1929).

Report of the Court of Enquiry (Chairman: J.C. Higgins, 7 January 1939), *Report of the Board of Conciliation* (K.K. Hajra, 8 August 1939) and *Report of the Committee of Enquiry* (M.M. Mukerjee, 25 November 1939) into the Affairs at Digboi, Government of Assam, Shillong.

Report of the Line System Committee, Vols. 1–2 (Hockenhull Committee, Shillong, 1938).

Annual Reports on the Land Revenue Administration (Shillong).

Director, Department of Land Records and Agriculture, *Assam Valley Reassessment Report* (Shillong, 1893).

Laine, A.J., D.C. of Goalpara, *An Account of the Land Revenue System of Goalpara: with Criticisms of the Existing Rent Law and Suggestions for Its Improvements* (Shillong, 1917).

'Annual Government Resolutions on Immigrant Labour in Assam' (Shillong).

Assam Gazette (Shillong), select issues, Parts II and VI.

Government of East Bengal and Assam, 1905–12

Report of the Administration of East Bengal and Assam 1905–06 (Shillong, 1907) and other *Annual Administration Reports* of the province.

'Annual Government Resolutions on Immigrant Labour in the Assam Districts of East Bengal and Assam' (Shillong).

Proceedings of Eastern Bengal and Assam Legislative Council, 1906–12.

Gupta, G.N., *A Survey of the Industries and Resources of Eastern Bengal and Assam for 1907–08* (1908).

Eastern Bengal and Assam Gazette, Part VI, select issues.

Government of Bengal, up to 1873

Proceedings of Bengal Legislative Council, select years.

Proceedings of the Legislative Department, 1867, and other *Proceedings*, as mentioned in relevant footnotes, State Archives of West Bengal.

Annual Administration Reports.

Report on the Revenue Administration of the Lower Province, 1870–71.

Selections from the Records of the Government of Bengal, Vol. 57 (Calcutta, 1861).

Report of the Commissioners on the Tea Cultivation of Assam, 1868.

Papers Relating to the Tea Industry of Bengal (Calcutta, 1873).

Mills, A.J.M., *Report on the Province of Assam* (Calcutta, 1854).

Government of India

Home Public, Home Political, Foreign Secret and Foreign Political Proceedings as well as Reforms Office and Legislative Department in the National Archives of India. [Only relevant documents for our period were consulted.]

Abstract of the Proceedings of the Council of the Governor-General of India, 1894, Vol. 33 (Calcutta, 1895) and other *Proceedings of the Imperial Legislative Council.*

India in 1920: A Report Prepared for Presentation to Parliament (Calcutta, 1921).

India in 1921–22: A Report Prepared for Presentation to Parliament (Calcutta, 1922).

India in 1928–29: A Report Prepared for Presentation to Parliament (Calcutta, 1929).

'Conditions of the People of Assam', No. 10, pp. 1–92 in Government of India, *Proceedings of the Revenue and Agricultural Department for December 1888, Famine Reports on the Condition of the Lower Classes of the Population in India*, Nos. 1–24, Confidential (National Archives of India).

Annual Reports on Immigrant Labour in the Assam Valley and the Surma Valley Divisions.

Annual Reports on the Working of Tea Districts Emigrants Act (XXII of 1932).

Report on an Enquiry into Conditions of Labour in Plantations in India (Labour Investigation Committee, Chairman: D.V. Rege, 1946).

Assam Labour Enquiry Committee, 1906: Proceedings in the Recruiting and Labour Districts.

Indian Labour Year-Book, 1947–48.

Report of the Assam Banking Enquiry Committee, 1929–30, Vols. 1–2.

Bureau of Public Information, Government of India, *Provincial Autonomy: Ministries and Parties in Assam, 1937–45* (National Archives of India).

Note on Land Transfers and Agricultural Indebtedness in India, 1895.

The Naga Problem (External Publicity Division, Ministry of External Affairs, New Delhi, n.d.).

Summary of the Report of the Commission of Enquiry into the RIN Mutiny, February 1946 (Government of India Press, New Delhi, 1946).

Imperial Gazetteers of India, Vols 1 and 4 (second edition, 1885).

Census of India, relevant volumes on Assam.

Government of UK

Official Reports Fifth Series, *Parliamentary Debates Commons*, 1934–35, Vol. 299.

East India/Indian Constitutional Reforms, *Views of Local Governments on the Working of the Reforms dated 1927* (London, 1928).

———, *Return Showing the Results of Elections in India* 1923 (presented to Parliament, London, 1924).

———, *Return Showing the Results of Elections in India 1925 and* 1926 (London, 1927).

—————, *Return Showing the Results of Elections in India* 1937 (Delhi, 1937).

—————, *Return Showing the Results of Elections to the Central Legislative Assembly and the Provincial Legislatures 1945–46* (Delhi, 1948).

—————, *Report of the Indian Franchise Committee, 1932, Vol. I* (London, 1932).

—————, Southborough Committee, Vol. I, *The Franchise Committee 1918–19* (London, 1919).

—————, *Letter from the Government of India dated 5th March 1919 and Enclosures on the Questions Raised in the Report on Indian Constitutional Reform* (London, 1919).

—————, *Return Showing the Results of Election in India 1923* (presented to Parliament, London, 1924).

Royal Commission on Labour in India, *Written Evidence*, Vol. 6, Part I, *Assam and the Douars* (London, 1930).

Royal Commission on Opium, *Report and Minutes of Evidences 1892–93*, Vols 1–7 (London, 1894).

The Transfer of Power, 1942–47, Vols I–V (London, 1970–74).

Newspapers and Periodicals

English

Weekly Assam Tribune (Dibrugarh), 1939–46.

Daily Assam Tribune (Gauhati), 1946–47.

Amrita Bazar Patrika (Calcutta), select issues.

The Statesman (Calcutta), select issues.

Shillong Times (Weekly), 1946–47.

People's War (Weekly, Bombay), July 1942–November 1945.

People's Age (Weekly that replaced *People's War*), November 1945–1948.

[There was no locally published daily newspaper in the nineteenth century or even during World War II. In fact, excepting for a new years, Assam had no local daily during the entire period under review in this book.]

The Bengalee, Friend of India, Hindoo Patriot, Indian Echo, Indian Nation, Indian Mirror and the Mussalman. [Only selections of news and views from these newspapers, as reproduced serially in *Daily Assam Tribune*, 1965–74, have been consulted.]

Also, Press Information Bureau, India, *Annual Reports*, 1917–18 to 1924–25.

Bengali

Samachar-darpan (Serampore) and *Somprakash* (Changripota) in *Selections*, published by Brajendranath Bandopadhyay and Binoy Ghosh, respectively, in several volumes.

Assamese

Asamiiya (Weekly, Dibrugarh/later Gauhati), 1918–47; a few volumes are missing in the collection of the DHAS, Gauhati.

[Files of Assamese newspapers are not easily available, even if extant. A stray copy of *Dainik Batori* (Jorhat) was checked for me by Munindranath Barkataki of the Department of Journalism, the University of Gauhati.]

Files of *Arunoday* (Sibsagar), *Mau* (Calcutta) and *Asam Bandhu* (Calcutta) – monthlies – were consulted at the British Museum/India Office libraries, London, in 1961. Selections from *Arunoday* are also available in Birinchi Kumar Barua, comp., *Arunodair Dhalphal* (Jorhat, 1965).

Avahan (Monthly, Calcutta), 1929–40.

Dinanath Sharma, *Soviet Biplav Aru Asamiya Sahitya* (Gauhati, 1973); O.K. Das, comp., *Banhiir Pratiddhani* (Dhekiajuli, 1968); Sashi Sharma, comp., *Lenin, Rus Biplav aru Bharat* (Gauhati, 1971) – there are other references containing extracts or reprints from Assamese monthlies.

Other Works and Reports

English

Assam Citizens' Association (compiled by Dhubri Head Office, Gauhati, 1940).

Assam Congress Opium Enquiry Report (Jorhat, 1925).

The Assam Directory and Tea Areas Hand-book (Annual publication, Calcutta).

Report of the Indian National Congress held at Calcutta, 1886, and similar reports on the annual sessions that followed. [There is a fairly complete collection of these reports in the Servants of India Society Library, Poona.]

Indian National Congress, 1920–23 (anonymous compiler, Allahabad, 1924).

Iswara Dutt, K., *The Congress Cyclopaedia: The Indian National Congress 1885–1920*, Vol. 1 (New Delhi, n.d.)

Sharma, J.S., *Indian Struggle for Freedom: Select Documents and Sources*, Vols 2–3 (Delhi, 1965).

Communist Party of India, Assam Provincial Organizing Committee, *Assam Fights for Freedom and Democracy: Draft Resolutions of Assam Communists* (Gauhati, n.d.).

Indian Annual Register, 1919–47 (edited by H.N. Mitra, and later, N.N. Mitra; Annual publication, Calcutta). For some years it was also called *Indian Quarterly Register*.

Aditya, R.N., *From the Corridors of Memory* (Calcutta, 1970).

Antrobus, H.A., *A History of the Assam Company 1839–1953* (Edinburgh, 1957).

———, *A History of the Jorehaut Tea Co. Ltd., 1859–1946* (London, 1948).

Assam Legislative Assembly, *Who's Who 1956* (Assembly Secretariat, Shillong, July 1956).

Azad, Abul Kalam, *India Wins Freedom: An Autobiographical Narrative* (Calcutta, 1959).

Barpujari, H.K., ed., *The Golden Jubilee Volume: Cotton College* (Gauhati, 1951–52).

Cotton, Sir Henry, *Indian and Home Memories* (London, 1911).

Durga Das, ed., *Sardar Patel's Correspondence 1945–50*, Vols. 1–10 (Ahmedabad, 1971–74).

Fuller, Sir Bampfylde, *Some Personal Experiences* (London, 1930).

Ganguli, Dwaraka Nath, *Slavery in Indian Dominion*, edited by K.L. Chattopadhyay; reprints of thirteen articles published in the *Bengalee*, September 1886 to April 1887 (Calcutta, 1972).

Hallsworth, J., and A.A. Purcell, M.P., *Report on Labour Conditions in India* (Trade Union Congress General Council, London, 1928).

Moon, P., ed., *Wavell the Visoroy's Journal* (London, 1973).

Pal, Bipin Chandra, *Memoirs of My Life and Times*, Vols 1–2 (second revised edition, Calcutta, 1973).

Prasad, Rajendra, *India Divided* (Bombay, 1946).

———, *Autobiography* (Bombay, 1957).

Reid, Sir Robert, *Years of Change in Bengal and Assam* (London, 1967).

Tayyebulla, M., *Between the Symbol and the Idol at Last* (New Delhi, 1964).

Zaidi, A.M., *The Way Out to Freedom: An Enquiry into the Quit India Movement Conducted by Participants* (New Delhi, 1973). [Contains a summary (pp. 73–79) of the Assam Pradesh Congress Committee's enquiry report on the Quit India Movement in Assam.]

Assamese

Agarwala, T.K., ed., *Haribilas Agarwala Dangariiyar Atmajiivanii* (Gauhati, 1967).

Assam Sahitya Sabhar Bhashanawalii, Part I (Gauhati, 1955).

Bardoloi, K.C., ed., *Sadaramiinar Atmmajiivanii* (Gauhati, 1960).

Barthakur, Padmanath, *Swadhinata Ranar Samsparshat* (Dibrugarh, 1968).

Barua, Gunabhiram, *Anandaram Dhenkial Phukanar Jiivan Caritra* (second edition, Calcutta, 1915).

Bezbarua, Lakshminath, *Mor Jivan Sonvaran* (Jorhat, 1961).

———, *Bezbaruvar Dinalekha*, edited by M. Neog (Jorhat, 1969).

Communist Party of India, Assam Provincial Committee, *Bharatar Communist Party Asam Pradeshik Sanmilan Rajnaitik Prastav: Pratham Adhiveshan* (Gauhati, 11–14 February 1948).

Hajarika, Atulchandra, ed., *Bhashanmala: Asam Chatra Sammilanar Bhashan-Sangraha* (Gauhati, 1960).

Raychaudhury, Ambikagiri, *Svadhiin Pancayat Rashtragathanar Ancani* (second edition, Gauhati, 1946).

———, *Mor Jivan Dhumuhar Echati* (Gauhati, 1973).

———, *Rachanavali* (Guwahati, 1986).

Sharma, Benudhar, *Congressar Kanciali Ra'dat* (Gauhati, 1959).

Sharma, Brajanath, *Biplavii* (Gauhati, 1973).

Sharma, Krishnath, *Krishna Sharmar Dairy* (Gauhati, 1972).

Sharma, Purnachandra, *Mor Atiitar Sonvaranii aru Nagaon Zilat Mukti Samgram*, Vol. I, 1900–32 (Nowgong, 1973).

Sharma, S., ed., *Tyagabiir Hem Baruva Smriti grantha* (Gauhati, 1971).

Tayyebulla, M., *Karagarar Cithi* (Gauhati, 1962).

SECONDARY SOURCES

Books and Unpublished Theses

English

Aditya, R.N., *Fight for Freedom in Sylhet* (Karimganj, 1964).

Andrews, C.F., *Opium Evil in India* (London, 1926).

Bamford, P.C., *Histories of the Non-Cooperation and Khilafat Movements* (Delhi, 1925).

Banerjee D.N., *East Pakistan: A Case Study in Muslim Politics* (Delhi, 1969).

Bareh, Hamlet, *The History and Culture of the Khasi People* (Shillong, 1967).

Barpujari, H.K., *Assam in the Days of the Company 1826–1858* (Gauhati, 1963).

Barooah, N.K., *David Scott in North East India: A Study in British Paternalism* (New Delhi, 1970).

Bhuyan, A.C., 'The Second World War and Indian Nationalism: A Study of the Quit India Movement' (unpublished Ph.D. thesis, School of International Studies, Jawaharlal Nehru University, New Delhi, 1972).

Bhuyan, S.K., *Anglo-Assamese Relations 1771–1826* (Gauhati, 1949).

Borra, J.N., *Bolinarayan Borrah: His Life, Work and Musings* (Calcutta, 1967).

Bose, Sanat Kumar, *Capital and Labour in the Indian Tea Industry* (All India Trade Union Congress, Bombay, 1954).

Broomfield, J.H., *Elite Conflicts in a Plural Society: Twentieth Century Bengal* (Bombay, 1968).

Brown, Judith M., *Gandhiji's Rise to Power: Indian Politics 1915–1922* (Cambridge, 1972).

Centenary Volume, C.F. Andrews 1871–1971 (Deenabandhu Andrews Centenary Committee, Calcutta, 1972).

Chamanlal, D., *Coolie: the Story of Labour and Capital in India* (Lahore, 1932).

Chandra, Bipan, *The Rise and Growth of Economic Nationalism in India* (New Delhi, 1966; reprinted, 1969).

Chattopadhyay, Gautam, *Communism and Bengal's Freedom Movement*, Vol. 1: 1917–29 (New Delhi/Bombay, 1970).

Chaube, S., *Hill Politics in North-East India* (Calcutta, 1973).

———, *Constituent Assembly of India: Spring-board of Revolution* (New Delhi, 1973).

Coupland, R., *The Constitutional Problem of India*, Part III (Oxford University Press, 1944).

Das, R.K., *Plantation Labour in India* (Calcutta, 1931).

Devi Charan Barua Birth Centenary Souvenir 1964 (Jorhat, 1964).

Dutt, K.N., *Landmarks of the Freedom Struggle in Assam* (Gauhati, 1958; reprinted, 1969).

Dutt, R. Palme, *India Today* (second Indian edition, Calcutta, 1970).

Elwin, Verrier, *Nagaland* (Shillong, 1961).

Gait, E.A., *A History of Assam* (second edition, Calcutta/Simla, 1926).

Galagher, J., G. Johnson and Anil Seal, *Locality, Province and Nation 1870–1940* (Cambridge, 1973).

Gopal, S., *British Policy in India 1858–1905* (Cambridge, 1965).

Gordon, L.A., *Bengal: the Nationalist Movement 1876–1970* (Delhi, 1974).

Goswami, P.C., *The Economic Development of Assam* (Bombay, 1963).

Griffiths, P., *The History of the Indian Tea Industry* (London, 1967).

Hardy, P. *The Muslims of British India* (Cambridge, 1972).

Jha, M., *Role of Central Legislature in the Freedom Struggle* (New Delhi, 1972).

Kar, Parimalchandra, *British Annexation of Garo Hills* (Calcutta, 1970).

Khaliquzzaman, Chowdhry, *Pathway to Pakistan* (Lahore, 1961).

Lahiri, R.M., *The Annexation of Assam 1824–54* (Calcutta, 1954).

Longer, V., *Red Coats to Olive Green: A History of the Indian Army* (Bombay, 1974).

Mazumdar, B.B., *Indian Political Associations and Reform of Legislature 1818–1917* (Calcutta, 1965).

McCall, Major A.G., *Lushai Chrysalis* (London, 1949).

Mukherjee, H. and Uma Mukherjee, *Bipin Chandra Pal and India's Struggle for Swaraj* (Calcutta, 1958).

Sarkar, Sumit, *The Swadeshi Movement in Bengal 1903–1908* (New Delhi, 1973).

Sayeed, Khalid B., *Pakistan: the Formative Phase 1857–1948* (second edition, New York/Karachi, 1968).

Sen, S.P., ed., *Dictionary of National Biography*, Vols 1–4 (Calcutta, 1972–74).

Sharma, Benudhar, *The Rebellion of 1857 vis-à-vis Assam* (Gauhati, 1957).

Sharma, Atulchandra, 'A Study of Assam Finances – Structure and Trend, 1947–48 to 1965–66' (unpublished D.Phil. thesis, Gauhati University, 1971).

Srinivas, M.N., *Social Change in Modern India* (Berkeley, 1966).

Stalin, J.V., *Works,* Vol. 2, *1907–13* (Moscow, 1953).

Tarachand, *History of the Freedom Movement in India*, Vols 3–4 (New Delhi, 1972).

Thomas, M.M. and R.W. Taylor, eds, *Tribal Awakening: A Group Study* (Bangalore, 1965).

Tripathi, Amales, *The Extremist Challenge in India between 1890–1910* (Calcutta, 1967).

Venkata Rao, V., *A Hundred Years of Local Self Government in Assam* (second edition, Gauhati, 1965).

Assamese

Agarwala, Jyotiprasad, *Candrakumar Agarwala* (Gauhati, 1967).

Ali, Najar, *Mor Jiivanar Kichu Katha* (Mangaldai, 1969).

Bardoloi, Gopinath, *Gandhiji* (Gauhati, 1969).

Barua, Atulchandra *et al., Saratcandra Gosvamiir Camu Jiivani* (Gauhati, n.d.).

Barua, Golokeshvar, *Suryya Aru Suryyabipra* (Gauhati, 1974).

Barua, Harendranath, *et al.*, eds, *Bharatar Mukti Yujat Asam* (Gauhati, 1972).

Barua, Prafullachandra, *Uttamcandra Baruvar Jiivanii* (Gauhati, 1962).

Bhattacharya, Narendrakumar, *Karmmayogii Bhuban Gagai* (Sibsagar, 1956).

Bhuyan, Nakulchandra, *Radhakanta Sandiqai Dangariiya* (Jorhat, 1961).

Bhuyan, Suryakumar, *Anandaram Baruva Jiivan Carit* (Gauhati, 1955).

Bhuyan, Suryakumar, ed., *Asamiiya Alocaniit Prakashita Buranjiimulak Pravan-dhavaliir Talika*, Part I (Assam Sahitya Sabha, Jorhat, 1955).

Bora, Lakshmiram, comp., *Asamar Sankhshep Itihas* (Gauhati, 1875).

Chaudhuri, Dilip, *Nilmani Phukanar Cintadhara* (Gauhati, 1972).

Communist Party of India, Assam State Council, *Silver Jubilee Souvenir* (Gauhati, May 1969).

———, *Janamat* (Weekly, Gauhati), Vol. 15, special issue, 22 December 1975.

Das, Tilakchandra, *Ambikagirii Aru Teonr Jiivan Darshan*, Vol. I (Gauhati, 1952).

Gohain-Barua, Padmanath, ed., *Jiivanii Sangraha* (enlarged edition, Gauhati, 1969).

Goswami, J., *Jagannath Baruva* (Jorhat, 1976).

Goswami, Pandit Pratapchandra, *Jiivan Smriti Aru Kamrupii Samaj* (Gauhati, 1971).

Goswami, Prafulladatta, *Manikcandra Baruva Aru Teonr Yug* (Gauhati, 1970).

Hajarika, Atulchandra and H. Sharma, eds, *Kamrup Ratnamala* (Gauhati, 1973).

Kalita, Benudhar, *Phulagurir Dhewa* (Deurigaon, Nowgong, 1961).

Kalita, Dandinath, *Karmmabiir Candranath* (Tezpur, 1846 *shaka*).

Neog, Hariprasad, *Pramathanath Cakravartii* (Jorhat, 1968).

———, *Radhakanta Handiqui* (Asam Sahitya Sabha, Jorhat, 1960).

Neog, Hariprasad, ed., *Herambaprasad Baruva: Smriti-nivandha* (Golaghat, 1968).

———, *Asam Sahitya Sabhar Pancash Bacar* (Asam Sahitya Sabha, Jorhat, n.d.).

Phukan, Lakshminath, *Mahatmarpara Rupkonwaralai* (Calcutta, 1969).

Saikia, Chandraprasad, ed., *Asamat Mahatma* (Gauhati, 1969).

———, *Radhanath Changkakatii* (Gauhati, 1971).

———, *Bimalaprasad Caliha* (Gauhati, 1972).

———, *Smriti-grantha : Karmmabiir Nabiincandra Bardaloi* (Gauhati, 1975).

Rajkhowa, Benudhar, *Mor Jiivan Dapon* (Gauhati, 1969).

Raychaudhury, Ambikagiri, *Dekadekeriir Ved* (Gauhati, 1958).

Saikia, Chidananda, ed., *Dhiren Datta Smritigrantha* (Golaghat, 1974).

Sharma, Benudhar, *Maniram Devan* (Gauhati, 1950).

———, *Gangagovinda Phukan* (Gauhati, 1948).

Sharma, Dineshwar, *Patharughatar Ran* (Mangaldai, 1957).

Talukdar, Nanda, *Kanaklal Baruva* (Gauhati, 1972).

Bengali

Ahmad, Abul Mansur, *Amar Dekha Rajnitir Pancas Bacar* (Dacca, 1970).

Bhattacharya, Ajoy, *Nankar Vidroha*, Vol. 1 (Dacca, 1973).

Bhattacharya (Vidyaratna), Ramkumar, *Udasii Satyashrabar Asam Bhraman* (Calcutta, 1880).

Dhekial-Phukan, Anandaram, *Ain O Byabastha Sangraha: Notes on Laws of Bengal*, Vol. I (Calcutta, 1855).

Dhekial-Phukan, Haliram, *Asam Buranji*, Parts I–IV (Calcutta, 1829); edited by J. Bhattacharya (Gauhati, 1962).

Guha, N.K., *Banglay, Biplabvad* (fourth edition, Calcutta, 1376 BS).

Gupta-Chaudhury, N., ed., *Shriihatta Pratibha* (Sylhet, 1961).

Walliullah, M., *Yugabicitra* (Dacca, 1967).

Hindi

Sahajananda, Saraswati Swami, *Mera Jiivan Sangharsha* (*Patna*, 1952).

Articles and Papers

English

Bardaloi, N.C., 'Conditions of Labour in the Tea Gardens of Assam', *India* (London), 14 November 1919.

Barpujari, H.K., 'Facts behind the Jaintia rebellion 1862–64', *Journal of Indian History*, 51, Part I (April 1873).

Barua Harendranath, 'The Development Scheme: Position of Indigenous People', *Assam Tribune*, 29 August 1941.

Chattopadhyay, Gautam, 'The Almost Revolution: India in February 1946', *Indian Left Review*, 3 (April 1974).

Chaudhury, B.N., 'Democracy in Action', *Assam Tribune*, 11 April 1941.

Desai, S.P., 'My Thirty-Five Years in Assam', K.L. Punjabi, ed., *The Civil Servant in India* (Bombay, 1965).

Gohain, Hiren, 'Origins of the Assamese Middle Class', *Social Scientist*, 2 (August 1973).

Guha, Amalendu, 'Colonization of Assam: Years of Transitional Crisis (1825–40)', *Indian Economic and Social Hitory Review (IESHR)*, 5 (June 1968).

———, 'Colonization of Assam: Second Phase 1840–1859', *IESHR*, 4 (December 1967).

———, 'Socio-economic Change in Agrarian Assam', in M.K. Chaudhuri, ed., *Trends in Socio-Economic Change in India 1871–1961* (Simla, 1967).

———, 'The McMahon Line in Contemporary History', in M.S. Rajan, ed., *Studies in Politics: National and International* (Delhi, 1970).

———, 'Impact of Bengal Renaissance on Assam 1825–75', *IESHR*, 9 (September 1972).

———, 'Geography behind History: An Introduction to Socio-economic Study of North-east India', *Northeastern Affairs*, 2 (Annual, 1973).

———, 'Bhasani and East Bengal Immigrants in Assam Politics: 1928–47', paper presented to the 35th session of the Indian History Congress, Calcutta, December 1974; see *Indian History Congress Thirtyfifth Session: Summaries of Papers* (Jadavpur University, December 1974).

Kar, Parimalchandra, 'A Point of View on the Garos in Transition', in Pannalal Dasgupta, ed., *A Common Perspective for North-East India* (Calcutta, 1967).

Kar, M., 'Muslim Politics in Assam', *Northeastern Affairs*, 2 (July–December 1973).

———, 'Assam's Language Question in Retrospect', *Social Scientist*, 4 (September 1975).

Majumdar, D.N., 'A Glimpse of Garo Politics', *Northeastern Affairs*, 2 (Annual, 1973).

Misra, Prafulla, 'Communist Movement in Assam', *Northeastern Affairs*, 1 (July–September 1972).

Phukan, Nilmani, 'Notes on the Domicile Question', *Assam Tribune*, 6 October 1939.

Prasad, R.N., 'Evolution of Party Politics in Mizoram', *Northeastern Affairs*, 2 (Annual, 1973).

Sarma, G.C., 'Trade Union Movement: A Study of Assam Chah Karmachari Sangha', *The North Eastern Research Bulletin* (Dibrugarh), 5 (Summer 1974).

Srinivas, M.M., 'The Cohesive Role of Sanskritization' (mimeographed, University of Delhi, 1966).

———, 'Note on Sanskritization and Westernization', *Far Eastern Quarterly*, 15, No. 4 (1956).

Assamese

Baruah, Hemchandra, 'Asamar jatiiya andolan aru cah khetiak-sakalar biruddha-caran', *Asamiiya*, 25 May 1929.

Bora, Jnananath, 'Asam desh aru Congress', *Dainik Batori*, 24 October 1937.

———, 'Asam desh Bharatbarshar bhitarat thakiba kiya', *Avahan*, 10 (1938).

Bora, Mahidhar, 'Biyallish biplavar eta aitihasik din', *Saptahik Niilacal* (Gauhati), 14 August 1974.

Chaliha, Sadananda, 'Barak banam Brahmaputra', *Saptahik Niilacal*, serialized, 20 December 1972 and other issues.

Das, Omeo Kumar, 'Jiivan Smriti', *Maniddiip* (Gauhati), 6–7 (September 1966–January 1967).

———, 'Rajniiti Kshetrat Jyotiprasad', in *Jyoti Pratibha*, edited by Rupaliim Sanskritik Santha (Shillong, 1967), pp. 76–88.

Dhekial-Phukan, Anandaram, 'Inglandar bivaran', *Arunoday* (Sibsagar), 2, No. 4 (April 1947).

Kakati, Banikanta, 'Ambikagirii Raycaudhuriir vyaktitvat ebhumuki', *Manidiip*, 1 (January 1961).

Raychaudhri, Prabuddha, 'Uttar Kamrup aru darangar Krishak bidroha', *Paravaha* (Gauhati), 1, Nos. 6–8 (1956).

Sharma, Ajitkumar, 'Asamar cah udyogat bideshii muldhan', *Sadiniiya Navyug* (Gauhati), 30 October 1963.

Bengali

Anonymous, 'Banglay svadhiinata sangram', *Anandabazar Patrika* (Calcutta), Autumn special issue, 1338 *sal* (1931).

[Books consulted for information outside our period and standard official volumes of statistics referred to marginally, are not mentioned in the above bibliography.]

Interviews and Correspondence

Akram, Md.: left-oriented student Muslim leaguer in the 1940s and currently a Congressman, Jorhat. Interviewed on 12 August 1974, Assam House, Calcutta.

Ali Ahmed, Fakhruddin: Congress leader. Interviewed on 6 August 1974, Assam House, Calcutta.

Bhattacharya, Achintyakumar: ex-terrorist and communist leader. Interviewed on 1 July 1974, CPI(M) Office, Gauhati.

Bhattacharya, Gaurishankar: ex-communist and founder of Assam Peoples' Democratic Party, now practising law at Gauhati. Wrote to me on 20 August 1974.

Bhattacharya, Jagannath: a founder of the CPI in the Brahmaputra Valley, now in Calcutta. Interviewed on 21 August 1974, Calcutta. Wrote to me on 23 September 1974.

Biswas, Hemanga: communist and a co-founder of the Indian Peoples' Theatre Association. Interviewed on 19 February 1976 at 8D, Asgar Mistri Lane, Calcutta.

Biswas, Praneshchandra: ex-communist, now practising law at Shillong. Interviewed on 7 August 1973, Shillong.

Chaliha (Mrs Basu), Minakshi: daughter of Jadavprasad Chaliha and exponent of Manipuri dance, Calcutta. Interviewed on 24 April 1974, Calcutta. Wrote to me on 13 May 1974.

Chaliha, Parag: son of Padmadhar Chaliha and Principal of Sibsagar College, Sibsagar. Wrote to me on 5 November 1974.

Dam-Ray, Sibendrakumar: ex-Congressman and ex-communist of Sylhet, now a teacher at Shillong. Interviewed on 7 August 1973, Shillong.

Das, Omeo Kumar: Congress leader. Interviewed on 10 July 1973, Gauhati. Wrote, in reply to my questions, several letters, the last one being received on 25 September 1974.

Dasgupta, Amiya: a CPI student leader sent to the Brahmaputra Valley to draw communist activists into the party in 1939–40, now in Calcutta. Interviewed on 20 August 1974, Calcutta.

Deka, Haridas: an ex-leader of the Revolutionary Communist Party of India and now practising law at Gauhati. Interviewed on 27 February 1974, Gauhati. Wrote to me on 24 March 1974.

Desai, S.P.: member of the Indian Civil Service and retired Chief Secretary to the Government of Assam, now at Poona. Interviewed on 4 April 1973, Poona.

Lahiri, Brajamohan: resident of Gauhati till 1948 and currently living in Calcutta. Interviewed on 7 March 1974 at Calcutta.

Mahanta, Dadhi: CPI leader, editor of the erstwhile weekly, *Natun Asam* (Gauhati), and currently of its successor, *Janamat* (Gauhati). Interviewed on 7 October 1975.

Nandy, Jyotirmay: CPI leader of Sylhet, now in Calcutta. Interviewed on 3 August 1974.

Talukdar, Pranjit: Son of Dhaniram Talukdar and Principal, M.C. College, Barpeta. Wrote to me on 5 and 28 September 1974.

Tripathi, K.P.: A leading Congressman of the province and INTUC leader. Interviewed at Calcutta on 19 October 1975.

[The above short-list of interviewees was drawn up with the object of filling only certain specific gaps in our pool of documented information. However, I alone am responsible for any omission or errors of fact and understanding.]

SUPPLEMENT TO BIBLIOGRAPHY

Barooah, N.K., 'Mohinii', in *Kalaar Chhabi* (in Assamese) (Gauhati, 1997).

Bhuyan, A.C. and S. De, eds, *Political History of Assam, Vol. III: 1940–47* (Government of Assam, Gauhati, 1980).

Census of India, Vol. 12, Part II A (1951).

Cotton, H., *Colonization of Wastelands in the Province of Assam* (1899).

Government of Assam, *Political History of Assam* (Gauhati, 1977, 1978, 1980).

Mitra, Ashok, Article in *Oitihya Aru Itihas (Heritage and History), Amalendu Guha Abhindan Grantha* (in Assamese mainly) (Gauhati, 2005).

Molla, M.K.U., *The New Province of Eastern Bengal and Assam* (Rajshahi University, 1981).

Proceedings of the Company's Calcutta Board, 28.10.1859, Manuscript No. 9925, Vol. 10, Guildhall Library, London.

Saikia, Rajen, *Social and Economic History of Assam 1853–1921* (Delhi, 2000).

———, Articles in *Gariiyasii*, VI (in Assamese) (Gauhati, May and September, 1999).

Syed, Abul Maksud, *Maolana Abdul Hamid Khan Bhasani* (in Bengali) Bangla Academy, Dhaka, 1994).

Index